PandoraHearts

Jun Mochizuki

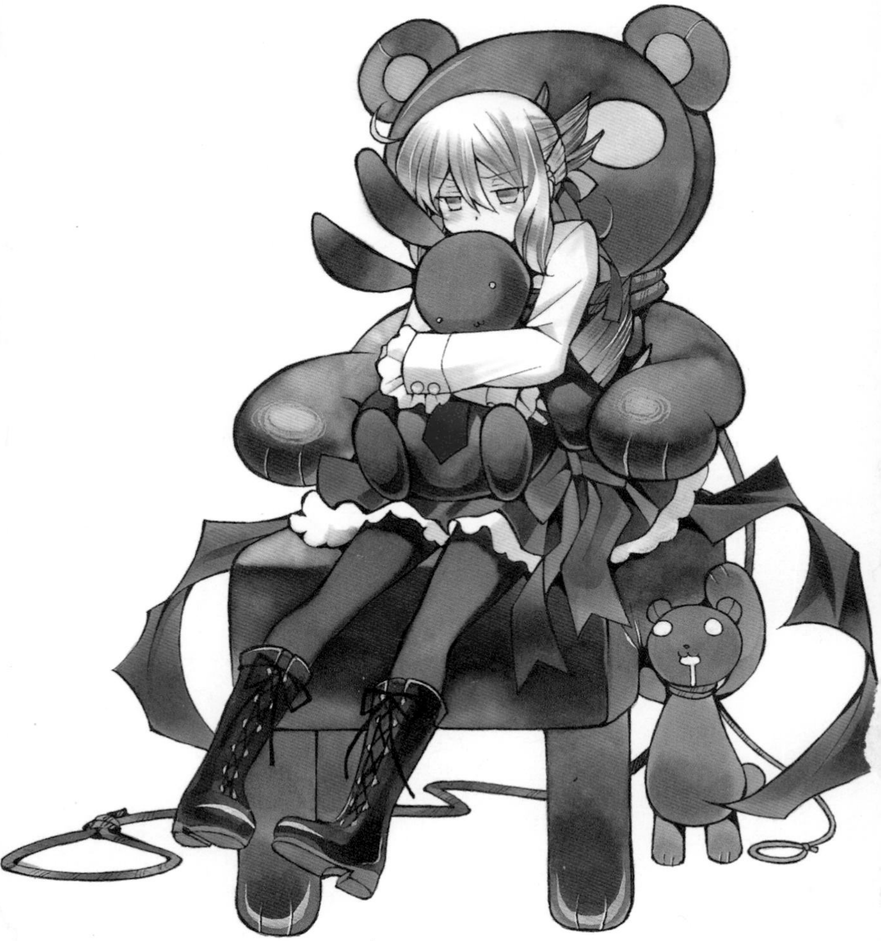

CONTENTS

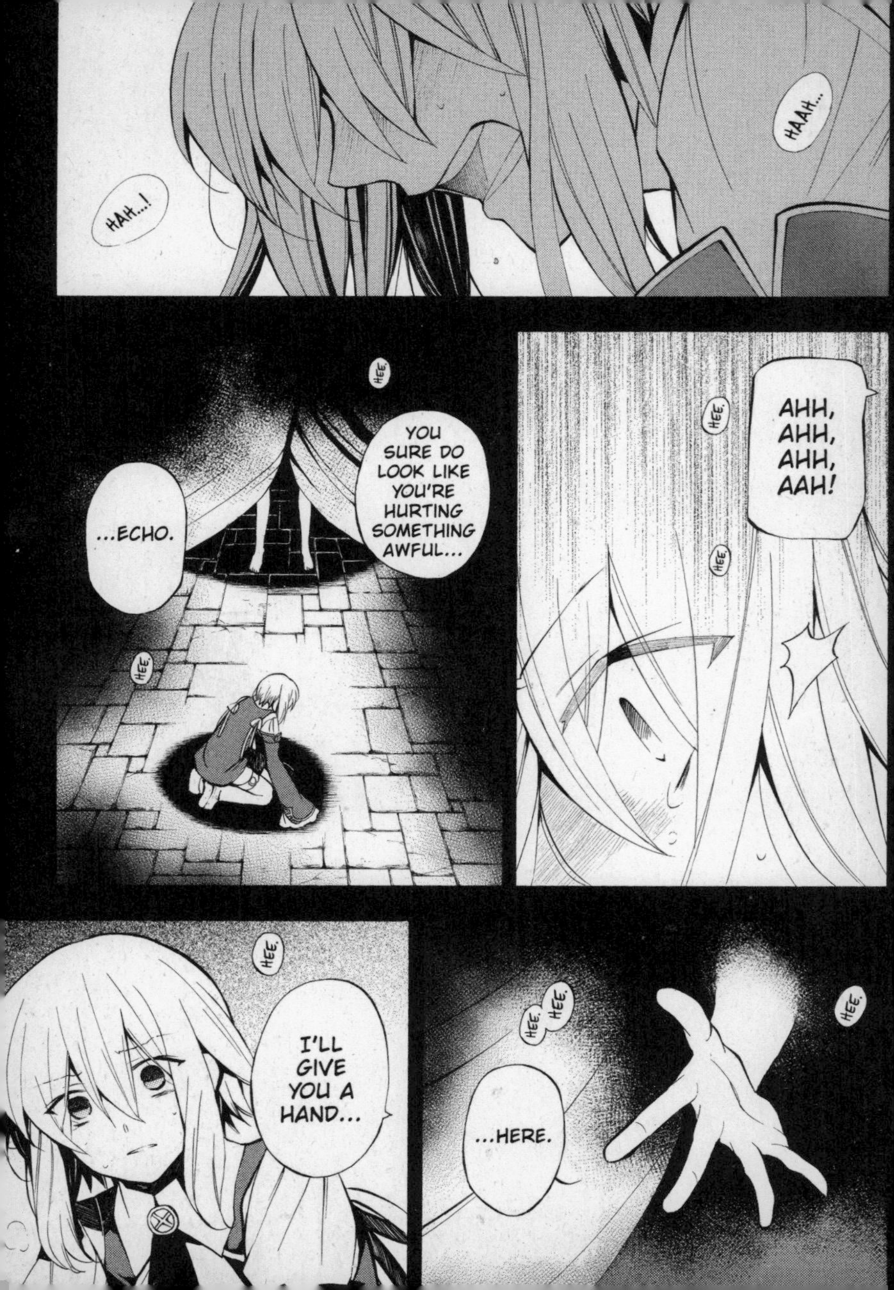
HAAH...
HAH...!
AHH, AHH, AHH, AAH!
HEE.
HEE.
HEE.
YOU SURE DO LOOK LIKE YOU'RE HURTING SOMETHING AWFUL...
...ECHO.
HEE.
HEE.
HEE.
HEE.
...HERE.
HEE.
I'LL GIVE YOU A HAND...

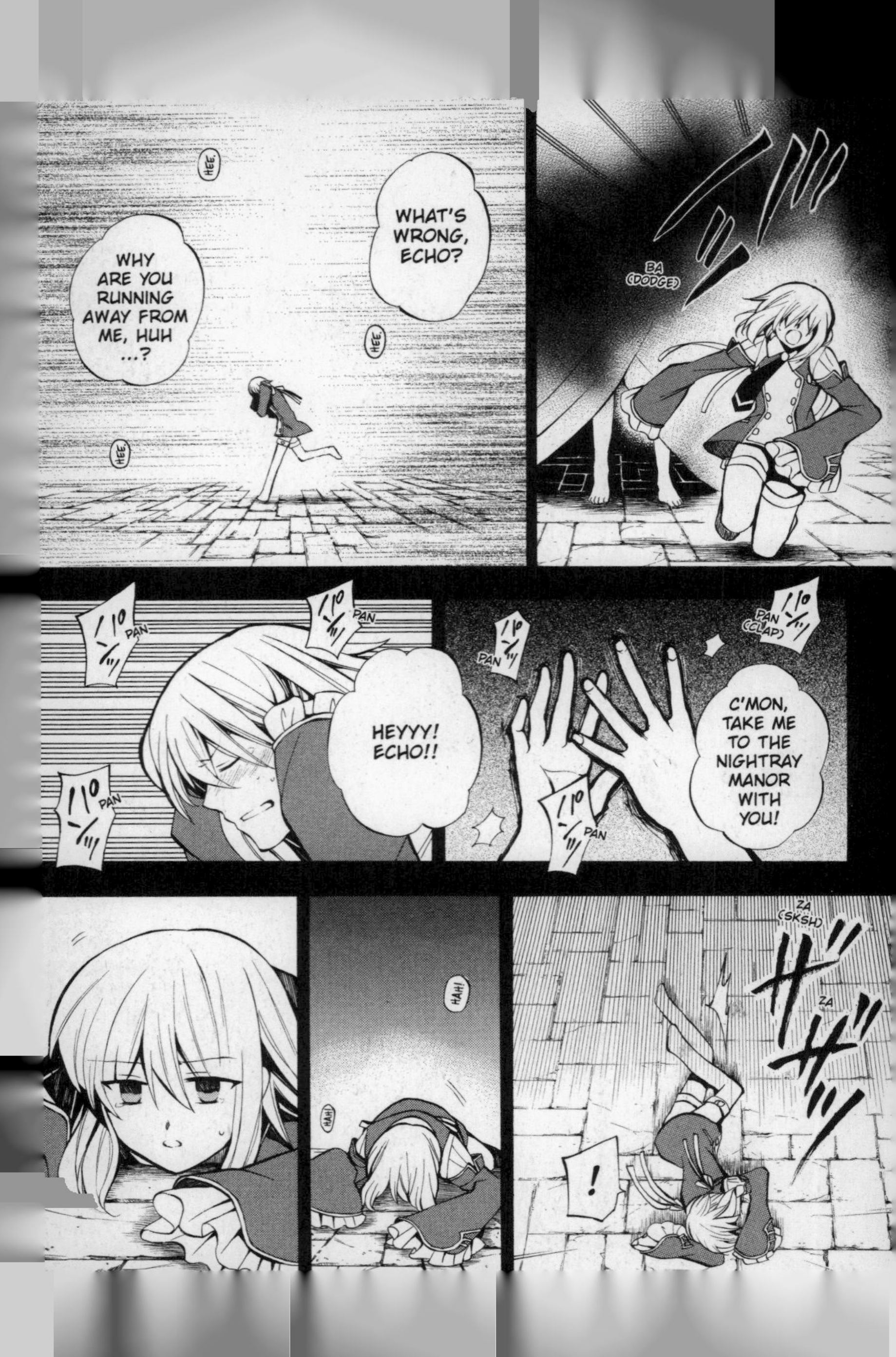
BA (DODGE)
HEE.
WHAT'S WRONG, ECHO?
WHY ARE YOU RUNNING AWAY FROM ME, HUH ...?
HEE.
HEE.
PAN (CLAP)
PAN
C'MON, TAKE ME TO THE NIGHTRAY MANOR WITH YOU!
PAN
PAN
PAN
HEYYY! ECHO!!
PAN
ZA (SKSH)
ZA
!
HAH!
HAH!

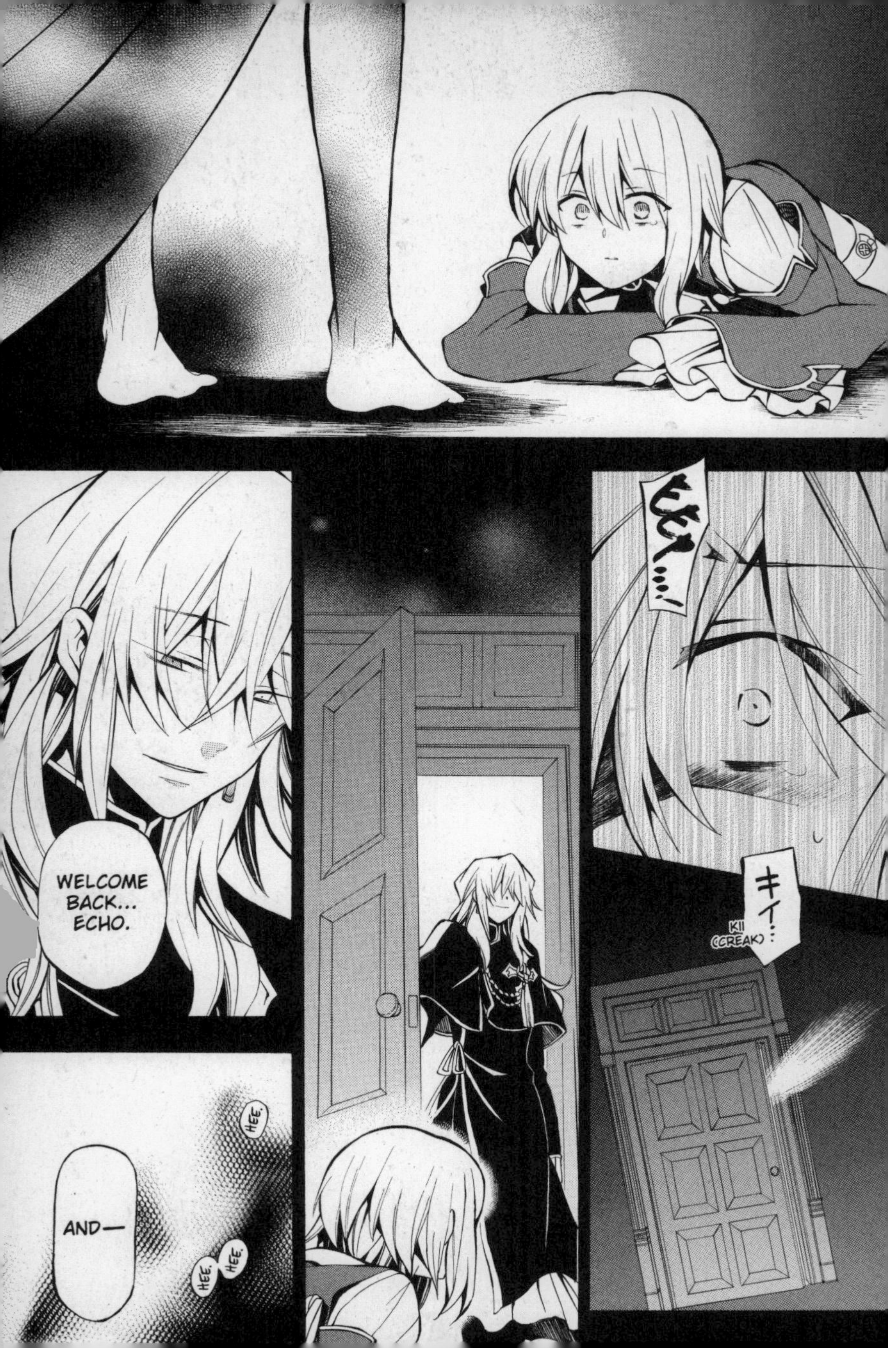
キイ…
KII (CREAK)
WELCOME BACK... ECHO.
HEE.
AND—
HEE. HEE.

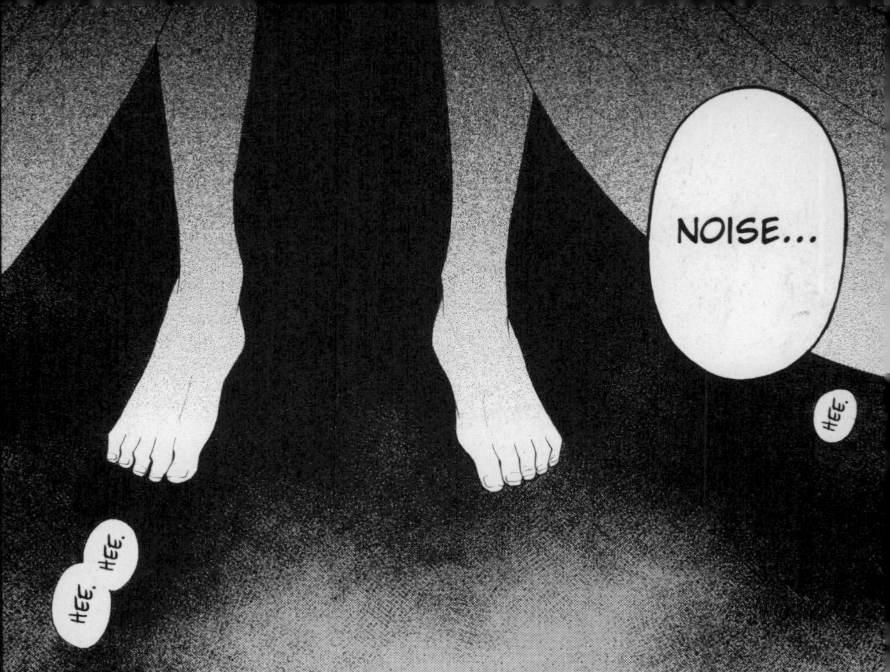
NOISE...
HEE.
HEE.
HEE.

Retrace:XXXIV Noise of Echo

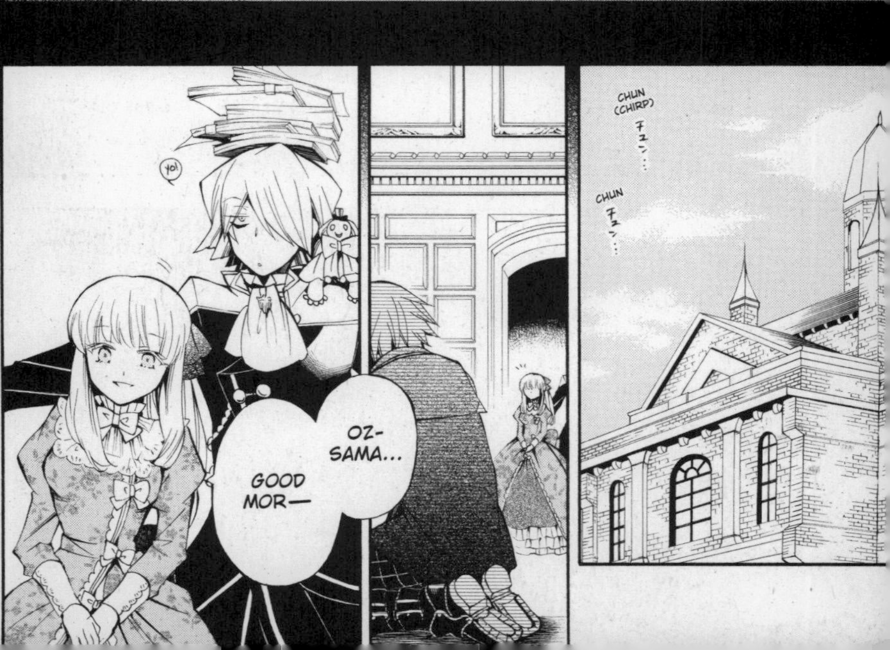
CHUN (CHIRP)
チュン…
CHUN
チュン…
YO!
OZ-SAMA...
GOOD MOR—

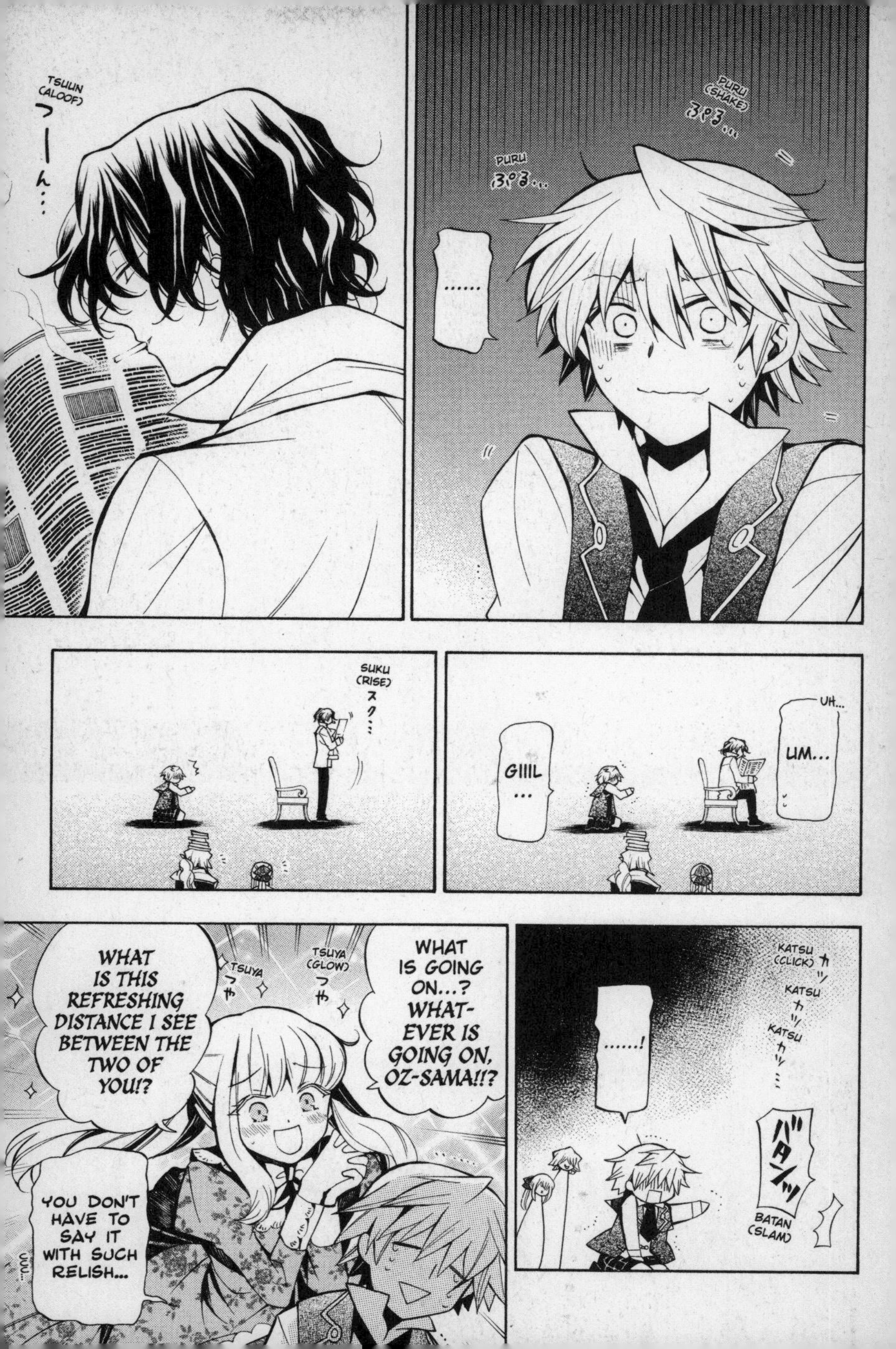
PURU (SHAKE)
ぷるる…
PURU
ぷる…
……
TSUUN (ALOOF)
つーん…
UH...
UM...
GIIIL ...
SUKU (RISE)
スク…
......!
KATSU (CLICK)
カッ
KATSU
カッ
KATSU
カッ…
バタンッ
BATAN (SLAM)
WHAT IS GOING ON...? WHAT-EVER IS GOING ON, OZ-SAMA!!?
TSUYA (GLOW)
つや
TSUYA
つや
WHAT IS THIS REFRESHING DISTANCE I SEE BETWEEN THE TWO OF YOU!?
YOU DON'T HAVE TO SAY IT WITH SUCH RELISH...
UUU...

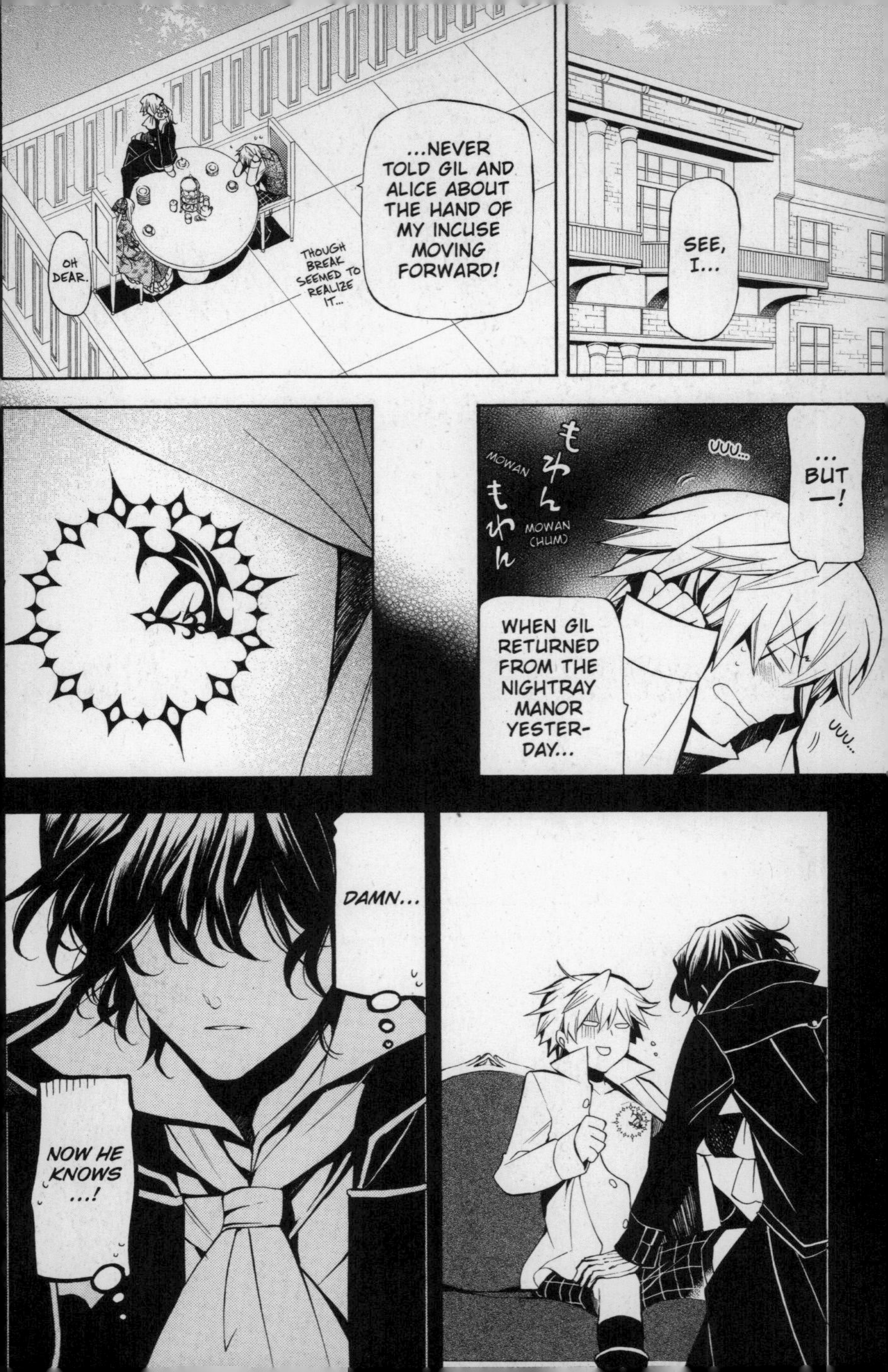
SEE, I...
...NEVER TOLD GIL AND ALICE ABOUT THE HAND OF MY INCUSE MOVING FORWARD!
THOUGH BREAK SEEMED TO REALIZE IT...
OH DEAR.
...BUT—!
UUU...
もわん
MOWAN
もわん
MOWAN (HUM)
WHEN GIL RETURNED FROM THE NIGHTRAY MANOR YESTER-DAY...
UUU...
DAMN...
NOW HE KNOWS ...!

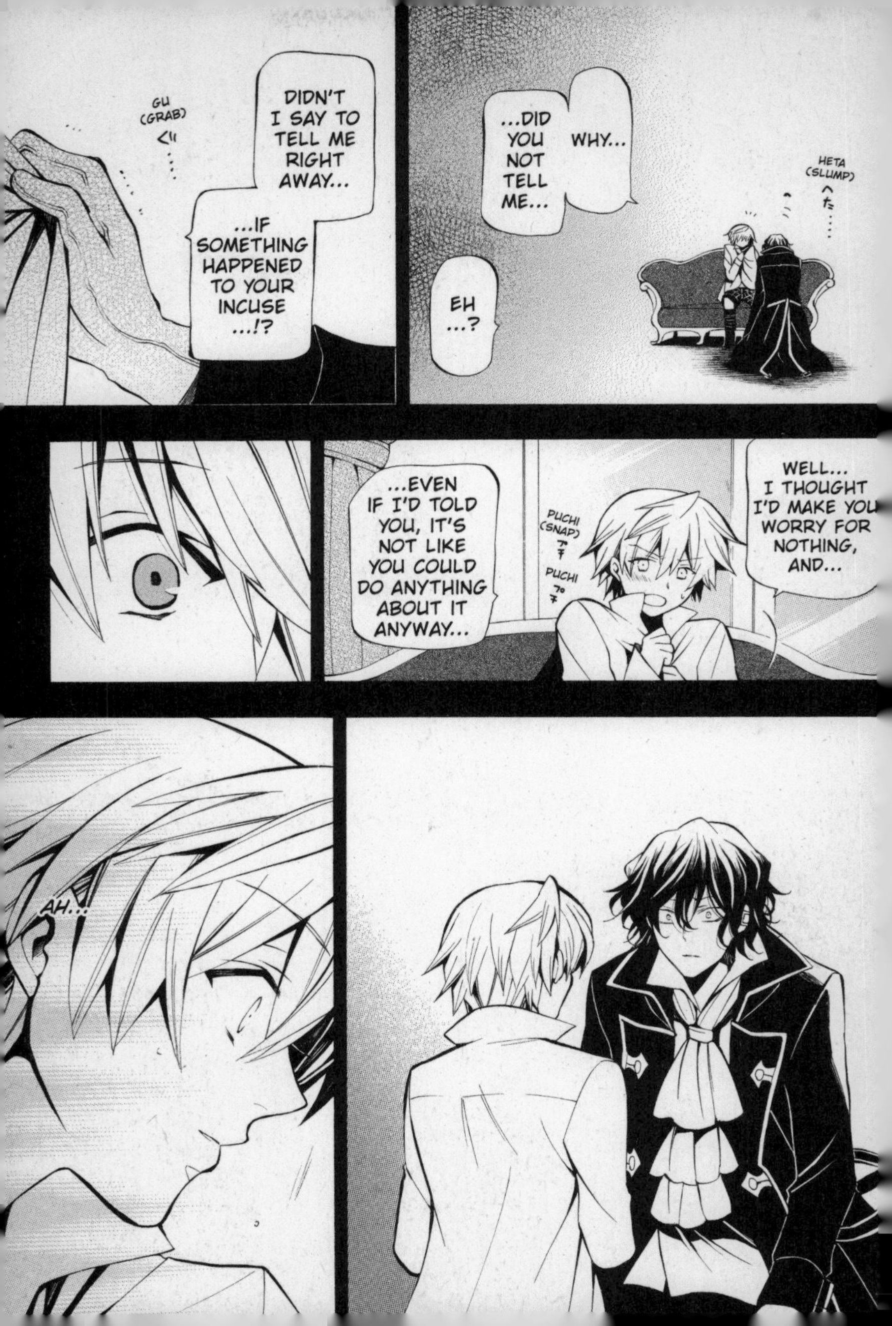
HETA (SLUMP)
WHY...
...DID YOU NOT TELL ME...
EH ...?
GU (GRAB)
DIDN'T I SAY TO TELL ME RIGHT AWAY...
...IF SOMETHING HAPPENED TO YOUR INCUSE ...!?
WELL... I THOUGHT I'D MAKE YOU WORRY FOR NOTHING, AND...
PUCHI (SNAP)
PUCHI
...EVEN IF I'D TOLD YOU, IT'S NOT LIKE YOU COULD DO ANYTHING ABOUT IT ANYWAY...
AH...

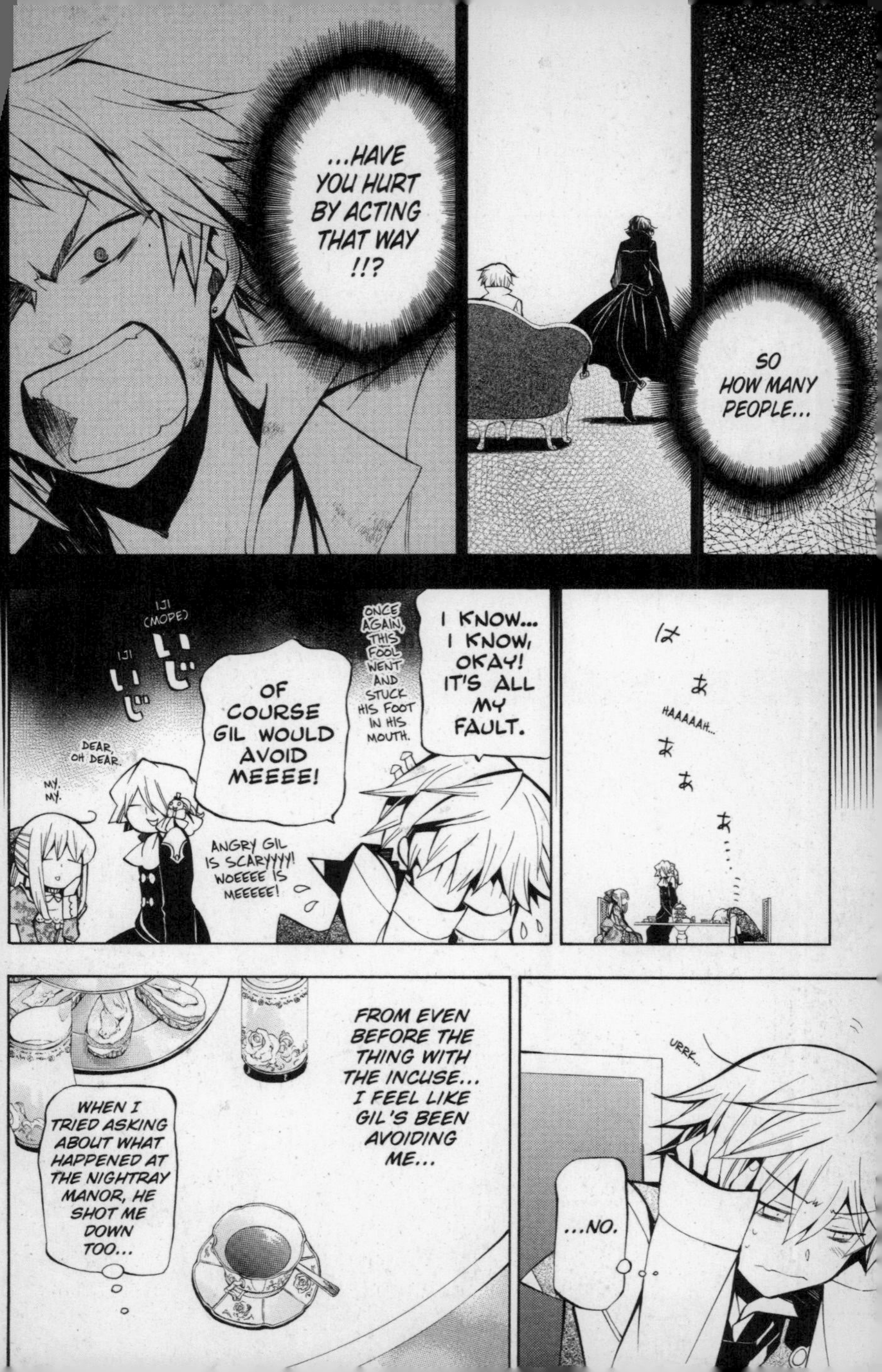
SO HOW MANY PEOPLE...
...HAVE YOU HURT BY ACTING THAT WAY !!?
はあ
HAAAAAH...
あああ...
I KNOW... I KNOW, OKAY! IT'S ALL MY FAULT.
ONCE AGAIN, THIS FOOL WENT AND STUCK HIS FOOT IN HIS MOUTH.
OF COURSE GIL WOULD AVOID MEEEE!
IJI (MOPE)
いじ
IJI
いじ
ANGRY GIL IS SCARYYYY! WOEEEE IS MEEEEE!
DEAR, OH DEAR.
MY, MY.
URRK...
...NO.
FROM EVEN BEFORE THE THING WITH THE INCUSE... I FEEL LIKE GIL'S BEEN AVOIDING ME...
WHEN I TRIED ASKING ABOUT WHAT HAPPENED AT THE NIGHTRAY MANOR, HE SHOT ME DOWN TOO...

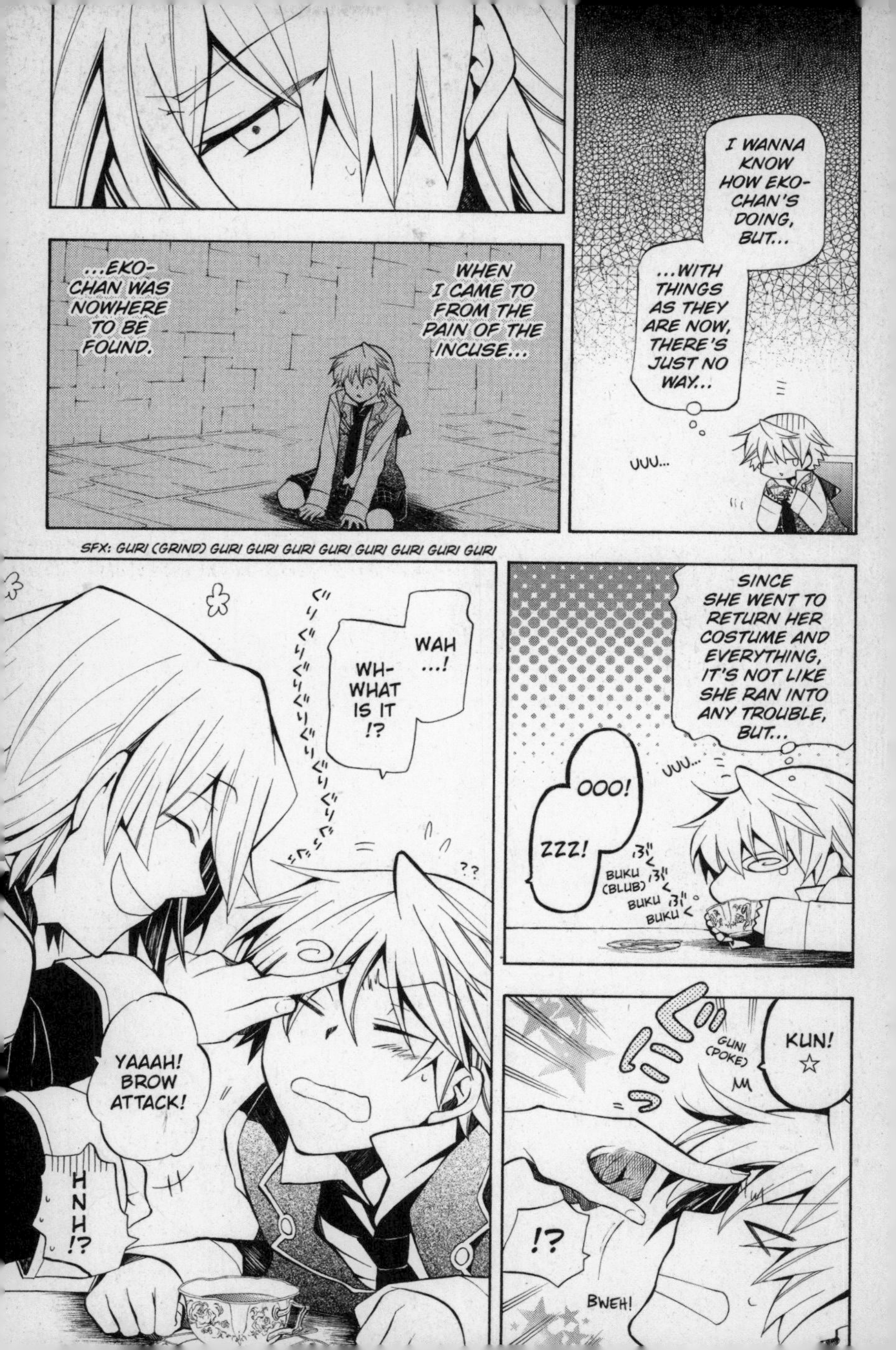
I WANNA KNOW HOW EKO-CHAN'S DOING, BUT...
...WITH THINGS AS THEY ARE NOW, THERE'S JUST NO WAY...
UUU...
WHEN I CAME TO FROM THE PAIN OF THE INCUSE...
...EKO-CHAN WAS NOWHERE TO BE FOUND.
SFX: GURI (GRIND) GURI GURI GURI GURI GURI GURI GURI GURI
SINCE SHE WENT TO RETURN HER COSTUME AND EVERYTHING, IT'S NOT LIKE SHE RAN INTO ANY TROUBLE, BUT...
UUU...
OOO! ZZZ!
BUKU (BLUB) BUKU BUKU
KUN! ☆
GUNI (POKE)
!?
BWEH!
WAH...!
WH-WHAT IS IT!?
YAAAH! BROW ATTACK!
HNH!?

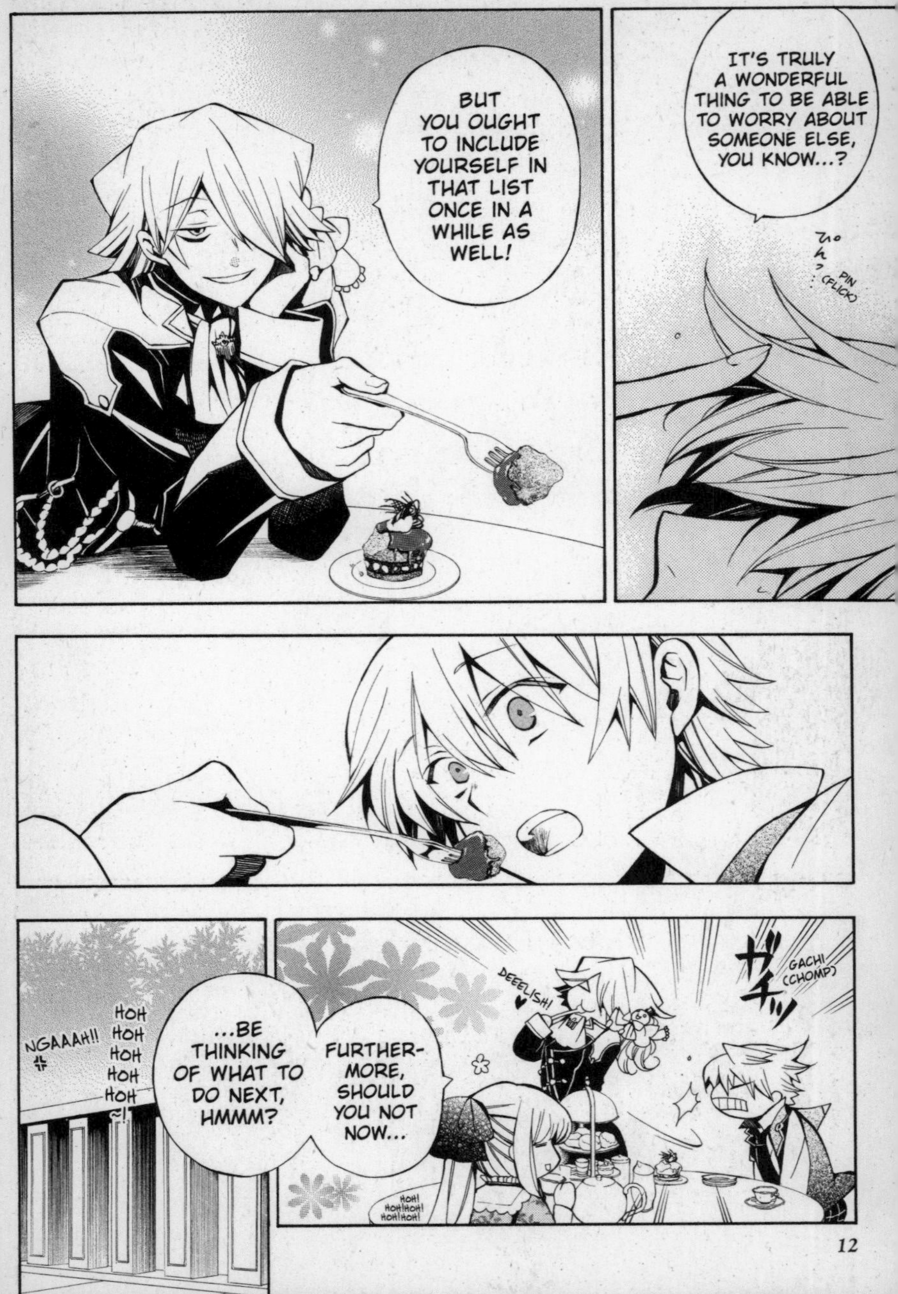
IT'S TRULY A WONDERFUL THING TO BE ABLE TO WORRY ABOUT SOMEONE ELSE, YOU KNOW...?
ぴん…
PIN (FLICK)
BUT YOU OUGHT TO INCLUDE YOURSELF IN THAT LIST ONCE IN A WHILE AS WELL!
ガチッ
GACHI (CHOMP)
DEEELISH!
FURTHER-MORE, SHOULD YOU NOT NOW...
HOH! HOH!HOH! HOH!HOH!
...BE THINKING OF WHAT TO DO NEXT, HMMM?
HOH HOH HOH HOH HOH ~!
NGAAAH!!

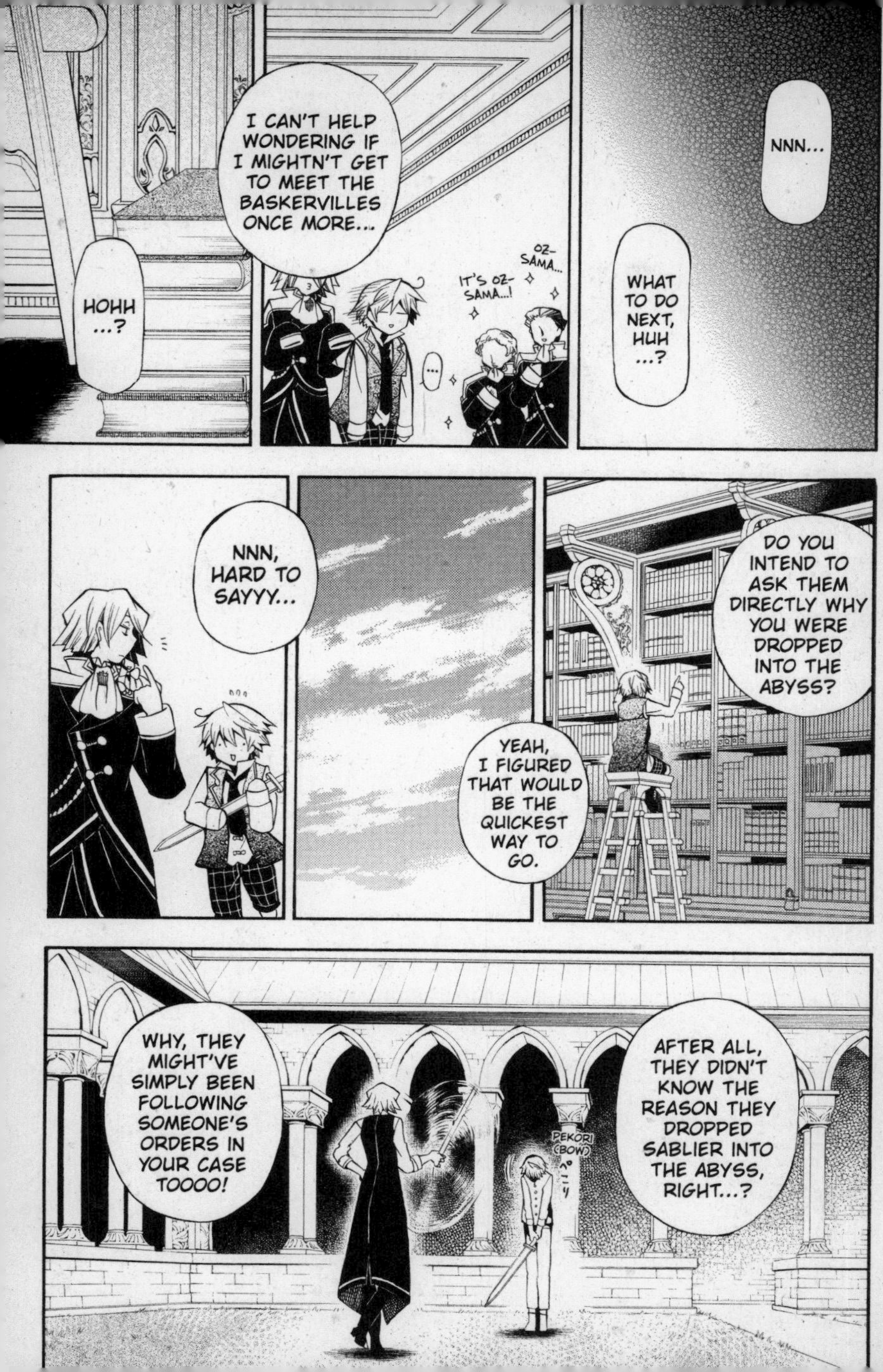
NNN...
WHAT TO DO NEXT, HUH...?
I CAN'T HELP WONDERING IF I MIGHTN'T GET TO MEET THE BASKERVILLES ONCE MORE...
OZ-SAMA...
IT'S OZ-SAMA...!
...
HOHH...?
DO YOU INTEND TO ASK THEM DIRECTLY WHY YOU WERE DROPPED INTO THE ABYSS?
YEAH, I FIGURED THAT WOULD BE THE QUICKEST WAY TO GO.
NNN, HARD TO SAYYY...
AFTER ALL, THEY DIDN'T KNOW THE REASON THEY DROPPED SABLIER INTO THE ABYSS, RIGHT...?
PEKORI (BOW)
WHY, THEY MIGHT'VE SIMPLY BEEN FOLLOWING SOMEONE'S ORDERS IN YOUR CASE TOOOO!

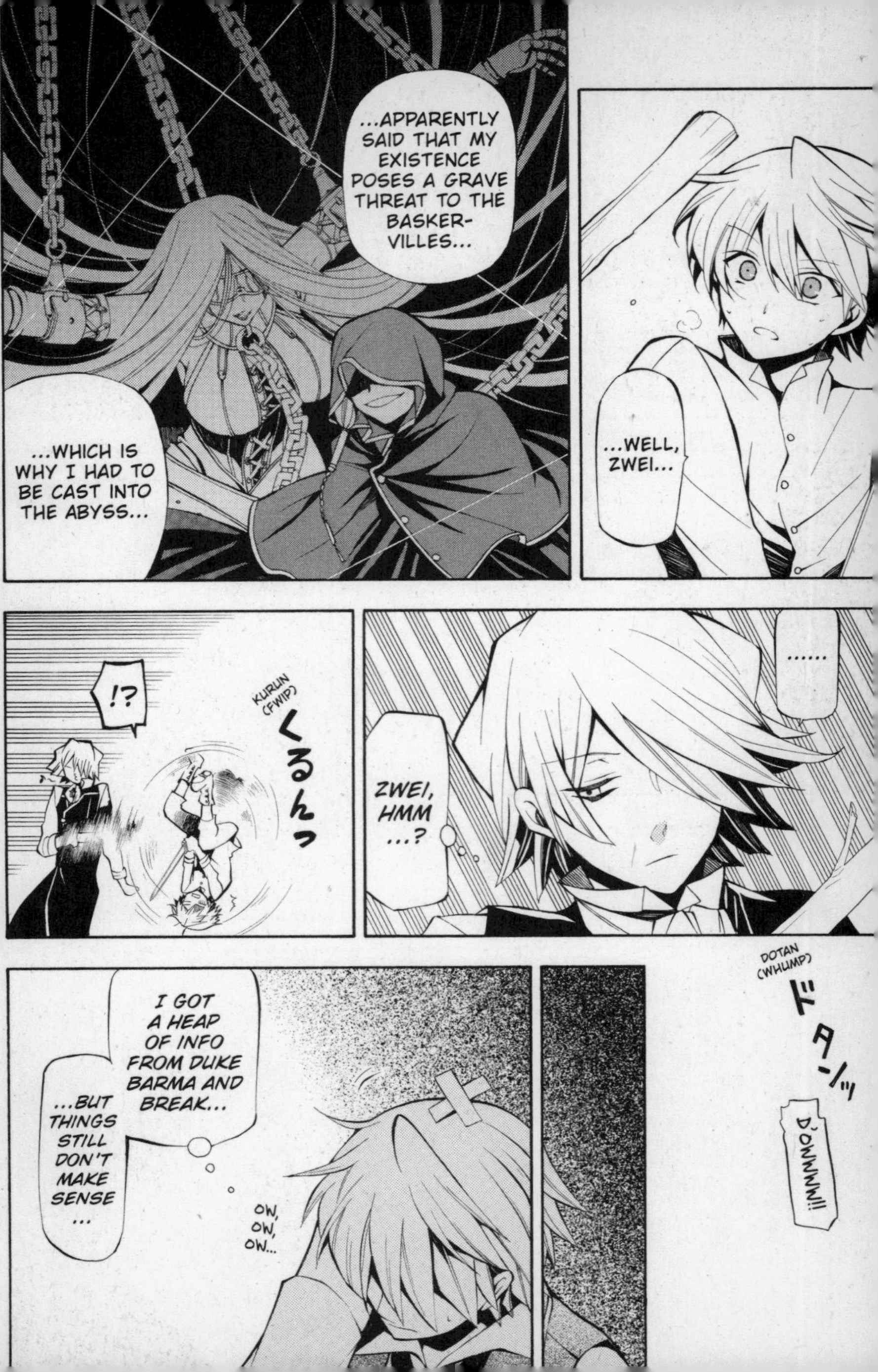
...WELL, ZWEI...
...APPARENTLY SAID THAT MY EXISTENCE POSES A GRAVE THREAT TO THE BASKER-VILLES...
...WHICH IS WHY I HAD TO BE CAST INTO THE ABYSS...
......
ZWEI, HMM ...?
KURUN (FWIP)
くるんっ
!?
DOTAN (WHUMP)
ドターンッ
DOWWW!!
I GOT A HEAP OF INFO FROM DUKE BARMA AND BREAK...
...BUT THINGS STILL DON'T MAKE SENSE ...
OW, OW, OW...

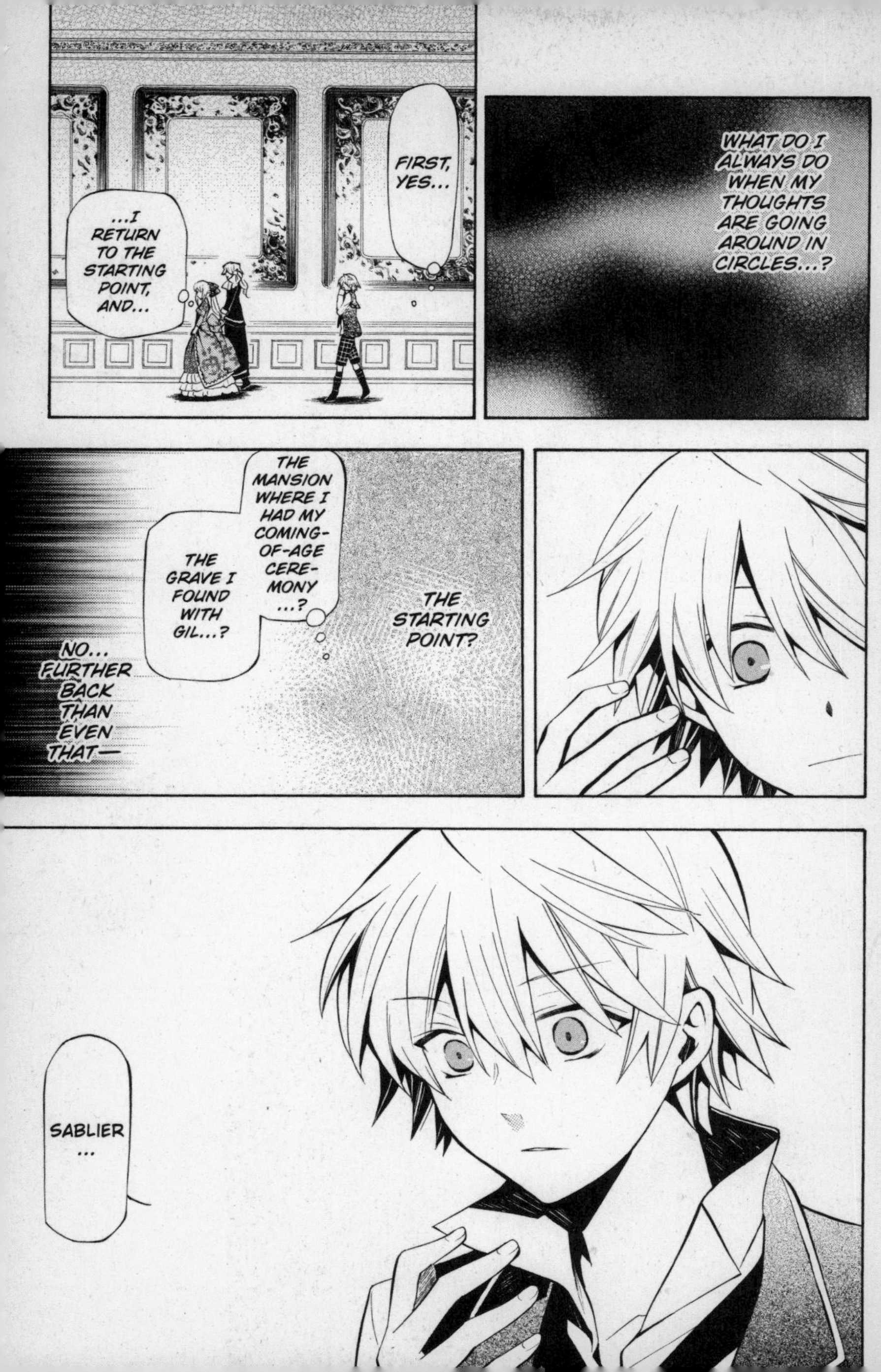
WHAT DO I ALWAYS DO WHEN MY THOUGHTS ARE GOING AROUND IN CIRCLES...?
FIRST, YES...
...I RETURN TO THE STARTING POINT, AND...
THE STARTING POINT?
THE MANSION WHERE I HAD MY COMING-OF-AGE CEREMONY...?
THE GRAVE I FOUND WITH GIL...?
NO... FURTHER BACK THAN EVEN THAT—
SABLIER...

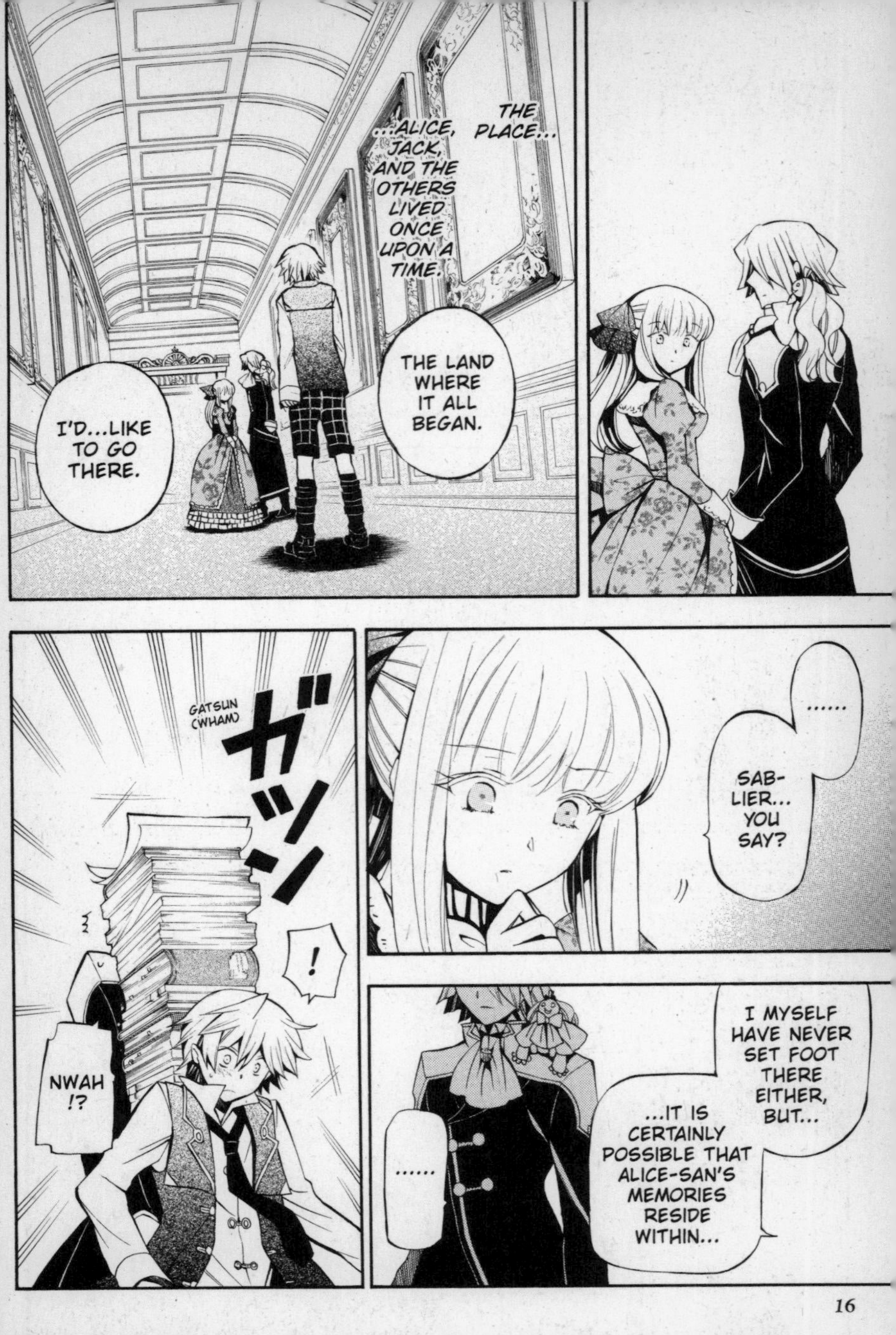

THE PLACE...
...ALICE, JACK, AND THE OTHERS LIVED ONCE UPON A TIME.
THE LAND WHERE IT ALL BEGAN.
I'D...LIKE TO GO THERE.
......
SABLIER... YOU SAY?
I MYSELF HAVE NEVER SET FOOT THERE EITHER, BUT...
...IT IS CERTAINLY POSSIBLE THAT ALICE-SAN'S MEMORIES RESIDE WITHIN...
......
GATSUN (WHAM)
ガツン
!
NWAH!?

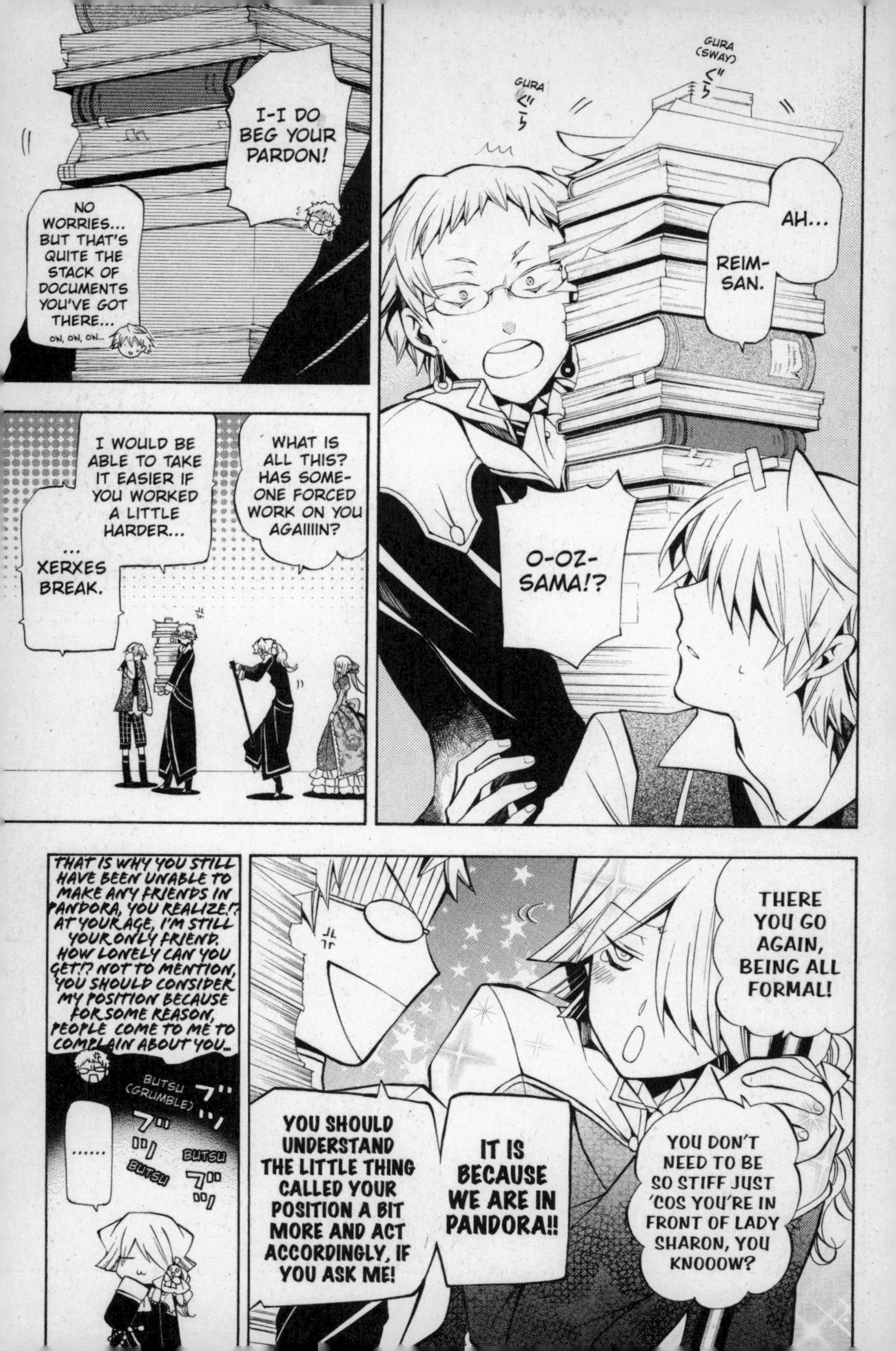
GURA (SWAY)
GURA
AH... REIM-SAN.
O-OZ-SAMA!?
I-I DO BEG YOUR PARDON!
NO WORRIES... BUT THAT'S QUITE THE STACK OF DOCUMENTS YOU'VE GOT THERE...
OW, OW, OW...
WHAT IS ALL THIS? HAS SOME-ONE FORCED WORK ON YOU AGAIIIIN?
I WOULD BE ABLE TO TAKE IT EASIER IF YOU WORKED A LITTLE HARDER...
... XERXES BREAK.
THERE YOU GO AGAIN, BEING ALL FORMAL!
YOU DON'T NEED TO BE SO STIFF JUST 'COS YOU'RE IN FRONT OF LADY SHARON, YOU KNOOOW?
IT IS BECAUSE WE ARE IN PANDORA!!
YOU SHOULD UNDERSTAND THE LITTLE THING CALLED YOUR POSITION A BIT MORE AND ACT ACCORDINGLY, IF YOU ASK ME!
THAT IS WHY YOU STILL HAVE BEEN UNABLE TO MAKE ANY FRIENDS IN PANDORA, YOU REALIZE!? AT YOUR AGE, I'M STILL YOUR ONLY FRIEND. HOW LONELY CAN YOU GET!? NOT TO MENTION, YOU SHOULD CONSIDER MY POSITION BECAUSE FOR SOME REASON, PEOPLE COME TO ME TO COMPLAIN ABOUT YOU...
BUTSU (GRUMBLE)
BUTSU
BUTSU
......

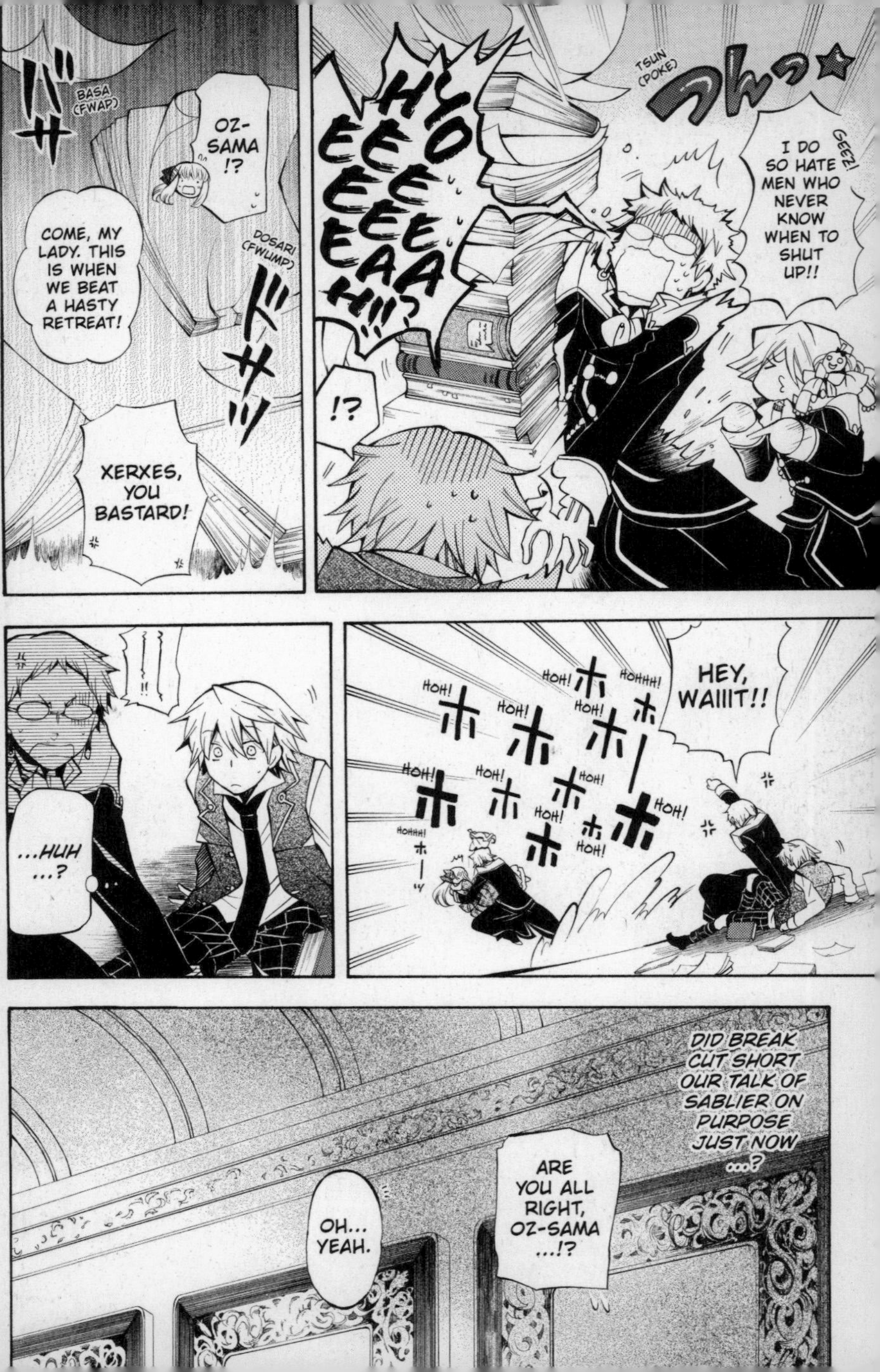

TSUN (POKE)
つんっ☆
GEEZ!
I DO SO HATE MEN WHO NEVER KNOW WHEN TO SHUT UP!!
HYOEEEEEEEAAH!!?
!?
BASA (FWAP)
バサ
OZ-SAMA!?
COME, MY LADY. THIS IS WHEN WE BEAT A HASTY RETREAT!
DOSARI (FWUMP)
ドサッ
XERXES, YOU BASTARD!
HEY, WAIIIT!!
HOHHH! HOH! HOH! HOH! HOH! HOH! HOH! HOH! HOH! HOH! HOHHH!
ホホホホホホホホホホー
...!!
...HUH...?
DID BREAK CUT SHORT OUR TALK OF SABLIER ON PURPOSE JUST NOW...?
ARE YOU ALL RIGHT, OZ-SAMA...!?
OH... YEAH.

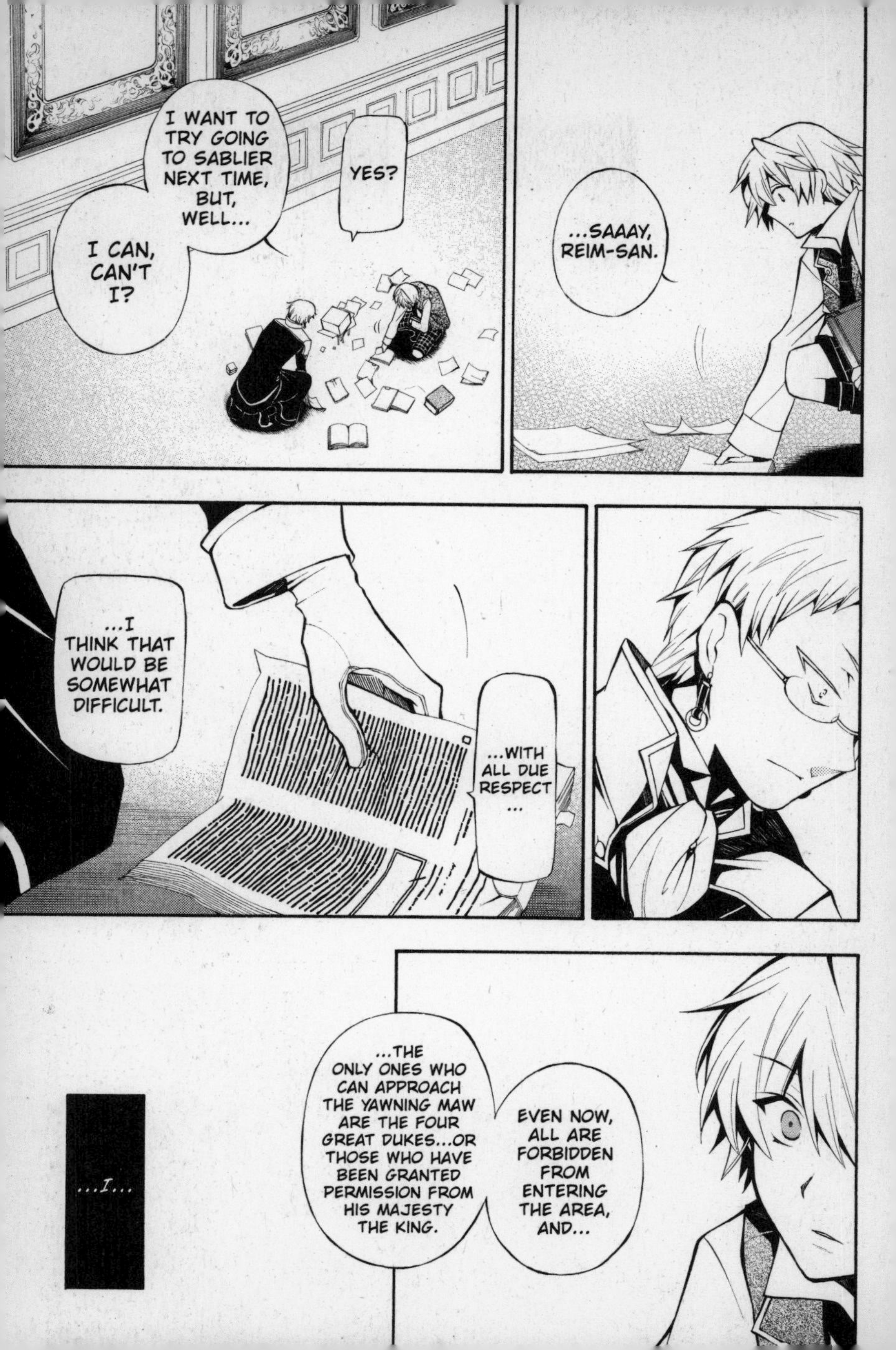
...SAAAY, REIM-SAN.
YES?
I WANT TO TRY GOING TO SABLIER NEXT TIME, BUT, WELL...
I CAN, CAN'T I?
...WITH ALL DUE RESPECT...
...I THINK THAT WOULD BE SOMEWHAT DIFFICULT.
EVEN NOW, ALL ARE FORBIDDEN FROM ENTERING THE AREA, AND...
...THE ONLY ONES WHO CAN APPROACH THE YAWNING MAW ARE THE FOUR GREAT DUKES...OR THOSE WHO HAVE BEEN GRANTED PERMISSION FROM HIS MAJESTY THE KING.
...I...

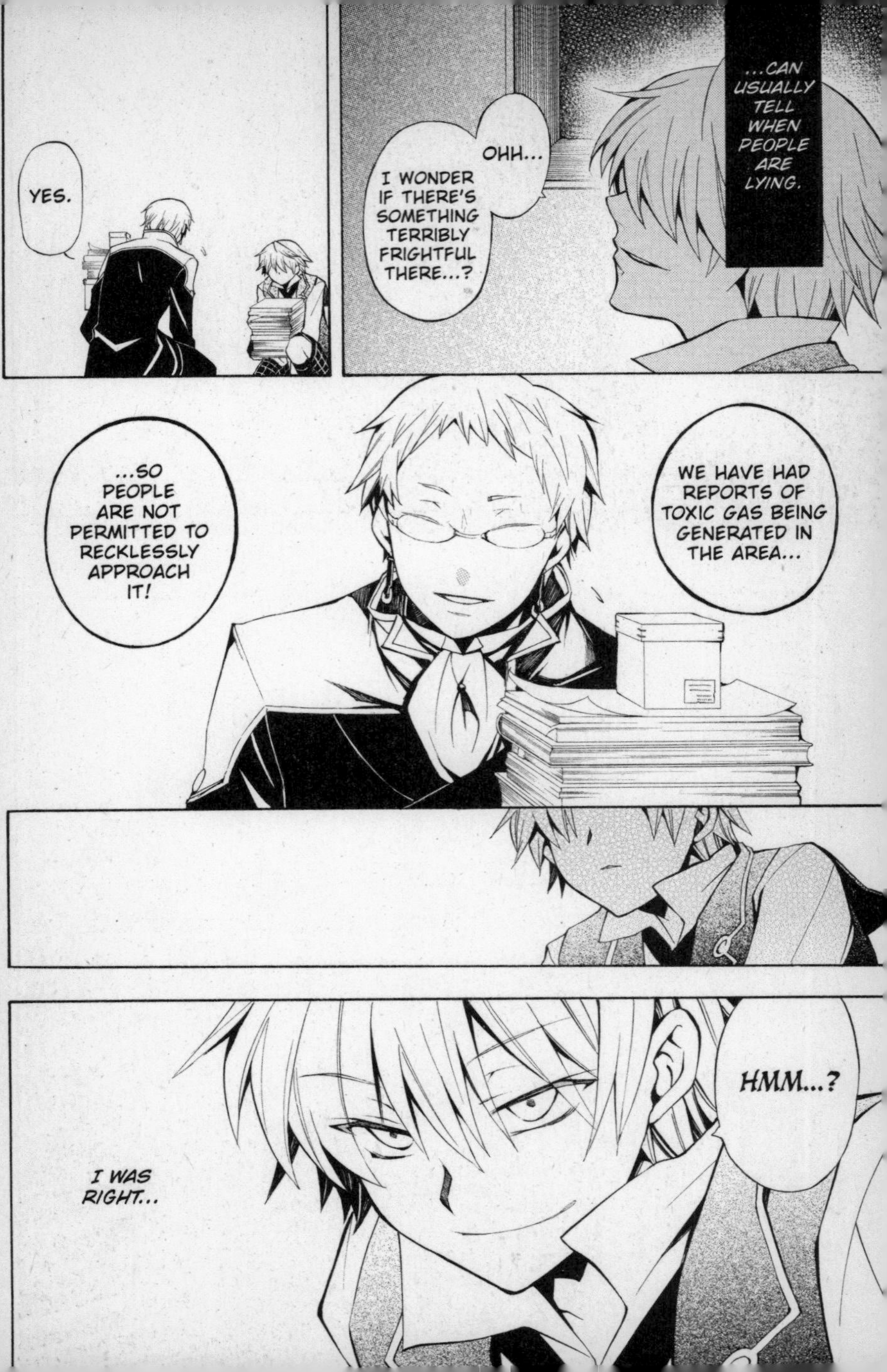
...CAN USUALLY TELL WHEN PEOPLE ARE LYING.
OHH... I WONDER IF THERE'S SOMETHING TERRIBLY FRIGHTFUL THERE...?
YES.
WE HAVE HAD REPORTS OF TOXIC GAS BEING GENERATED IN THE AREA...
...SO PEOPLE ARE NOT PERMITTED TO RECKLESSLY APPROACH IT!
HMM...?
I WAS RIGHT...

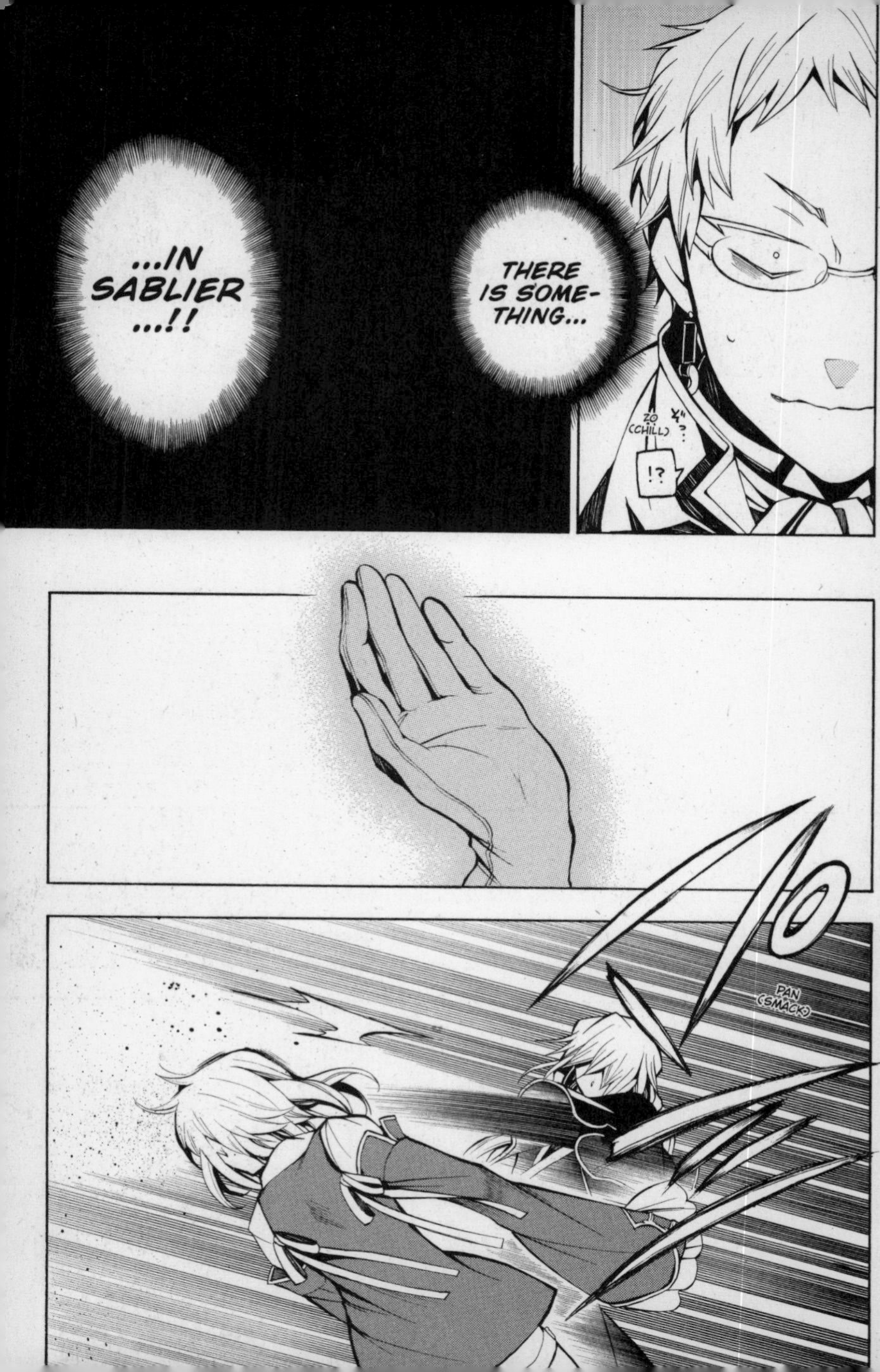
THERE IS SOME-THING...
...IN SABLIER ...!!
ZO (CHILL)
!?
PAN (SMACK)

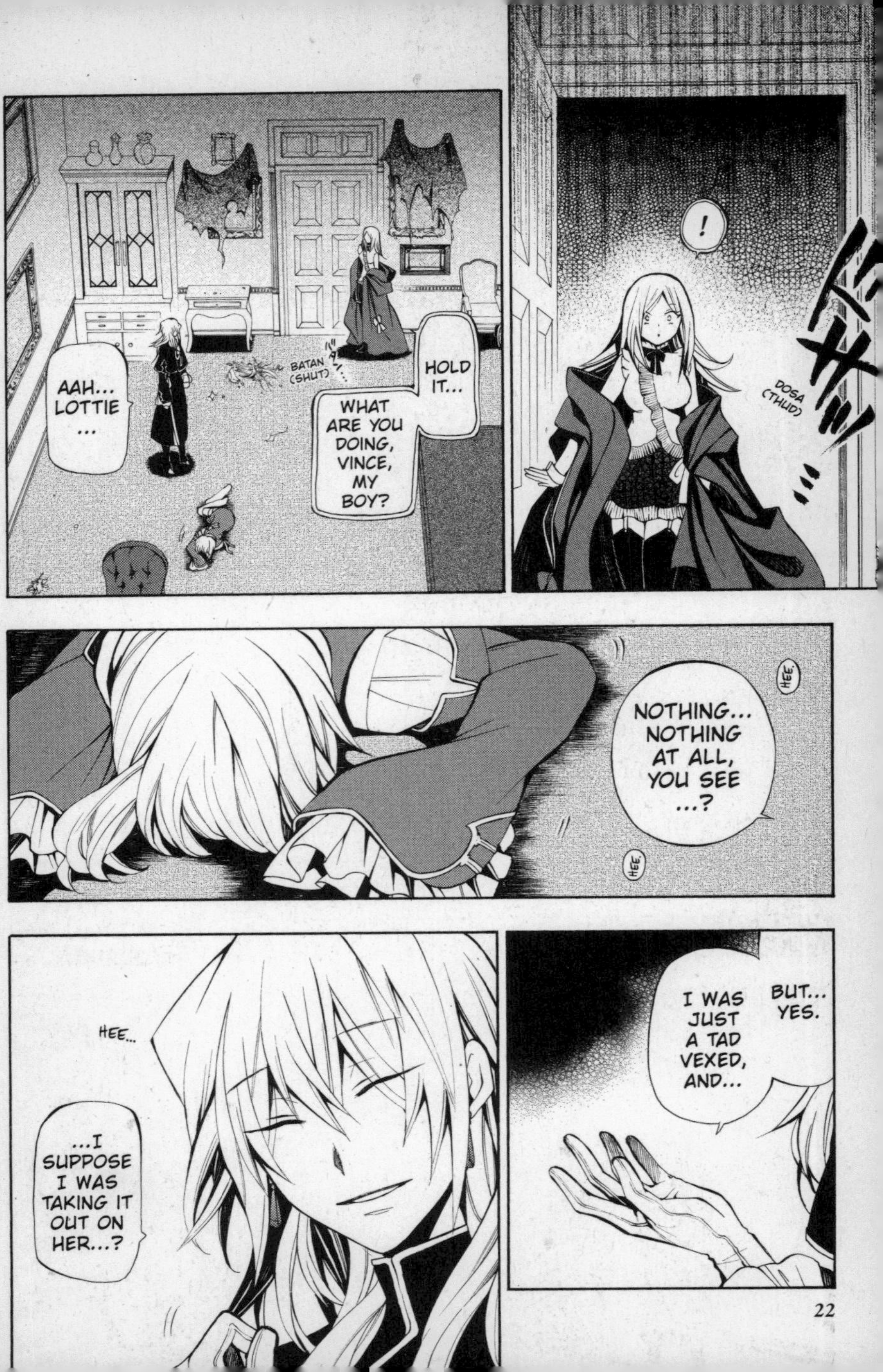
!
DOSA (THUD)
HOLD IT...
WHAT ARE YOU DOING, VINCE, MY BOY?
BATAN (SHUT)
AAH... LOTTIE ...
HEE.
NOTHING... NOTHING AT ALL, YOU SEE ...?
HEE.
BUT... YES.
I WAS JUST A TAD VEXED, AND...
HEE...
...I SUPPOSE I WAS TAKING IT OUT ON HER...?

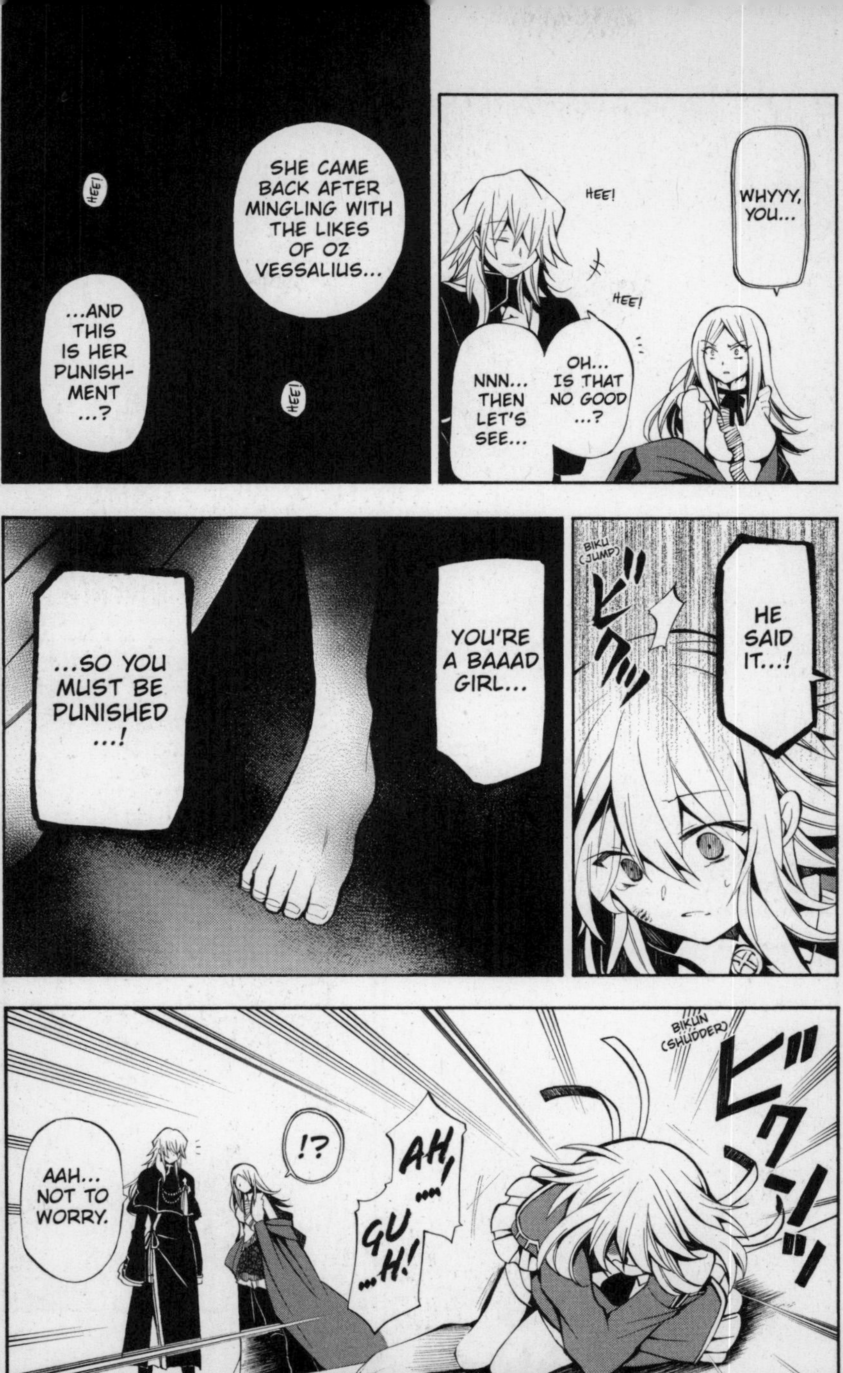
WHYYY, YOU...
HEE!
HEE!
OH... IS THAT NO GOOD ...?
NNN... THEN LET'S SEE...
HEE!
SHE CAME BACK AFTER MINGLING WITH THE LIKES OF OZ VESSALIUS...
...AND THIS IS HER PUNISHMENT ...?
HEE!
BIKU (JUMP)
HE SAID IT...!
YOU'RE A BAAAD GIRL...
...SO YOU MUST BE PUNISHED ...!
BIKUN (SHUDDER)
AH, ...GU ...H!
!?
AAH... NOT TO WORRY.

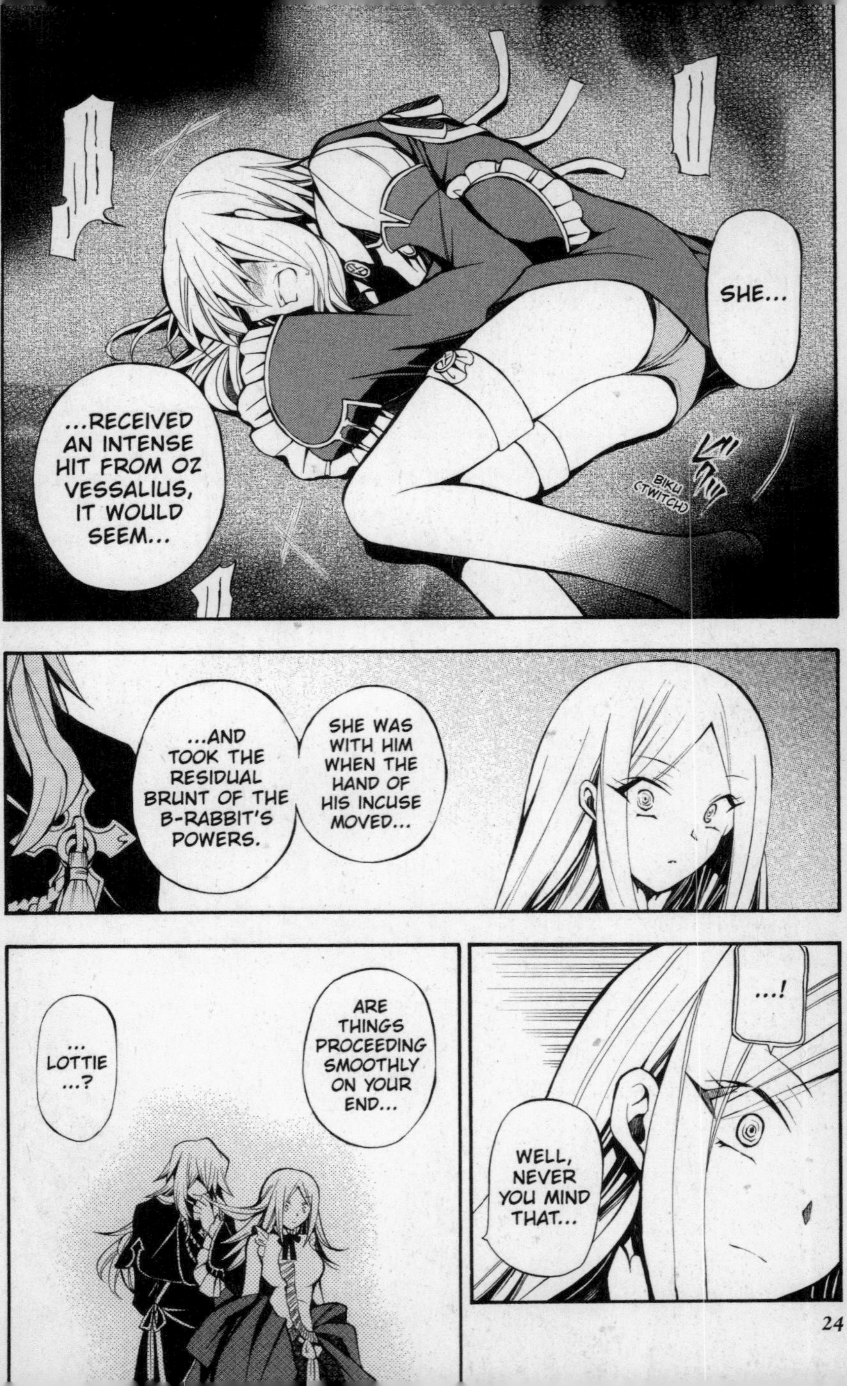
SHE...
...RECEIVED AN INTENSE HIT FROM OZ VESSALIUS, IT WOULD SEEM...
BIKU (TWITCH)
SHE WAS WITH HIM WHEN THE HAND OF HIS INCUSE MOVED...
...AND TOOK THE RESIDUAL BRUNT OF THE B-RABBIT'S POWERS.
...!
WELL, NEVER YOU MIND THAT...
ARE THINGS PROCEEDING SMOOTHLY ON YOUR END...
... LOTTIE ...?

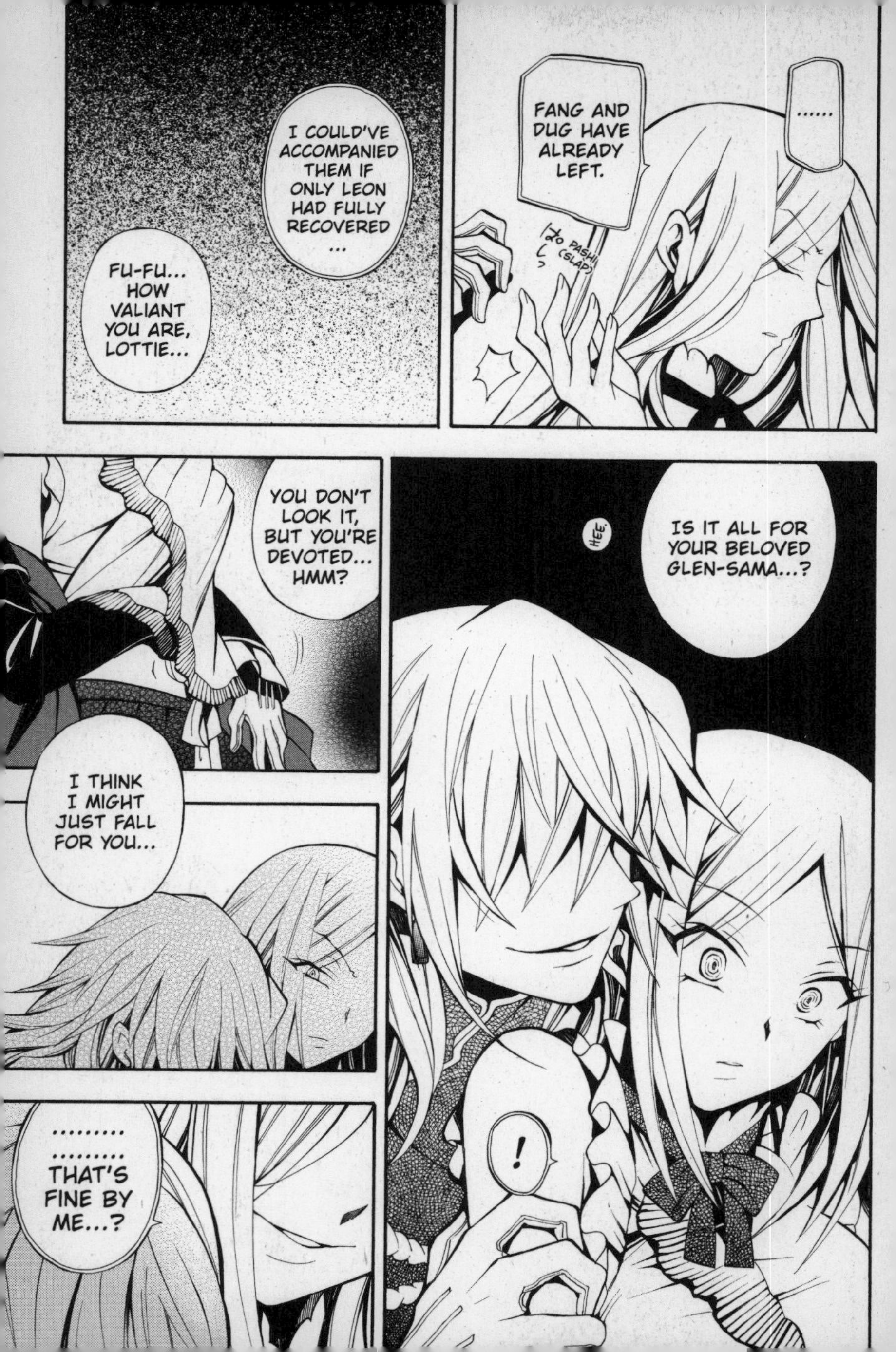

......
FANG AND DUG HAVE ALREADY LEFT.
PASHI (SLAP)
I COULD'VE ACCOMPANIED THEM IF ONLY LEON HAD FULLY RECOVERED ...
FU-FU... HOW VALIANT YOU ARE, LOTTIE...
IS IT ALL FOR YOUR BELOVED GLEN-SAMA...?
HEE.
!
YOU DON'T LOOK IT, BUT YOU'RE DEVOTED... HMM?
I THINK I MIGHT JUST FALL FOR YOU...
.... THAT'S FINE BY ME...?

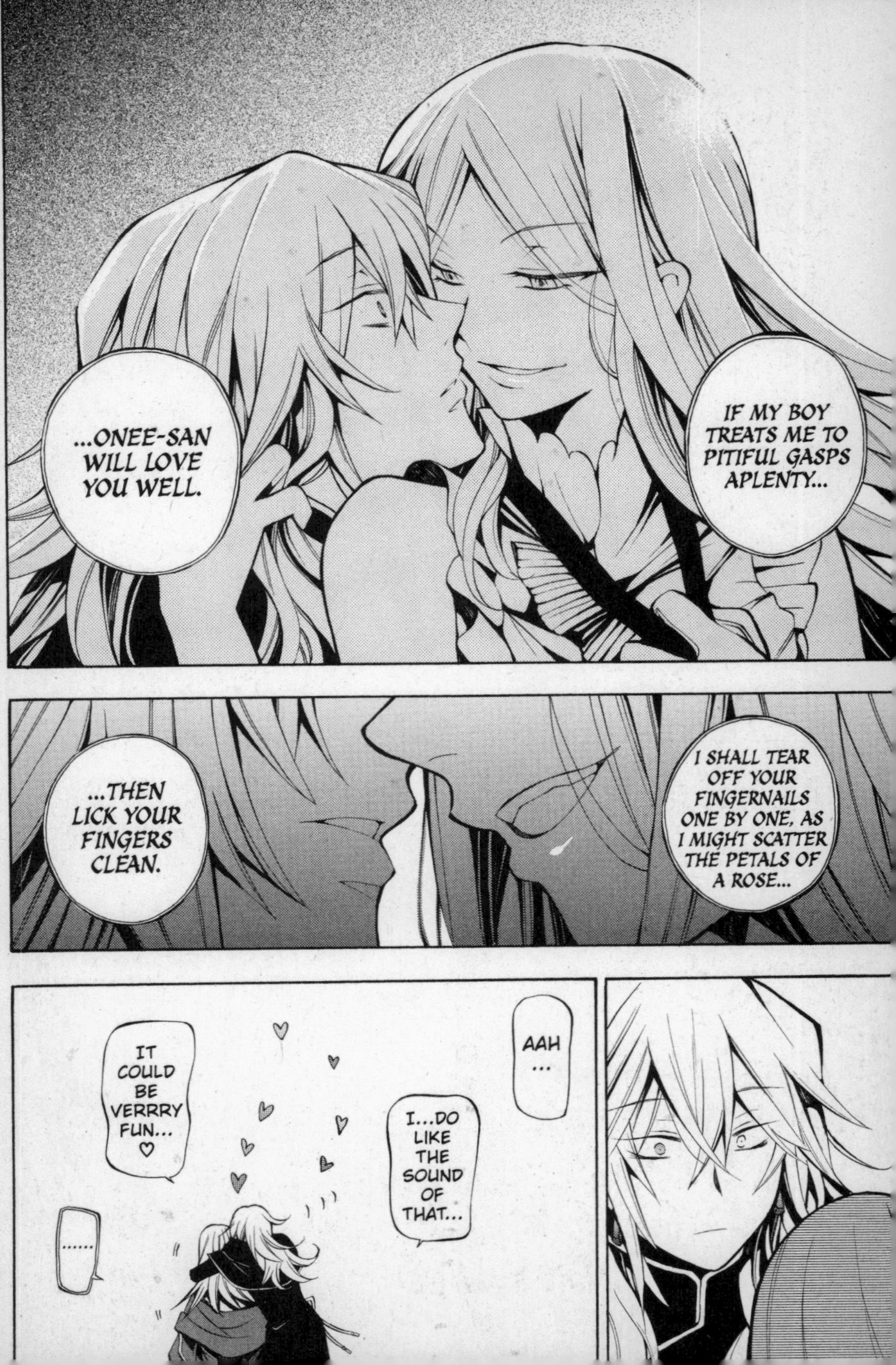
IF MY BOY TREATS ME TO PITIFUL GASPS APLENTY...
...ONEE-SAN WILL LOVE YOU WELL.
I SHALL TEAR OFF YOUR FINGERNAILS ONE BY ONE, AS I MIGHT SCATTER THE PETALS OF A ROSE...
...THEN LICK YOUR FINGERS CLEAN.
AAH...
I...DO LIKE THE SOUND OF THAT...
IT COULD BE VERRRY FUN...♡
......

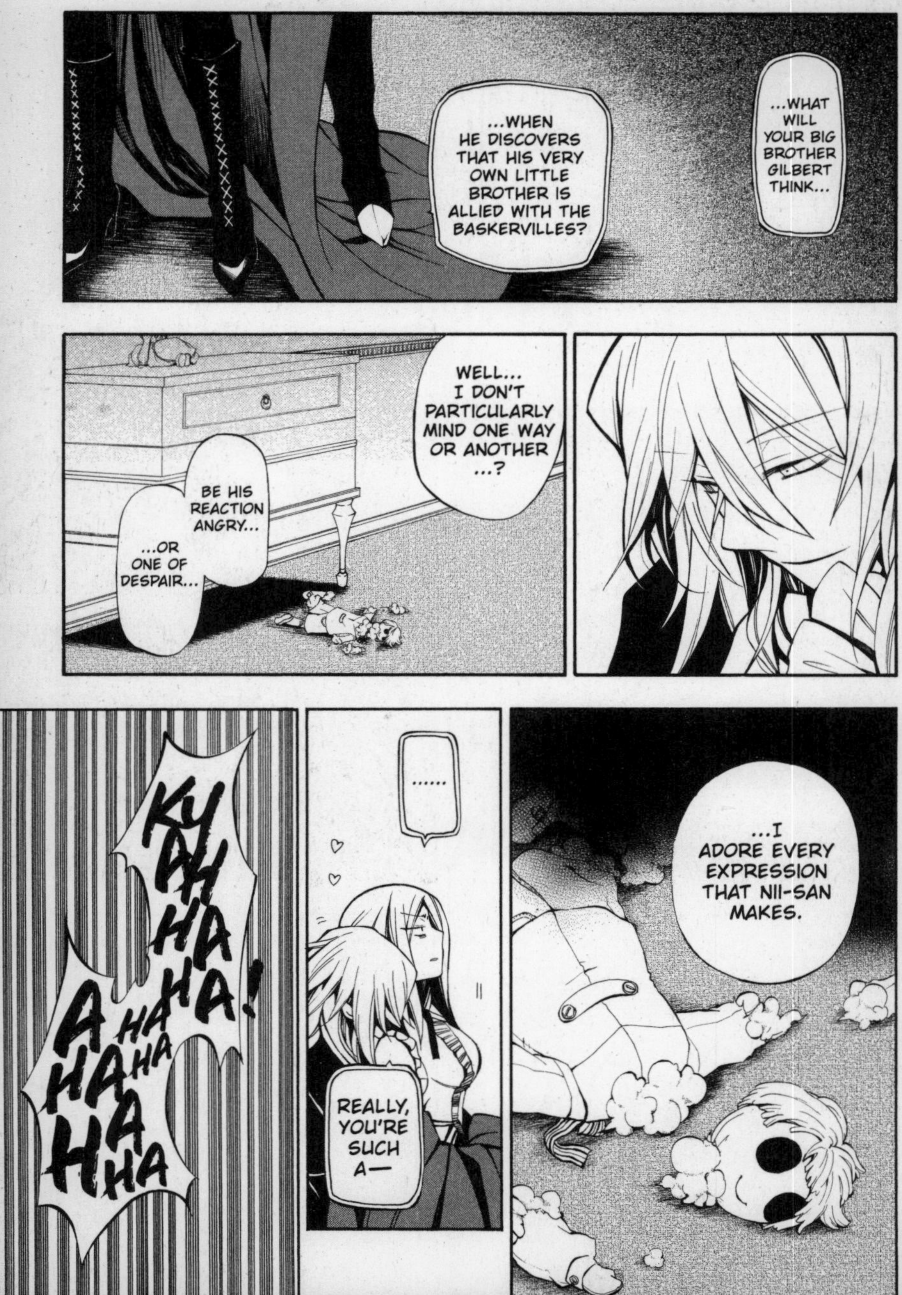
...WHAT WILL YOUR BIG BROTHER GILBERT THINK...
...WHEN HE DISCOVERS THAT HIS VERY OWN LITTLE BROTHER IS ALLIED WITH THE BASKERVILLES?
WELL... I DON'T PARTICULARLY MIND ONE WAY OR ANOTHER ...?
BE HIS REACTION ANGRY...
...OR ONE OF DESPAIR...
...I ADORE EVERY EXPRESSION THAT NII-SAN MAKES.
......
REALLY, YOU'RE SUCH A—
KYAHAHAHA!
AHAHAHAHAHAHA

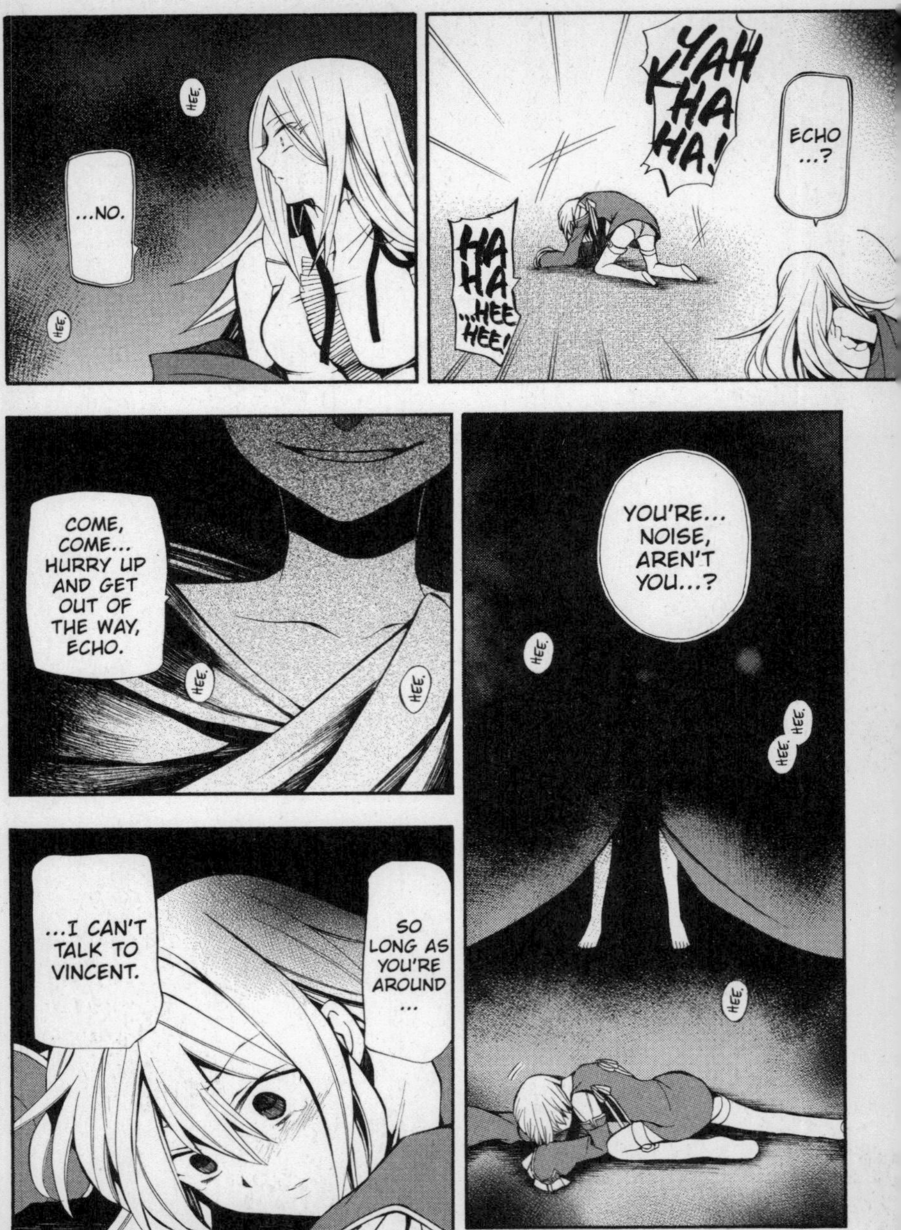
ECHO ...?
YAH KHA HA HA!
HA HA ...HEE HEE!
HEE.
...NO.
HEE.
YOU'RE... NOISE, AREN'T YOU...?
HEE.
HEE.
HEE.
HEE.
COME, COME... HURRY UP AND GET OUT OF THE WAY, ECHO.
HEE.
HEE.
SO LONG AS YOU'RE AROUND ...
...I CAN'T TALK TO VINCENT.

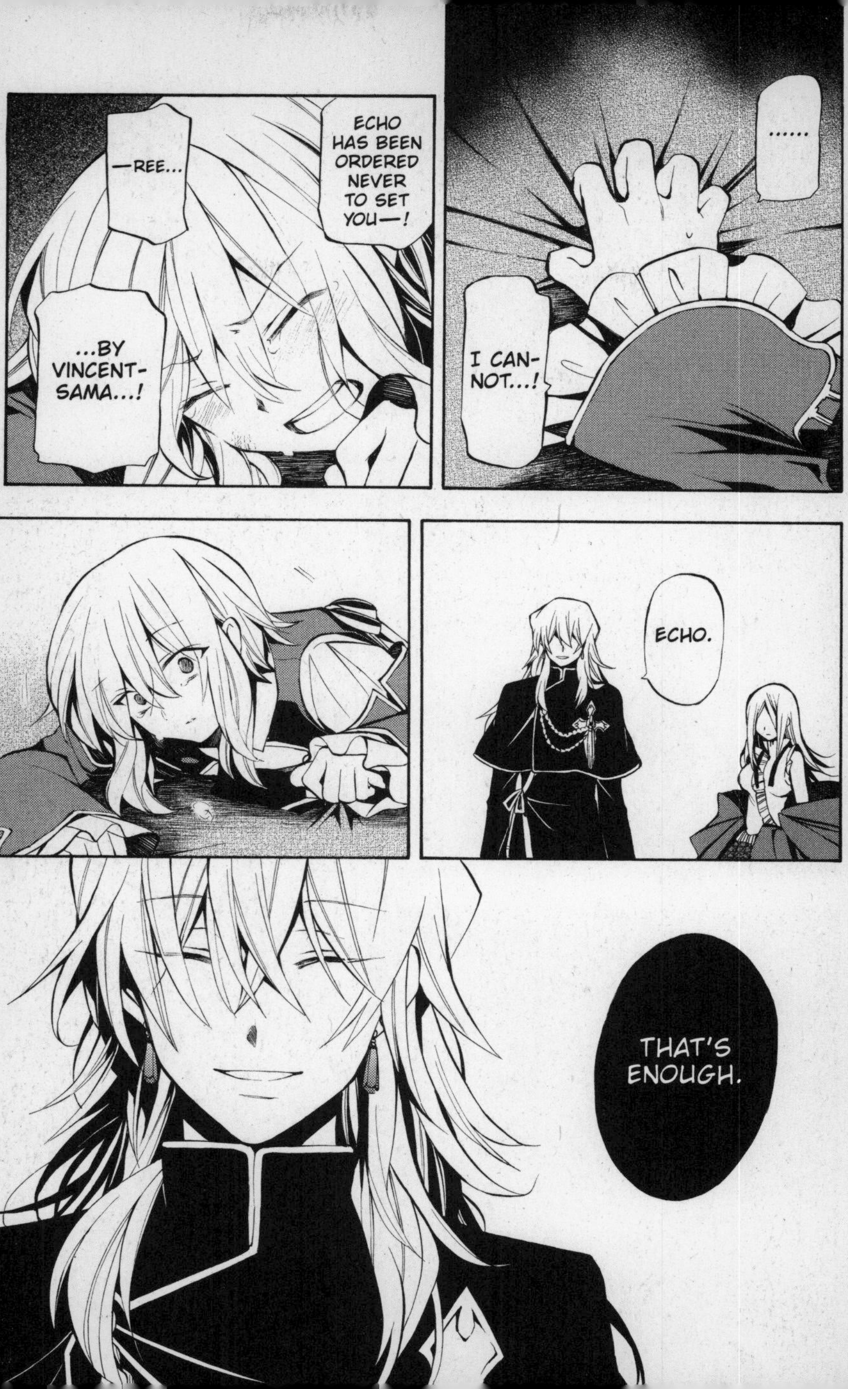
......
I CAN-NOT...!
ECHO HAS BEEN ORDERED NEVER TO SET YOU—!
—REE...
...BY VINCENT-SAMA...!
ECHO.
THAT'S ENOUGH.

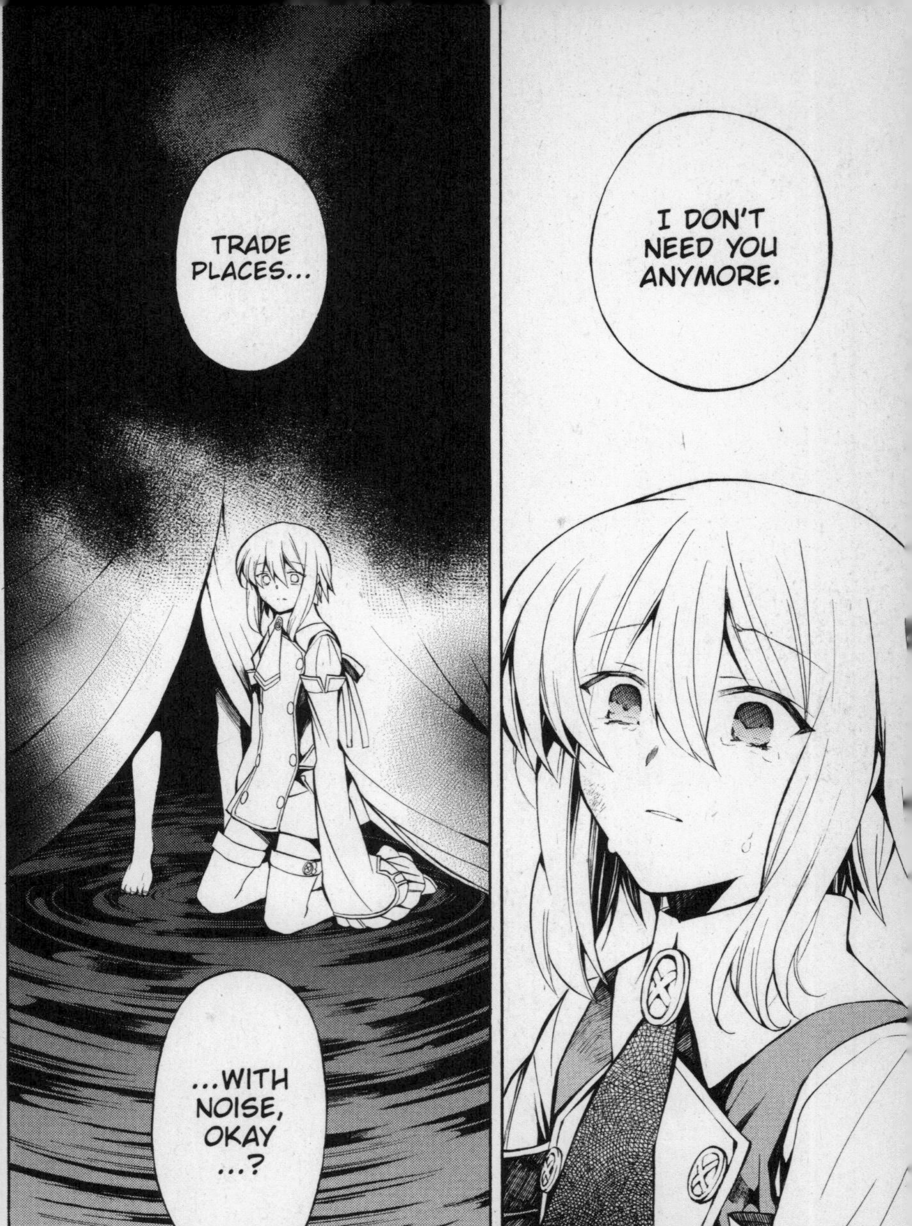
I DON'T NEED YOU ANYMORE.
TRADE PLACES...
...WITH NOISE, OKAY ...?

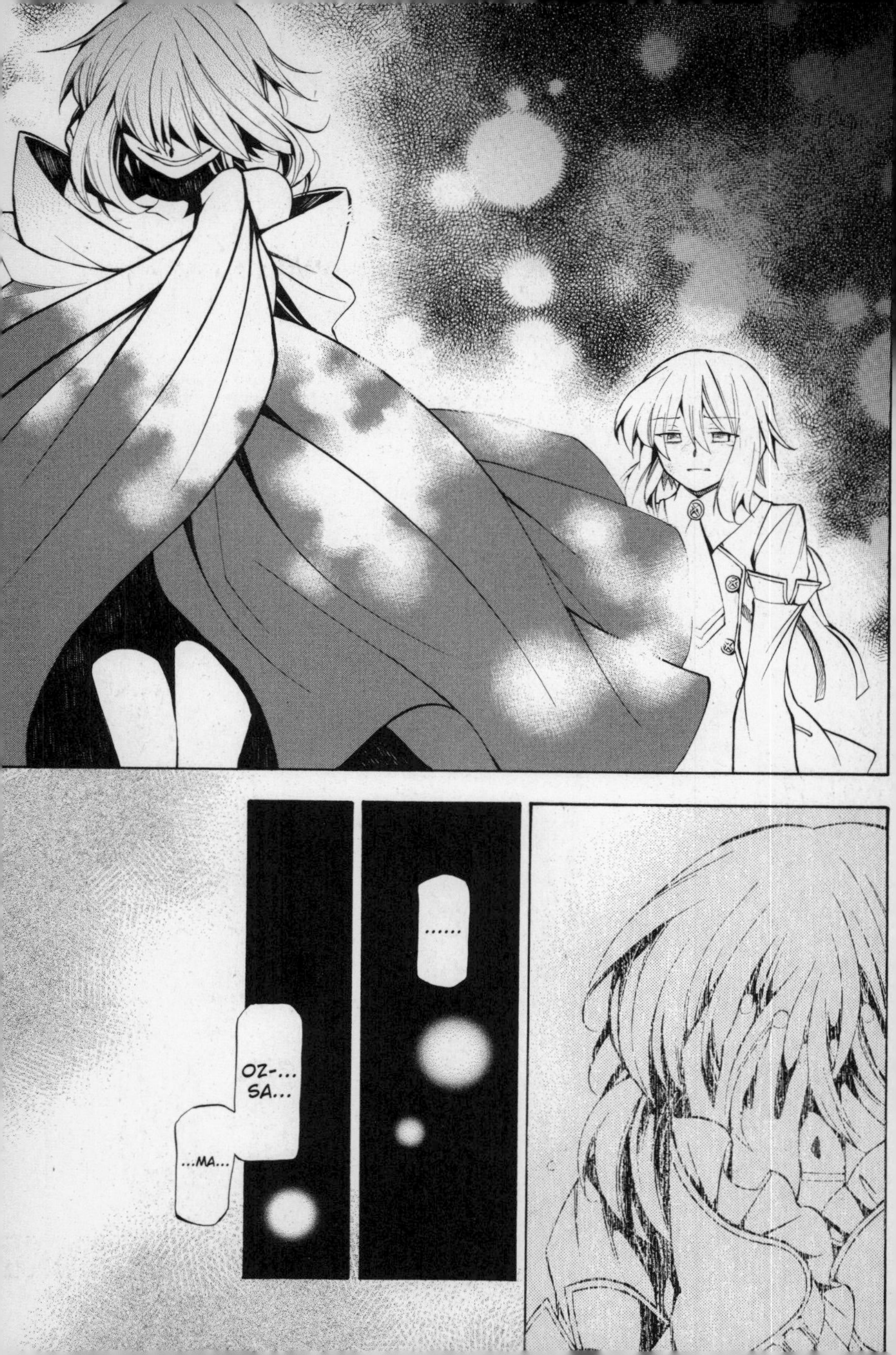
......
OZ-... SA...
...MA...

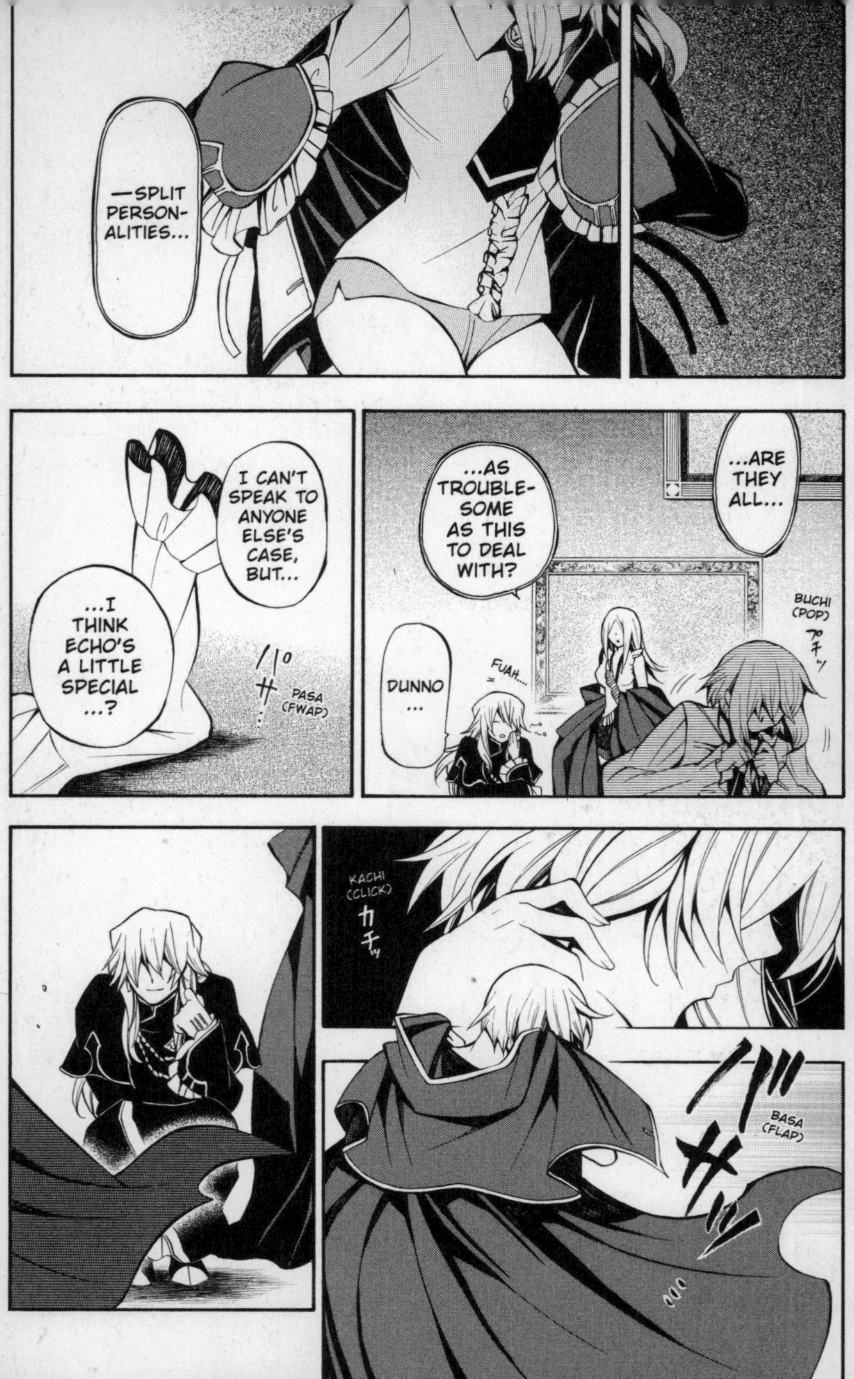
—SPLIT PERSONALITIES...
...ARE THEY ALL...
...AS TROUBLESOME AS THIS TO DEAL WITH?
BUCHI (POP)
FUAH...
DUNNO...
I CAN'T SPEAK TO ANYONE ELSE'S CASE, BUT...
PASA (FWAP)
...I THINK ECHO'S A LITTLE SPECIAL...?
KACHI (CLICK)
BASA (FLAP)

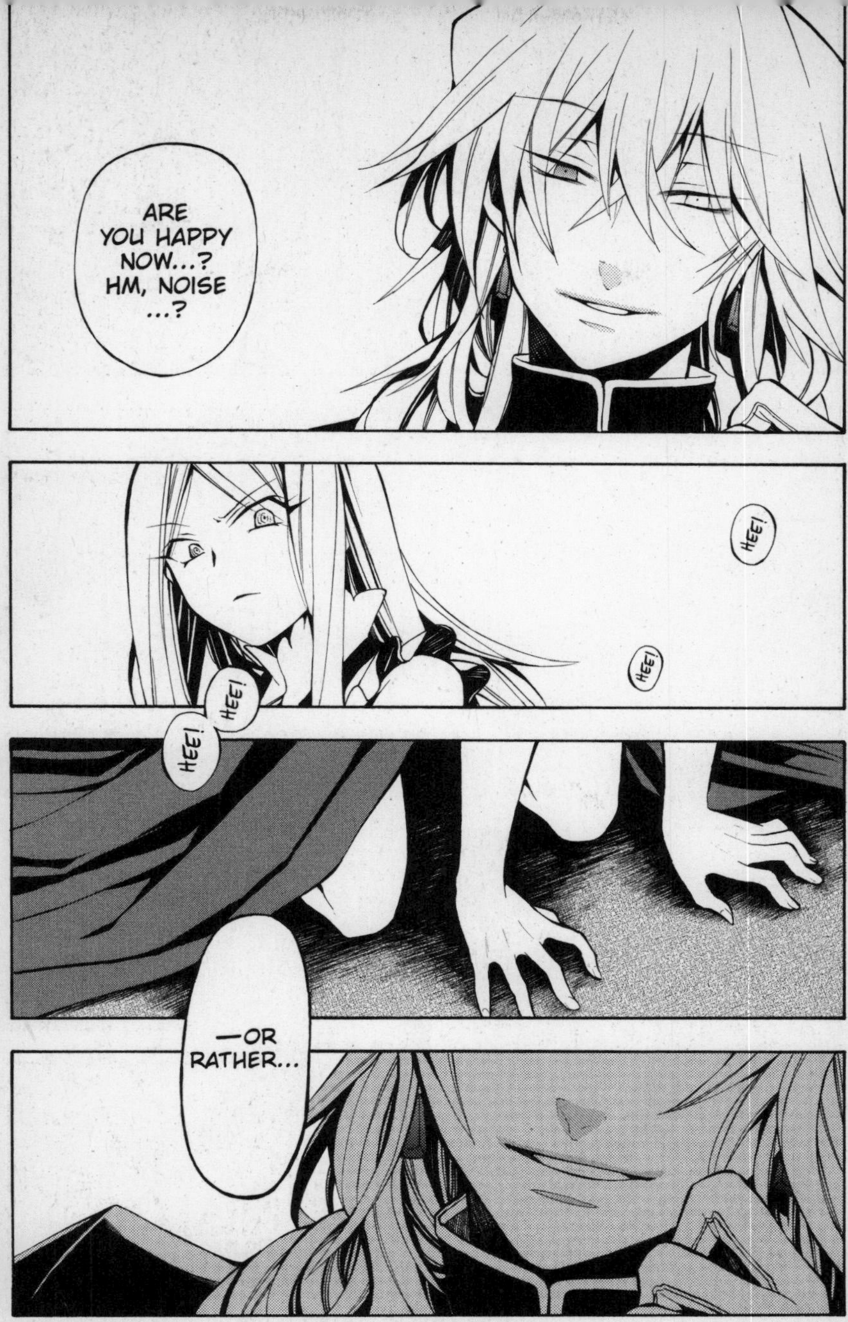
ARE YOU HAPPY NOW...? HM, NOISE ...?
HEE!
HEE!
HEE!
HEE!
—OR RATHER...

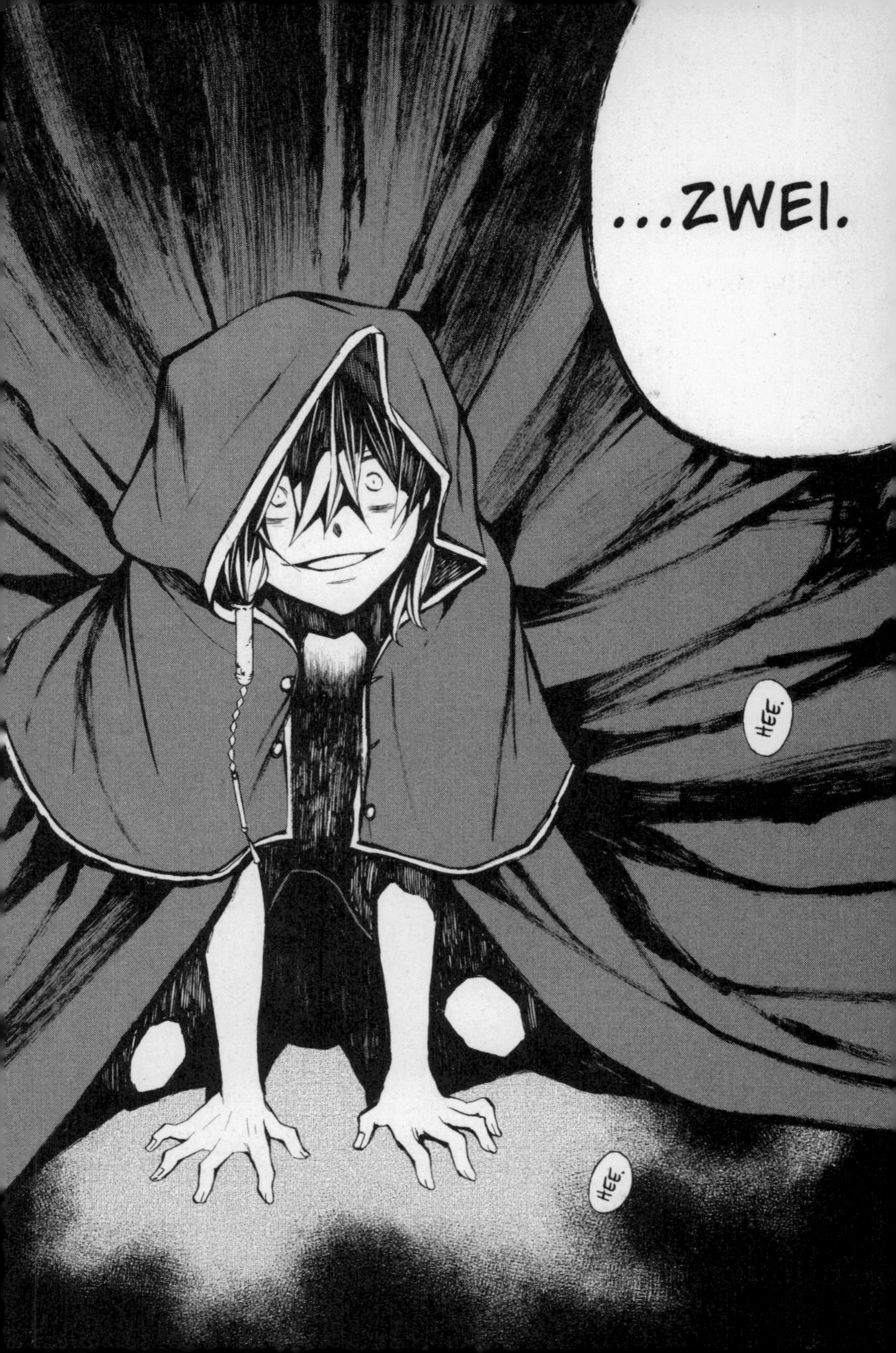
...ZWEI.
HEE.
HEE.

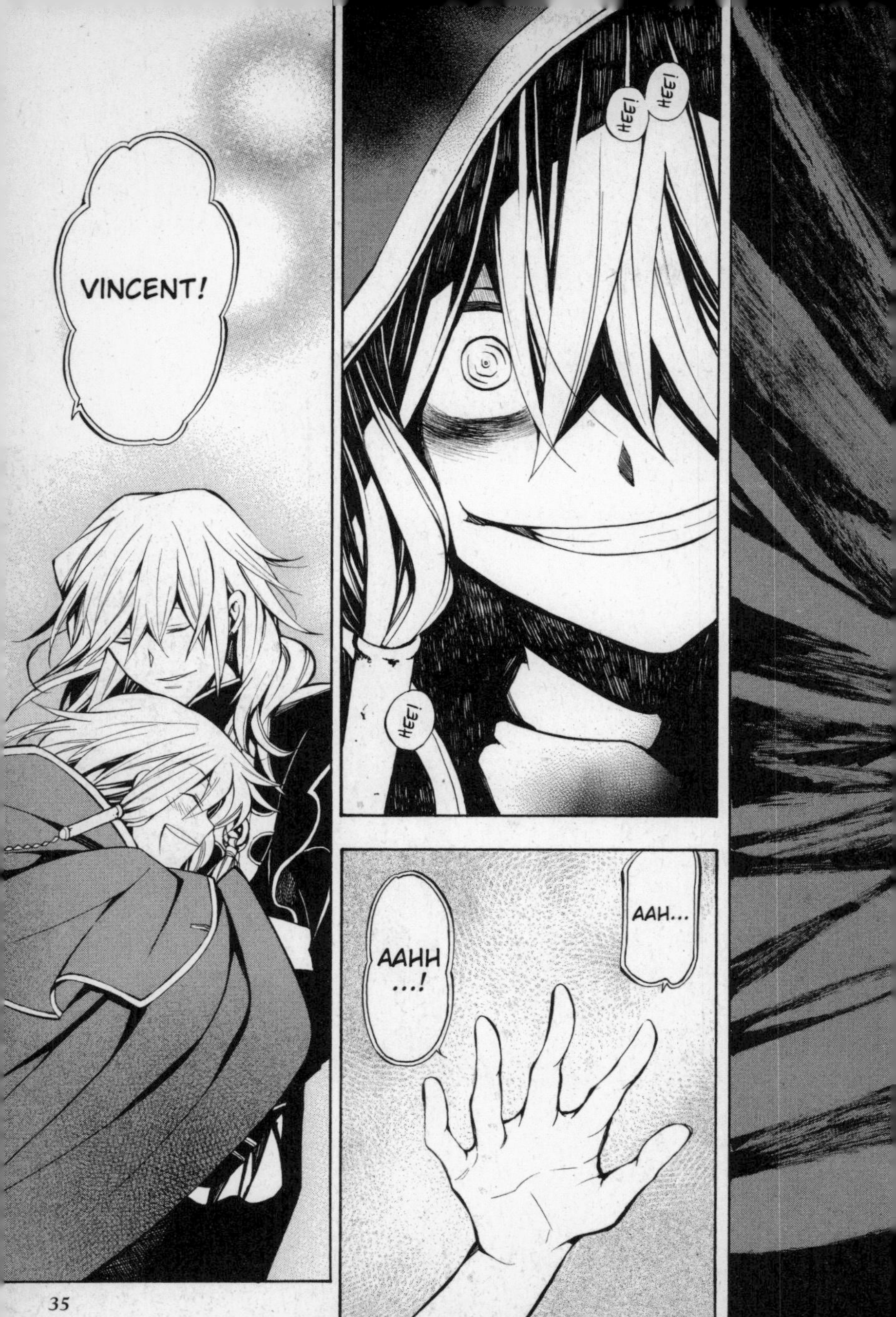
HEE!
HEE!
HEE!
AAH...
AAHH ...!
VINCENT!

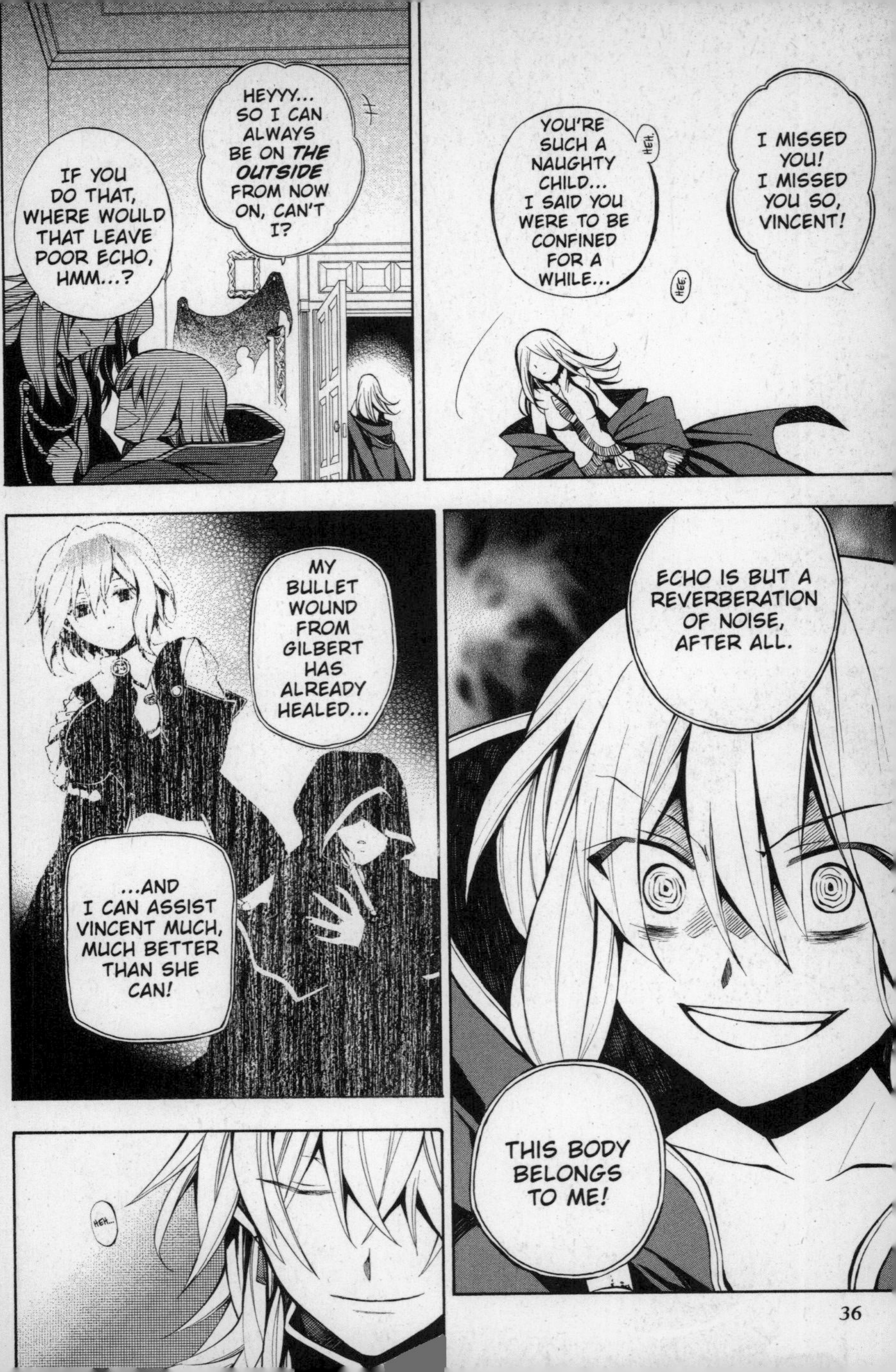
I MISSED YOU! I MISSED YOU SO, VINCENT!
HEH.
YOU'RE SUCH A NAUGHTY CHILD... I SAID YOU WERE TO BE CONFINED FOR A WHILE...
HEE.
HEYYY... SO I CAN ALWAYS BE ON *THE OUTSIDE* FROM NOW ON, CAN'T I?
IF YOU DO THAT, WHERE WOULD THAT LEAVE POOR ECHO, HMM...?
ECHO IS BUT A REVERBERATION OF NOISE, AFTER ALL.
THIS BODY BELONGS TO ME!
MY BULLET WOUND FROM GILBERT HAS ALREADY HEALED...
...AND I CAN ASSIST VINCENT MUCH, MUCH BETTER THAN SHE CAN!
HEH...

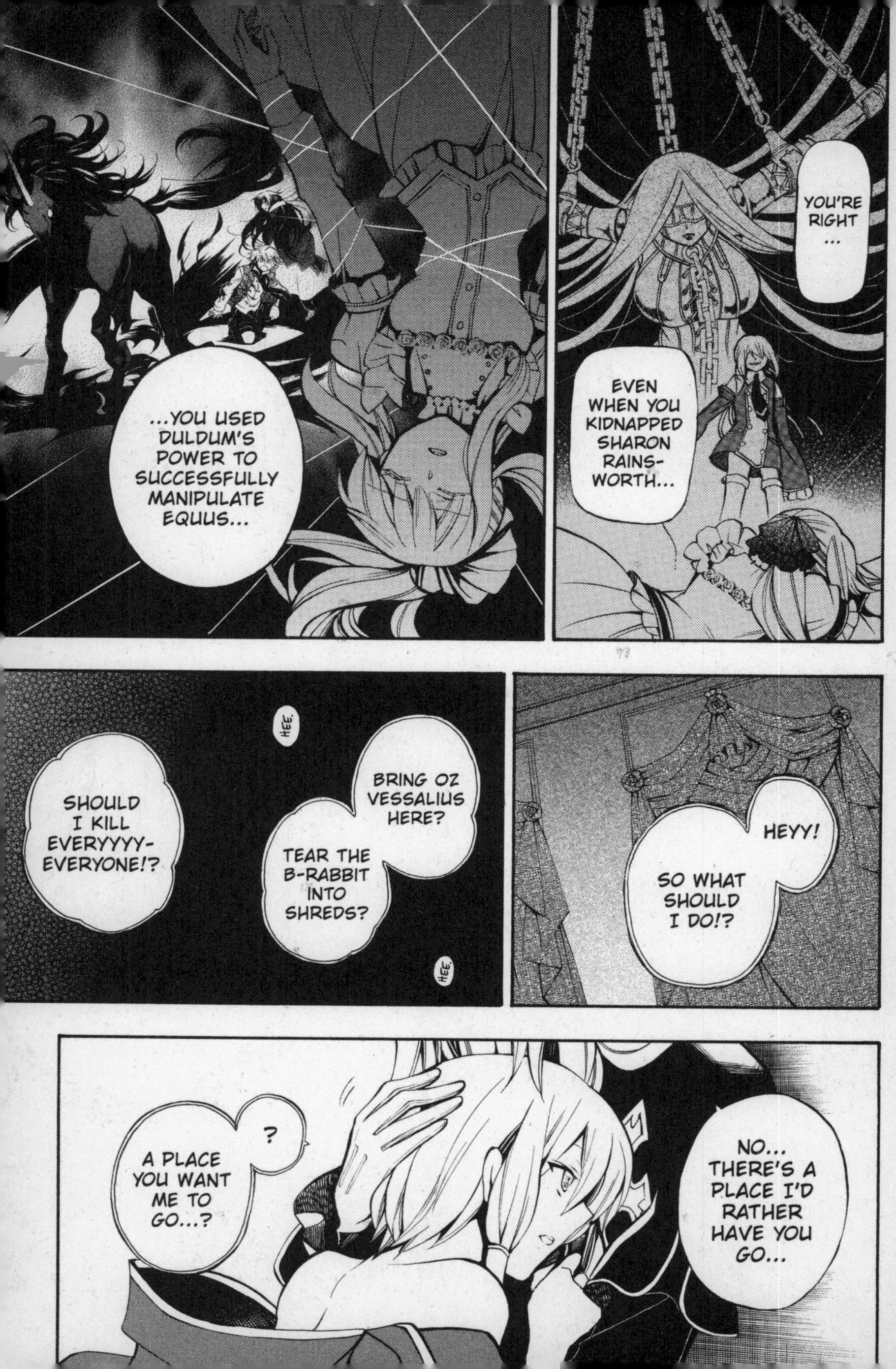
YOU'RE RIGHT ...
EVEN WHEN YOU KIDNAPPED SHARON RAINS-WORTH...
...YOU USED DULDUM'S POWER TO SUCCESSFULLY MANIPULATE EQUUS...
HEYY!
SO WHAT SHOULD I DO!?
HEE.
BRING OZ VESSALIUS HERE?
TEAR THE B-RABBIT INTO SHREDS?
HEE.
SHOULD I KILL EVERYYYY-EVERYONE!?
NO... THERE'S A PLACE I'D RATHER HAVE YOU GO...
?
A PLACE YOU WANT ME TO GO...?

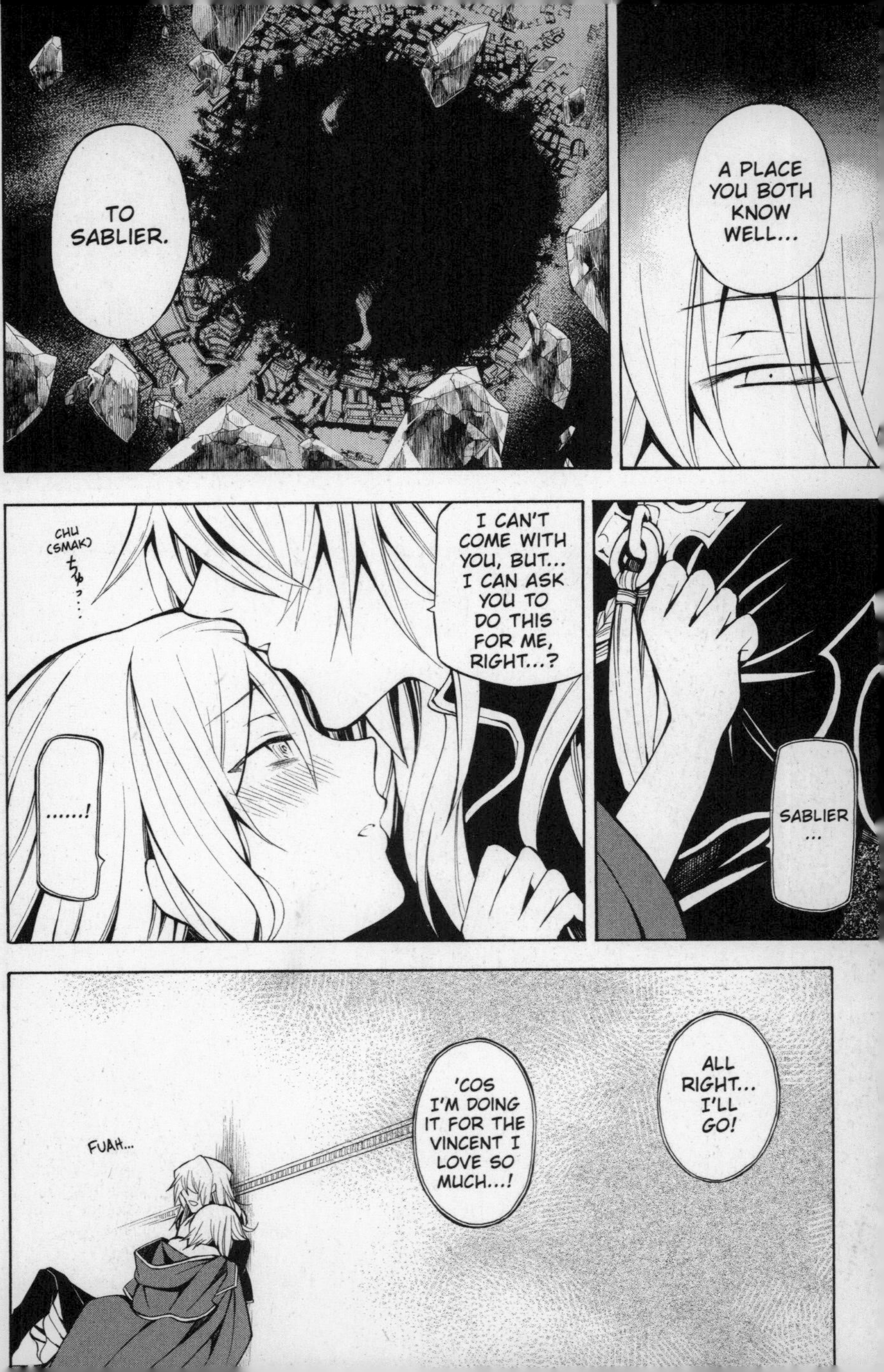
A PLACE YOU BOTH KNOW WELL...
TO SABLIER.
SABLIER...
I CAN'T COME WITH YOU, BUT... I CAN ASK YOU TO DO THIS FOR ME, RIGHT...?
CHU (SMAK)
ちゅっ…
......!
ALL RIGHT... I'LL GO!
'COS I'M DOING IT FOR THE VINCENT I LOVE SO MUCH...!
FUAH...

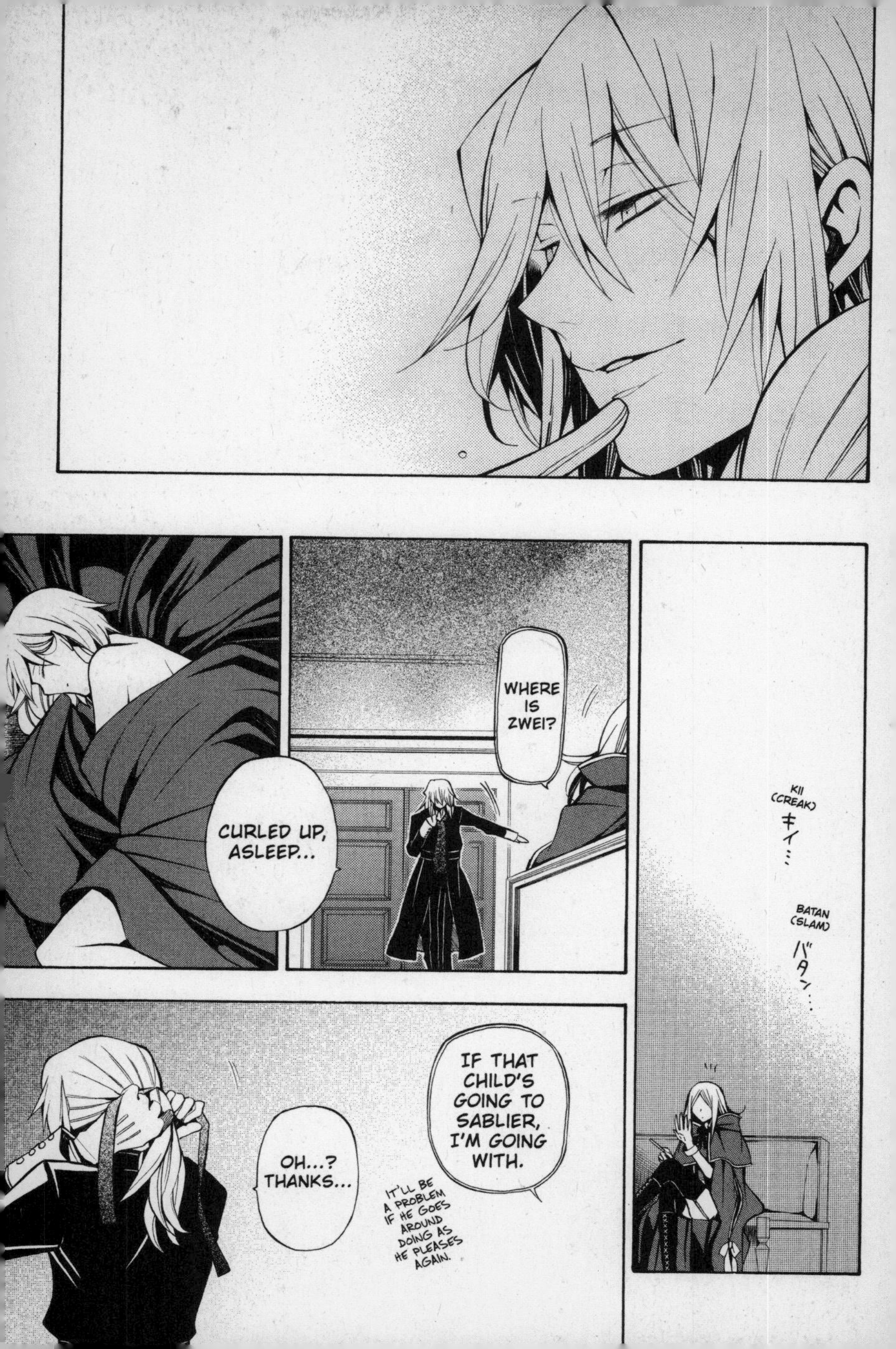
KII (CREAK)
キイ…
BATAN (SLAM)
バタン…
WHERE IS ZWEI?
CURLED UP, ASLEEP…
IF THAT CHILD'S GOING TO SABLIER, I'M GOING WITH.
IT'LL BE A PROBLEM IF HE GOES AROUND DOING AS HE PLEASES AGAIN.
OH…? THANKS…

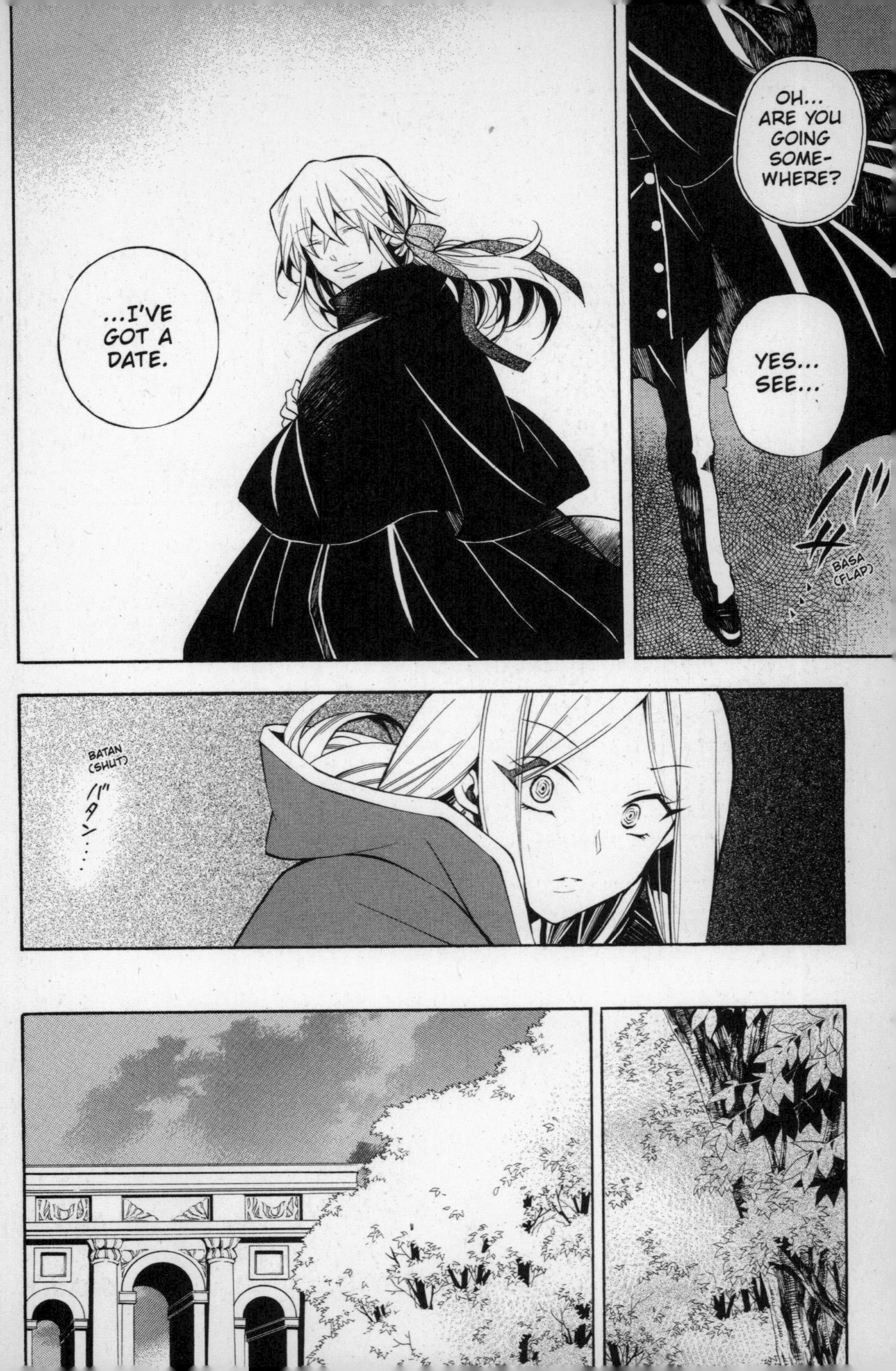
OH... ARE YOU GOING SOME-WHERE?
YES... SEE...
BASA (FLAP)
...I'VE GOT A DATE.
BATAN (SHUT)

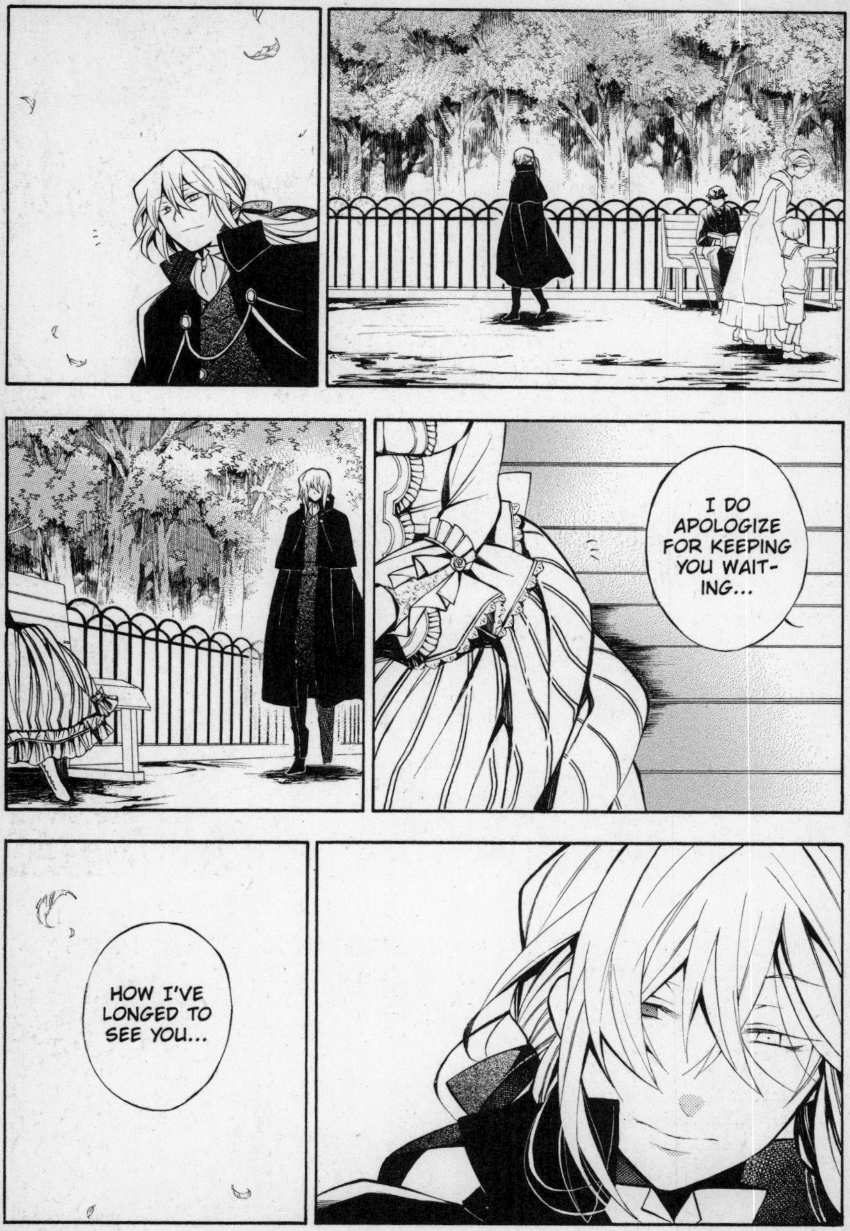
I DO APOLOGIZE FOR KEEPING YOU WAIT-ING...
HOW I'VE LONGED TO SEE YOU...

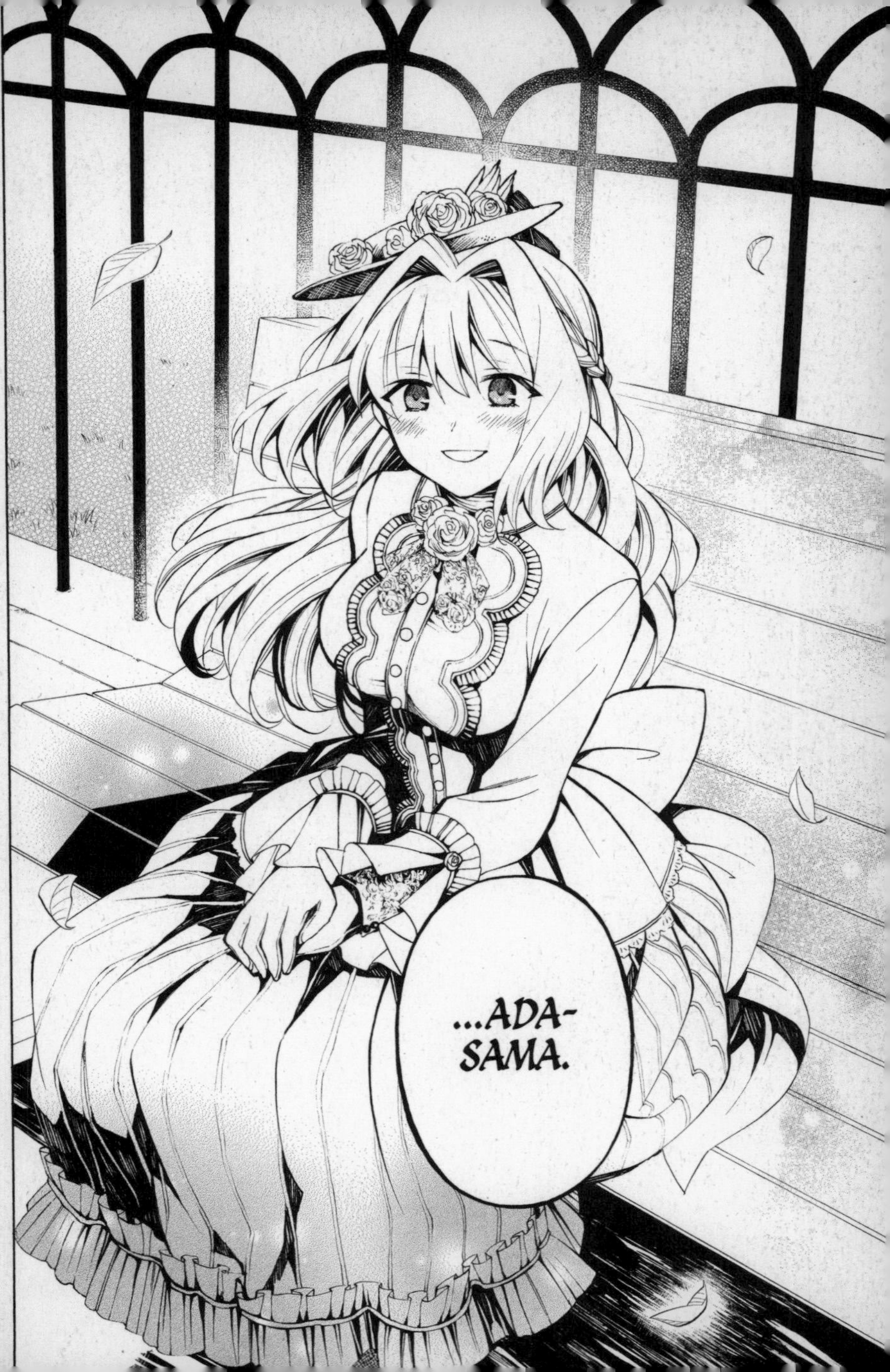
...ADA-SAMA.

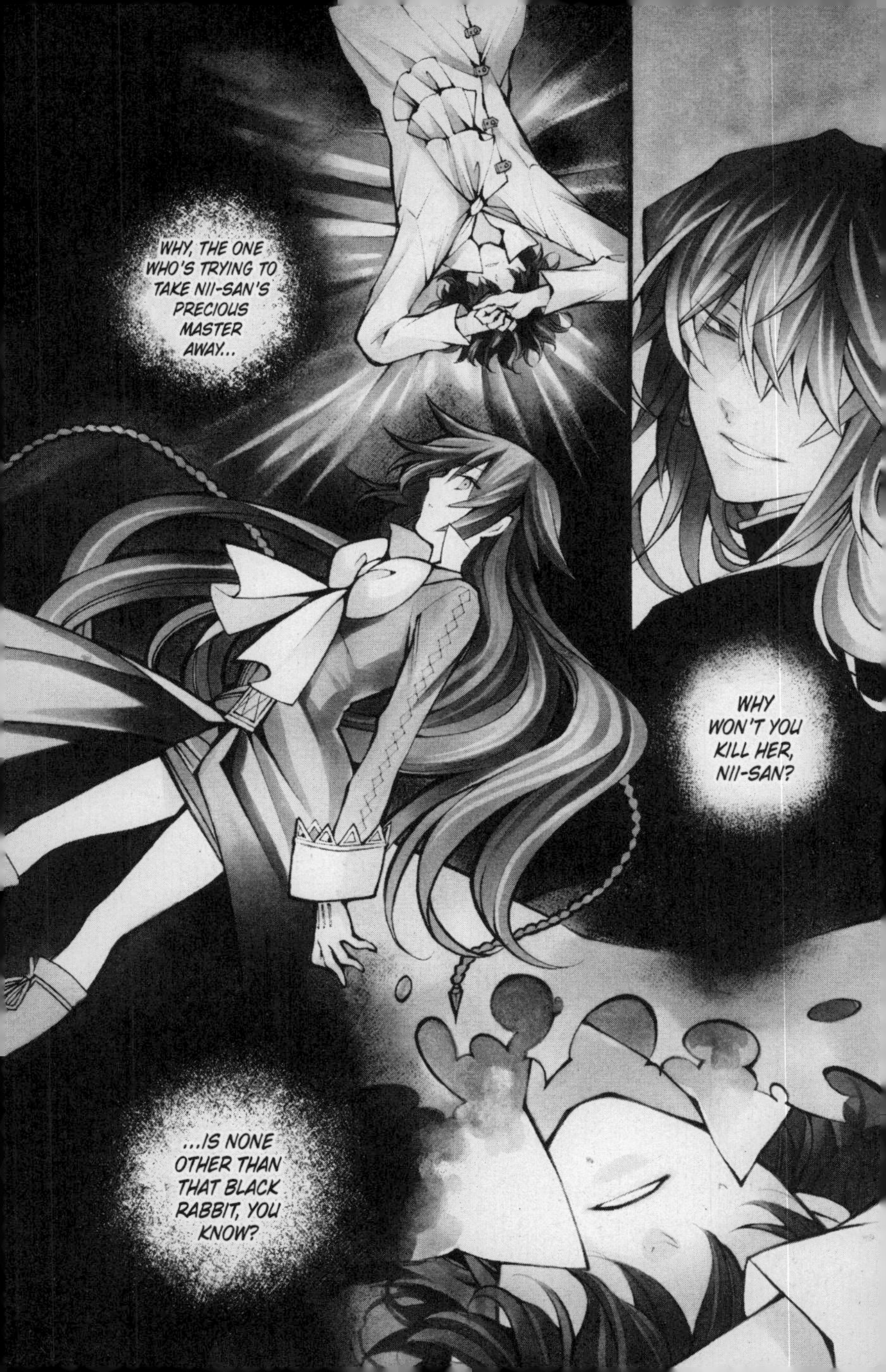
WHY WON'T YOU KILL HER, NII-SAN?
WHY, THE ONE WHO'S TRYING TO TAKE NII-SAN'S PRECIOUS MASTER AWAY...
...IS NONE OTHER THAN THAT BLACK RABBIT, YOU KNOW?

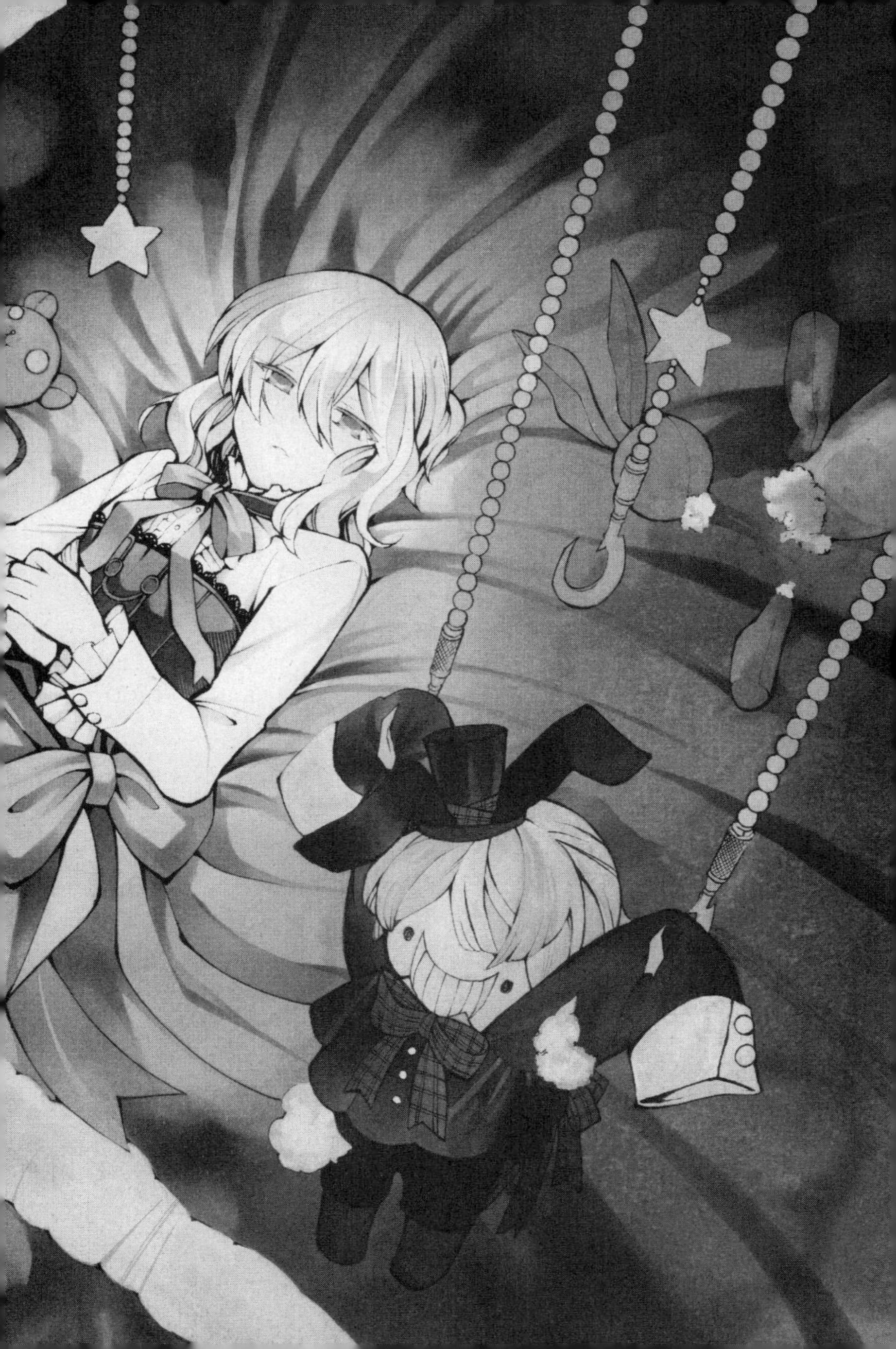

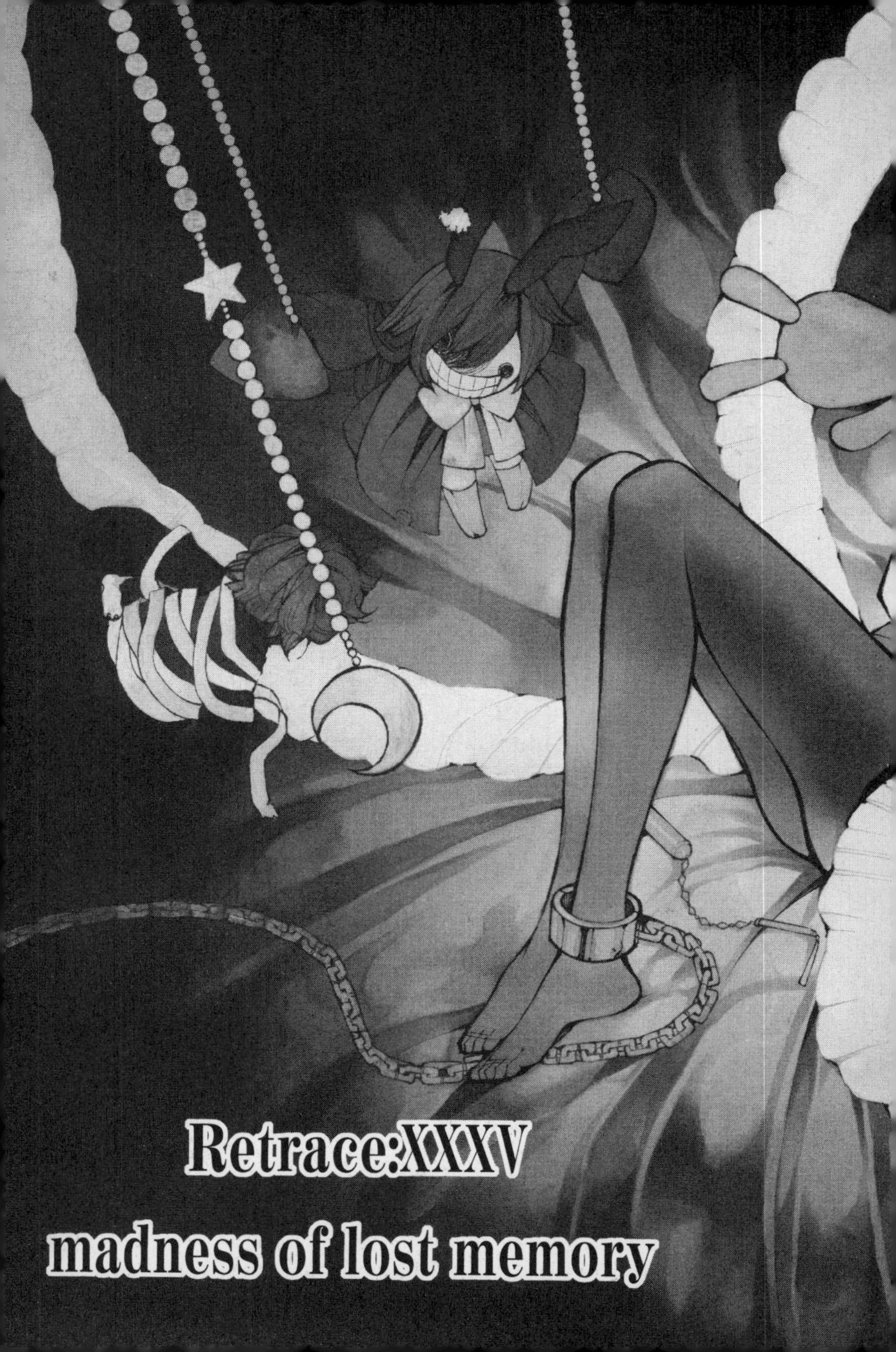
Retrace:XXXV
madness of lost memory

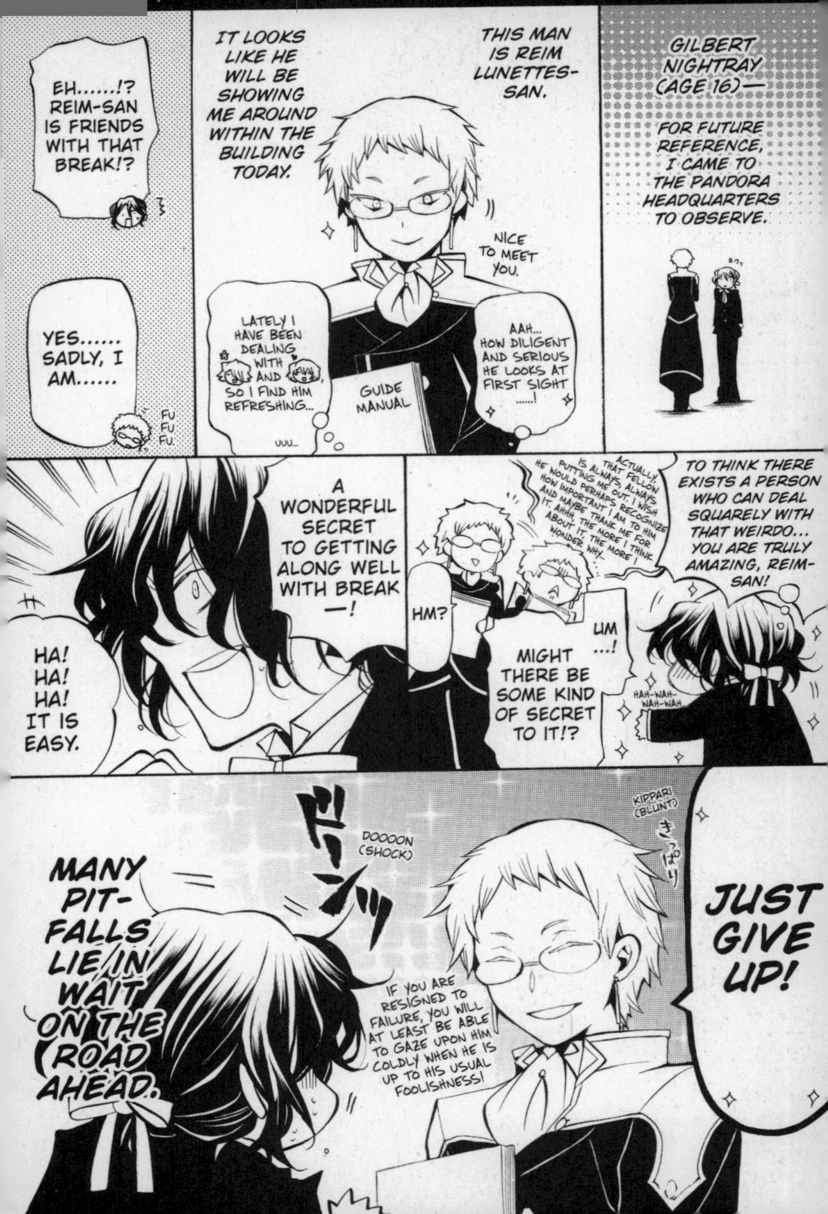
GILBERT NIGHTRAY (AGE 16)—
FOR FUTURE REFERENCE, I CAME TO THE PANDORA HEADQUARTERS TO OBSERVE.
THIS MAN IS REIM LUNETTES-SAN.
IT LOOKS LIKE HE WILL BE SHOWING ME AROUND WITHIN THE BUILDING TODAY.
NICE TO MEET YOU.
AAH... HOW DILIGENT AND SERIOUS HE LOOKS AT FIRST SIGHT ......!
LATELY I HAVE BEEN DEALING WITH AND SO I FIND HIM REFRESHING...
GUIDE MANUAL
UUU...
EH......!? REIM-SAN IS FRIENDS WITH THAT BREAK!?
YES...... SADLY, I AM......
FU FU FU.
TO THINK THERE EXISTS A PERSON WHO CAN DEAL SQUARELY WITH THAT WEIRDO... YOU ARE TRULY AMAZING, REIM-SAN!
ACTUALLY, THAT FELLOW IS ALWAYS, ALWAYS PUTTING ME OUT. I WISH HE WOULD PERHAPS RECOGNIZE HOW IMPORTANT I AM TO HIM AND MAYBE THANK ME FOR IT. AHHH, THE MORE I THINK ABOUT IT, THE MORE I WONDER WHY...
HAH-WAH-WAH
UM ...!
MIGHT THERE BE SOME KIND OF SECRET TO IT!?
HM?
A WONDERFUL SECRET TO GETTING ALONG WELL WITH BREAK—!
HA! HA! HA! IT IS EASY.
JUST GIVE UP!
KIPPARI (BLUNT)
IF YOU ARE RESIGNED TO FAILURE, YOU WILL AT LEAST BE ABLE TO GAZE UPON HIM COLDLY WHEN HE IS UP TO HIS USUAL FOOLISHNESS!
DOOOON (SHOCK)
MANY PIT-FALLS LIE IN WAIT ON THE ROAD AHEAD.

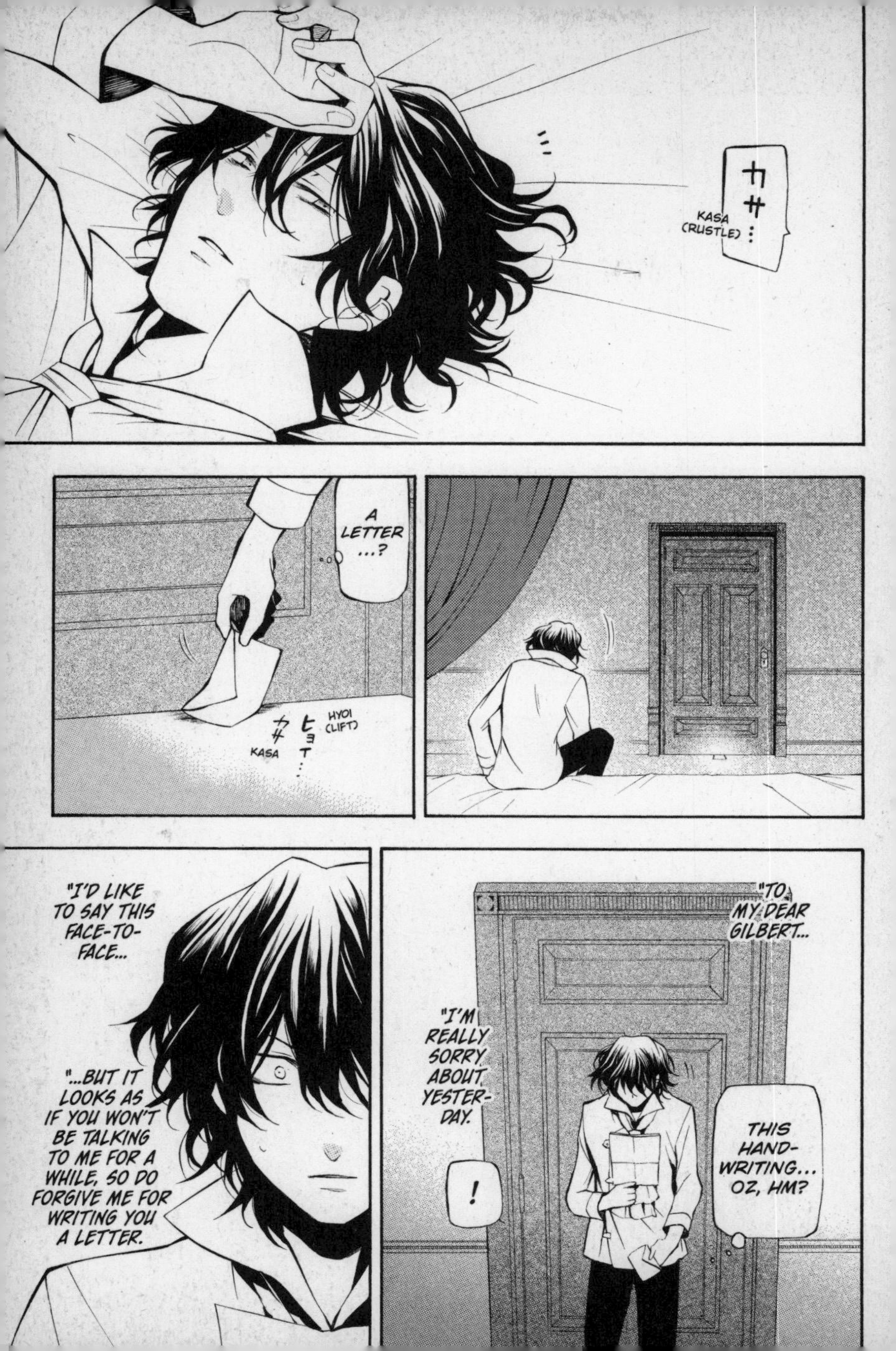
カサ…
KASA (RUSTLE)
A LETTER ...?
ヒョイ…
HYOI (LIFT)
カサ
KASA
"TO MY DEAR GILBERT...
THIS HAND-WRITING... OZ, HM?
"I'M REALLY SORRY ABOUT YESTER-DAY.
!
"I'D LIKE TO SAY THIS FACE-TO-FACE...
"...BUT IT LOOKS AS IF YOU WON'T BE TALKING TO ME FOR A WHILE, SO DO FORGIVE ME FOR WRITING YOU A LETTER.

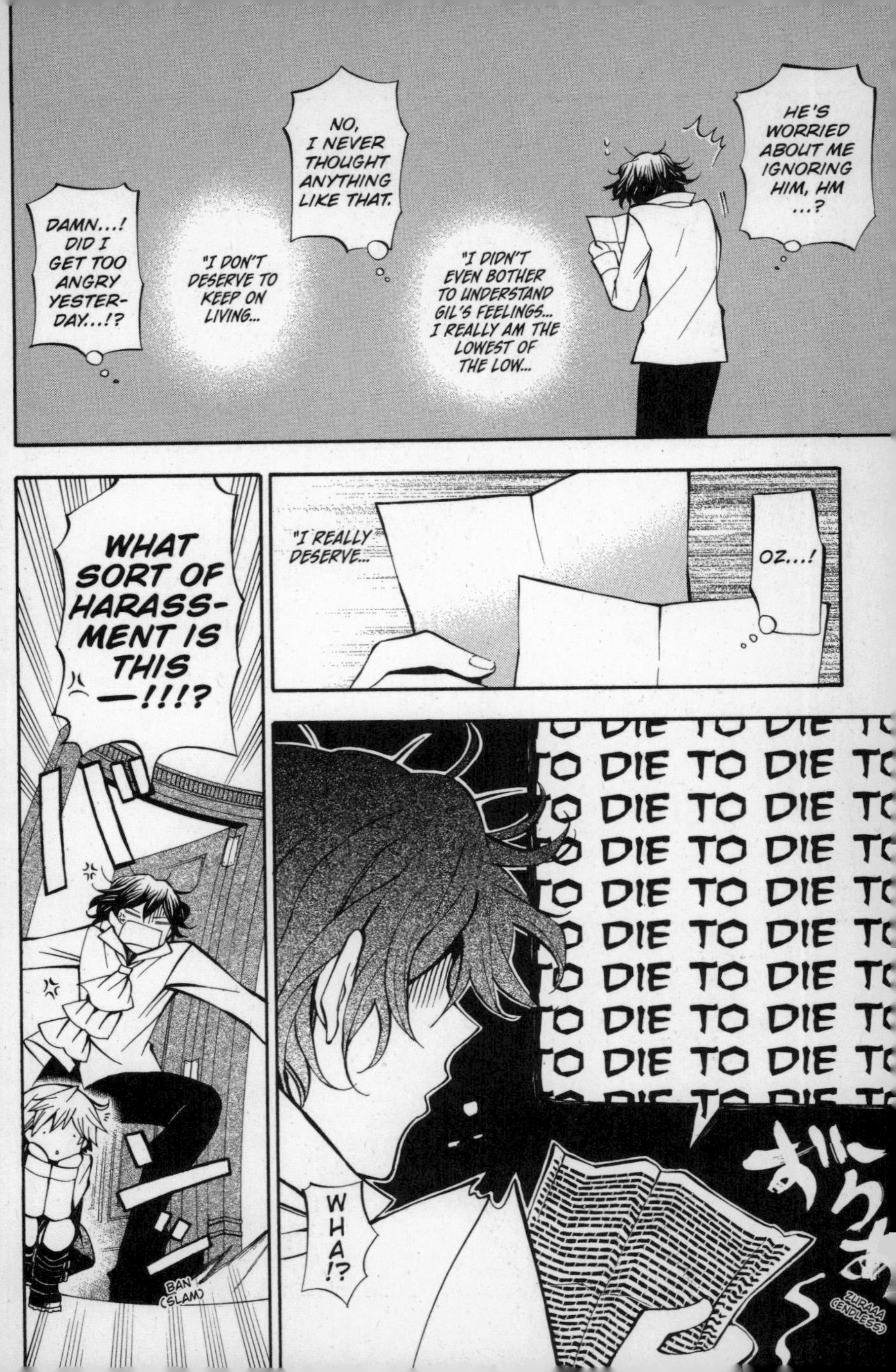
HE'S WORRIED ABOUT ME IGNORING HIM, HM ...?
"I DIDN'T EVEN BOTHER TO UNDERSTAND GIL'S FEELINGS... I REALLY AM THE LOWEST OF THE LOW...
NO, I NEVER THOUGHT ANYTHING LIKE THAT.
"I DON'T DESERVE TO KEEP ON LIVING...
DAMN...! DID I GET TOO ANGRY YESTER-DAY...!?
OZ...!
"I REALLY DESERVE...
TO DIE TO DIE TO DIE TO DIE TO DIE TO DIE TO DIE TO DIE TO DIE TO DIE TO DIE TO DIE TO DIE TO DIE TO DIE TO DIE
WHA!?
ZURAAA (ENDLESS)
WHAT SORT OF HARASS-MENT IS THIS —!!!?
BAN (SLAM)

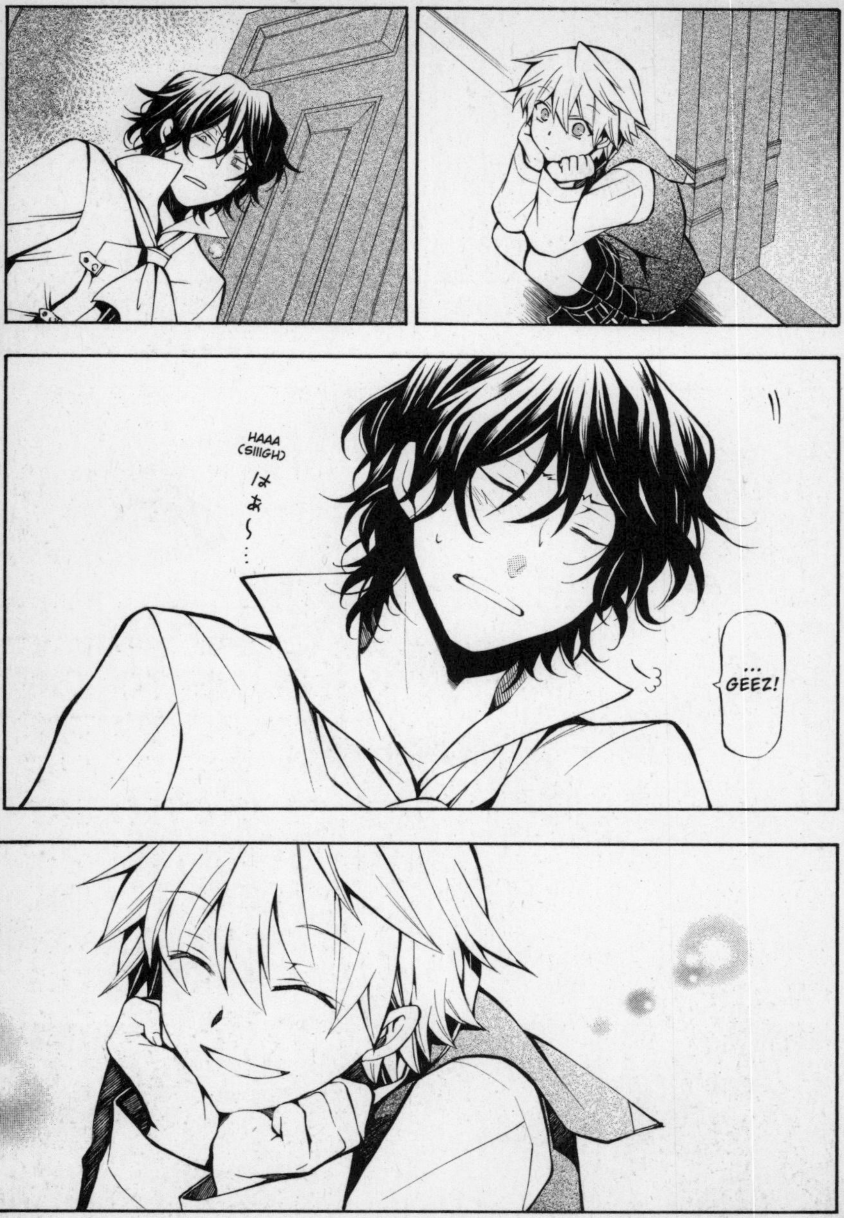
HAAA (SIIIGH)
はぁ～…
...GEEZ!

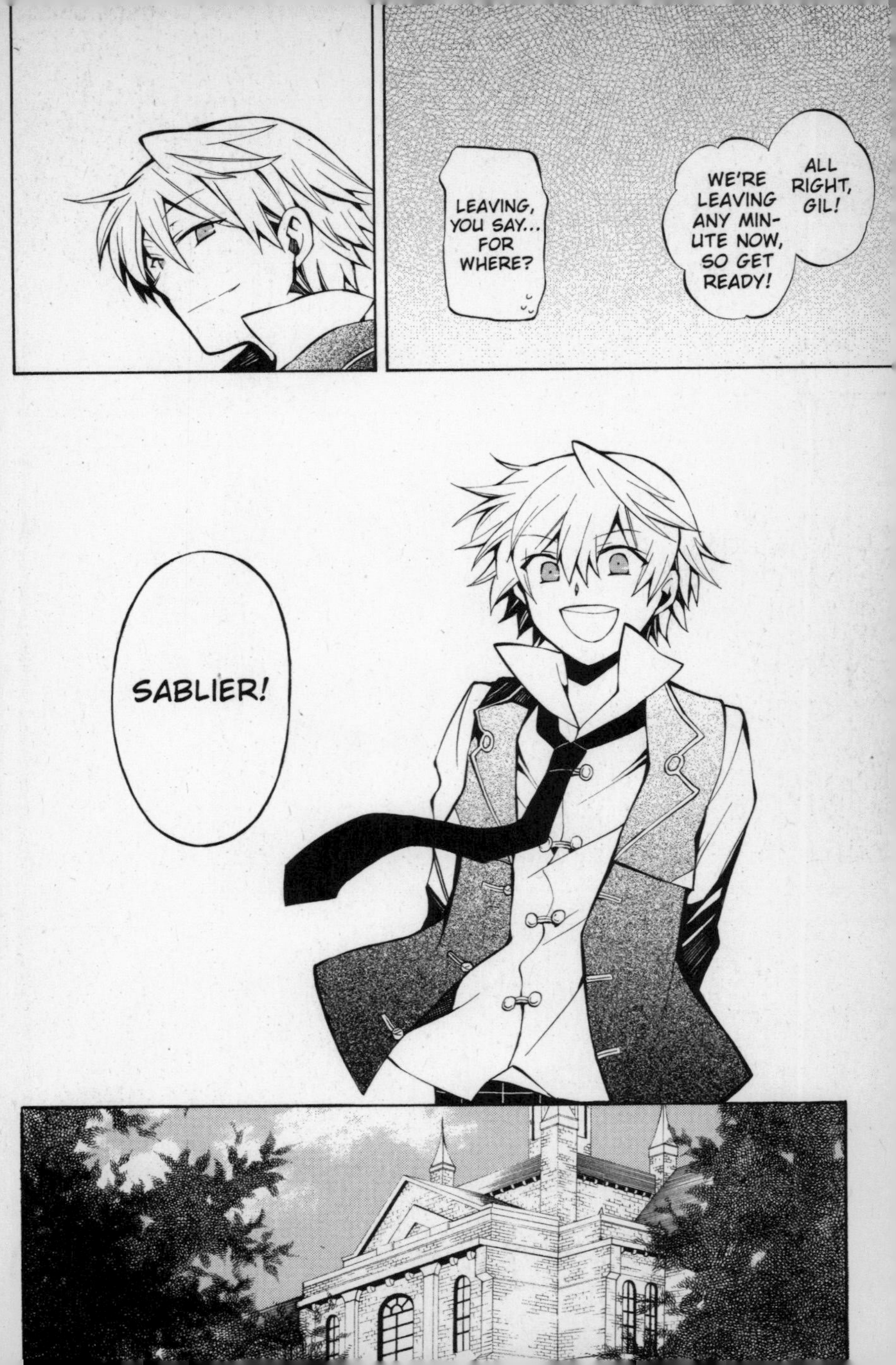
ALL RIGHT, GIL! WE'RE LEAVING ANY MIN-UTE NOW, SO GET READY!
LEAVING, YOU SAY... FOR WHERE?
SABLIER!

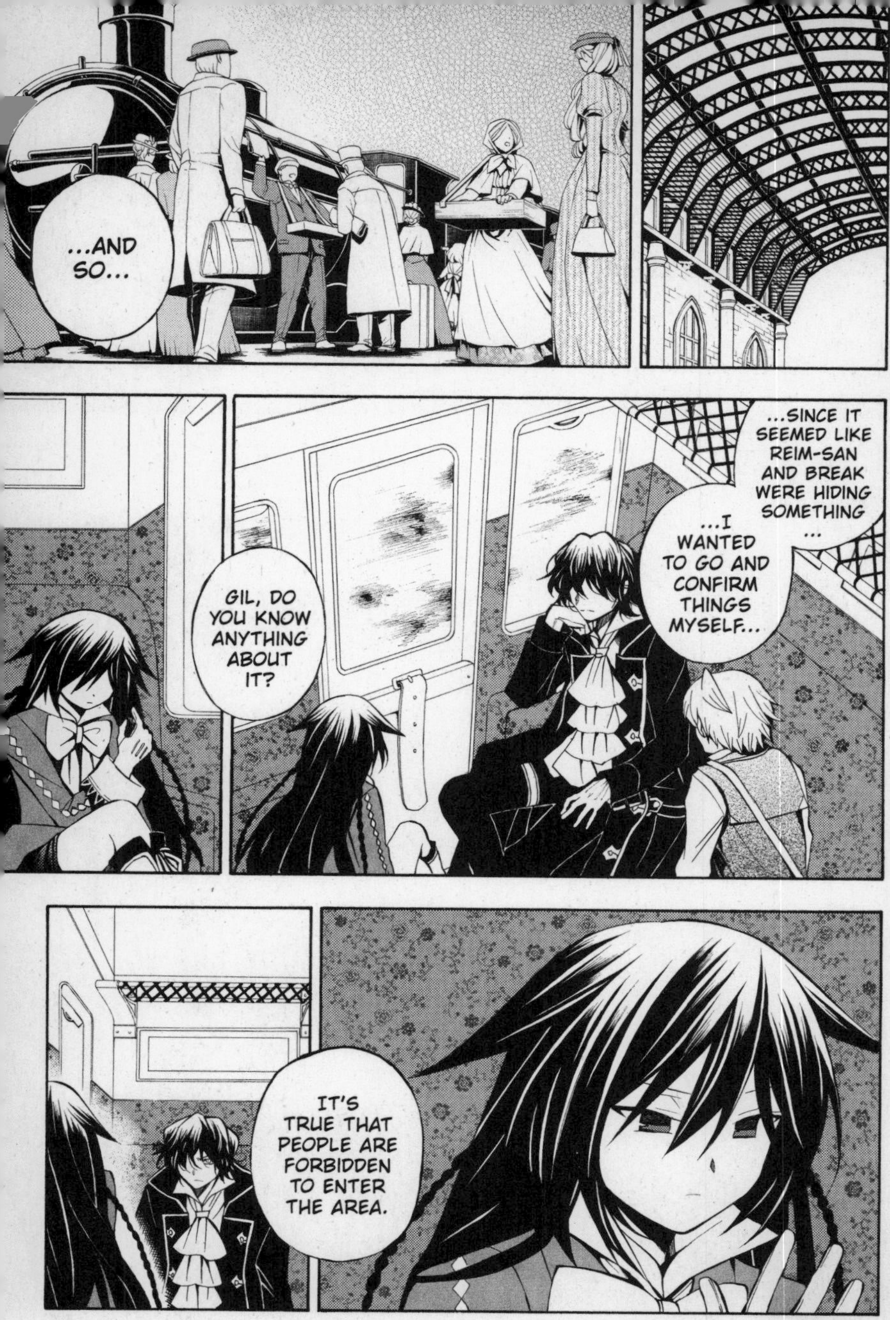
...AND SO...
...SINCE IT SEEMED LIKE REIM-SAN AND BREAK WERE HIDING SOMETHING ...
...I WANTED TO GO AND CONFIRM THINGS MYSELF...
GIL, DO YOU KNOW ANYTHING ABOUT IT?
IT'S TRUE THAT PEOPLE ARE FORBIDDEN TO ENTER THE AREA.

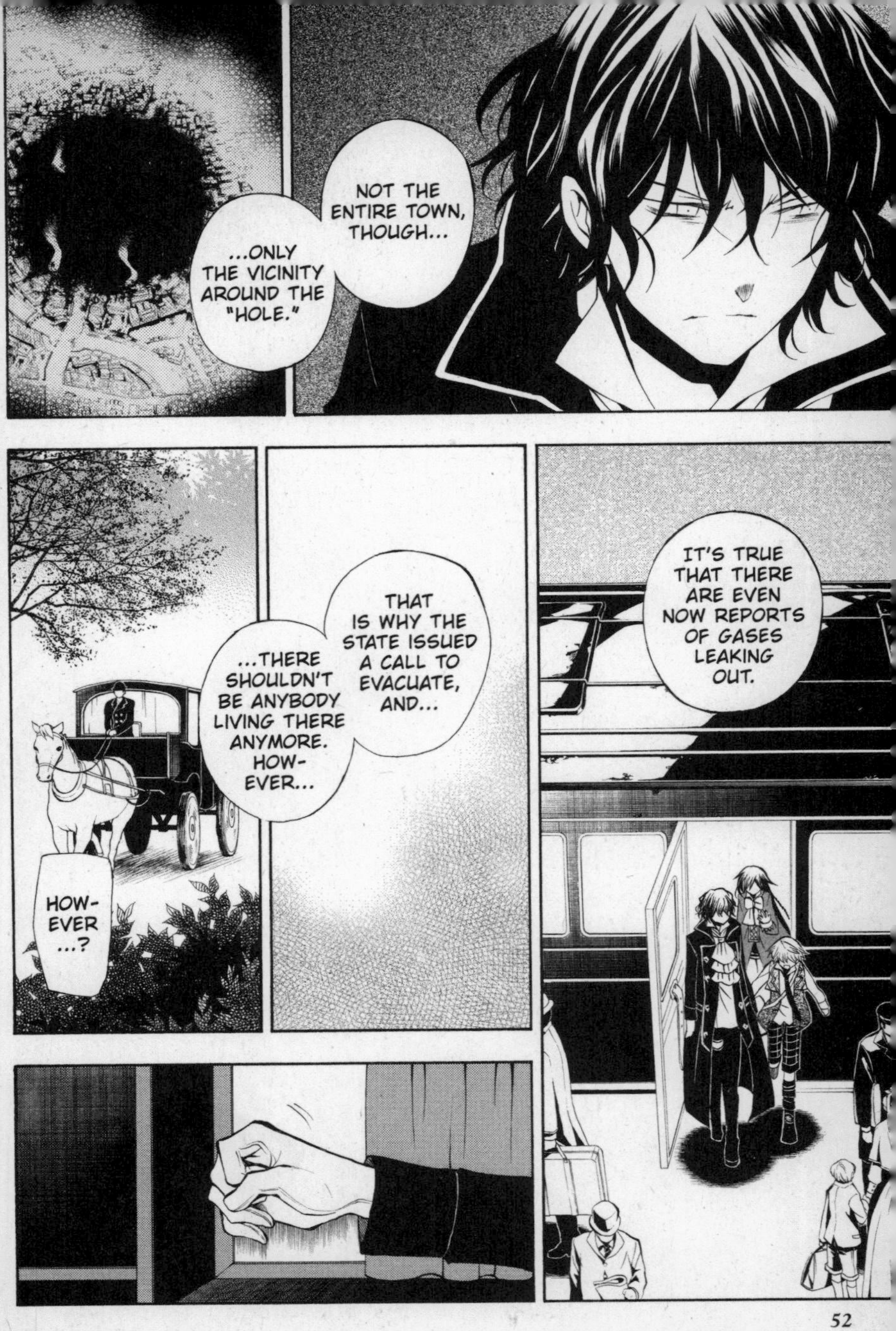
NOT THE ENTIRE TOWN, THOUGH...
...ONLY THE VICINITY AROUND THE "HOLE."
IT'S TRUE THAT THERE ARE EVEN NOW REPORTS OF GASES LEAKING OUT.
THAT IS WHY THE STATE ISSUED A CALL TO EVACUATE, AND...
...THERE SHOULDN'T BE ANYBODY LIVING THERE ANYMORE. HOW-EVER...
HOW-EVER ...?

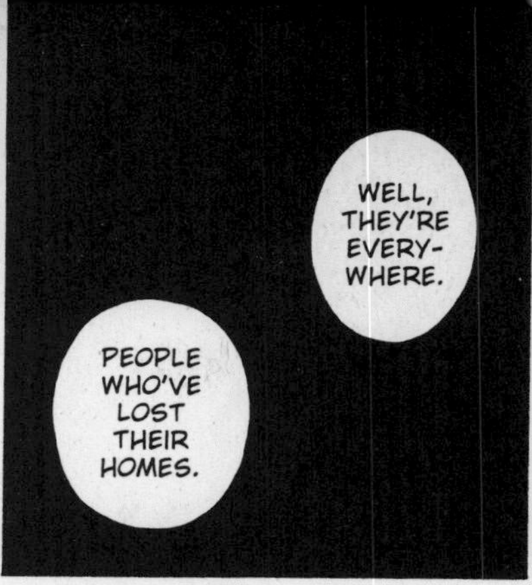
WELL, THEY'RE EVERY-WHERE.
PEOPLE WHO'VE LOST THEIR HOMES.
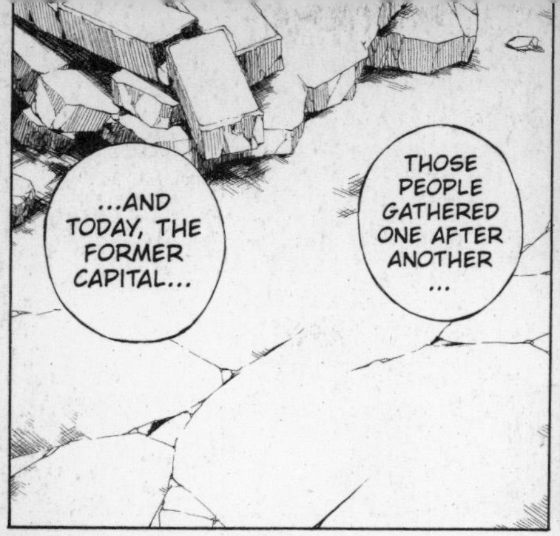
THOSE PEOPLE GATHERED ONE AFTER ANOTHER...
...AND TODAY, THE FORMER CAPITAL...
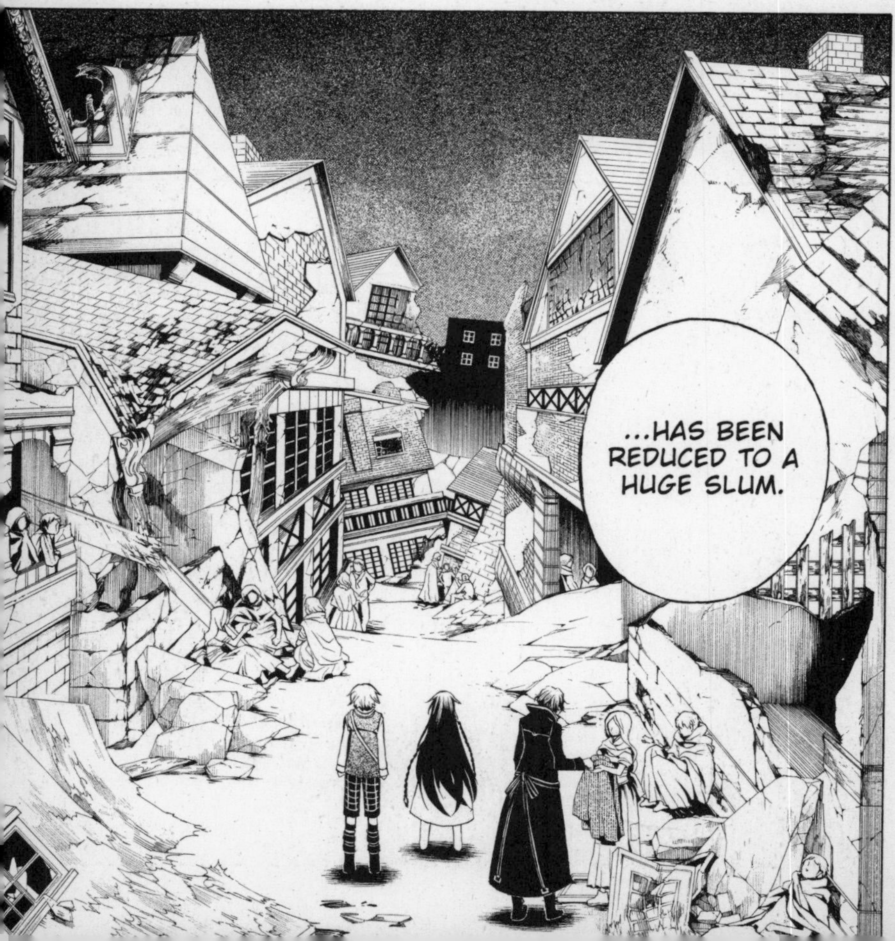
...HAS BEEN REDUCED TO A HUGE SLUM.

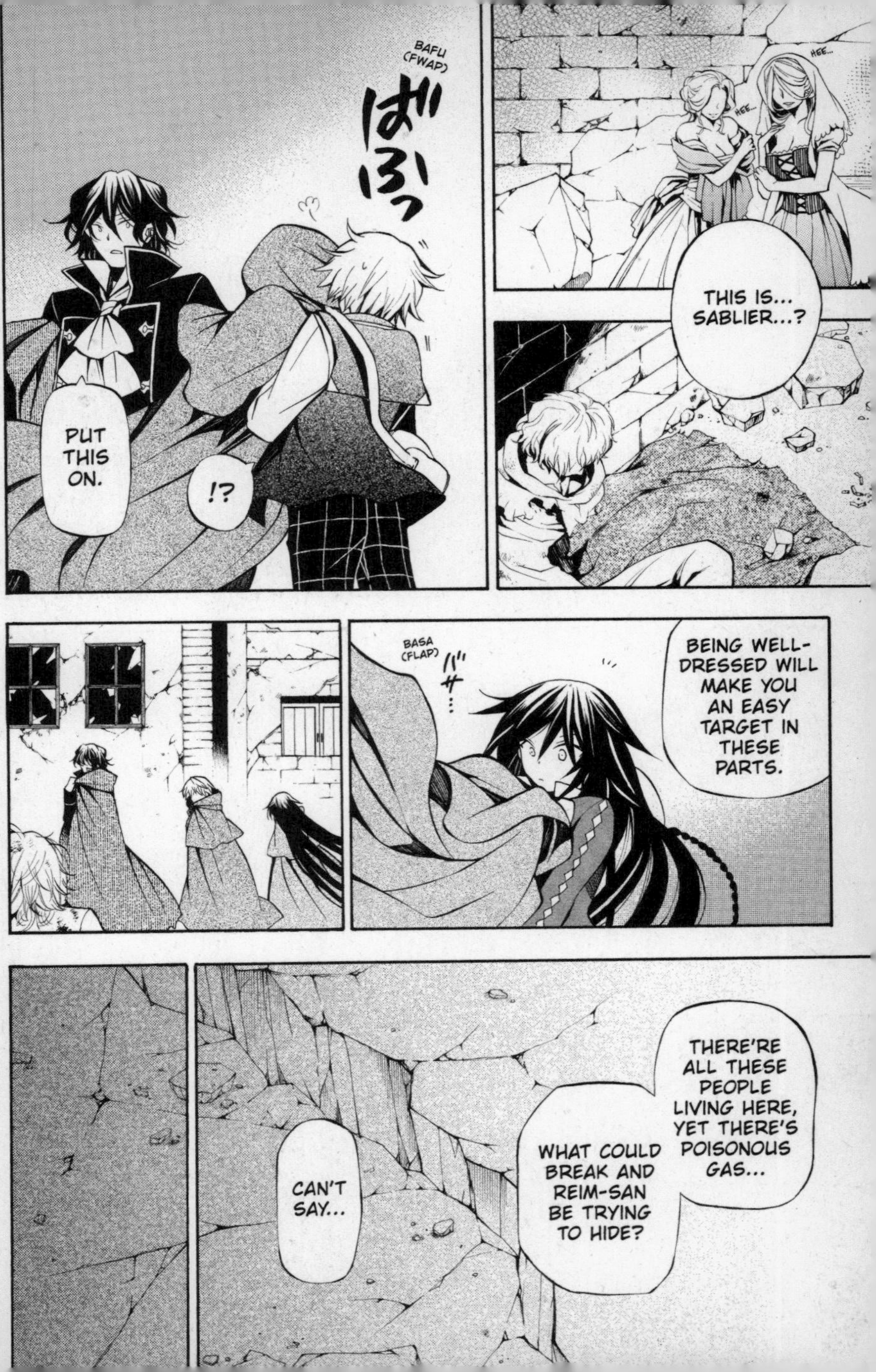
HEE...
HEE...
THIS IS... SABLIER...?
BAFU (FWAP)
ばふっ
PUT THIS ON.
!?
BASA (FLAP)
バサ…
BEING WELL-DRESSED WILL MAKE YOU AN EASY TARGET IN THESE PARTS.
THERE'RE ALL THESE PEOPLE LIVING HERE, YET THERE'S POISONOUS GAS...
WHAT COULD BREAK AND REIM-SAN BE TRYING TO HIDE?
CAN'T SAY...

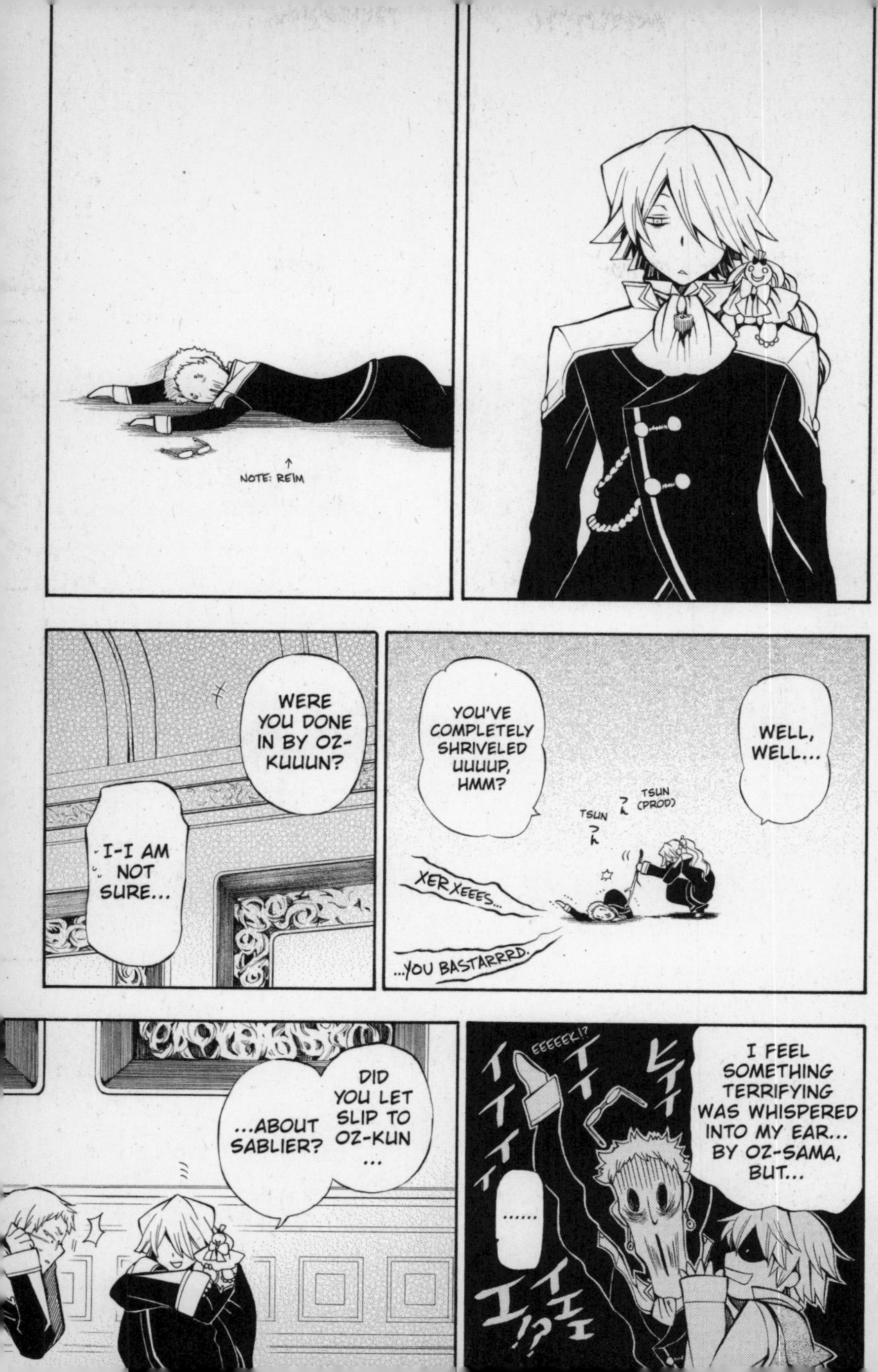
NOTE: REIM
WELL, WELL...
YOU'VE COMPLETELY SHRIVELED UUUUP, HMM?
TSUN (PROD)
TSUN
XERXEEES...
...YOU BASTARRRD.
WERE YOU DONE IN BY OZ-KUUUN?
I-I AM NOT SURE...
I FEEL SOMETHING TERRIFYING WAS WHISPERED INTO MY EAR... BY OZ-SAMA, BUT...
EEEEEK!?
......
DID YOU LET SLIP TO OZ-KUN ...
...ABOUT SABLIER?

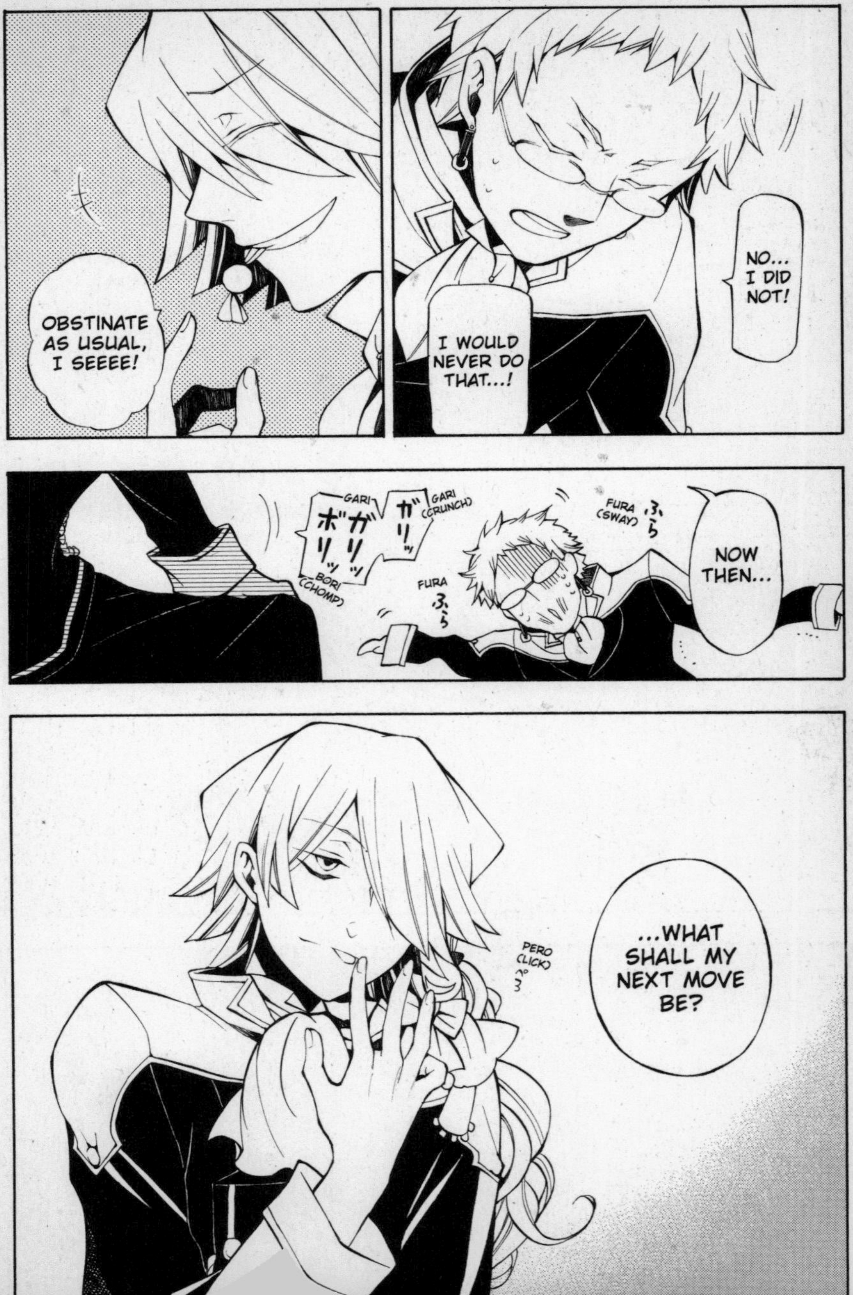
NO... I DID NOT!
I WOULD NEVER DO THAT...!
OBSTINATE AS USUAL, I SEEEE!
NOW THEN...
ふら FURA (SWAY)
ガリッ GARI (CRUNCH)
ガリッ GARI
ボリッ BORI (CHOMP)
ふら FURA
...WHAT SHALL MY NEXT MOVE BE?
ぺろ PERO (LICK)

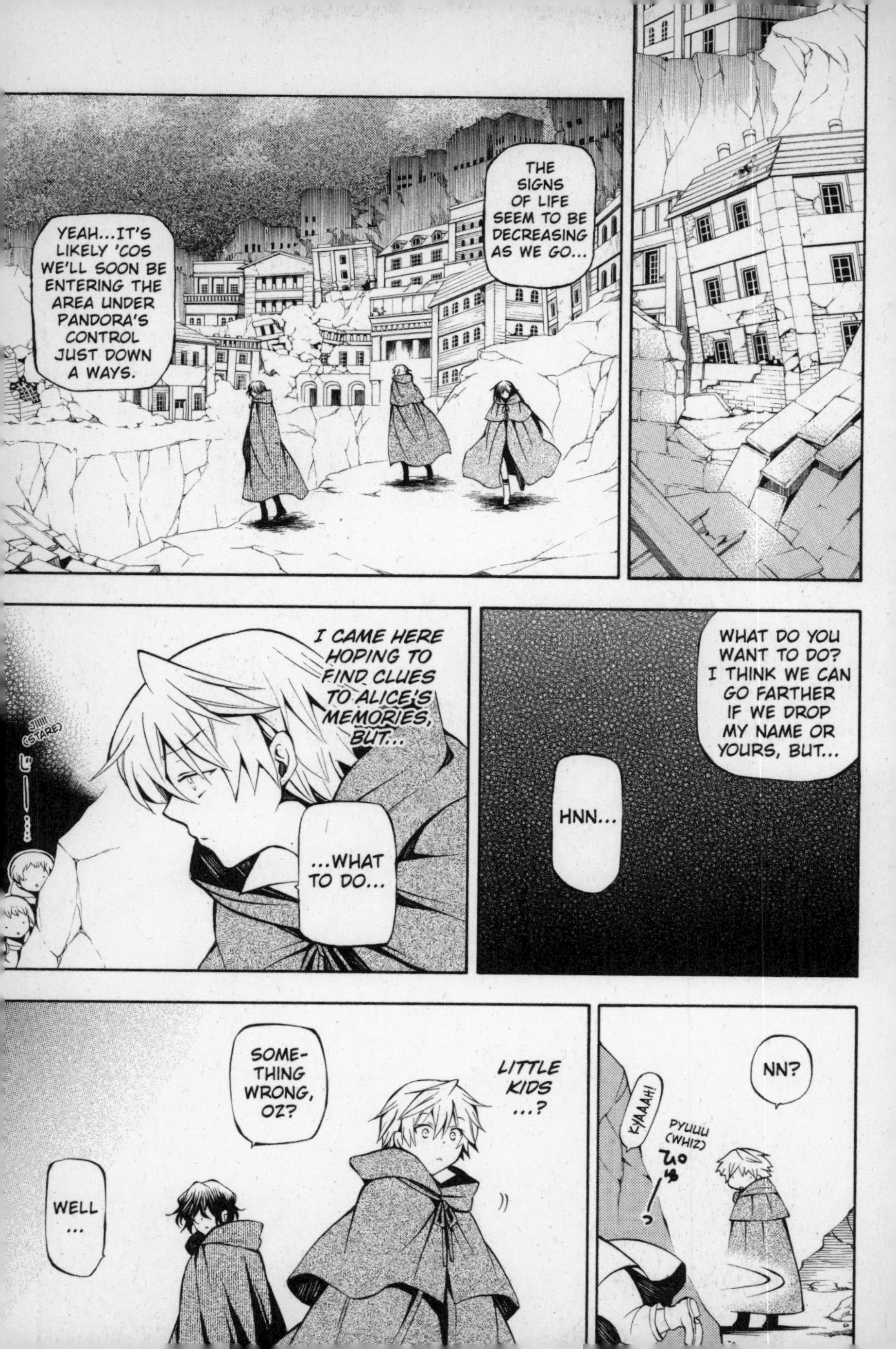
THE SIGNS OF LIFE SEEM TO BE DECREASING AS WE GO...
YEAH...IT'S LIKELY 'COS WE'LL SOON BE ENTERING THE AREA UNDER PANDORA'S CONTROL JUST DOWN A WAYS.
WHAT DO YOU WANT TO DO? I THINK WE CAN GO FARTHER IF WE DROP MY NAME OR YOURS, BUT...
HNN...
I CAME HERE HOPING TO FIND CLUES TO ALICE'S MEMORIES, BUT...
...WHAT TO DO...
JIIIII (STARE)
NN?
KYAAAH!
PYUUU (WHIZ)
LITTLE KIDS ...?
SOME-THING WRONG, OZ?
WELL ...

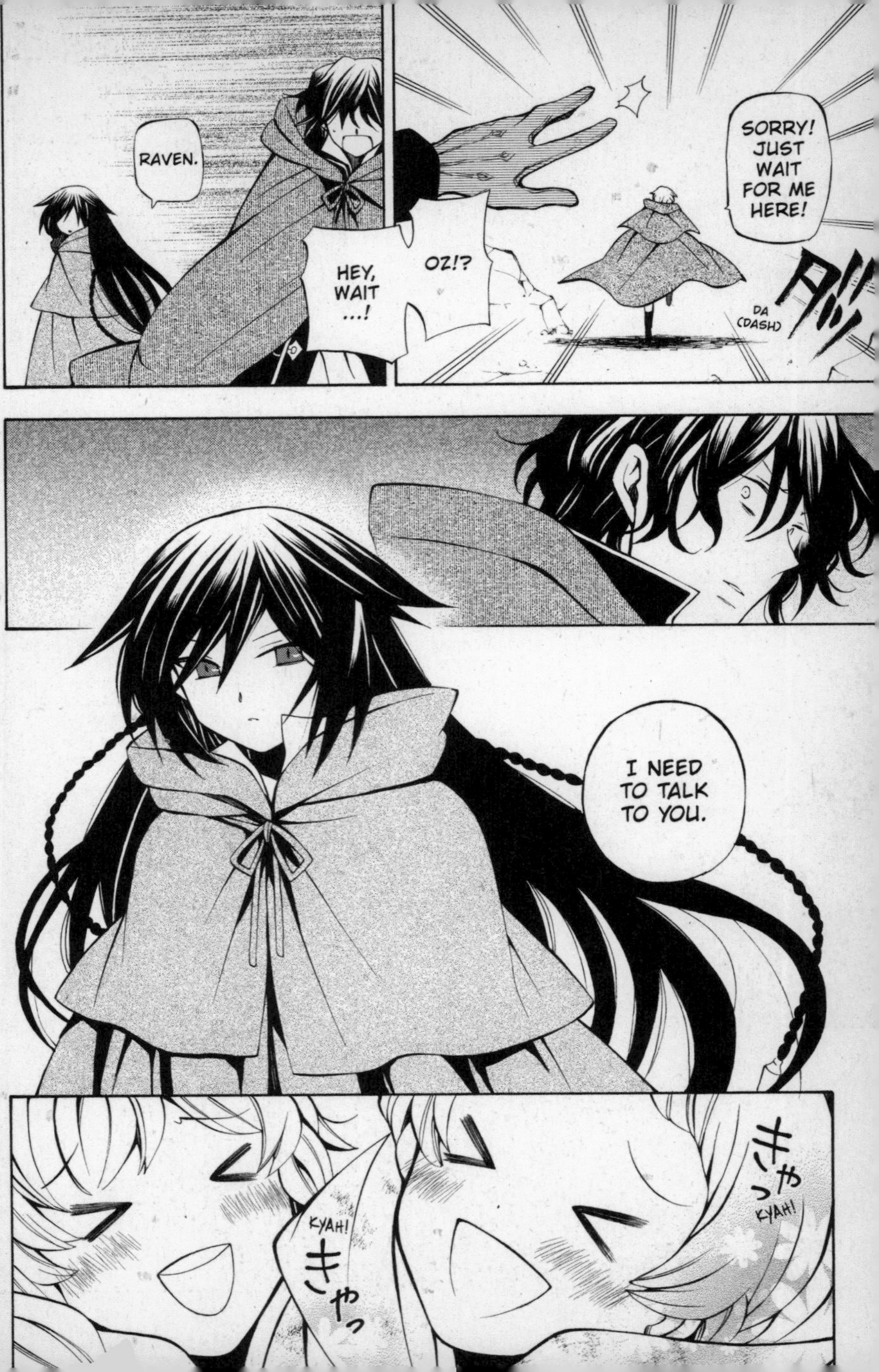
SORRY! JUST WAIT FOR ME HERE!
DA (DASH)
OZ!?
HEY, WAIT ...!
RAVEN.
I NEED TO TALK TO YOU.
きゃっ
KYAH!
KYAH!
きゃっ

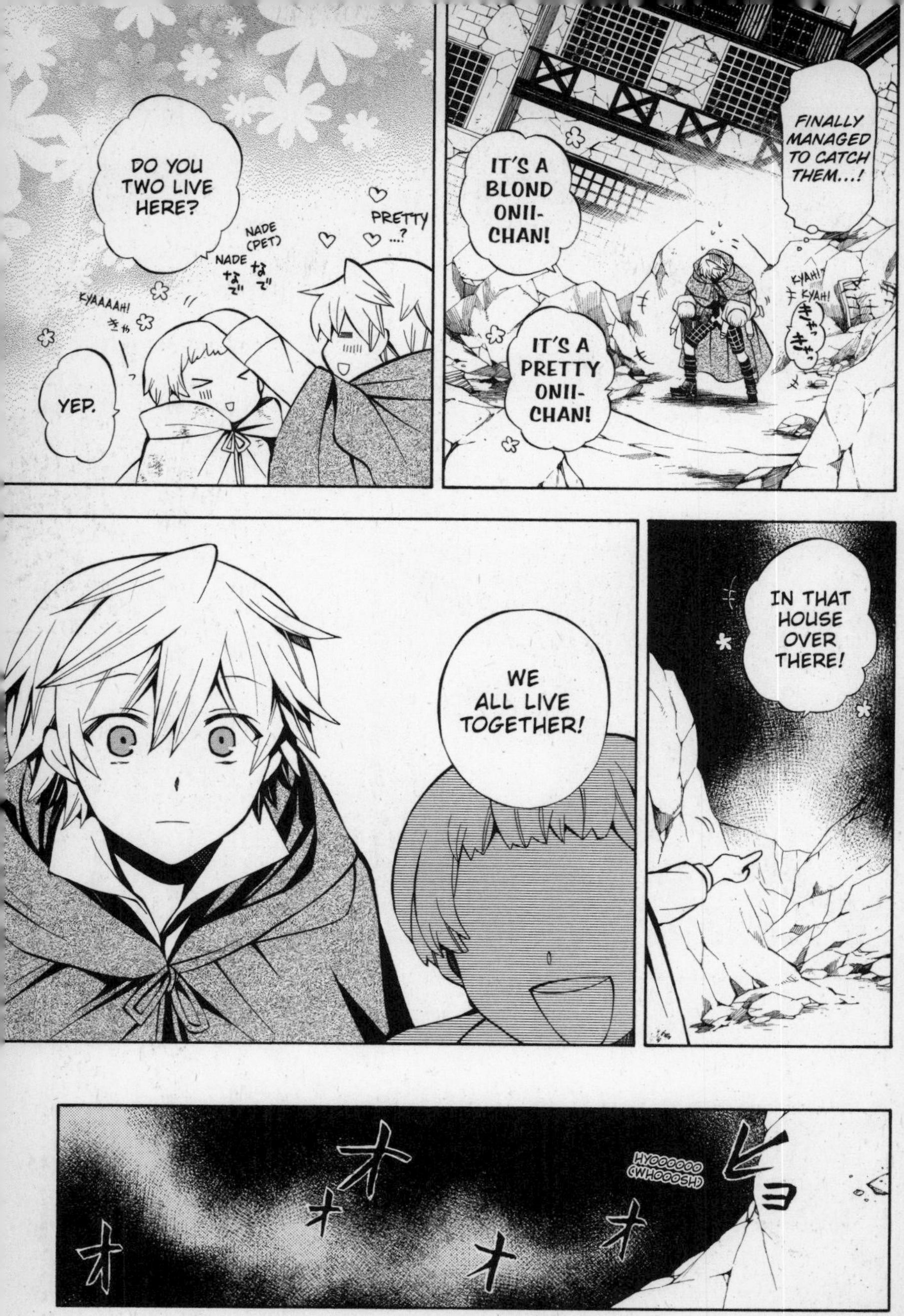
FINALLY MANAGED TO CATCH THEM...!
IT'S A BLOND ONII-CHAN!
IT'S A PRETTY ONII-CHAN!
KYAH! KYAH!
きゃっきゃっ
DO YOU TWO LIVE HERE?
PRETTY ...?
NADE (PET) NADE
なでなで
KYAAAAH!
きゃ
YEP.
IN THAT HOUSE OVER THERE!
WE ALL LIVE TOGETHER!
HYOOOOOO (WHOOOSH)
ヒョオオオオ

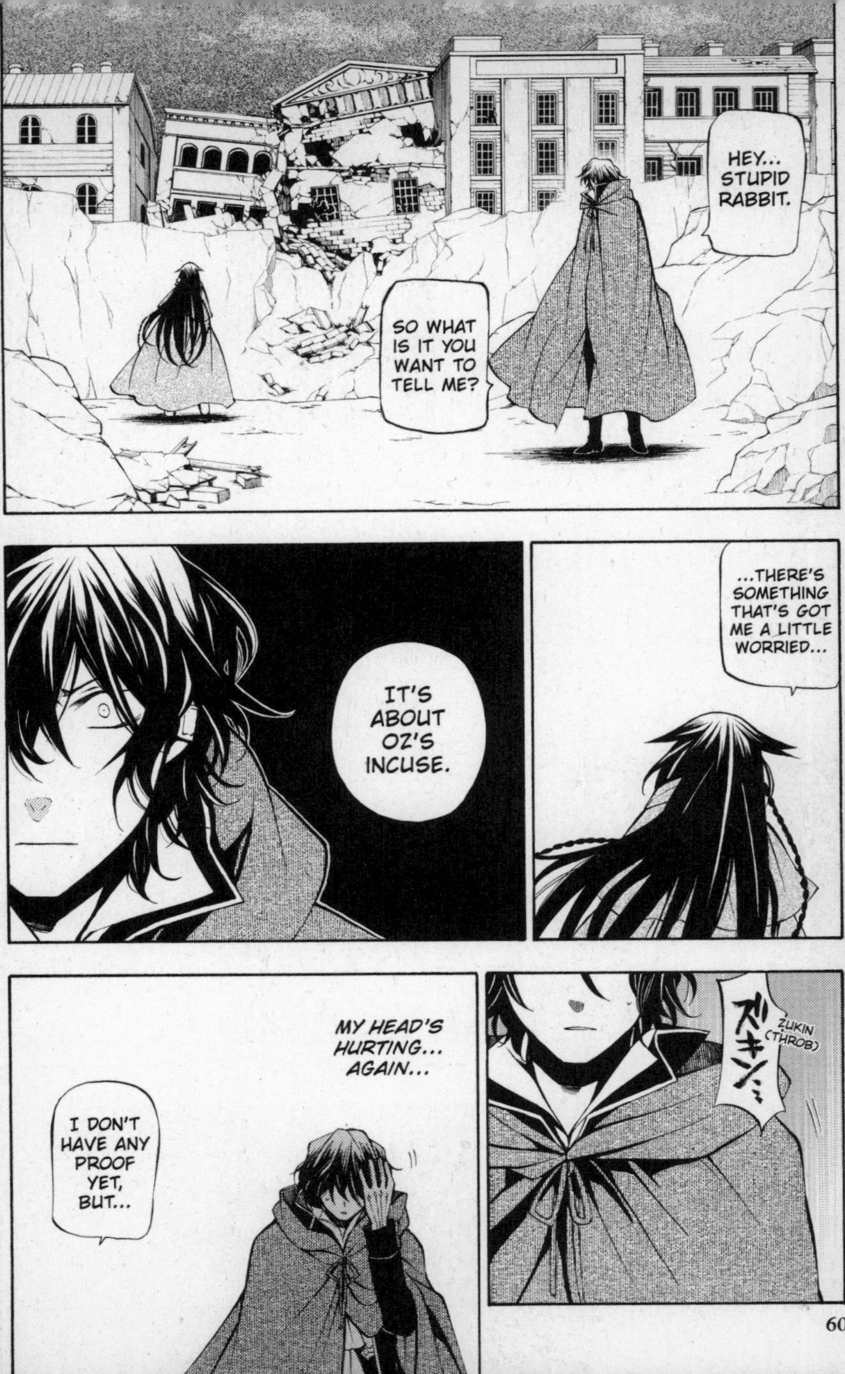
HEY... STUPID RABBIT.
SO WHAT IS IT YOU WANT TO TELL ME?
...THERE'S SOMETHING THAT'S GOT ME A LITTLE WORRIED...
IT'S ABOUT OZ'S INCUSE.
ズキン
ZUKIN (THROB)
MY HEAD'S HURTING... AGAIN...
I DON'T HAVE ANY PROOF YET, BUT...

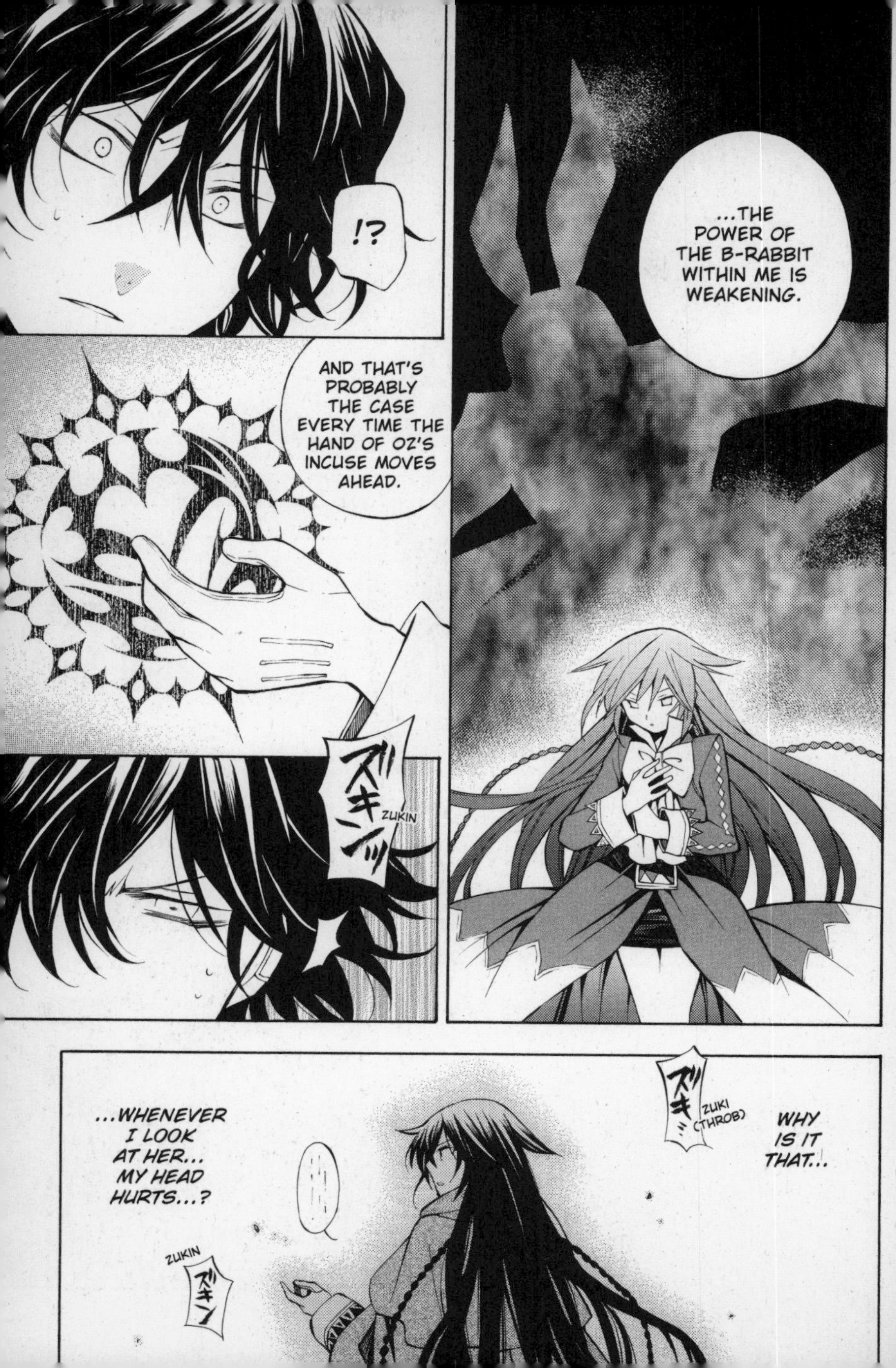
...THE POWER OF THE B-RABBIT WITHIN ME IS WEAKENING.
!?
AND THAT'S PROBABLY THE CASE EVERY TIME THE HAND OF OZ'S INCUSE MOVES AHEAD.
ズキンッ
ZUKIN
WHY IS IT THAT...
ズキ
ZUKI (THROB)
...WHENEVER I LOOK AT HER... MY HEAD HURTS...?
......
ズキン
ZUKIN

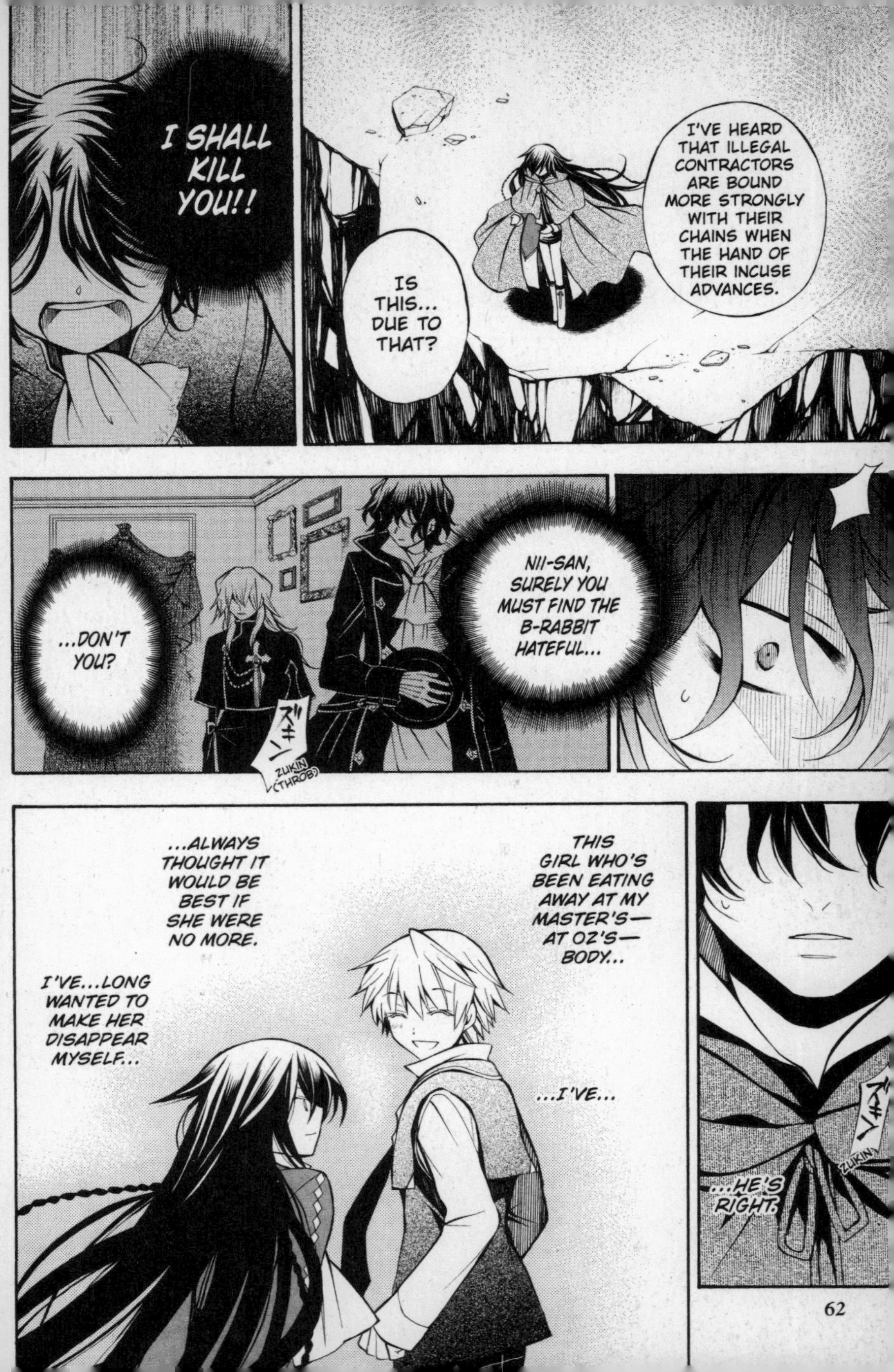

I'VE HEARD THAT ILLEGAL CONTRACTORS ARE BOUND MORE STRONGLY WITH THEIR CHAINS WHEN THE HAND OF THEIR INCUSE ADVANCES.
IS THIS... DUE TO THAT?
I SHALL KILL YOU!!
NII-SAN, SURELY YOU MUST FIND THE B-RABBIT HATEFUL...
...DON'T YOU?
ズキン
ZUKIN (THROB)
...HE'S RIGHT.
ズキン
ZUKIN
THIS GIRL WHO'S BEEN EATING AWAY AT MY MASTER'S—AT OZ'S—BODY...
...I'VE...
...ALWAYS THOUGHT IT WOULD BE BEST IF SHE WERE NO MORE.
I'VE...LONG WANTED TO MAKE HER DISAPPEAR MYSELF...

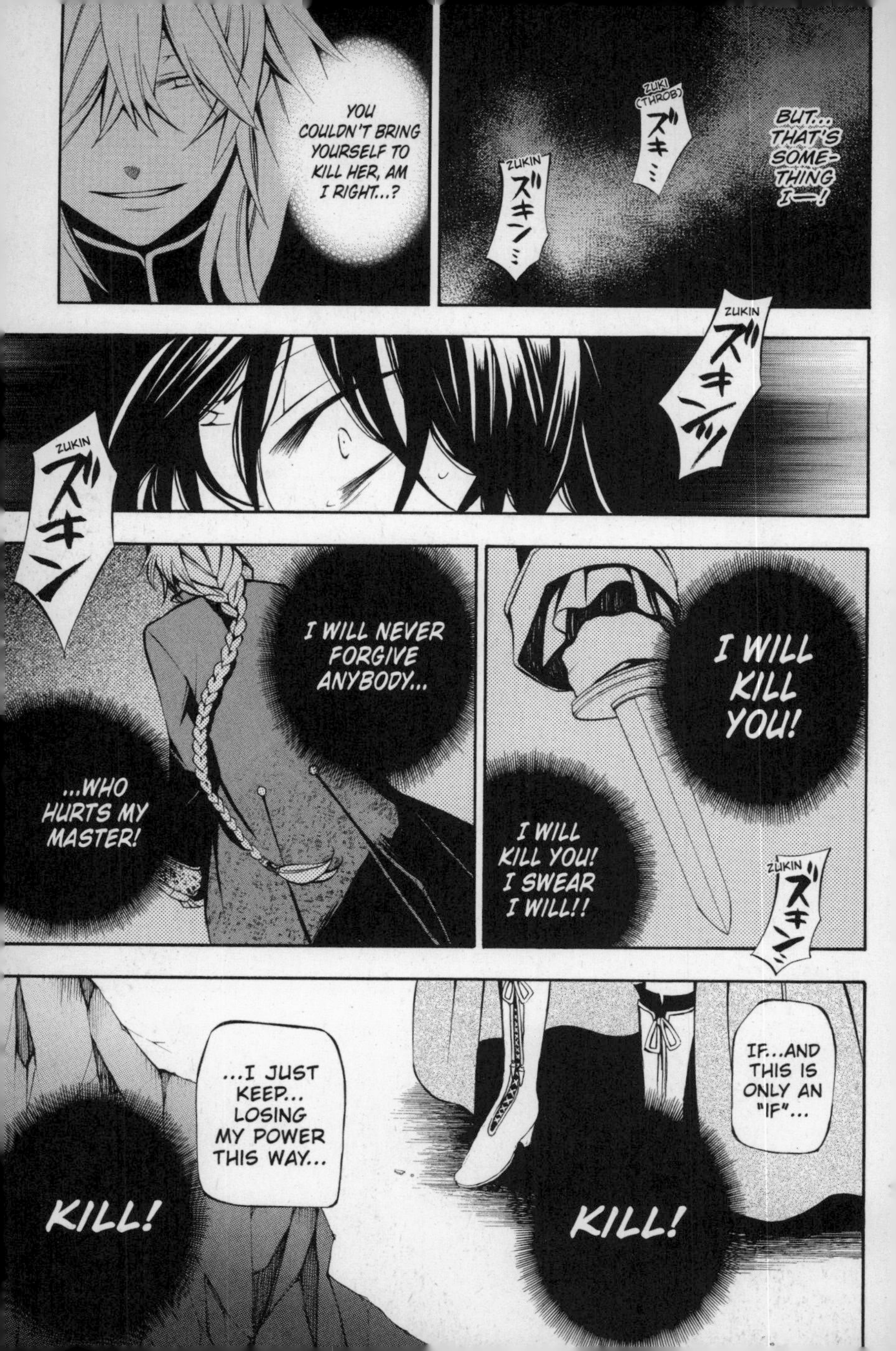
BUT... THAT'S SOME-THING I—!
ZUKI (THROB) ズキ…
ZUKIN ズキン…
YOU COULDN'T BRING YOURSELF TO KILL HER, AM I RIGHT...?
ZUKIN ズキンッ
ZUKIN ズキン
I WILL KILL YOU!
I WILL KILL YOU! I SWEAR I WILL!!
ZUKIN ズキン
I WILL NEVER FORGIVE ANYBODY...
...WHO HURTS MY MASTER!
IF...AND THIS IS ONLY AN "IF"...
KILL!
...I JUST KEEP... LOSING MY POWER THIS WAY...
KILL!

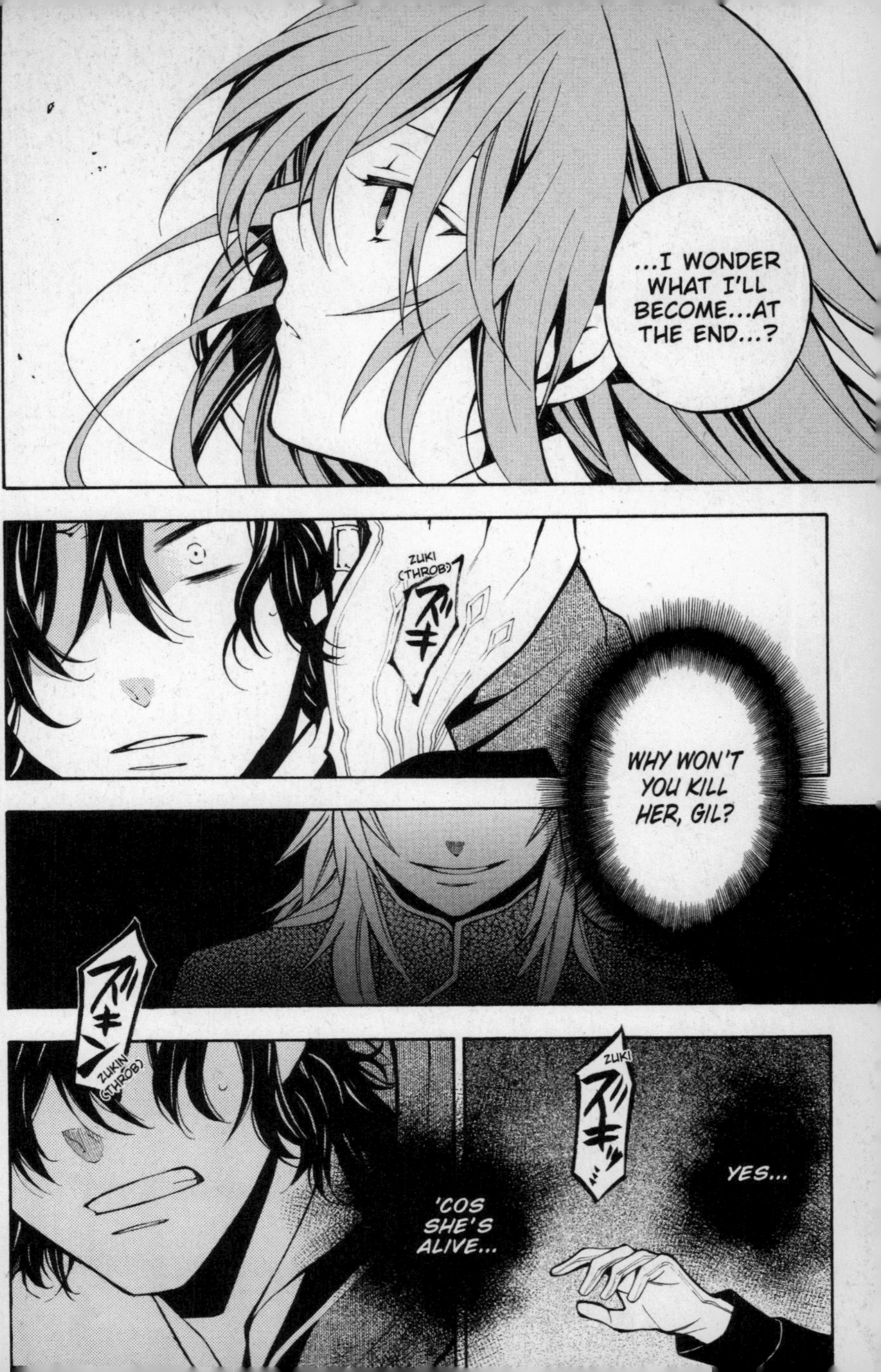
...I WONDER WHAT I'LL BECOME...AT THE END...?
ZUKI (THROB)
WHY WON'T YOU KILL HER, GIL?
ZUKI
YES...
'COS SHE'S ALIVE...
ZUKIN (THROB)

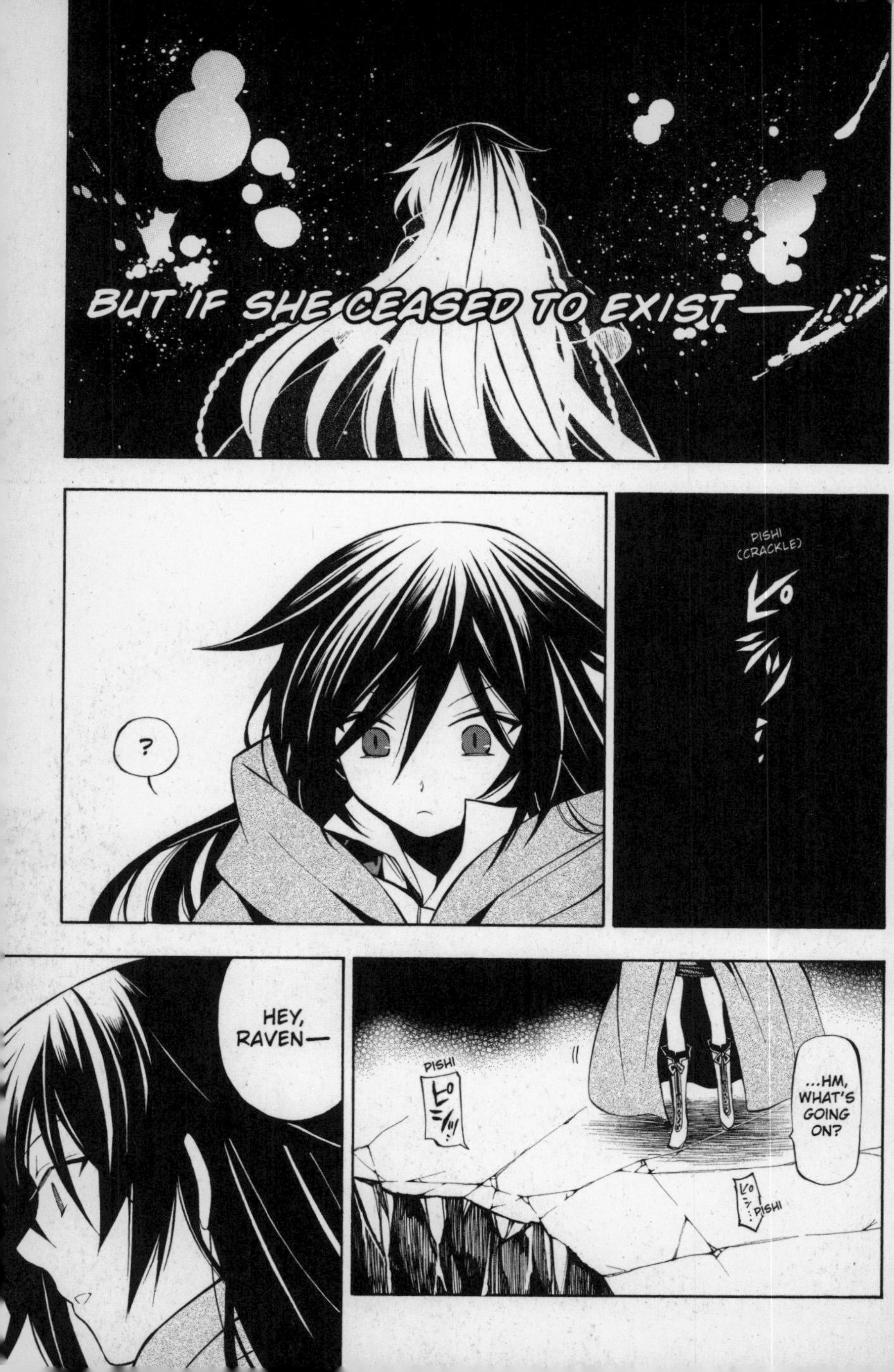
BUT IF SHE CEASED TO EXIST——!!
PISHI (CRACKLE)
?
PISHI
...HM, WHAT'S GOING ON?
PISHI
HEY, RAVEN—

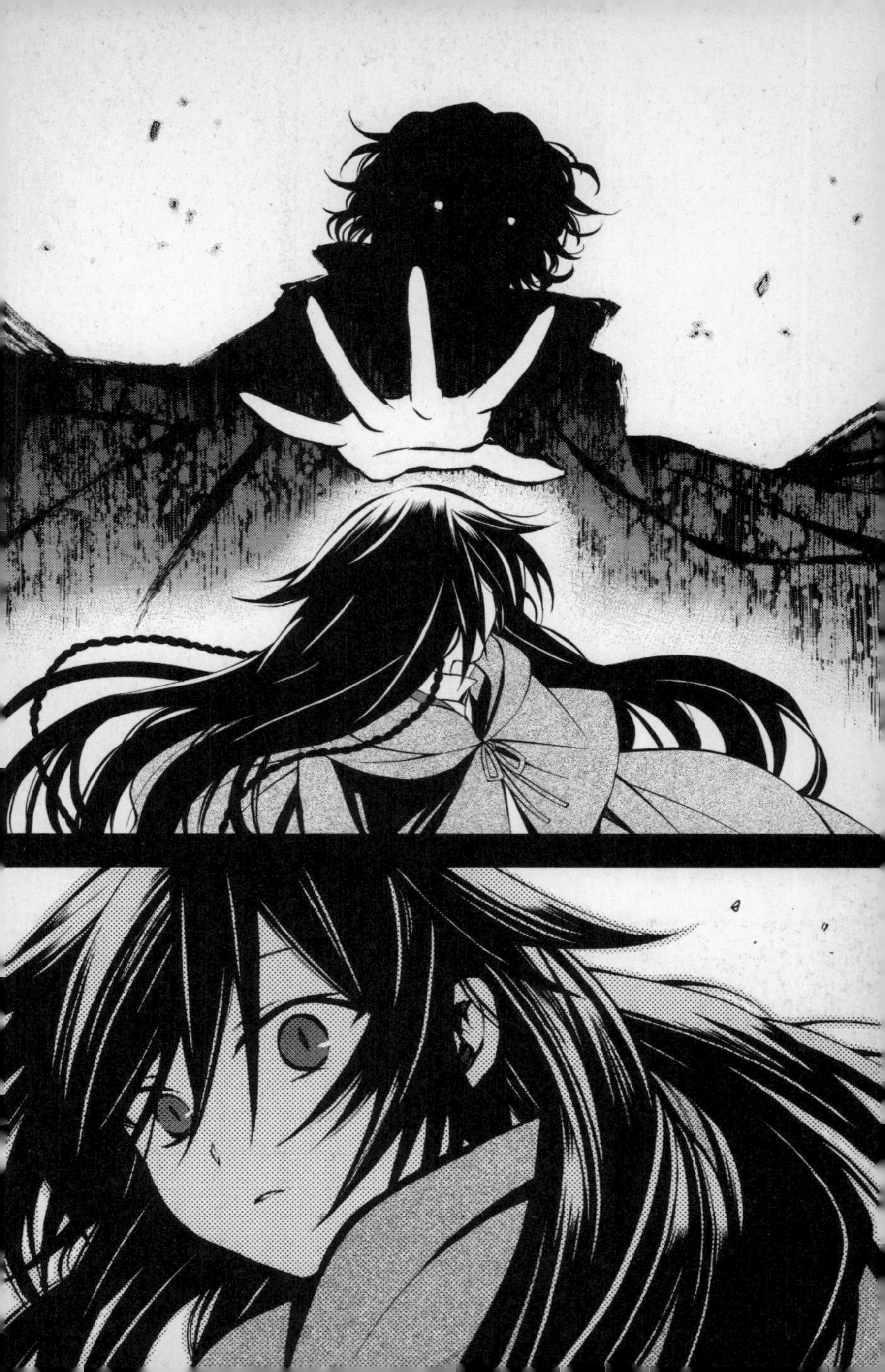

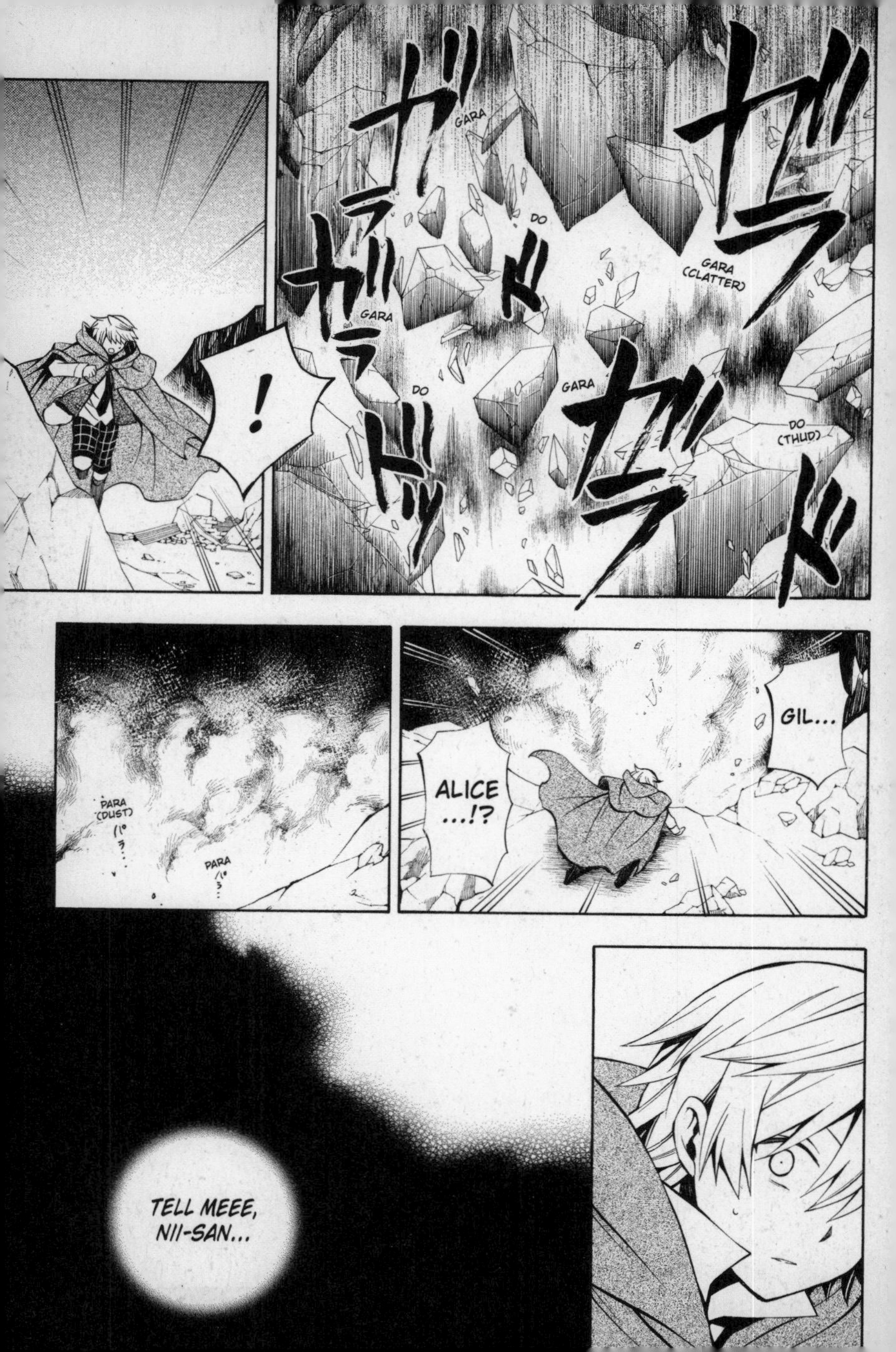
GARA (CLATTER)
DO (THUD)
GARA
DO
GARA
GARA
DO
!
GIL...
ALICE ...!?
PARA (DUST)
PARA
TELL MEEE, NII-SAN...

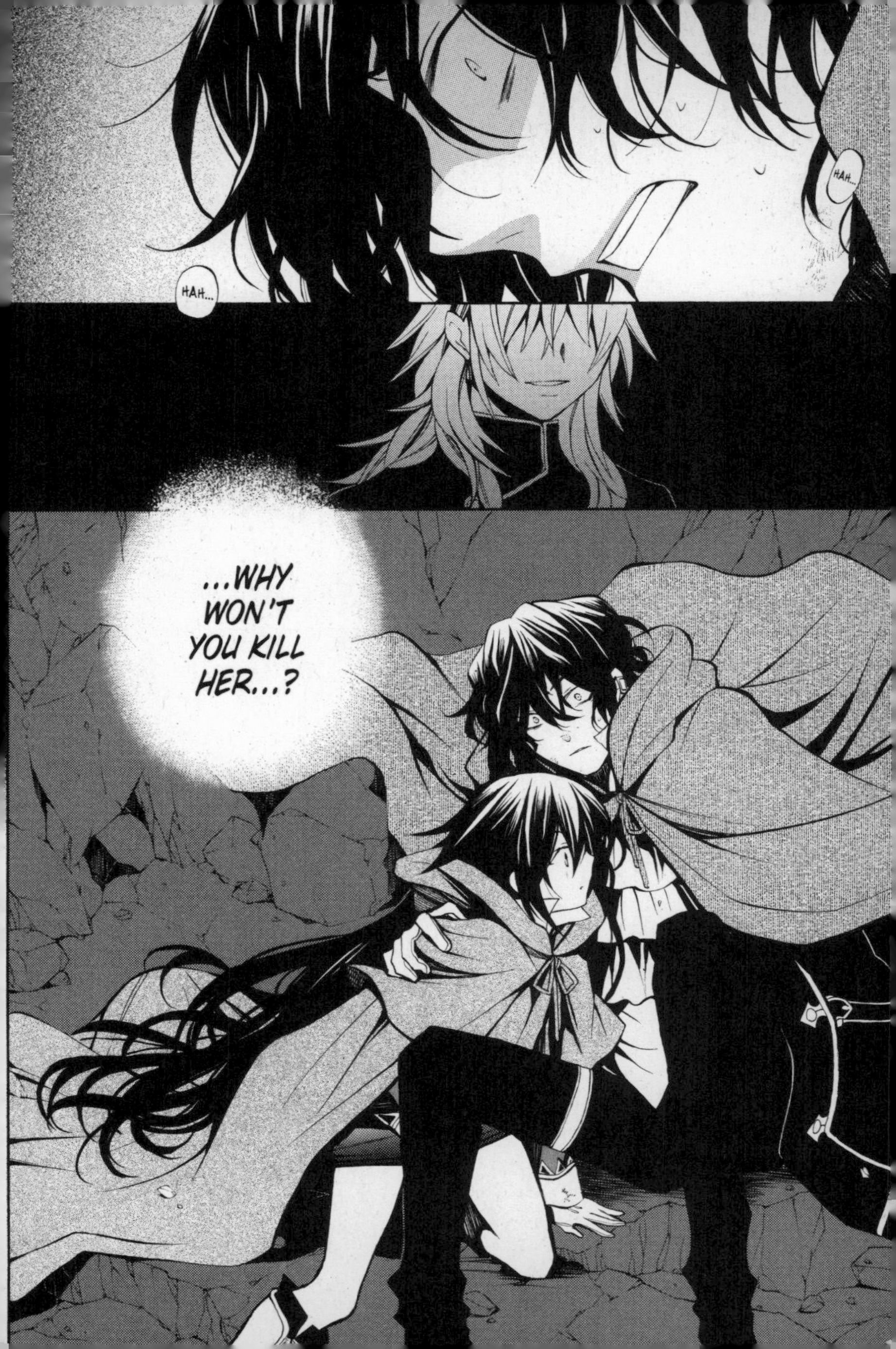
HAH...
HAH...
...WHY WON'T YOU KILL HER...?

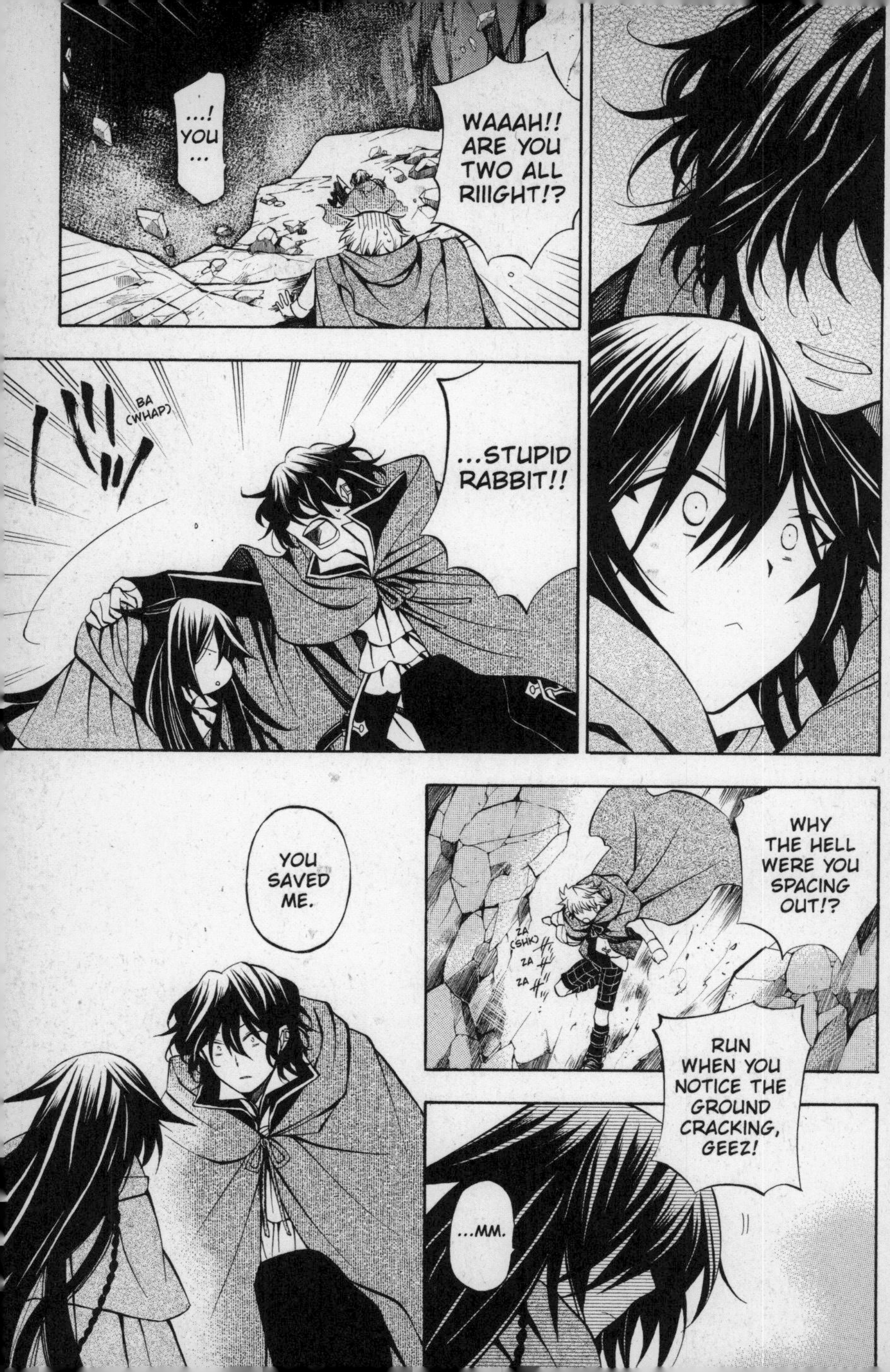
WAAAH!! ARE YOU TWO ALL RIIIGHT!?
...! YOU ...
...STUPID RABBIT!!
BA (WHAP)
WHY THE HELL WERE YOU SPACING OUT!?
ZA (SHK) ZA ZA
RUN WHEN YOU NOTICE THE GROUND CRACKING, GEEZ!
...MM.
YOU SAVED ME.

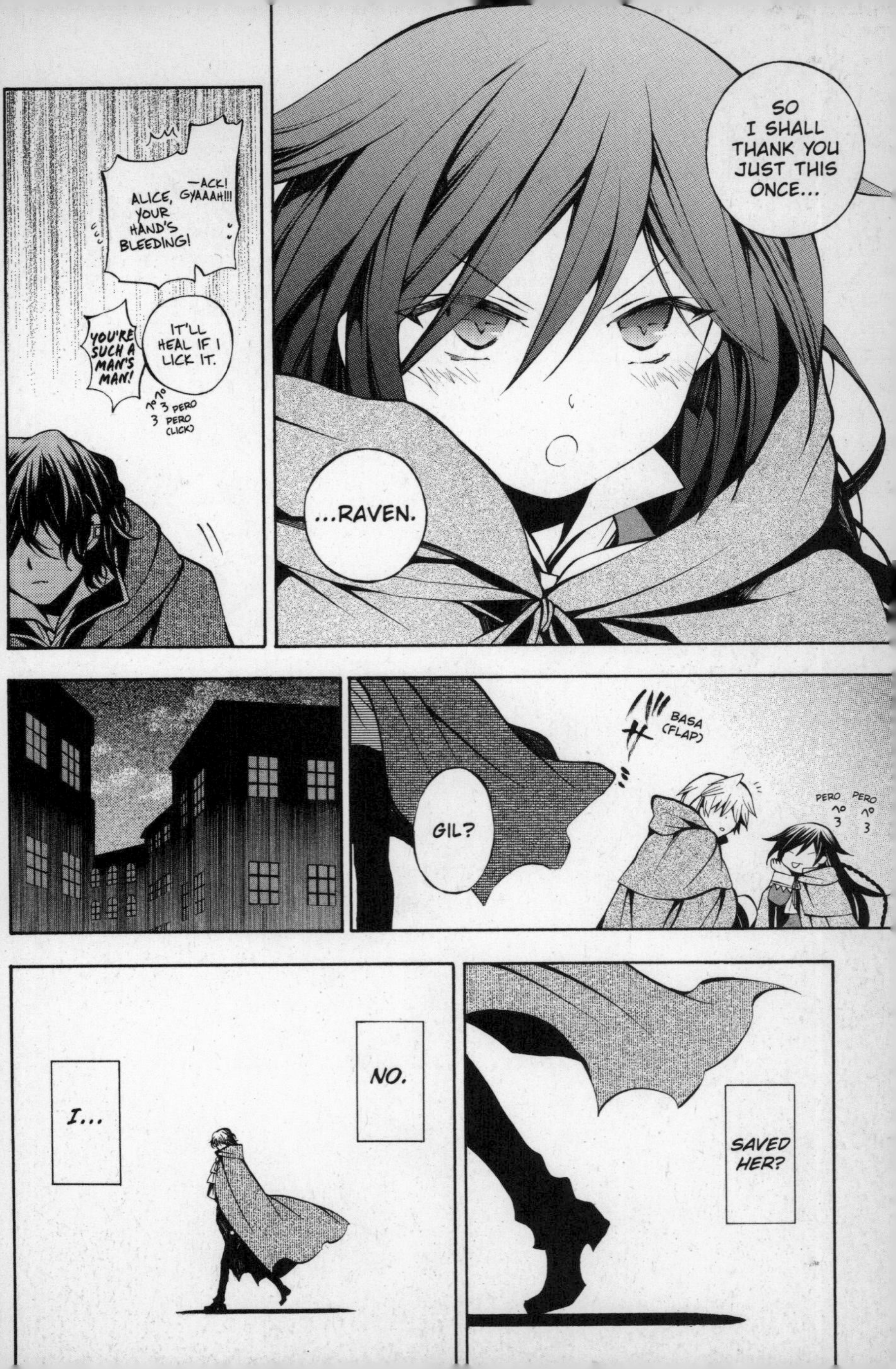
SO I SHALL THANK YOU JUST THIS ONCE...
...RAVEN.
—ACK! ALICE, YOUR HAND'S BLEEDING!
GYAAAH!!!
IT'LL HEAL IF I LICK IT.
YOU'RE SUCH A MAN'S MAN!
PERO PERO (LICK)
BASA (FLAP)
PERO PERO
GIL?
SAVED HER?
NO.
I...

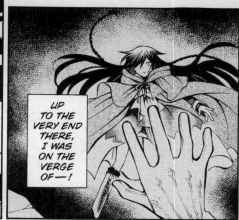

UP TO THE VERY END THERE, I WAS ON THE VERGE OF—!

I WILL KILL YOU ...!

BE QUIET ...

DAMN!!

DAN (SLAM)

SHUT UP!!

GILBERT.

GIL...

WHAT WOULD YOU HAVE ME DO?

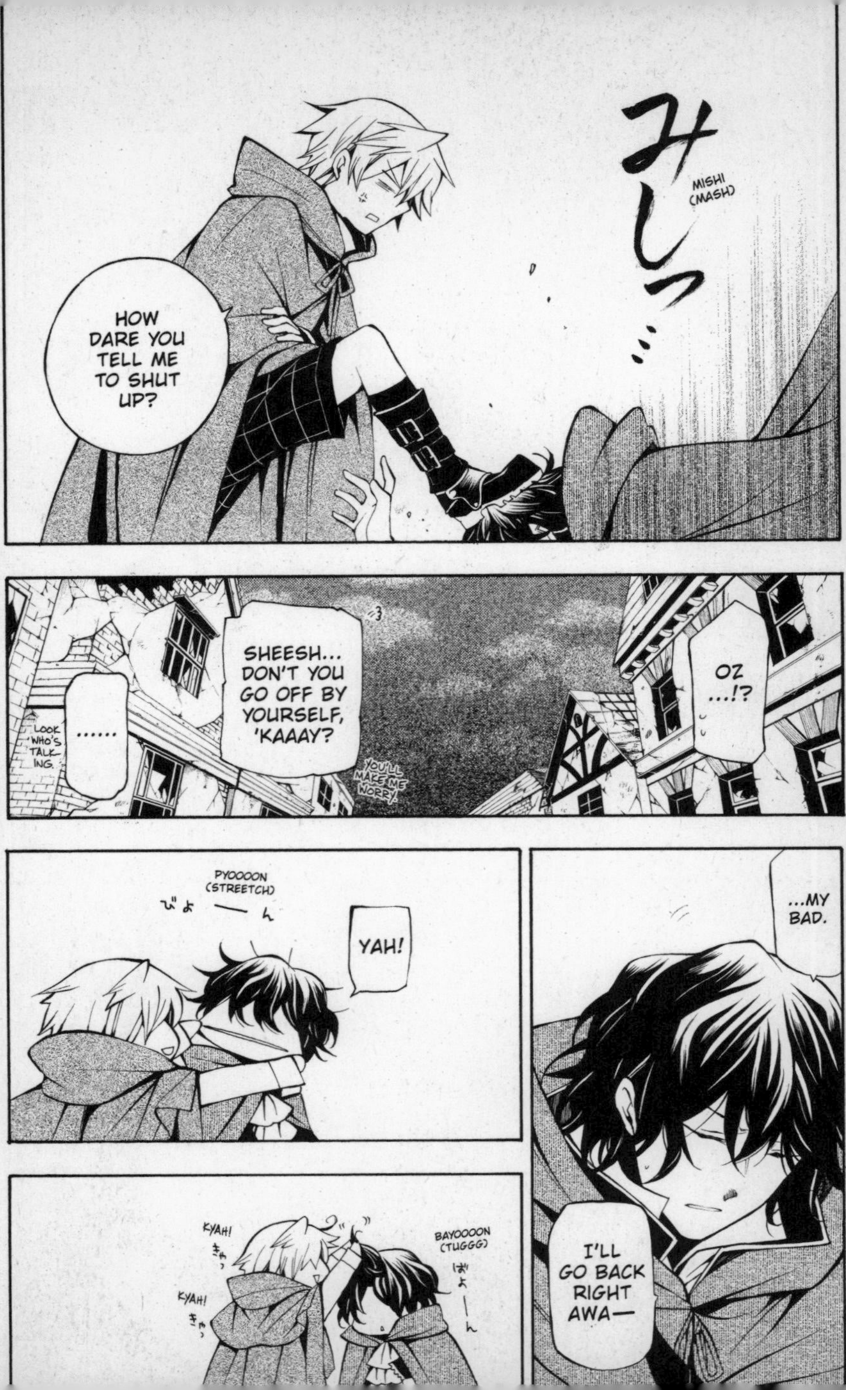

みしっ
MISHI (MASH)
HOW DARE YOU TELL ME TO SHUT UP?
OZ ...!?
SHEESH... DON'T YOU GO OFF BY YOURSELF, 'KAAAY?
YOU'LL MAKE ME WORRY.
......
LOOK WHO'S TALKING.
...MY BAD.
I'LL GO BACK RIGHT AWA—
びよーん
PYOOOON (STREETCH)
YAH!
ばよーん
BAYOOOON (TUGGG)
きゃっ
KYAH!
きゃっ
KYAH!

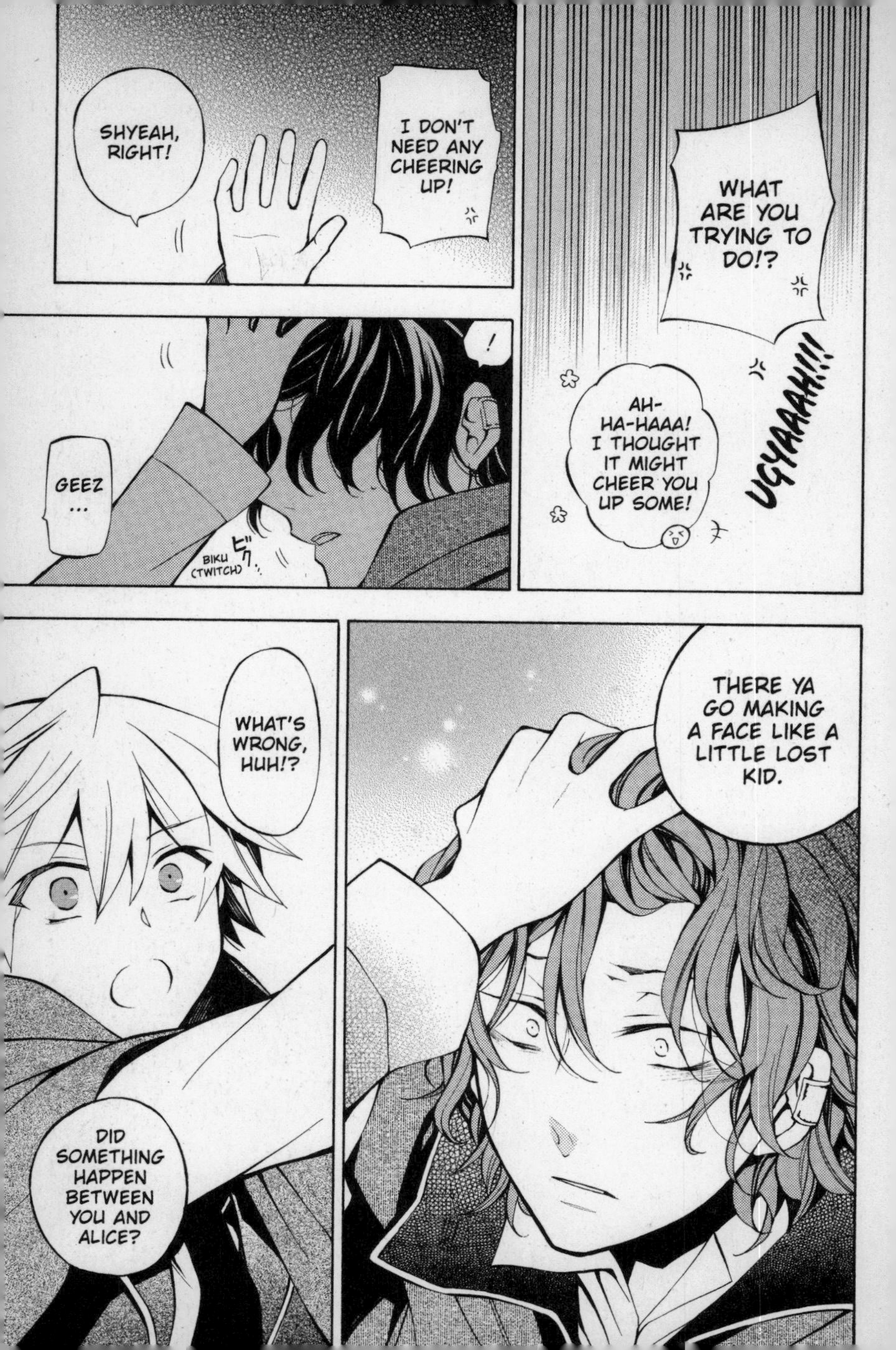
WHAT ARE YOU TRYING TO DO!?
UGYAAAH!!!
AH-HA-HAAA! I THOUGHT IT MIGHT CHEER YOU UP SOME!
I DON'T NEED ANY CHEERING UP!
SHYEAH, RIGHT!
!
GEEZ...
BIKU (TWITCH)
THERE YA GO MAKING A FACE LIKE A LITTLE LOST KID.
WHAT'S WRONG, HUH!?
DID SOMETHING HAPPEN BETWEEN YOU AND ALICE?

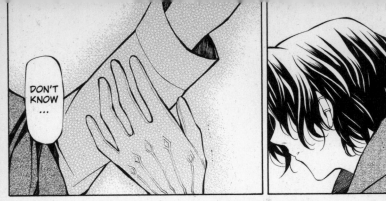

DON'T KNOW ...
LATELY ...
...I'VE BEEN REMEMBERING A LOT ABOUT THE PAST...
!
MY MEMORIES HAVEN'T RETURNED.
BUT ...
...THE FEELINGS THAT CAME FLOWING BACK TO ME...ARE PROVOKING MY BODY.
ARE THEY...MY EMOTIONS ...?
WHEN I RECALL EVERYTHING...
...WILL I BE ABLE TO KEEP BEING ME...!?

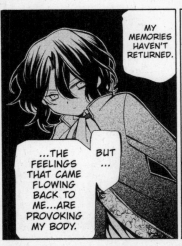

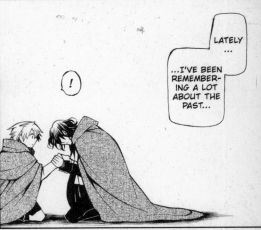

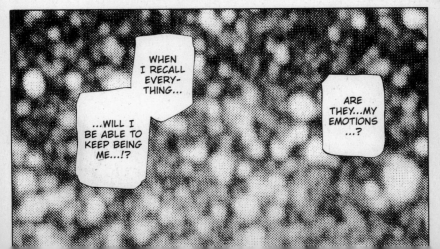

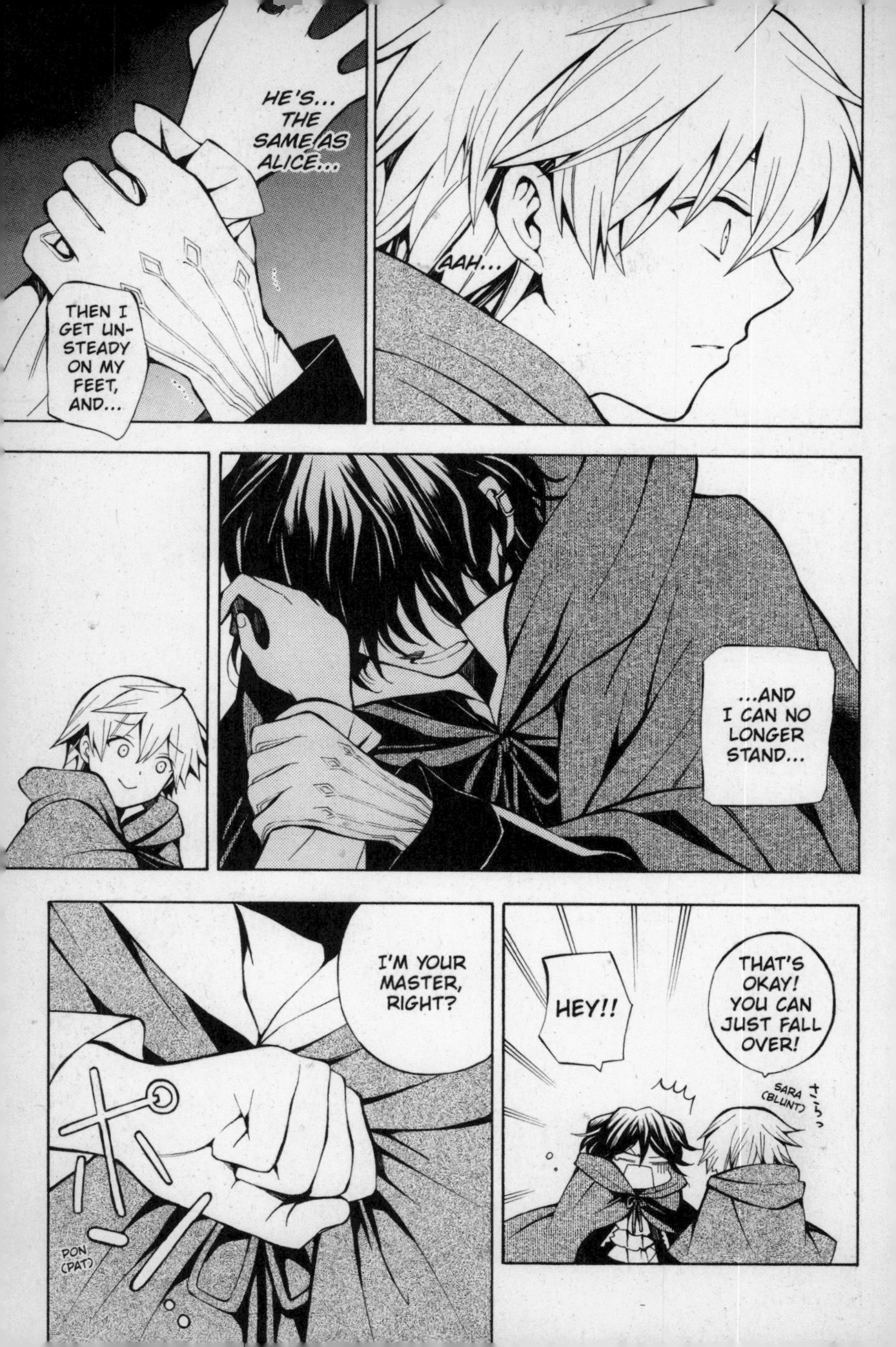
AAH...
HE'S... THE SAME AS ALICE...
....
THEN I GET UN-STEADY ON MY FEET, AND...
...AND I CAN NO LONGER STAND...
THAT'S OKAY! YOU CAN JUST FALL OVER!
HEY!!
SARA (BLUNT)
I'M YOUR MASTER, RIGHT?
PON (PAT)

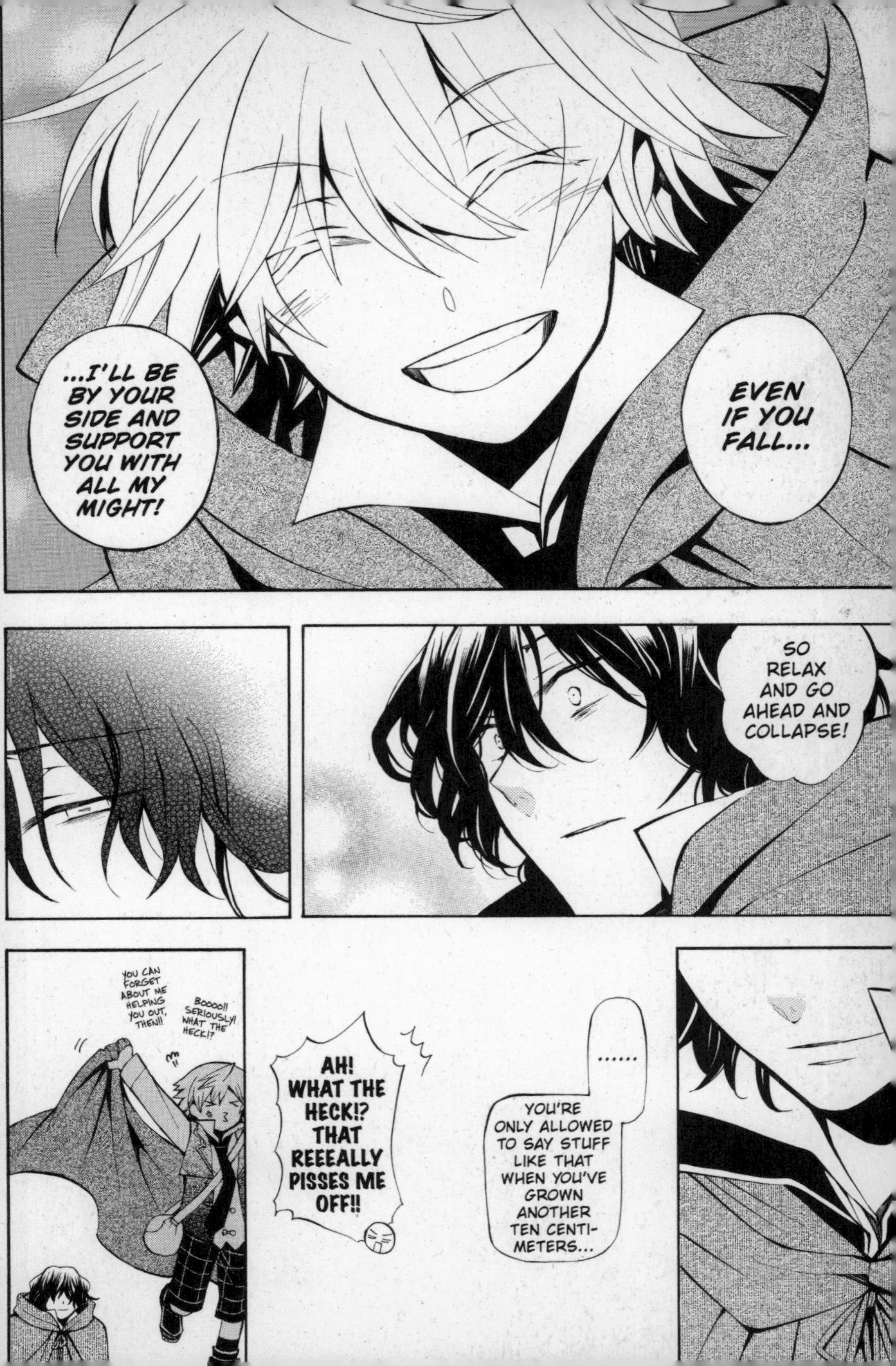
EVEN IF YOU FALL...
...I'LL BE BY YOUR SIDE AND SUPPORT YOU WITH ALL MY MIGHT!
SO RELAX AND GO AHEAD AND COLLAPSE!
......
YOU'RE ONLY ALLOWED TO SAY STUFF LIKE THAT WHEN YOU'VE GROWN ANOTHER TEN CENTI-METERS...
AH! WHAT THE HECK!? THAT REEEALLY PISSES ME OFF!!
BOOOOO!! SERIOUSLY! WHAT THE HECK!?
YOU CAN FORGET ABOUT ME HELPING YOU OUT, THEN!!

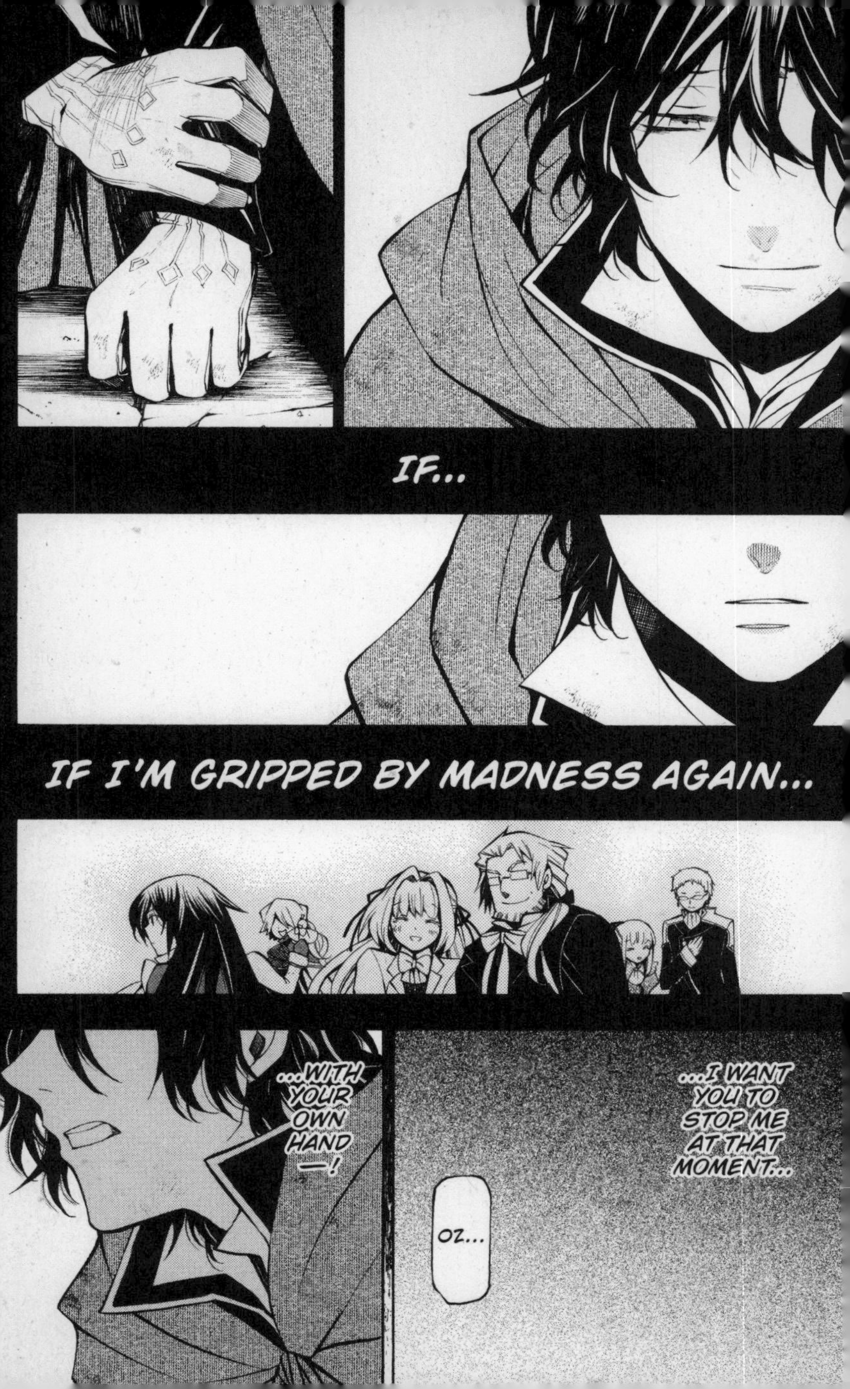
IF...
IF I'M GRIPPED BY MADNESS AGAIN...
...I WANT YOU TO STOP ME AT THAT MOMENT...
OZ...
...WITH YOUR OWN HAND—!

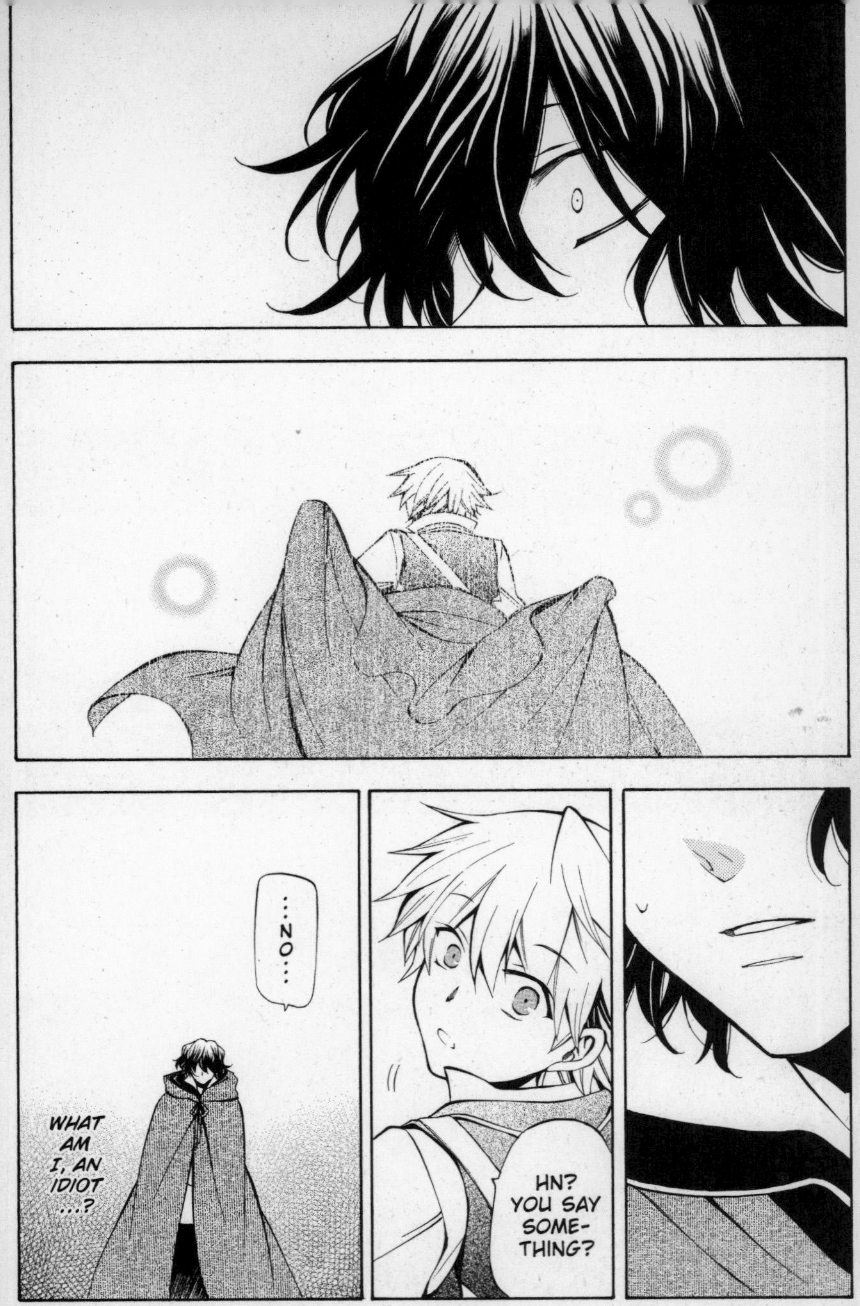
HN? YOU SAY SOME-THING?
...NO...
WHAT AM I, AN IDIOT ...?

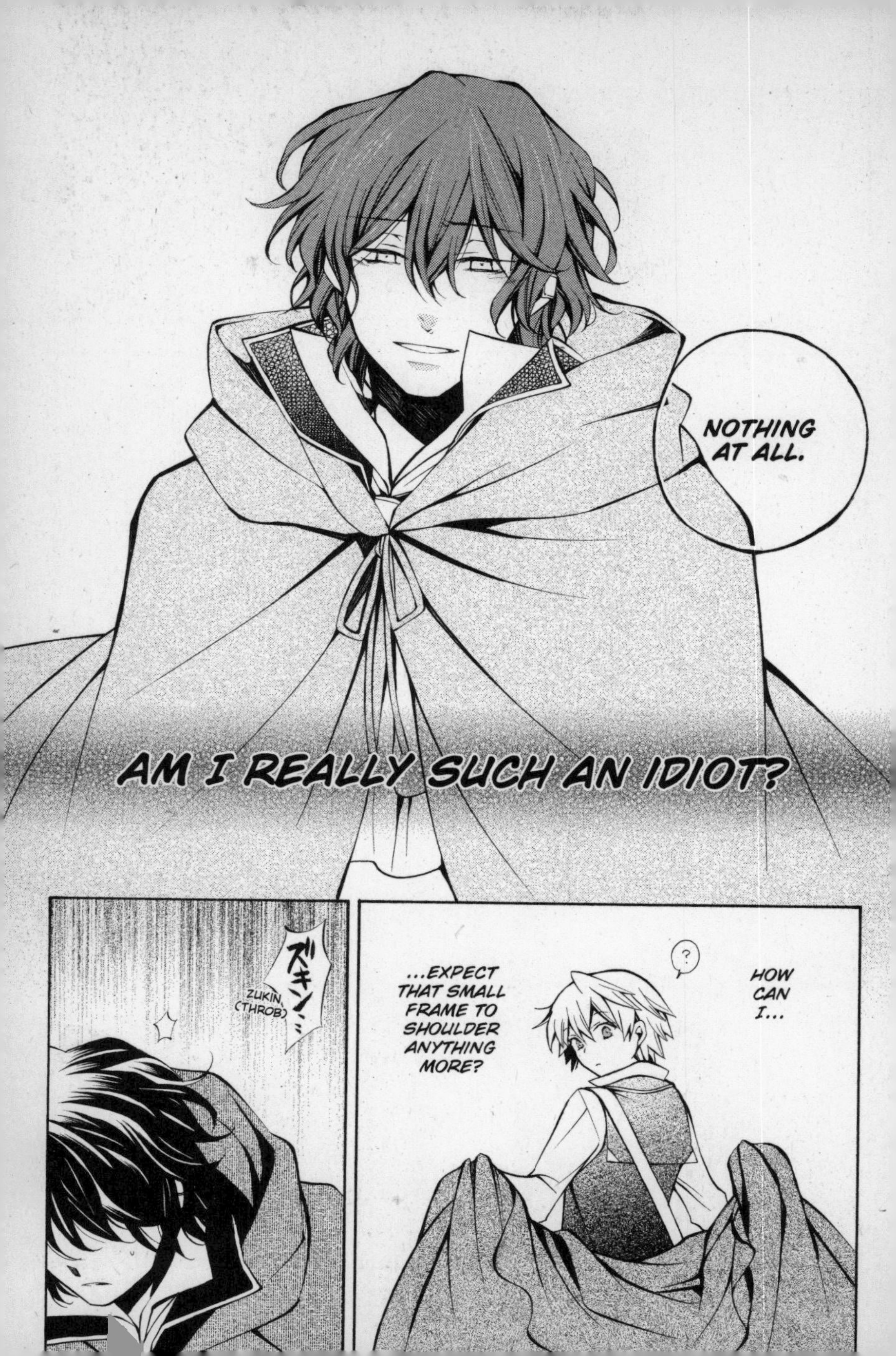
NOTHING AT ALL.
AM I REALLY SUCH AN IDIOT?
HOW CAN I...
?
...EXPECT THAT SMALL FRAME TO SHOULDER ANYTHING MORE?
ズキン
ZUKIN (THROB)

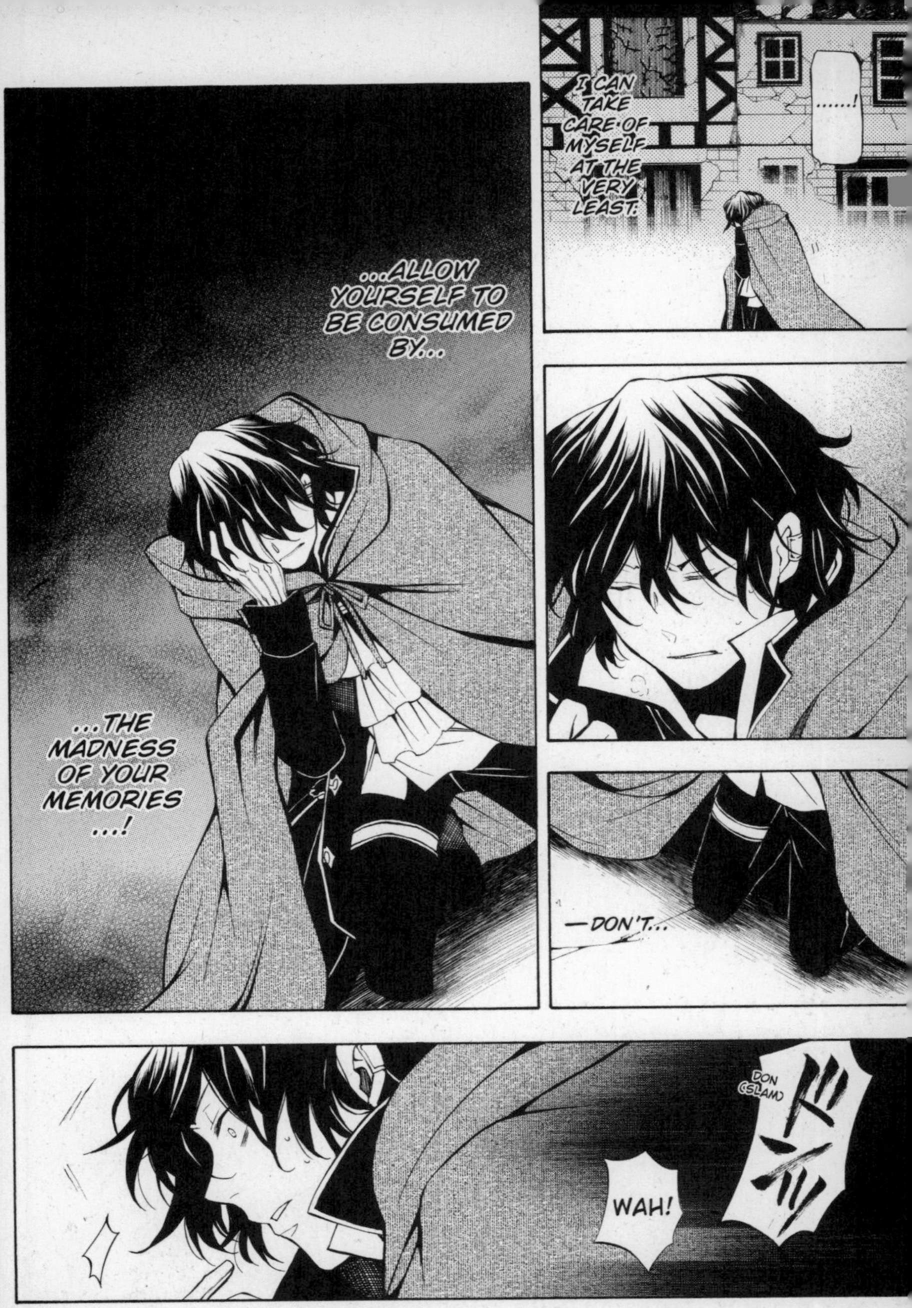
......!
I CAN TAKE CARE OF MYSELF AT THE VERY LEAST.
—DON'T...
...ALLOW YOURSELF TO BE CONSUMED BY...
...THE MADNESS OF YOUR MEMORIES ...!
DON (SLAM)
WAH!

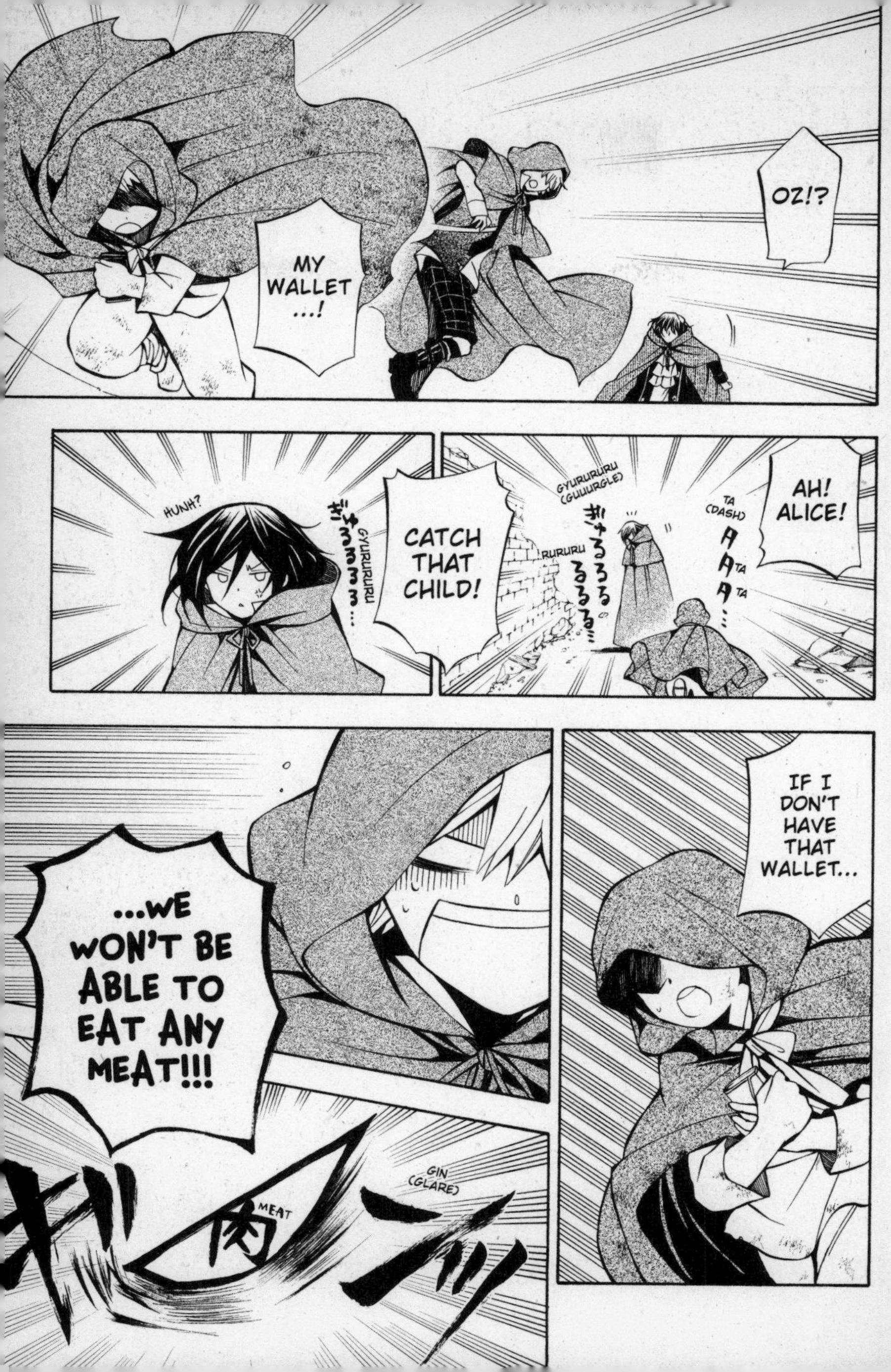
OZ!?
MY WALLET ...!
AH! ALICE!
TA (DASH)
TA
TA
CATCH THAT CHILD!
GYURURURU (GUUURGLE)
RURURU
GYURURURU
HUNH?
IF I DON'T HAVE THAT WALLET...
...WE WON'T BE ABLE TO EAT ANY MEAT!!!
GIN (GLARE)
MEAT

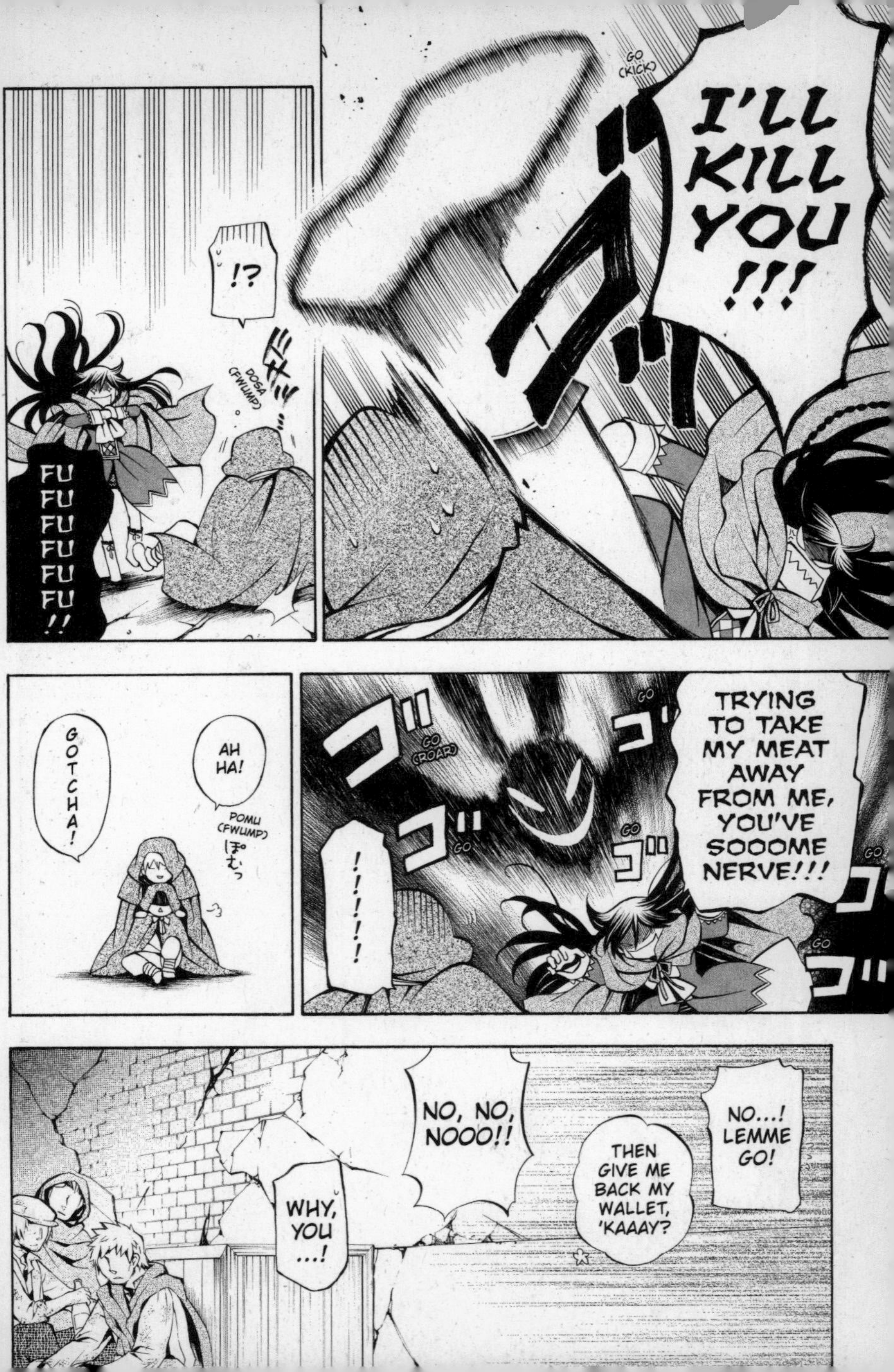
GO (KICK)
I'LL KILL YOU!!!
!?
DOSA (FWUMP)
FU FU FU FU FU FU!!
TRYING TO TAKE MY MEAT AWAY FROM ME, YOU'VE SOOOME NERVE!!!
GO
GO (ROAR)
GO
GO
GO
GO
!!!!!
AH HA!
POMU (FWUMP)
GOTCHA!
NO...! LEMME GO!
THEN GIVE ME BACK MY WALLET, 'KAAAY?
NO, NO, NOOO!!
WHY, YOU ...!

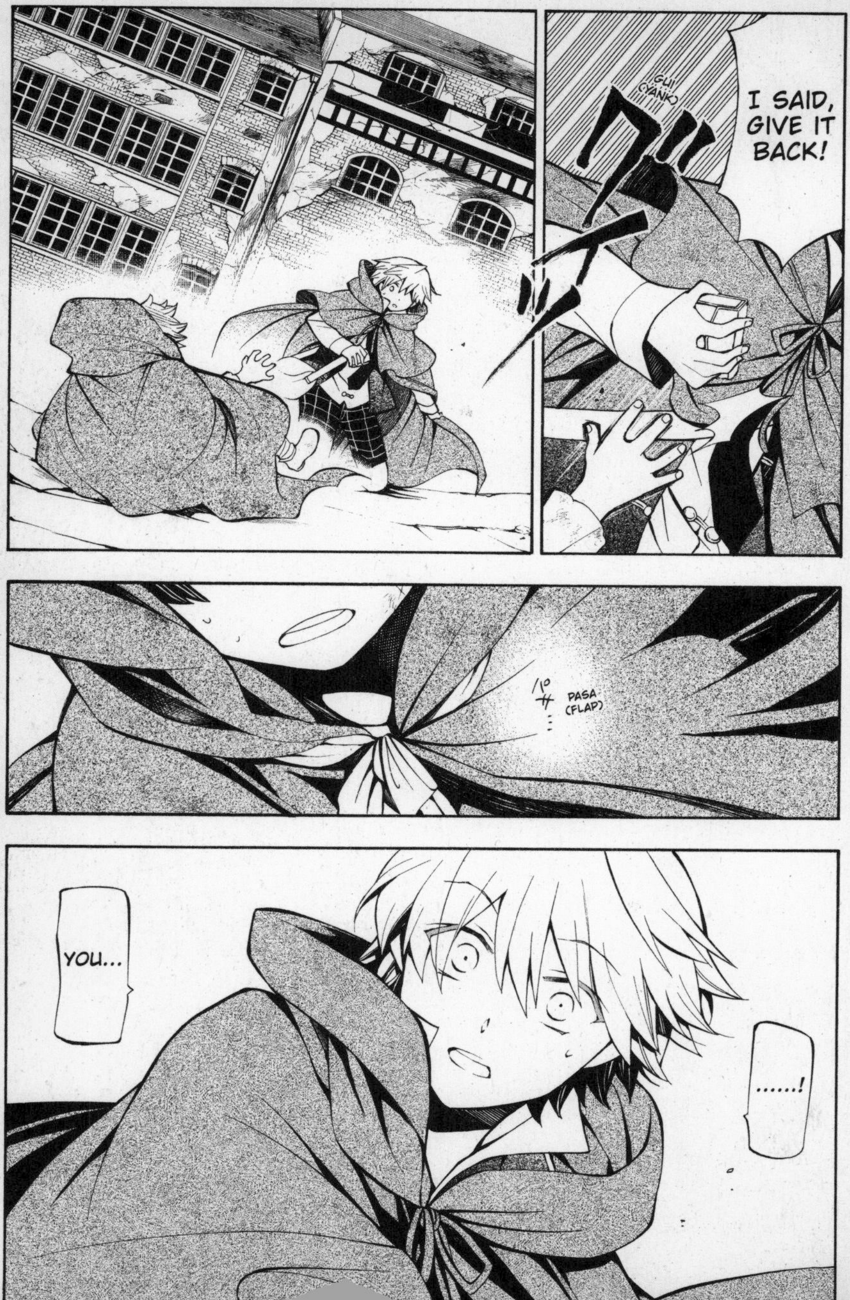

GUI (YANK)
I SAID, GIVE IT BACK!
PASA (FLAP)
......!
YOU...

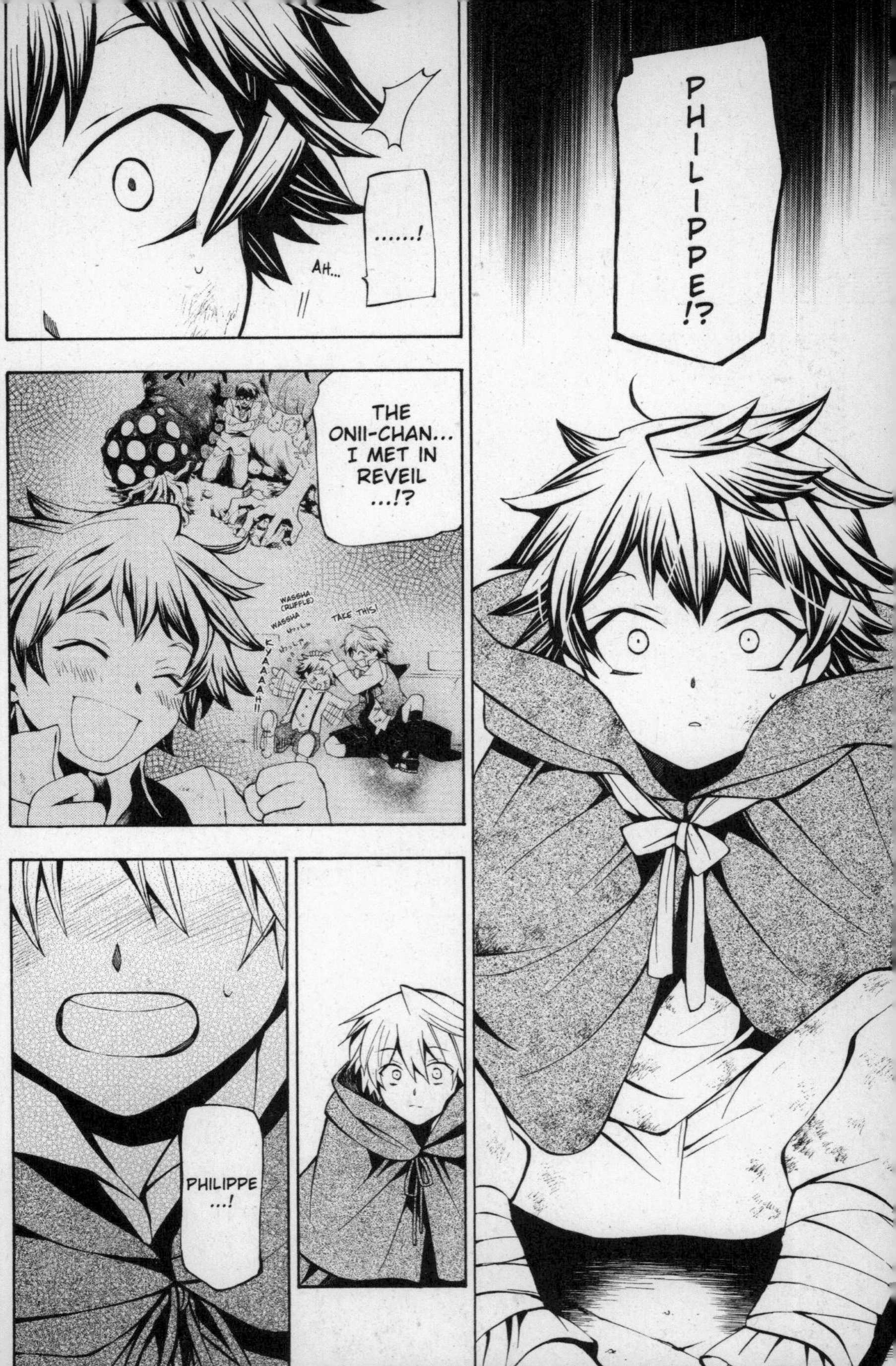
PHILIPPE!?
......!
AH...
THE ONII-CHAN... I MET IN REVEIL ...!?
TAKE THIS!
WASSHA (RUFFLE) WASSHA
KYAAAAAH!!
PHILIPPE ...!

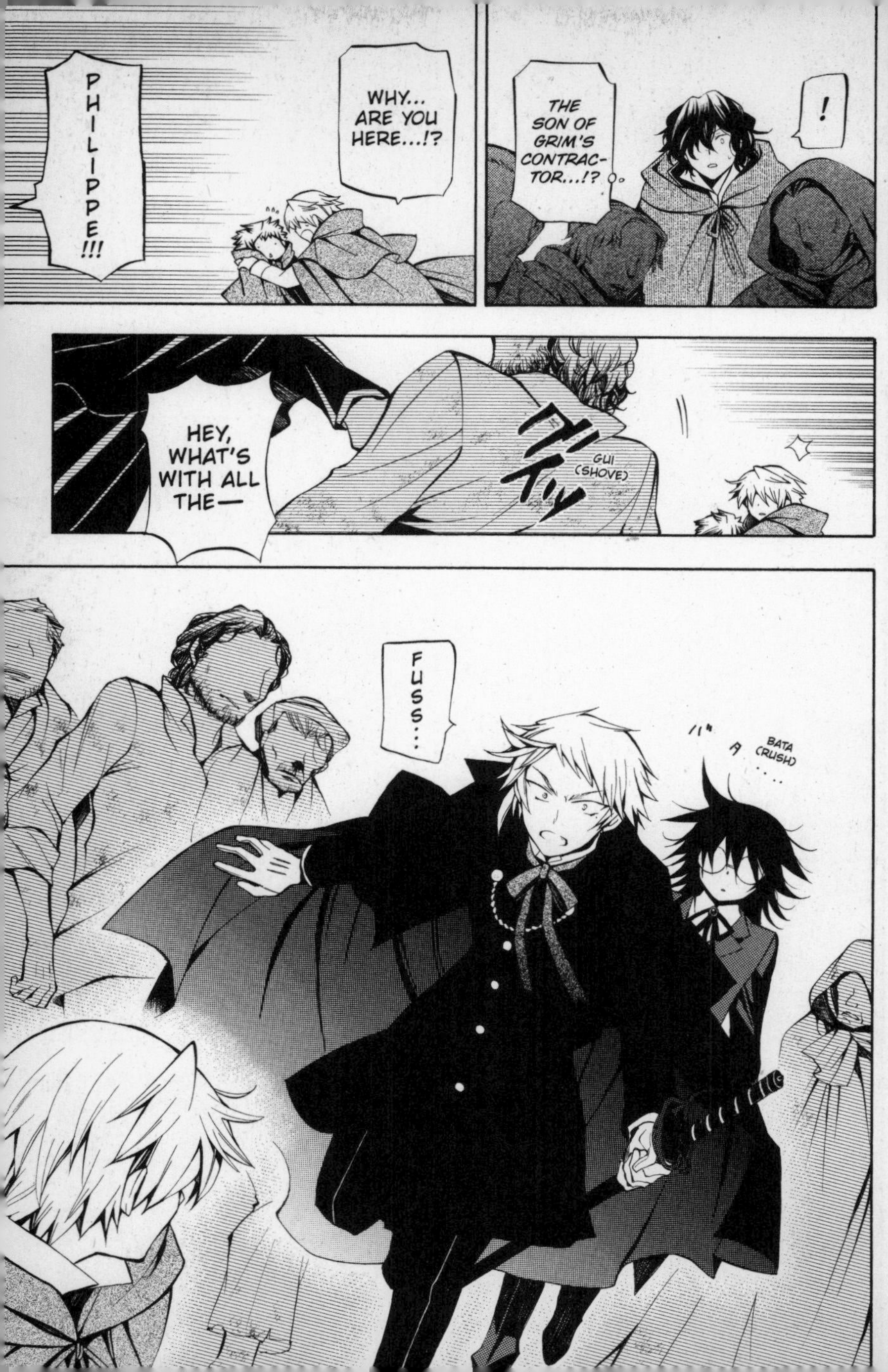
!
THE SON OF GRIM'S CONTRACTOR...!?
WHY... ARE YOU HERE...!?
PHILIPPE!!!
GUI (SHOVE)
HEY, WHAT'S WITH ALL THE—
BATA (RUSH)
FUSS...

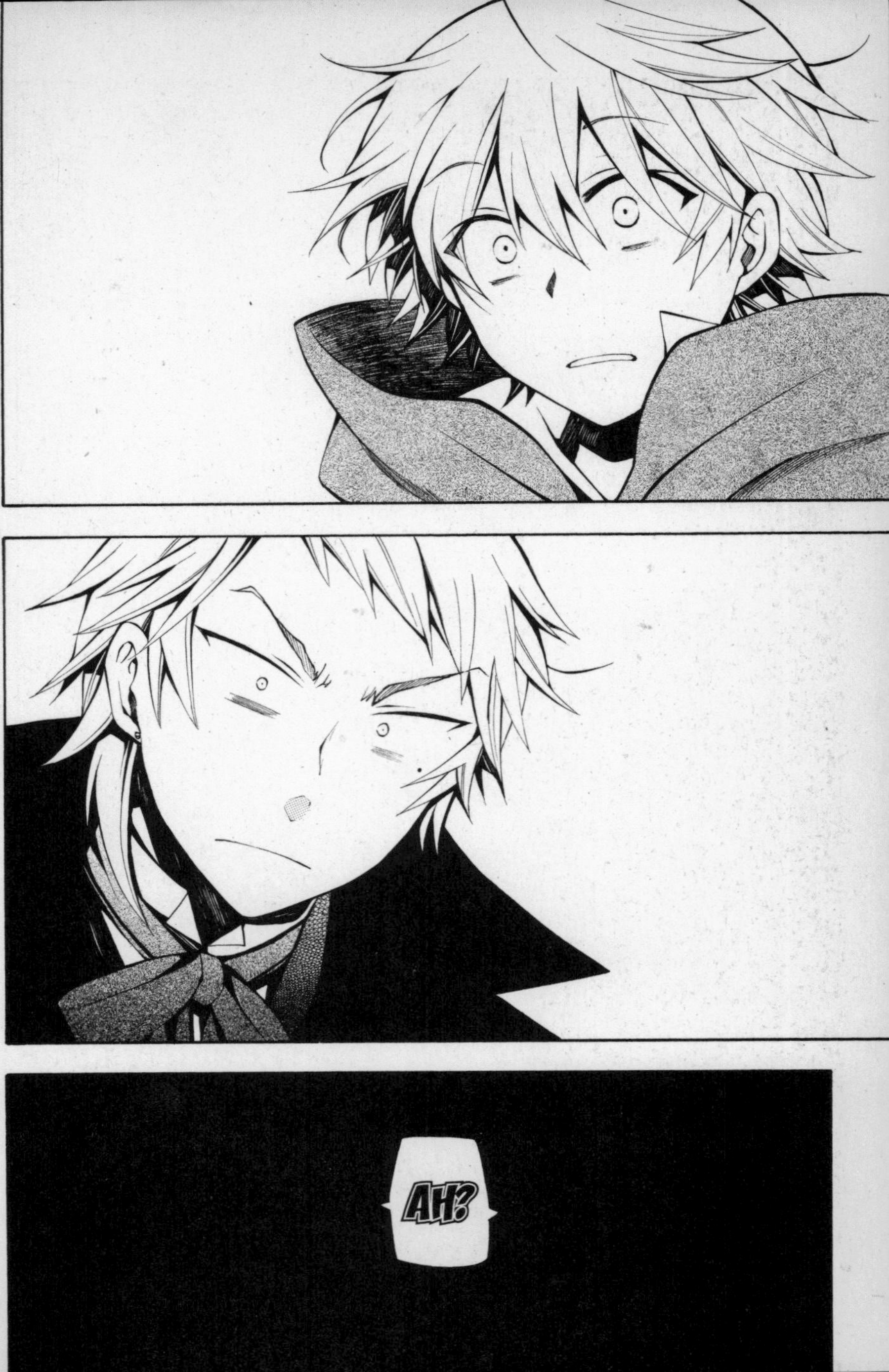
AH?

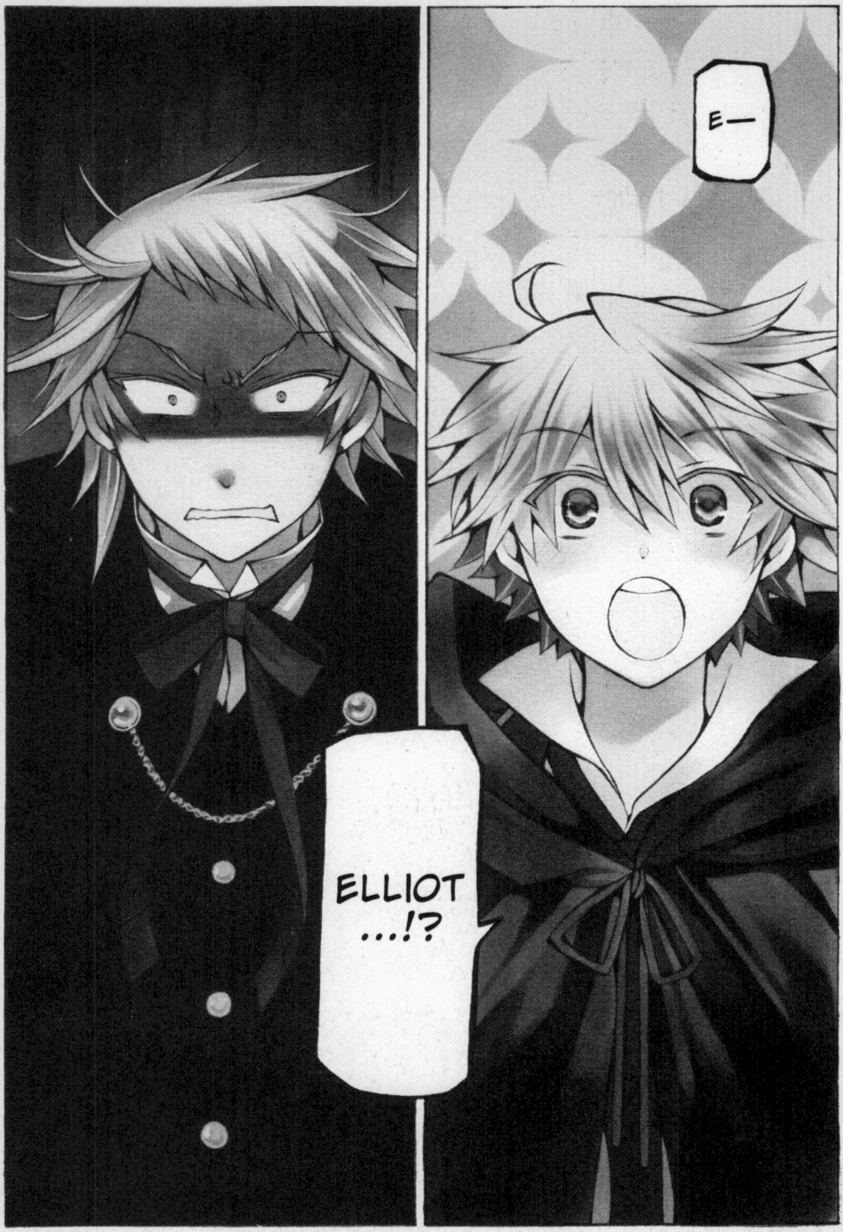
E—
ELLIOT ...!?

Retrace:XXXVI Sablier

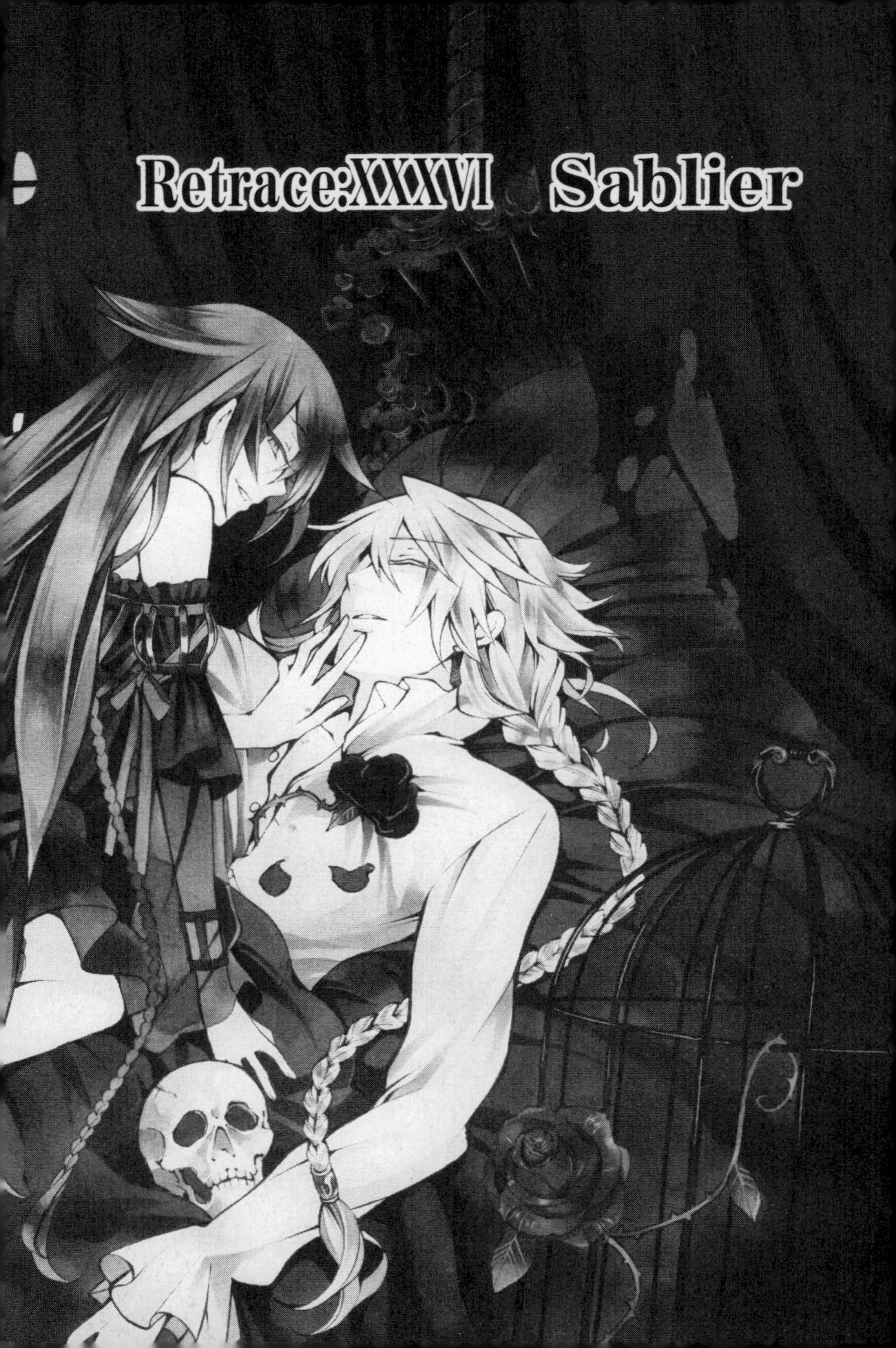

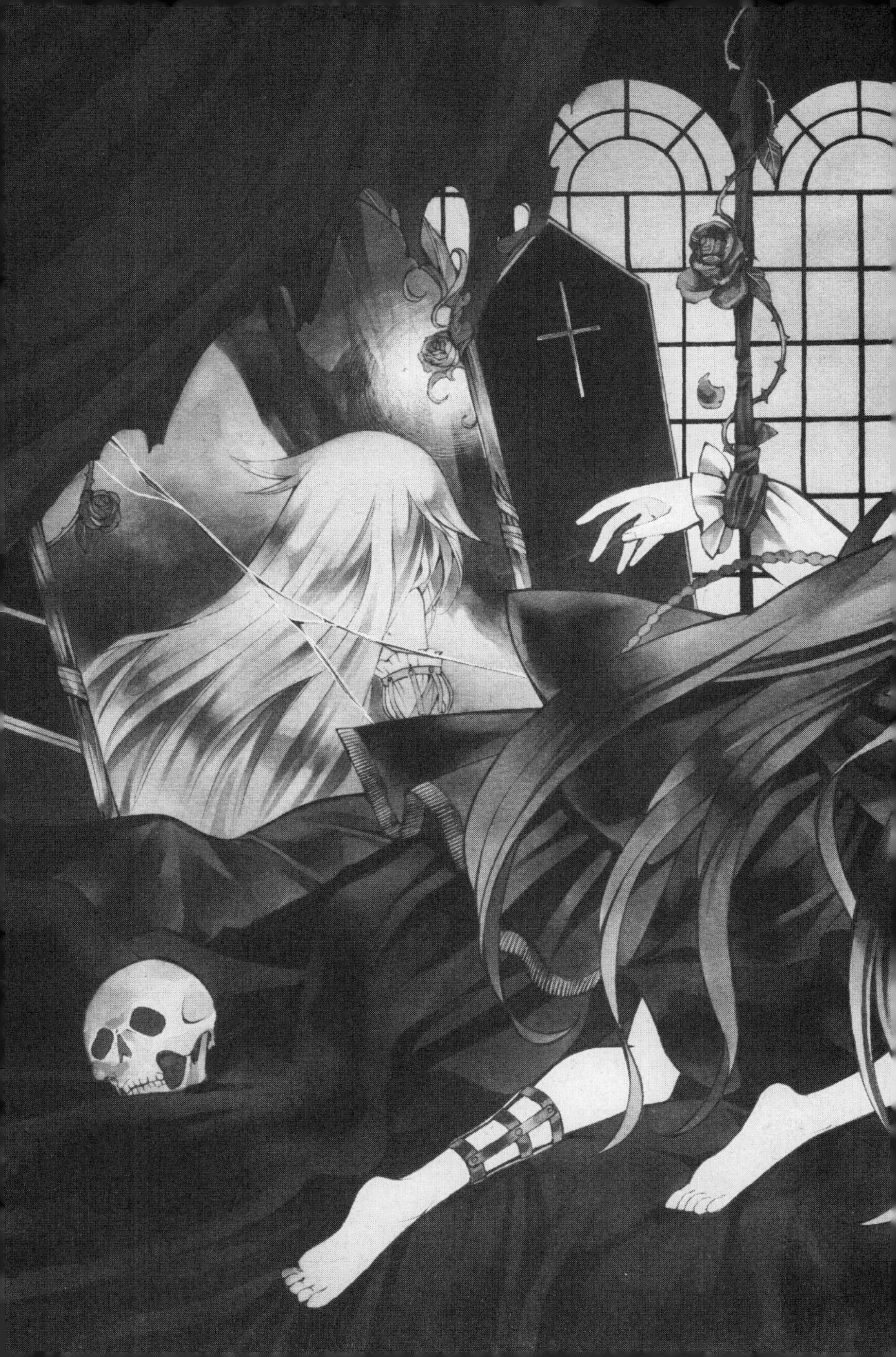

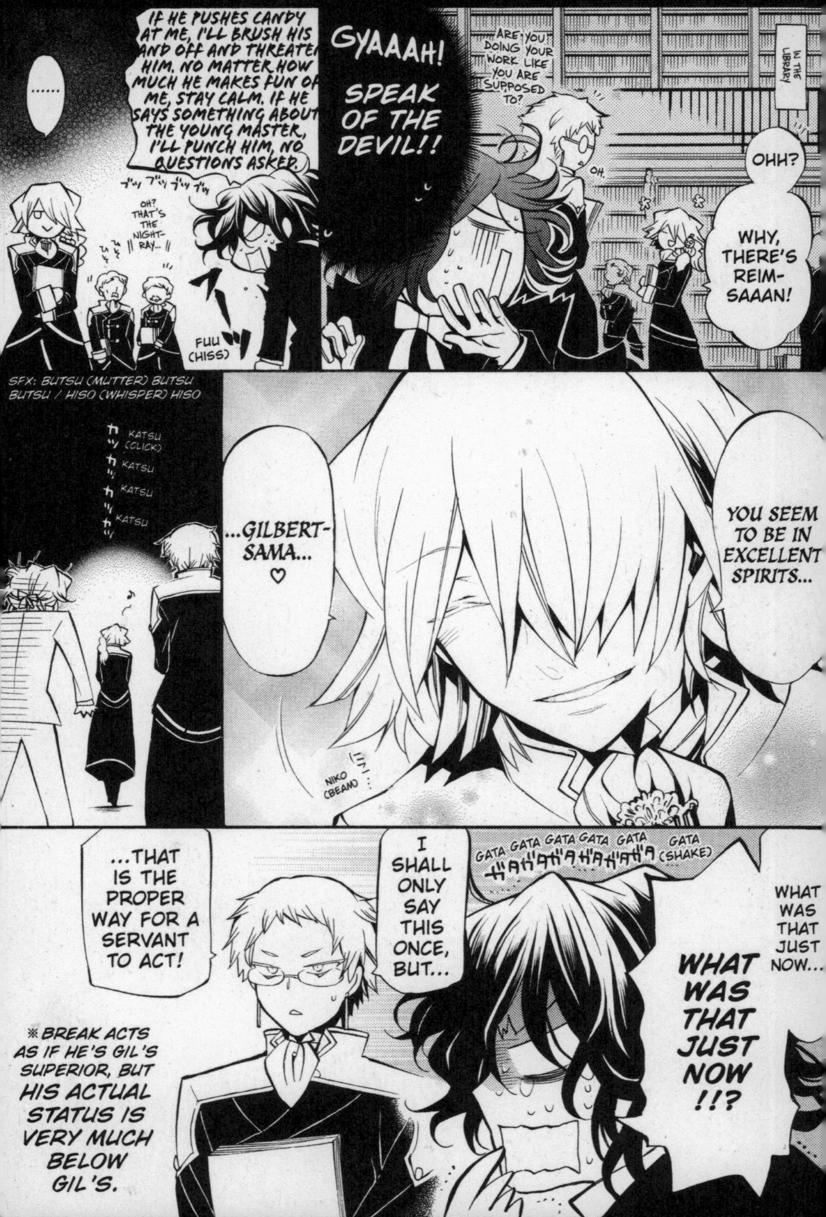
IN THE LIBRARY
OHH?
WHY, THERE'S REIM-SAAAN!
ARE YOU DOING YOUR WORK LIKE YOU ARE SUPPOSED TO?
OH.
GYAAAH! SPEAK OF THE DEVIL!!
IF HE PUSHES CANDY AT ME, I'LL BRUSH HIS HAND OFF AND THREATEN HIM. NO MATTER HOW MUCH HE MAKES FUN OF ME, STAY CALM. IF HE SAYS SOMETHING ABOUT THE YOUNG MASTER, I'LL PUNCH HIM, NO QUESTIONS ASKED.
......
OH? THAT'S THE NIGHTRAY...
FUU (HISS)
SFX: BUTSU (MUTTER) BUTSU BUTSU / HISO (WHISPER) HISO
YOU SEEM TO BE IN EXCELLENT SPIRITS...
...GILBERT-SAMA... ♡
NIKO (BEAM)
KATSU (CLICK)
KATSU
KATSU
KATSU
WHAT WAS THAT JUST NOW...
WHAT WAS THAT JUST NOW!!?
GATA GATA GATA GATA GATA GATA (SHAKE)
I SHALL ONLY SAY THIS ONCE, BUT...
...THAT IS THE PROPER WAY FOR A SERVANT TO ACT!
※BREAK ACTS AS IF HE'S GIL'S SUPERIOR, BUT HIS ACTUAL STATUS IS VERY MUCH BELOW GIL'S.

PLAYING GIL FOR A FOOL BEFORE THE OTHER ARISTOCRATS WILL MAKE ALL KINDS OF TROUBLE, SO HE ADDRESS

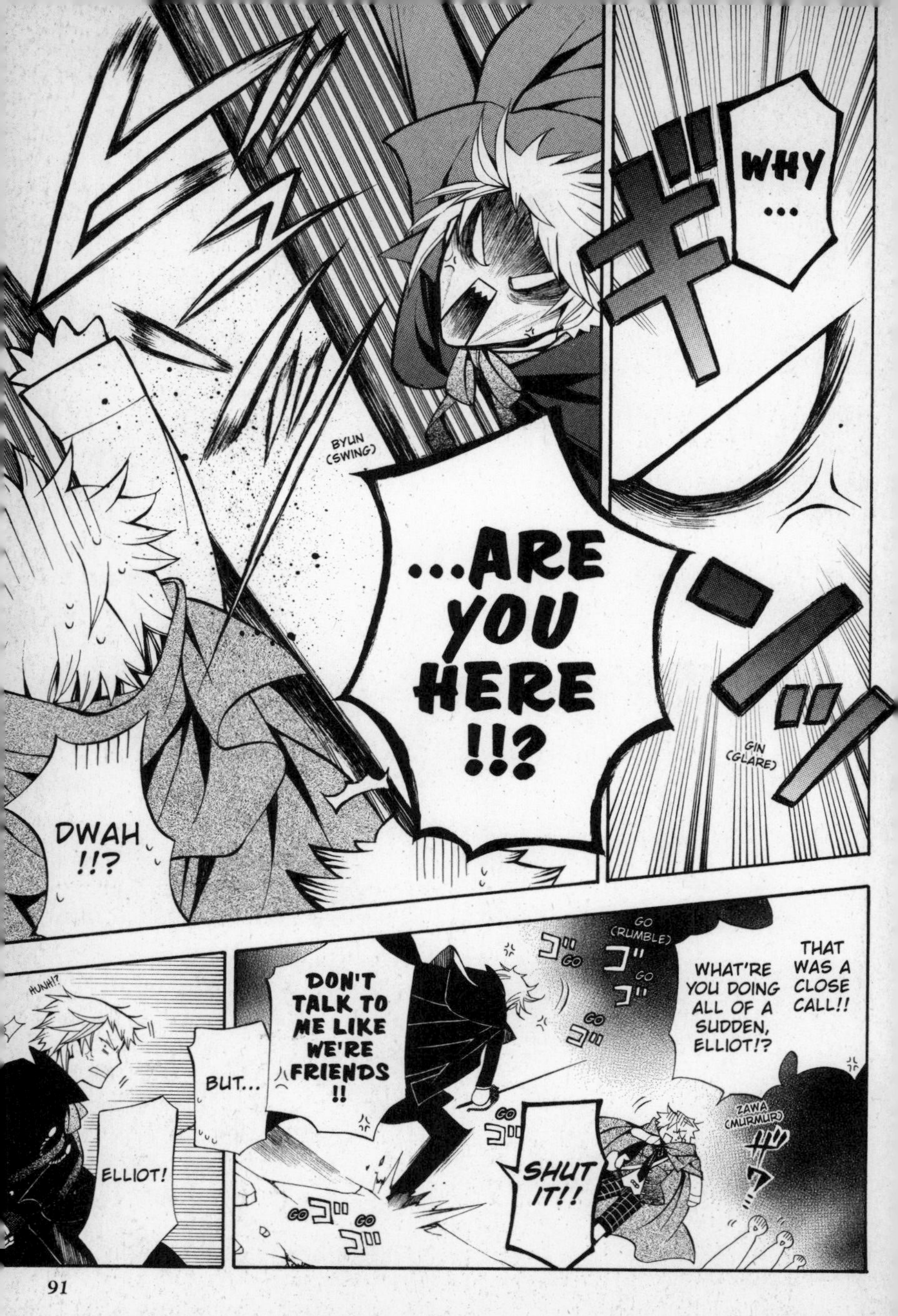
WHY ...
GIN (GLARE)
BYUN (SWING)
...ARE YOU HERE !!?
DWAH !!?
THAT WAS A CLOSE CALL!!
WHAT'RE YOU DOING ALL OF A SUDDEN, ELLIOT!?
GO (RUMBLE)
GO
GO
ZAWA (MURMUR)
DON'T TALK TO ME LIKE WE'RE FRIENDS !!
SHUT IT!!
GO
GO
GO
BUT...
HUNH!?
ELLIOT!

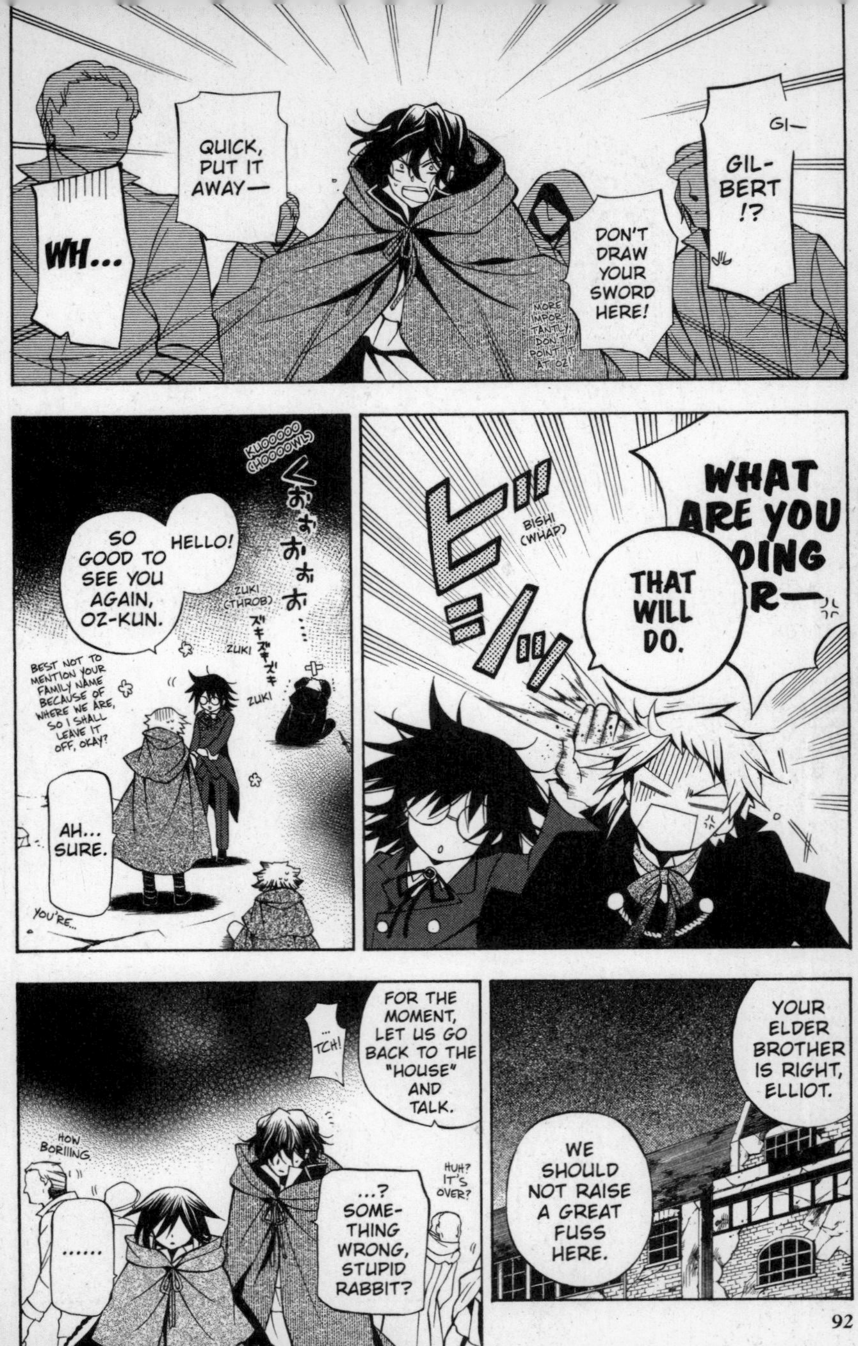
GI—
GILBERT!?
DON'T DRAW YOUR SWORD HERE!
MORE IMPORTANTLY, DON'T POINT IT AT OZ!
QUICK, PUT IT AWAY—
WH...
WHAT ARE YOU
OING
R—
BISHI (WHAP)
ビシッ
THAT WILL DO.
KUOOOOO (HOOOOWL)
くおぉおぉお…
HELLO!
SO GOOD TO SEE YOU AGAIN, OZ-KUN.
ZUKI (THROB)
ズキズキズキ
ZUKI
ZUKI
BEST NOT TO MENTION YOUR FAMILY NAME BECAUSE OF WHERE WE ARE, SO I SHALL LEAVE IT OFF, OKAY?
AH... SURE.
YOU'RE...
YOUR ELDER BROTHER IS RIGHT, ELLIOT.
WE SHOULD NOT RAISE A GREAT FUSS HERE.
FOR THE MOMENT, LET US GO BACK TO THE "HOUSE" AND TALK.
...TCH!
HUH? IT'S OVER?
...? SOMETHING WRONG, STUPID RABBIT?
HOW BORIIING.
......

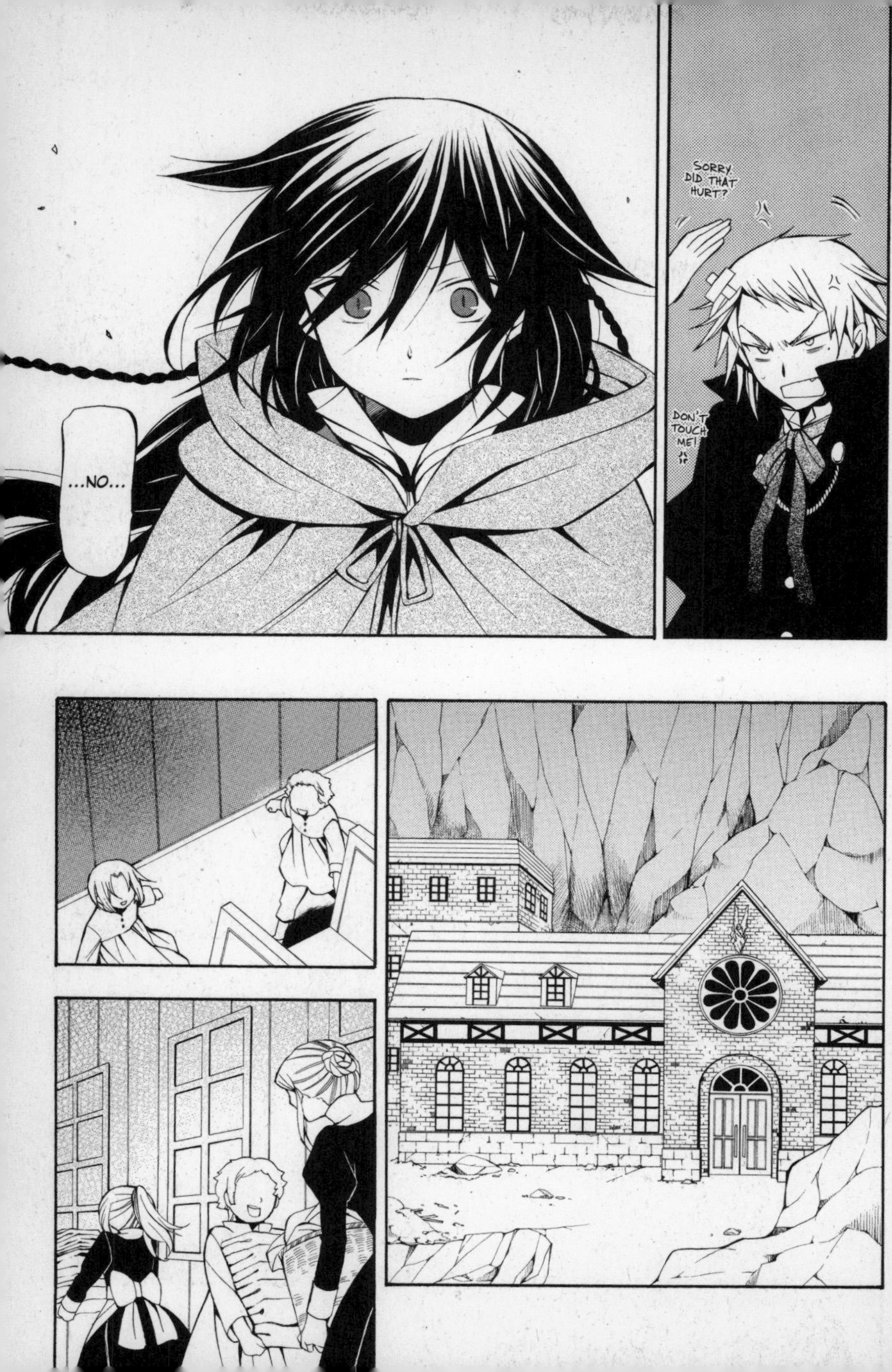
SORRY. DID THAT HURT?
DON'T TOUCH ME!
...NO...

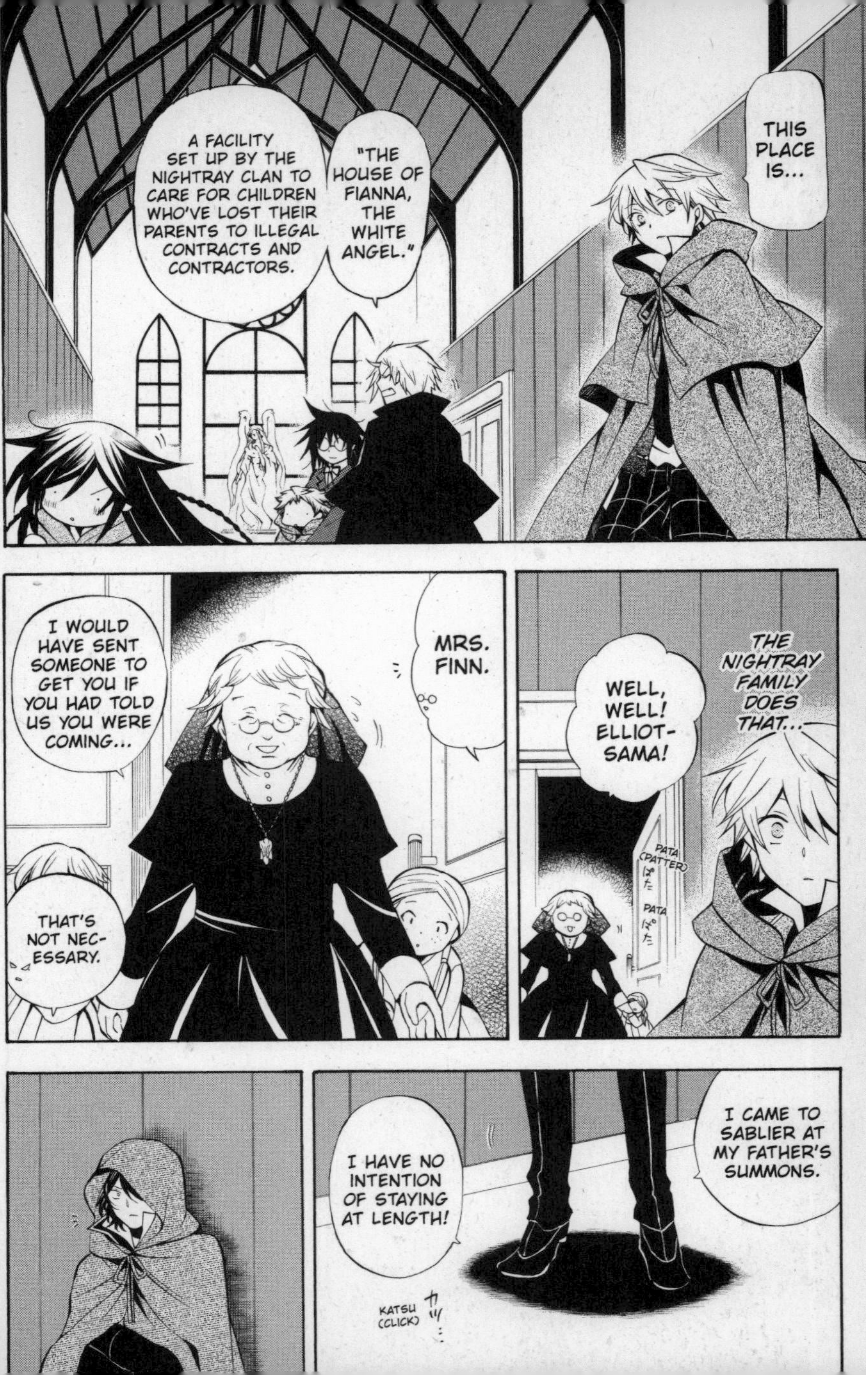
THIS PLACE IS...
"THE HOUSE OF FIANNA, THE WHITE ANGEL."
A FACILITY SET UP BY THE NIGHTRAY CLAN TO CARE FOR CHILDREN WHO'VE LOST THEIR PARENTS TO ILLEGAL CONTRACTS AND CONTRACTORS.
THE NIGHTRAY FAMILY DOES THAT...
WELL, WELL! ELLIOT-SAMA!
PATA (PATTER) PATA
MRS. FINN.
I WOULD HAVE SENT SOMEONE TO GET YOU IF YOU HAD TOLD US YOU WERE COMING...
THAT'S NOT NECESSARY.
I CAME TO SABLIER AT MY FATHER'S SUMMONS.
I HAVE NO INTENTION OF STAYING AT LENGTH!
KATSU (CLICK)

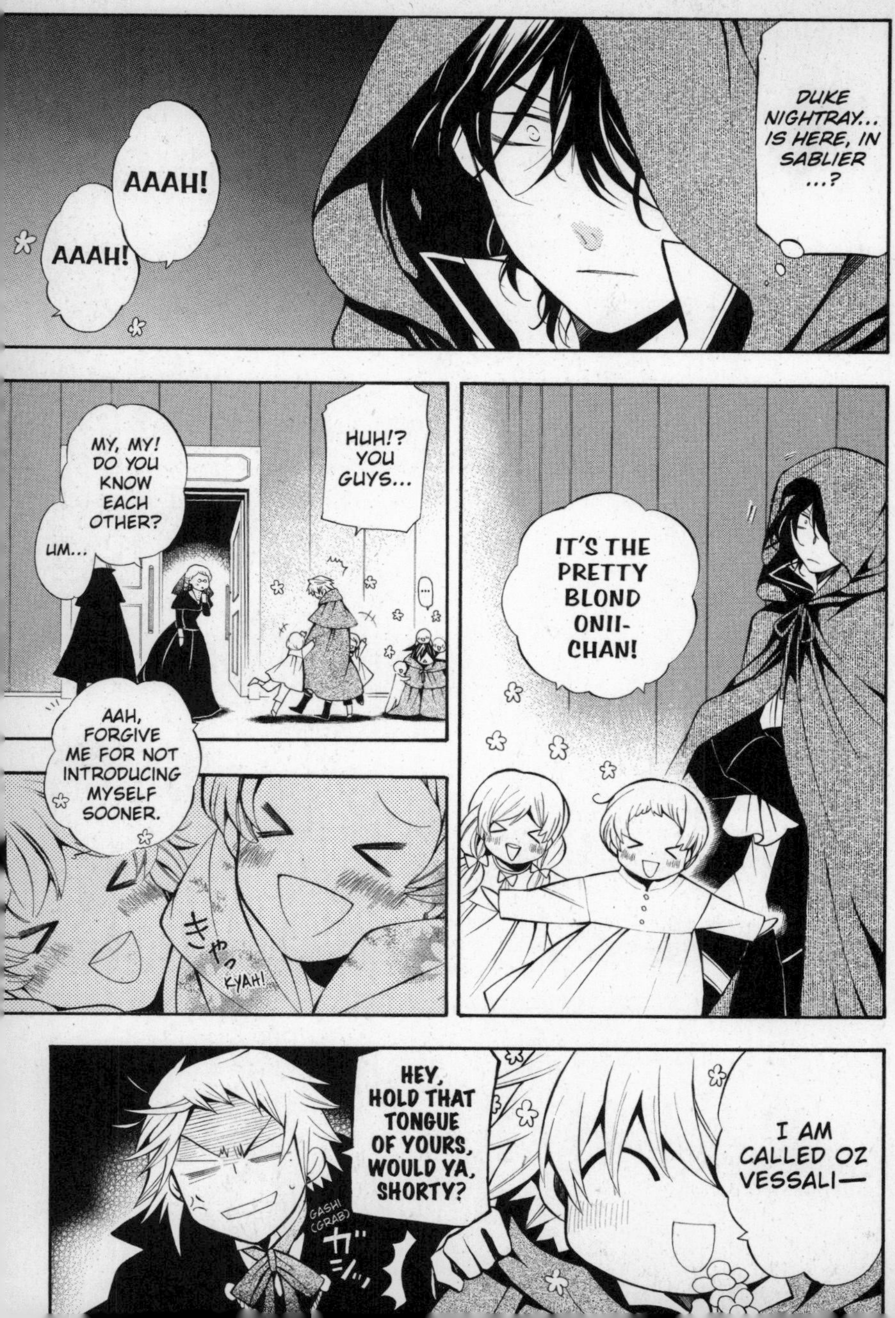
DUKE NIGHTRAY... IS HERE, IN SABLIER ...?
AAAH!
AAAH!
IT'S THE PRETTY BLOND ONII-CHAN!
HUH!? YOU GUYS...
...
MY, MY! DO YOU KNOW EACH OTHER?
UM...
AAH, FORGIVE ME FOR NOT INTRODUCING MYSELF SOONER.
きゃっ
KYAH!
I AM CALLED OZ VESSALI—
HEY, HOLD THAT TONGUE OF YOURS, WOULD YA, SHORTY?
ガシッ
GASHI (GRAB)

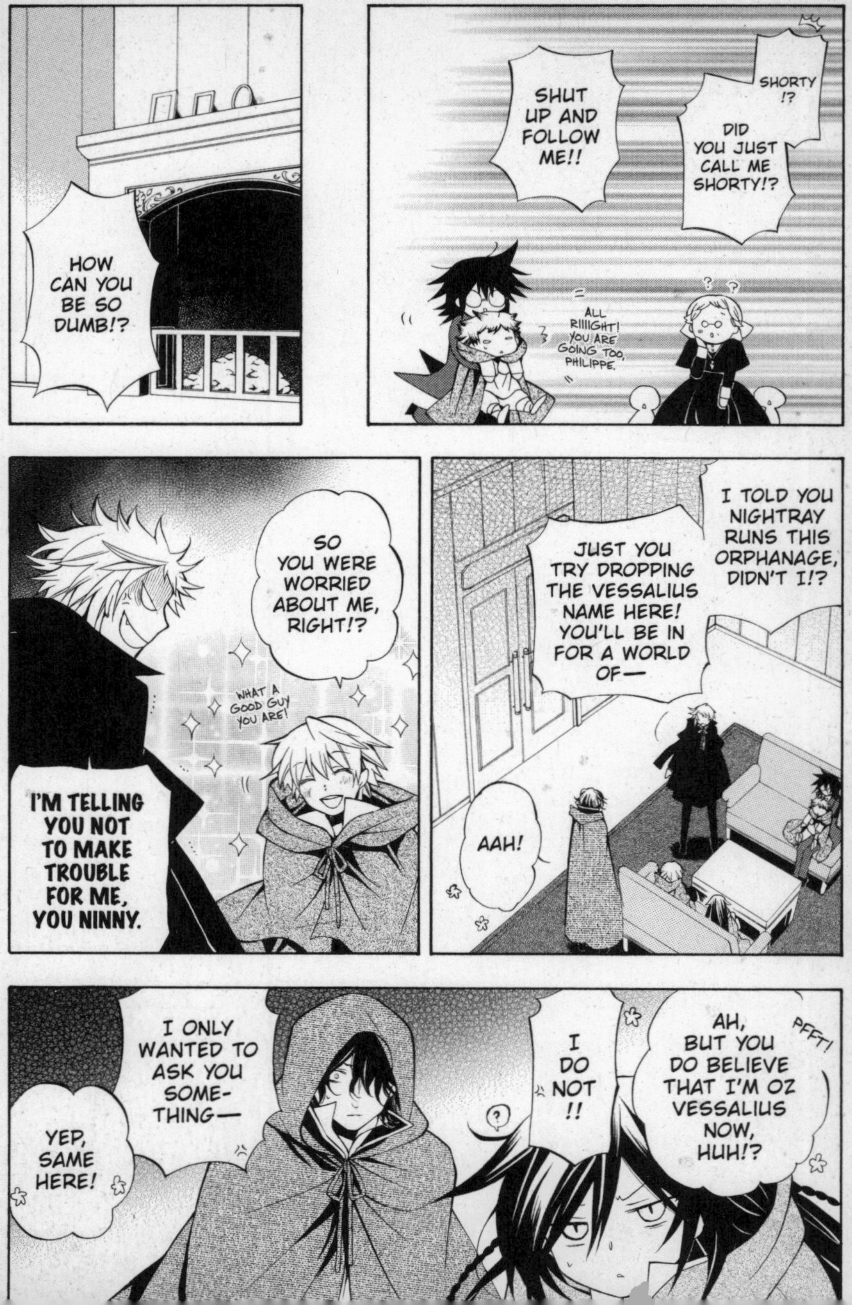
SHORTY!?
DID YOU JUST CALL ME SHORTY!?
SHUT UP AND FOLLOW ME!!
ALL RIIIIGHT! YOU ARE GOING TOO, PHILIPPE.
HOW CAN YOU BE SO DUMB!?
I TOLD YOU NIGHTRAY RUNS THIS ORPHANAGE, DIDN'T I!?
JUST YOU TRY DROPPING THE VESSALIUS NAME HERE! YOU'LL BE IN FOR A WORLD OF—
AAH!
SO YOU WERE WORRIED ABOUT ME, RIGHT!?
WHAT A GOOD GUY YOU ARE!
I'M TELLING YOU NOT TO MAKE TROUBLE FOR ME, YOU NINNY.
PFFT!
AH, BUT YOU DO BELIEVE THAT I'M OZ VESSALIUS NOW, HUH!?
I DO NOT!!
I ONLY WANTED TO ASK YOU SOME-THING—
YEP, SAME HERE!

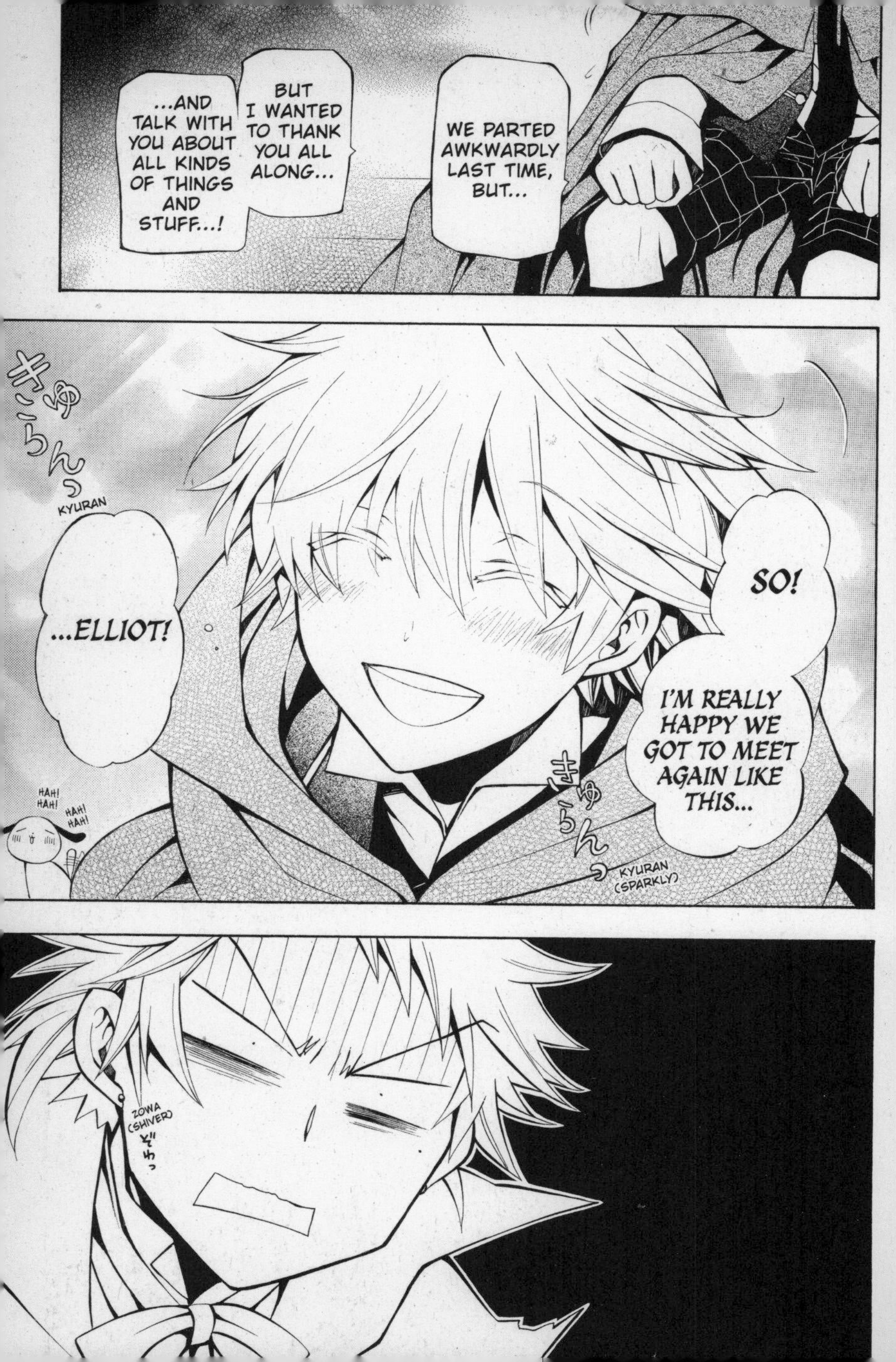
WE PARTED AWKWARDLY LAST TIME, BUT...
BUT I WANTED TO THANK YOU ALL ALONG...
...AND TALK WITH YOU ABOUT ALL KINDS OF THINGS AND STUFF...!
SO!
I'M REALLY HAPPY WE GOT TO MEET AGAIN LIKE THIS...
きゅらんっ
KYURAN (SPARKLY)
きゅらんっ
KYURAN
...ELLIOT!
HAH! HAH! HAH! HAH!
ぞわっ
ZOWA (SHIVER)

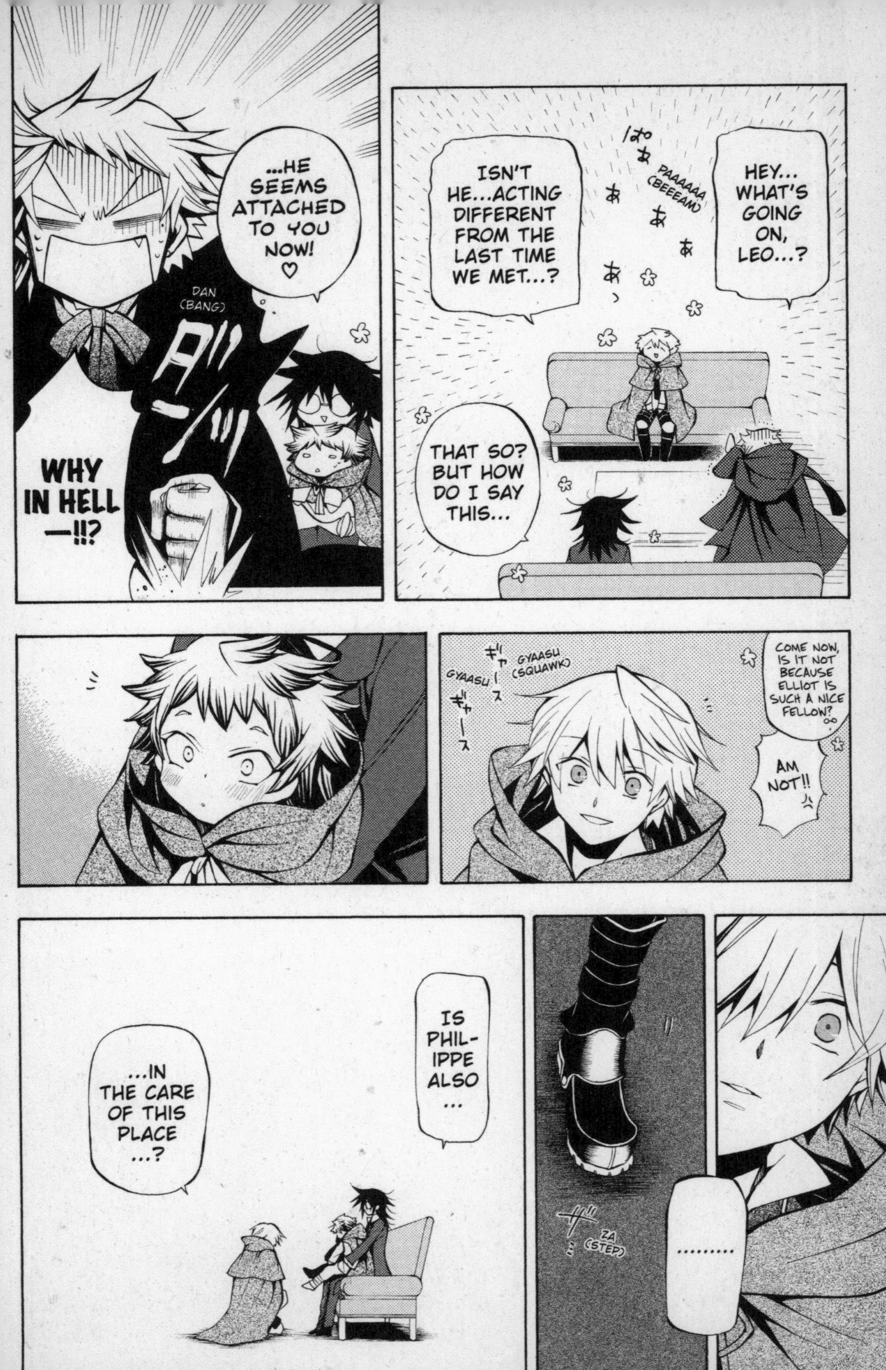

HEY... WHAT'S GOING ON, LEO...?
ぱぁぁぁぁっ
PAAAAAA (BEEEAM)
ISN'T HE...ACTING DIFFERENT FROM THE LAST TIME WE MET...?
THAT SO? BUT HOW DO I SAY THIS...
...HE SEEMS ATTACHED TO YOU NOW! ♡
DAN (BANG)
WHY IN HELL—!!?
COME NOW, IS IT NOT BECAUSE ELLIOT IS SUCH A NICE FELLOW?
AM NOT!!
GYAASU (SQUAWK)
GYAASU
....
ZA (STEP)
IS PHILIPPE ALSO ...
...IN THE CARE OF THIS PLACE ...?

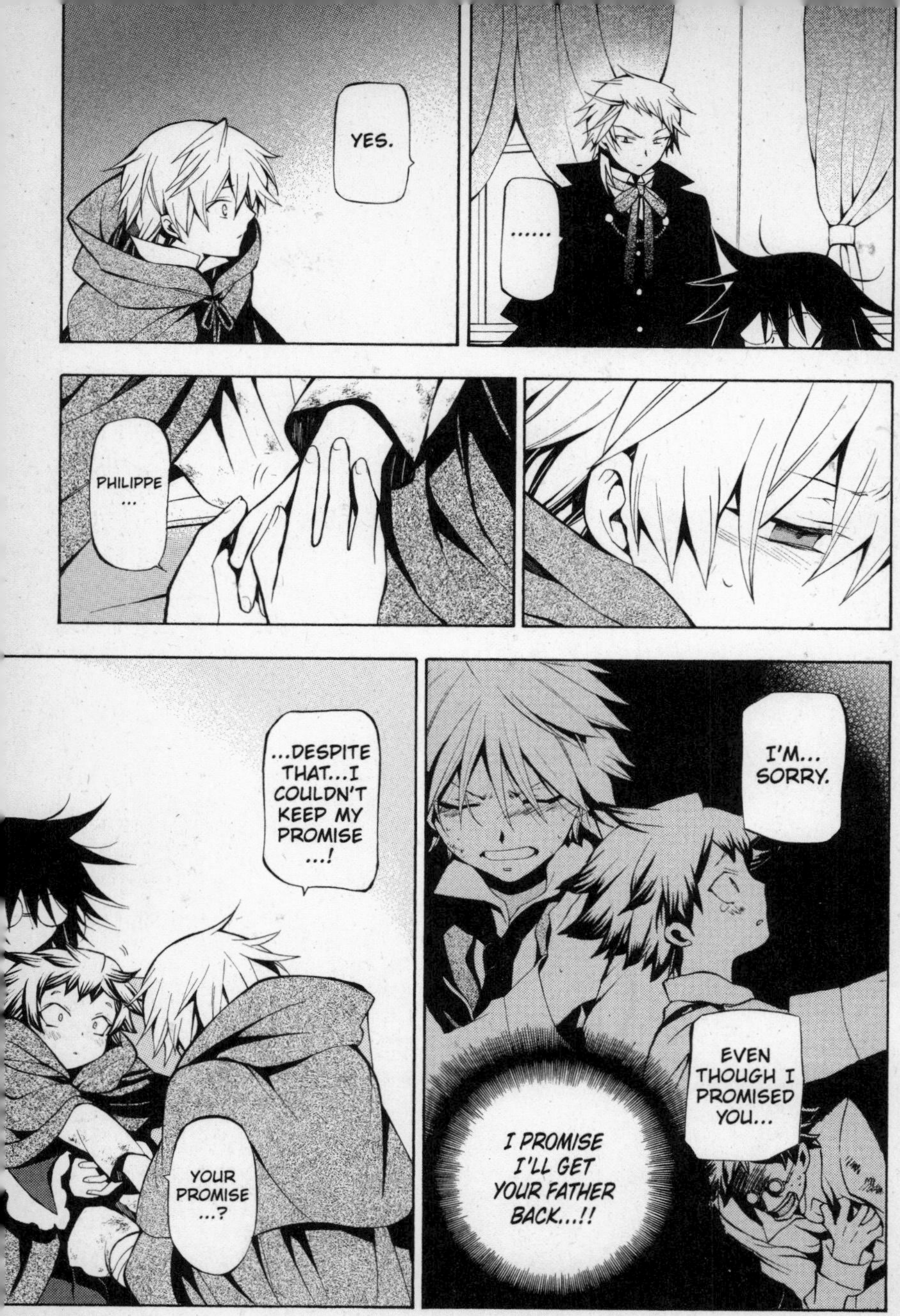
......
YES.
PHILIPPE ...
I'M... SORRY.
EVEN THOUGH I PROMISED YOU...
I PROMISE I'LL GET YOUR FATHER BACK...!!
...DESPITE THAT...I COULDN'T KEEP MY PROMISE ...!
YOUR PROMISE ...?

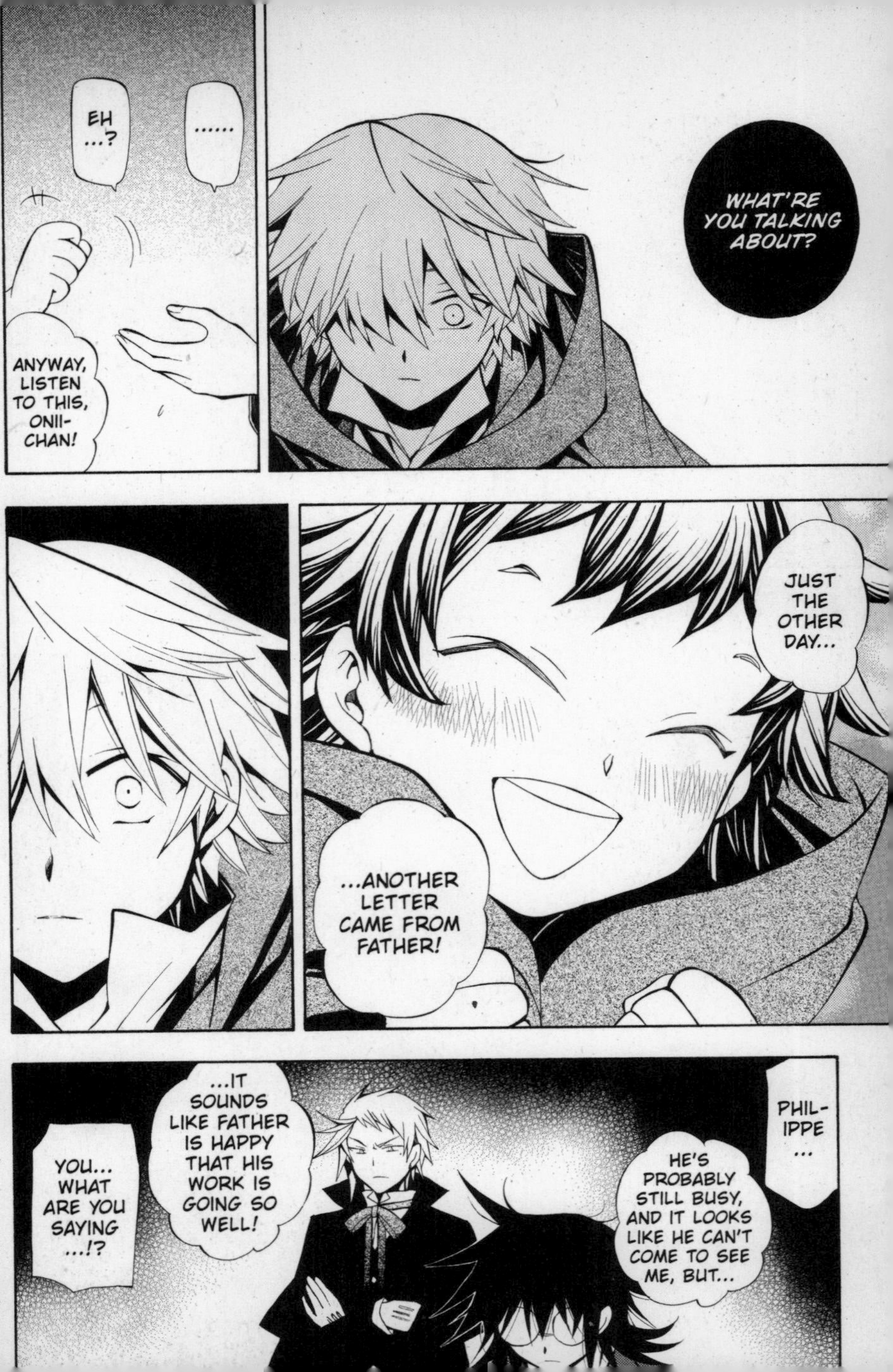
WHAT'RE YOU TALKING ABOUT?
......
EH ...?
ANYWAY, LISTEN TO THIS, ONII-CHAN!
JUST THE OTHER DAY...
...ANOTHER LETTER CAME FROM FATHER!
PHIL-IPPE ...
HE'S PROBABLY STILL BUSY, AND IT LOOKS LIKE HE CAN'T COME TO SEE ME, BUT...
...IT SOUNDS LIKE FATHER IS HAPPY THAT HIS WORK IS GOING SO WELL!
YOU... WHAT ARE YOU SAYING ...!?

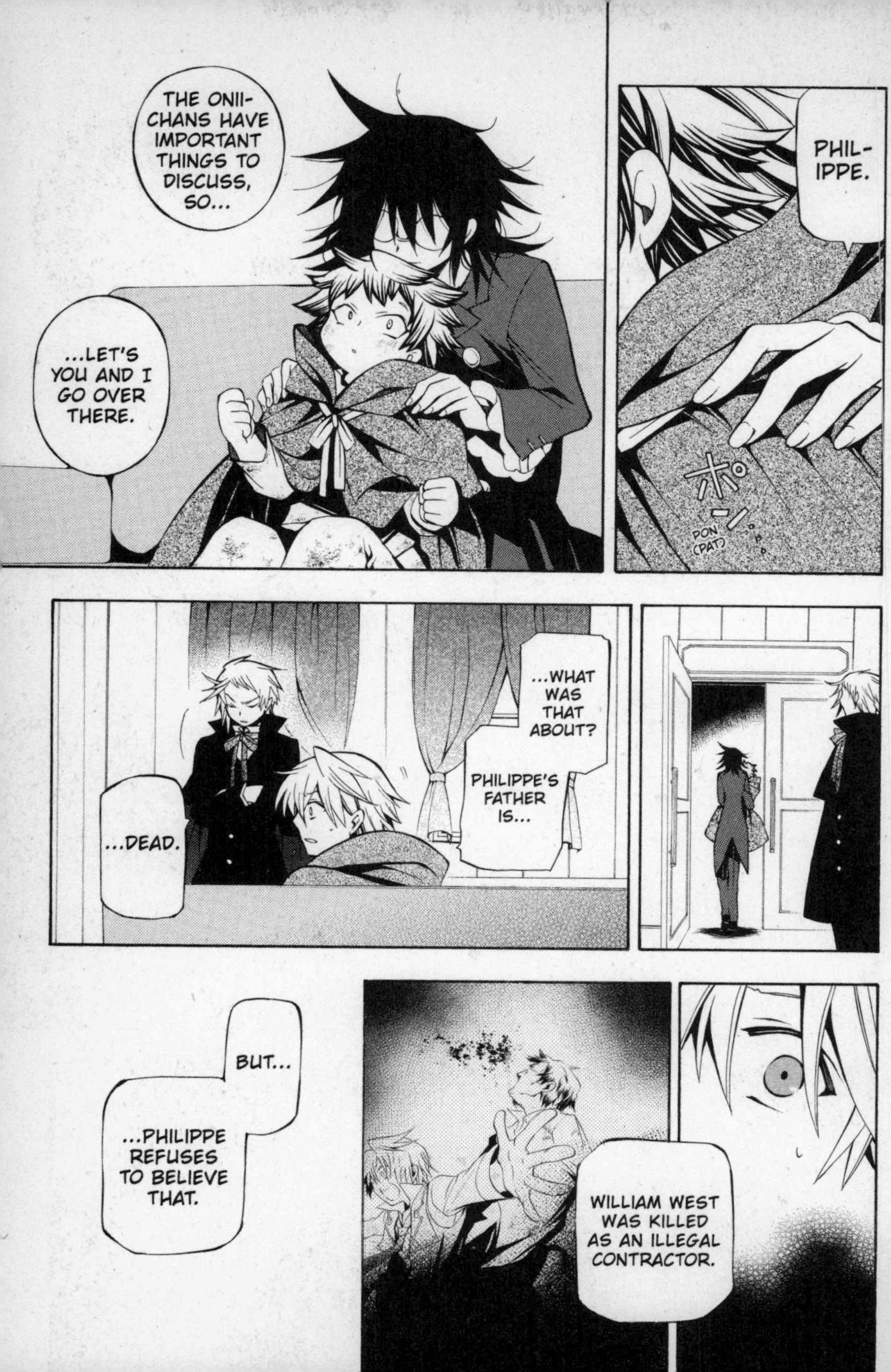
PHIL-IPPE.
ポン
PON (PAT)
THE ONII-CHANS HAVE IMPORTANT THINGS TO DISCUSS, SO...
...LET'S YOU AND I GO OVER THERE.
...WHAT WAS THAT ABOUT?
PHILIPPE'S FATHER IS...
...DEAD.
WILLIAM WEST WAS KILLED AS AN ILLEGAL CONTRACTOR.
BUT...
...PHILIPPE REFUSES TO BELIEVE THAT.

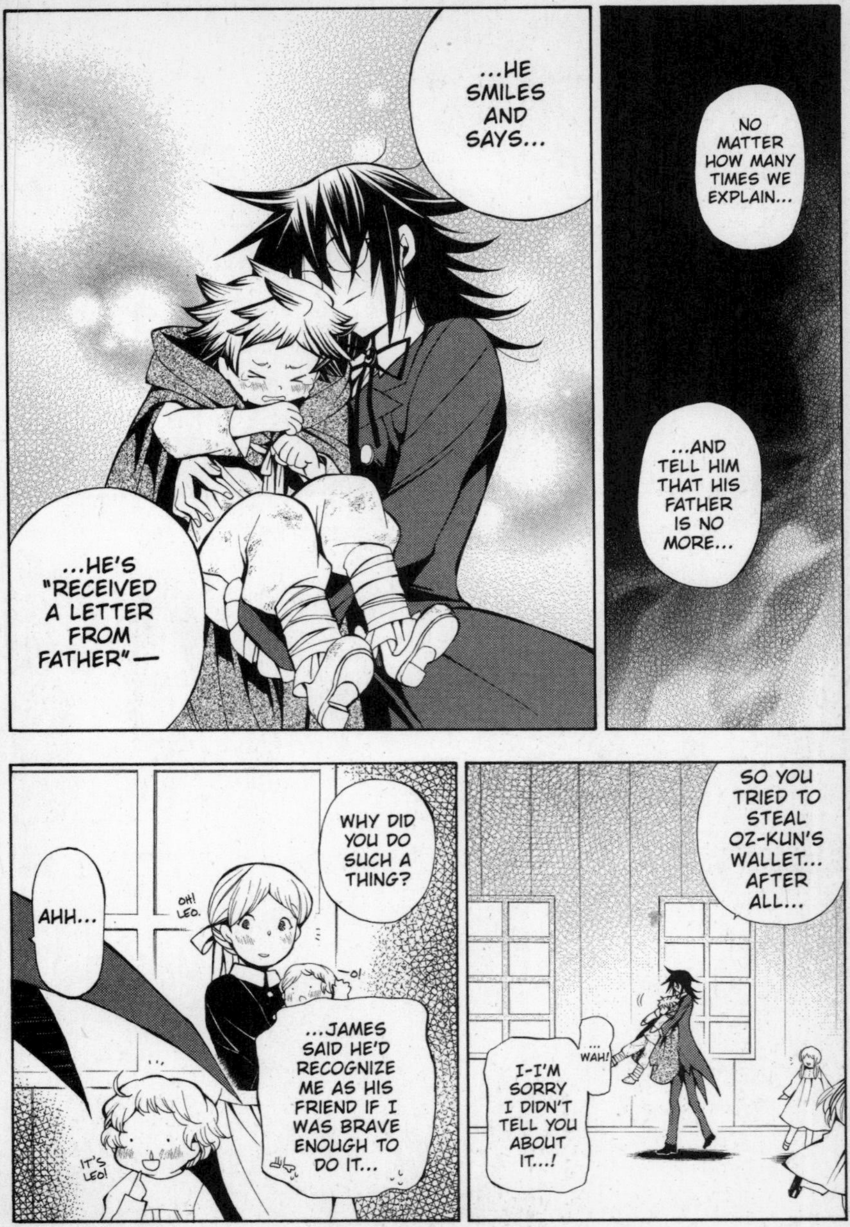
NO MATTER HOW MANY TIMES WE EXPLAIN...
...AND TELL HIM THAT HIS FATHER IS NO MORE...
...HE SMILES AND SAYS...
...HE'S "RECEIVED A LETTER FROM FATHER"—
SO YOU TRIED TO STEAL OZ-KUN'S WALLET... AFTER ALL...
... WAH!
I-I'M SORRY I DIDN'T TELL YOU ABOUT IT...!
WHY DID YOU DO SUCH A THING?
OH! LEO.
AHH...
—!
...JAMES SAID HE'D RECOGNIZE ME AS HIS FRIEND IF I WAS BRAVE ENOUGH TO DO IT...
IT'S LEO!

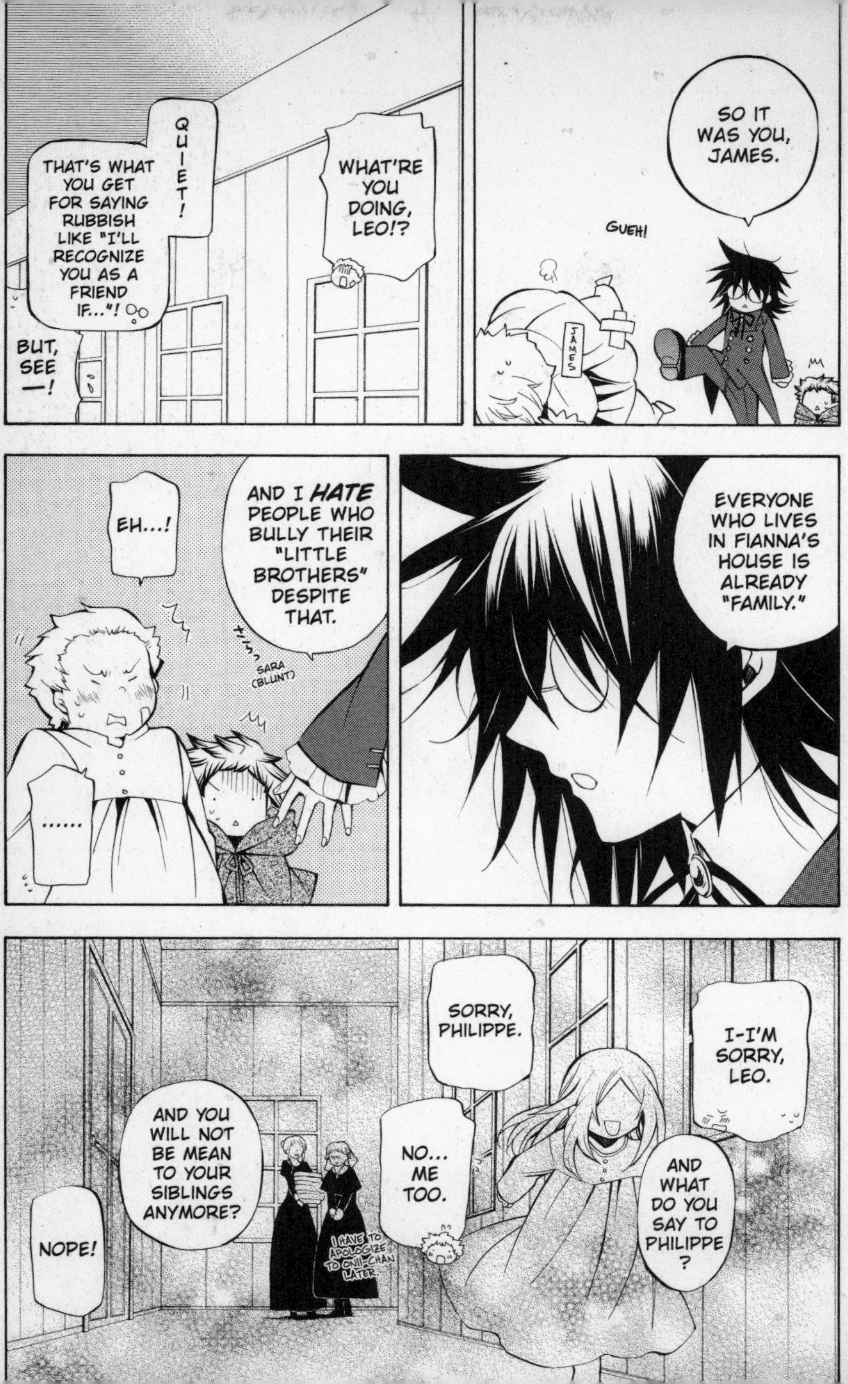
SO IT WAS YOU, JAMES.
GUEH!
JAMES
WHAT'RE YOU DOING, LEO!?
QUIET!
THAT'S WHAT YOU GET FOR SAYING RUBBISH LIKE "I'LL RECOGNIZE YOU AS A FRIEND IF..."!
BUT, SEE—!
EVERYONE WHO LIVES IN FIANNA'S HOUSE IS ALREADY "FAMILY."
AND I HATE PEOPLE WHO BULLY THEIR "LITTLE BROTHERS" DESPITE THAT.
SARA (BLUNT)
EH...!
......
I-I'M SORRY, LEO.
AND WHAT DO YOU SAY TO PHILIPPE?
SORRY, PHILIPPE.
NO... ME TOO.
I HAVE TO APOLOGIZE TO ONII-CHAN LATER.
AND YOU WILL NOT BE MEAN TO YOUR SIBLINGS ANYMORE?
NOPE!

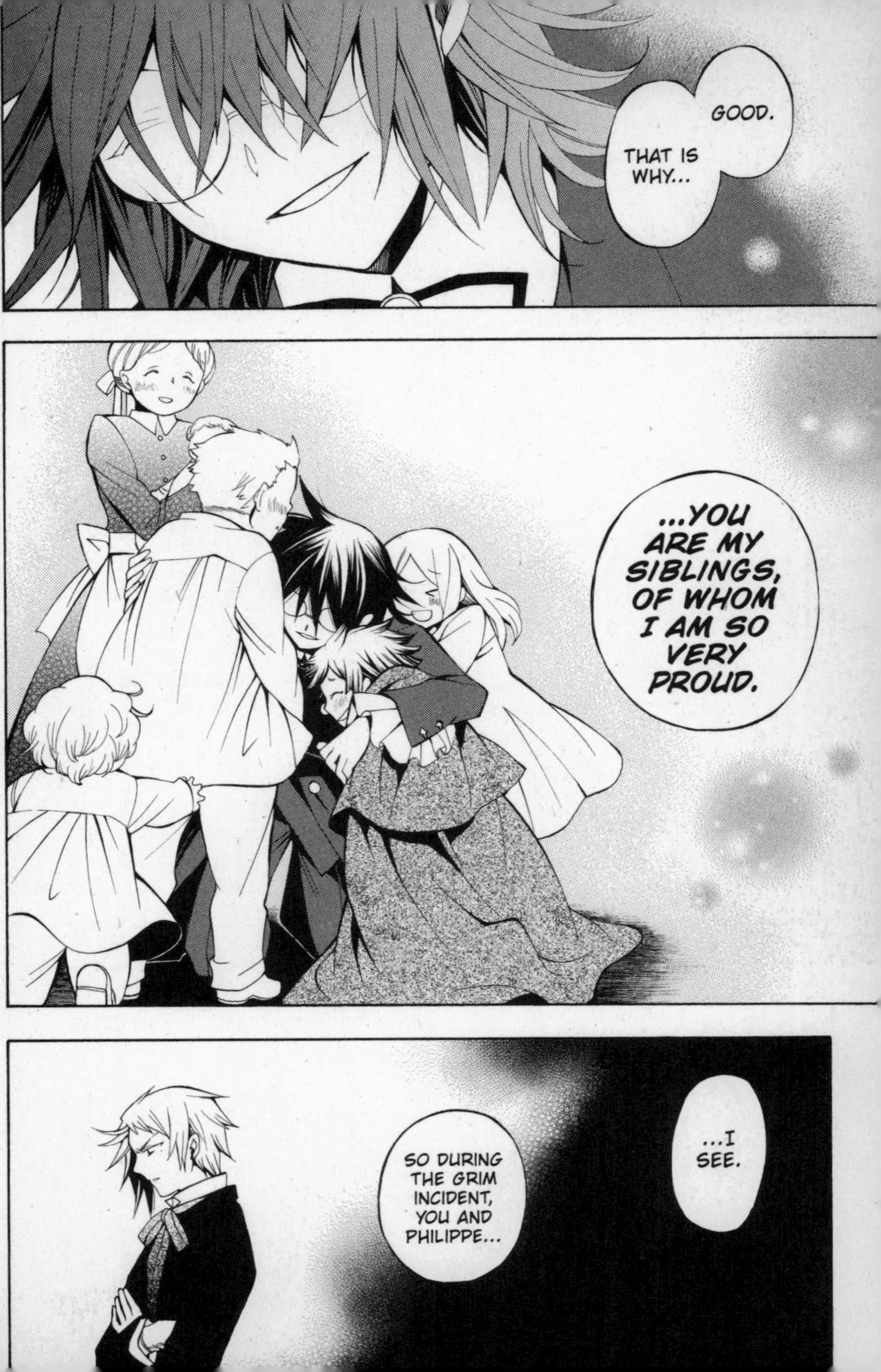
GOOD.
THAT IS WHY...
...YOU ARE MY SIBLINGS, OF WHOM I AM SO VERY PROUD.
...I SEE.
SO DURING THE GRIM INCIDENT, YOU AND PHILIPPE...

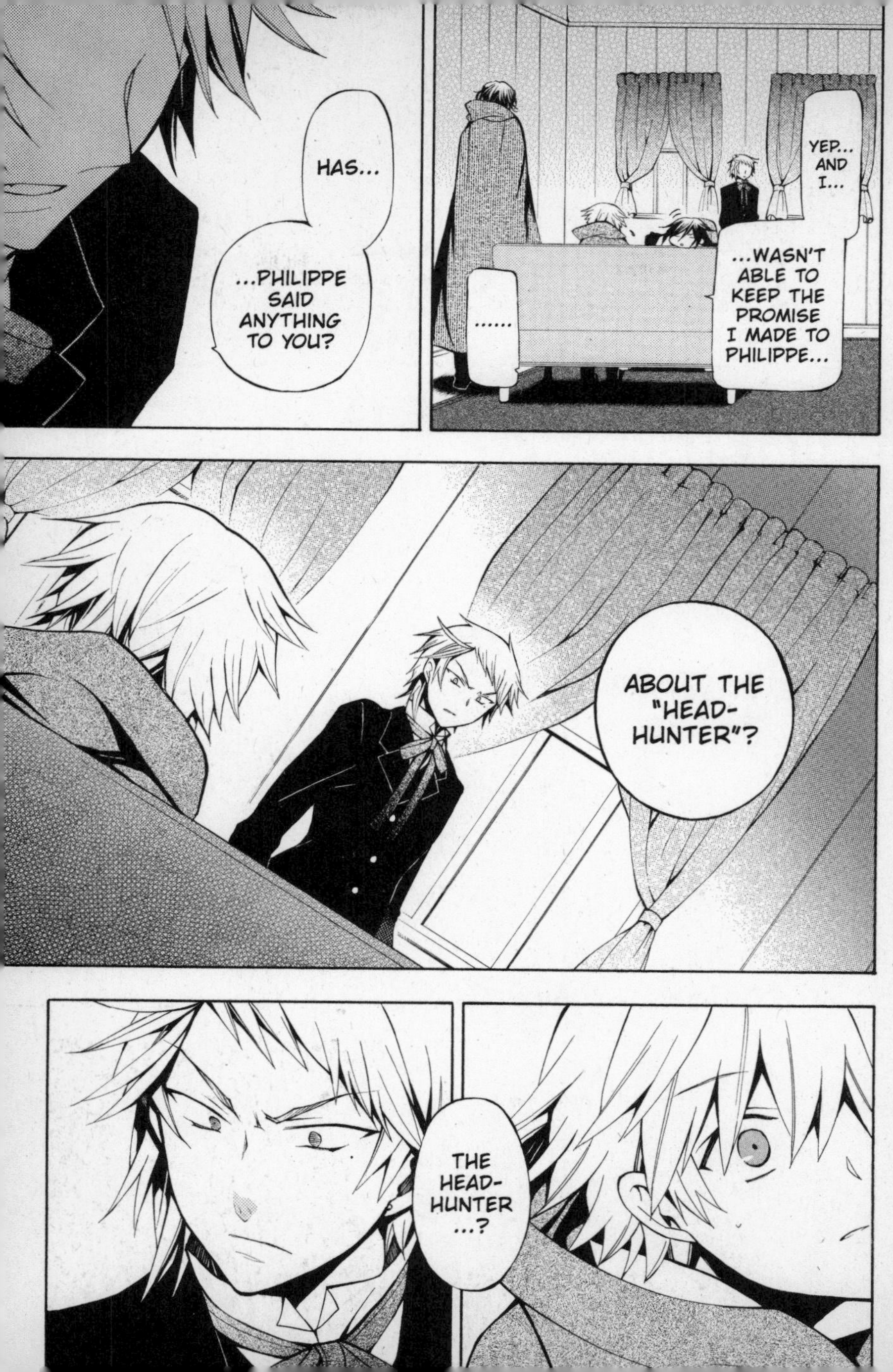
YEP... AND I...
...WASN'T ABLE TO KEEP THE PROMISE I MADE TO PHILIPPE...
......
HAS...
...PHILIPPE SAID ANYTHING TO YOU?
ABOUT THE "HEAD-HUNTER"?
THE HEAD-HUNTER ...?

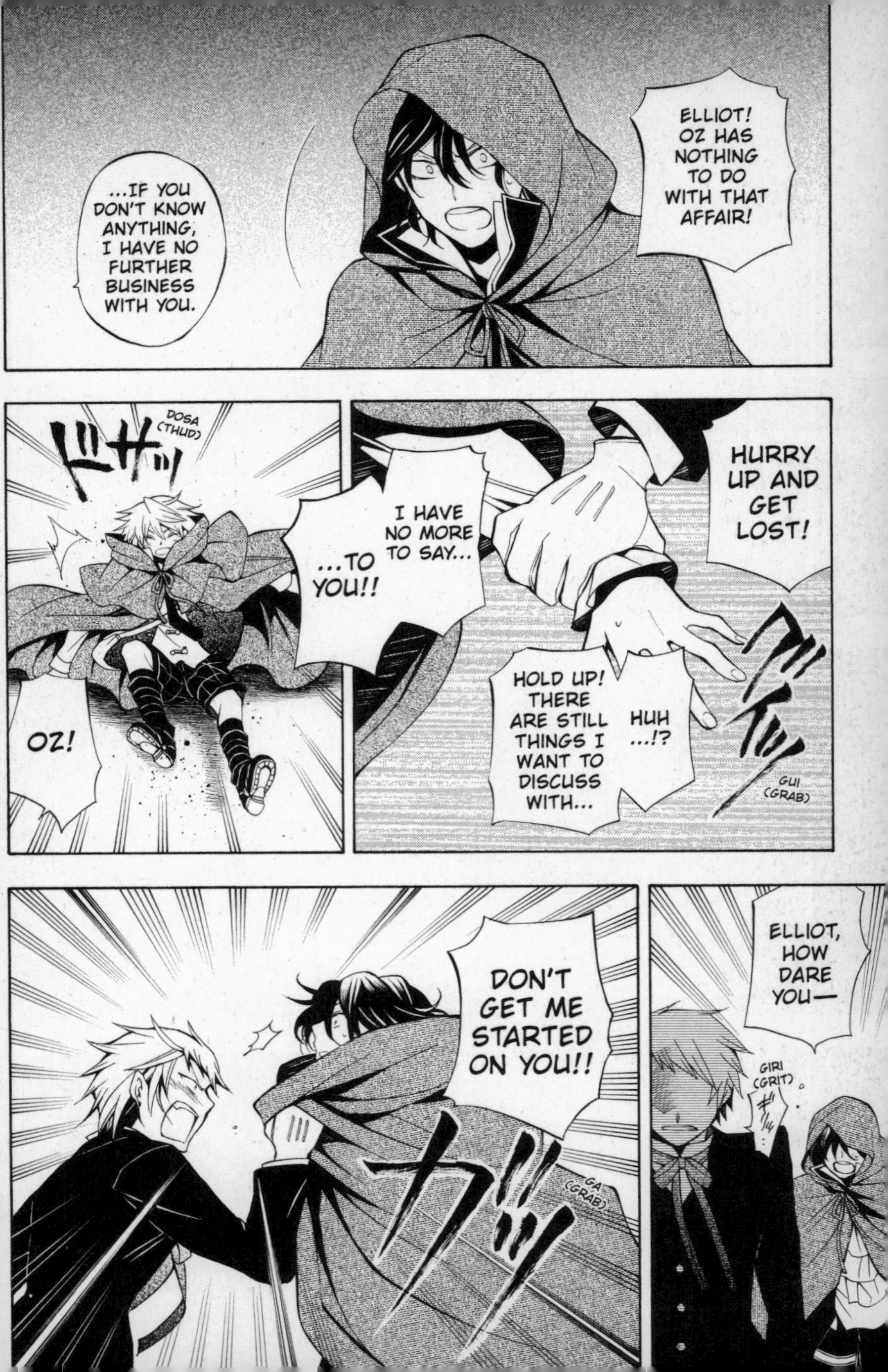

ELLIOT! OZ HAS NOTHING TO DO WITH THAT AFFAIR!
...IF YOU DON'T KNOW ANYTHING, I HAVE NO FURTHER BUSINESS WITH YOU.
HURRY UP AND GET LOST!
GUI (GRAB)
HOLD UP! THERE ARE STILL THINGS I WANT TO DISCUSS WITH...
HUH ...!?
I HAVE NO MORE TO SAY...
...TO YOU!!
DOSA (THUD)
OZ!
ELLIOT, HOW DARE YOU—
GIRI (GRIT)
DON'T GET ME STARTED ON YOU!!
GA (GRAB)

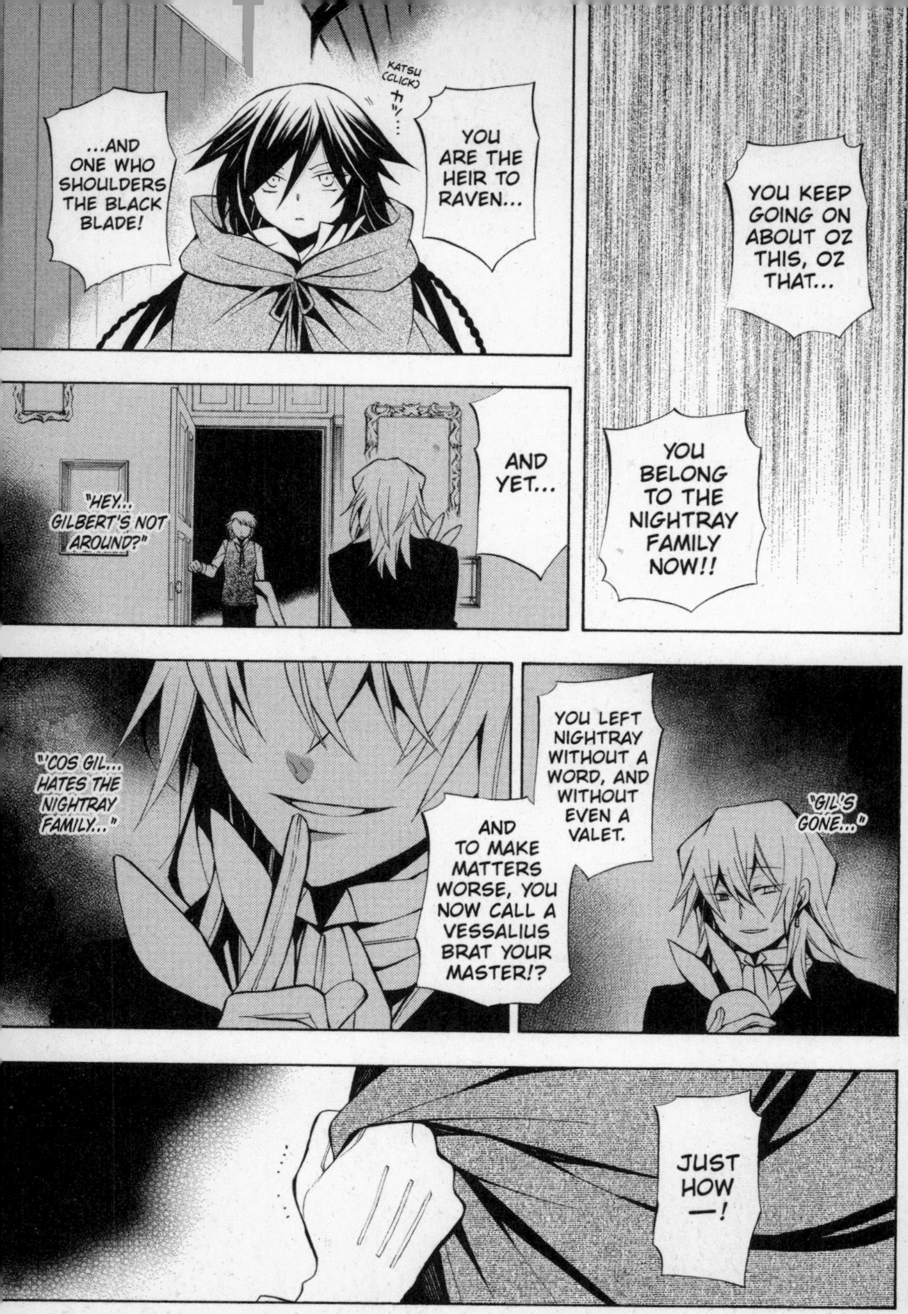
YOU KEEP GOING ON ABOUT OZ THIS, OZ THAT...
YOU BELONG TO THE NIGHTRAY FAMILY NOW!!
KATSU (CLICK)
YOU ARE THE HEIR TO RAVEN...
...AND ONE WHO SHOULDERS THE BLACK BLADE!
AND YET...
"HEY... GILBERT'S NOT AROUND?"
"GIL'S GONE..."
YOU LEFT NIGHTRAY WITHOUT A WORD, AND WITHOUT EVEN A VALET.
AND TO MAKE MATTERS WORSE, YOU NOW CALL A VESSALIUS BRAT YOUR MASTER!?
"'COS GIL... HATES THE NIGHTRAY FAMILY..."
JUST HOW—!
...

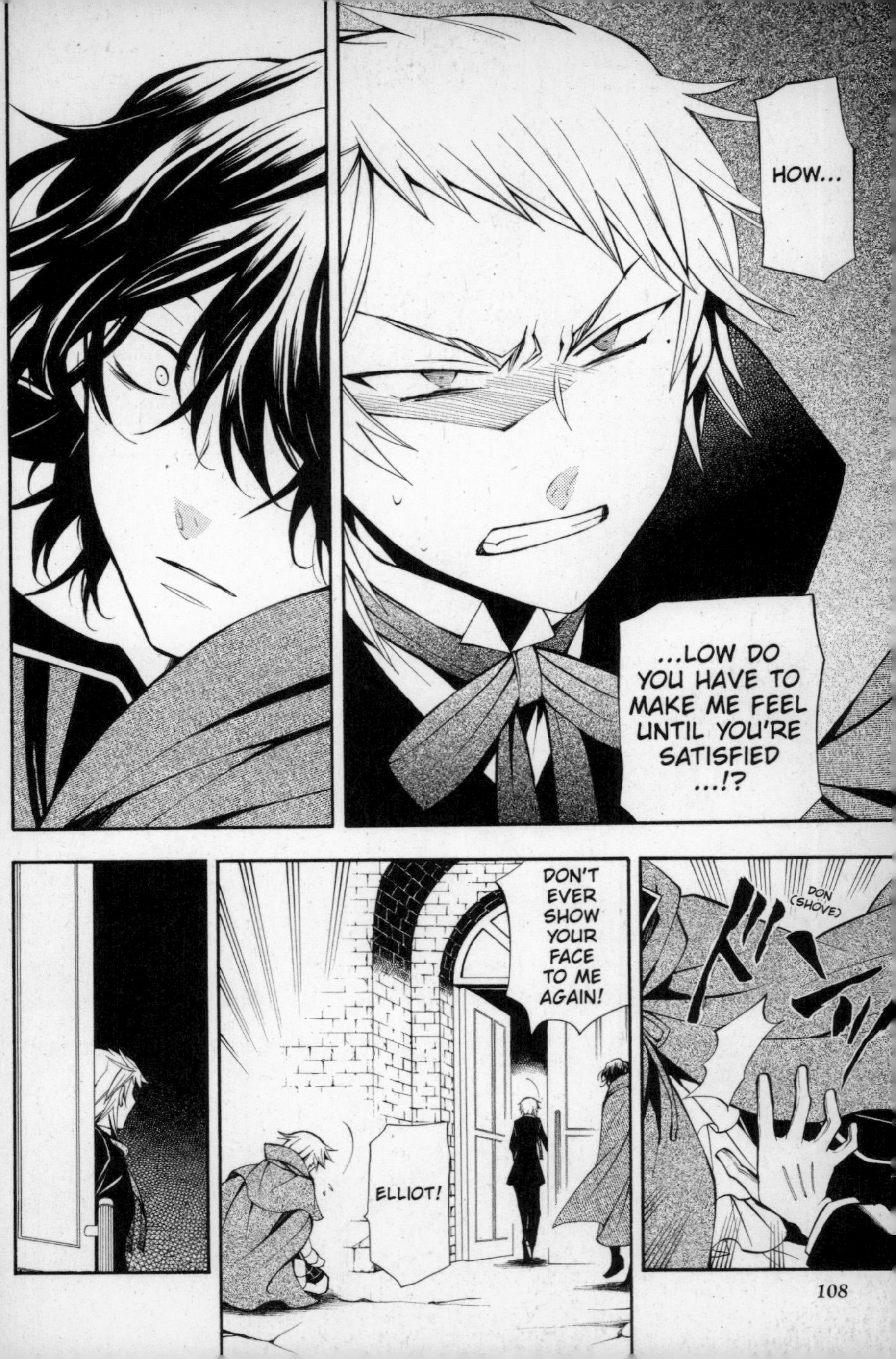
HOW...
...LOW DO YOU HAVE TO MAKE ME FEEL UNTIL YOU'RE SATISFIED ...!?
DON (SHOVE)
DON'T EVER SHOW YOUR FACE TO ME AGAIN!
ELLIOT!

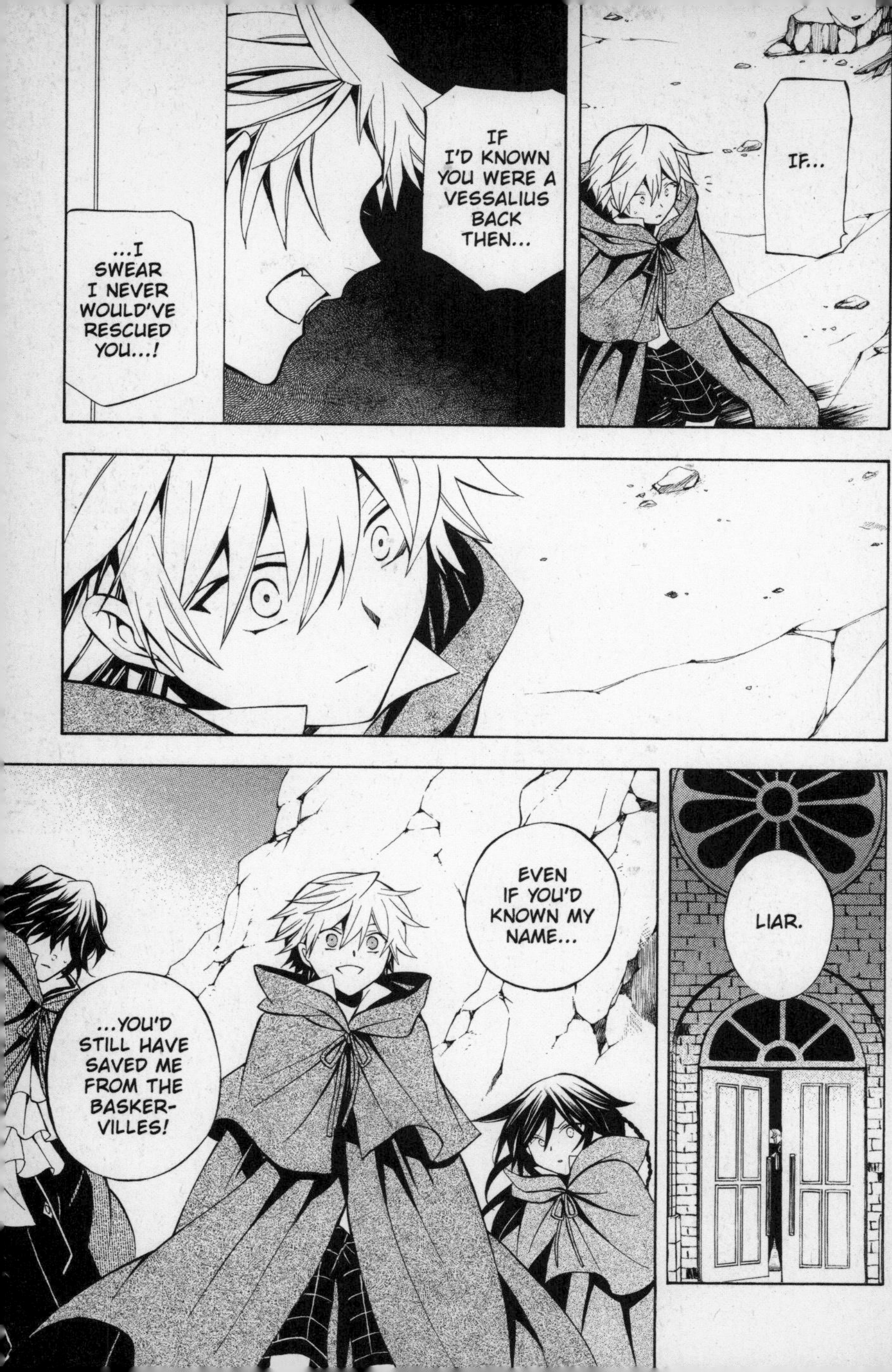
IF...
IF I'D KNOWN YOU WERE A VESSALIUS BACK THEN...
...I SWEAR I NEVER WOULD'VE RESCUED YOU...!
LIAR.
EVEN IF YOU'D KNOWN MY NAME...
...YOU'D STILL HAVE SAVED ME FROM THE BASKER-VILLES!

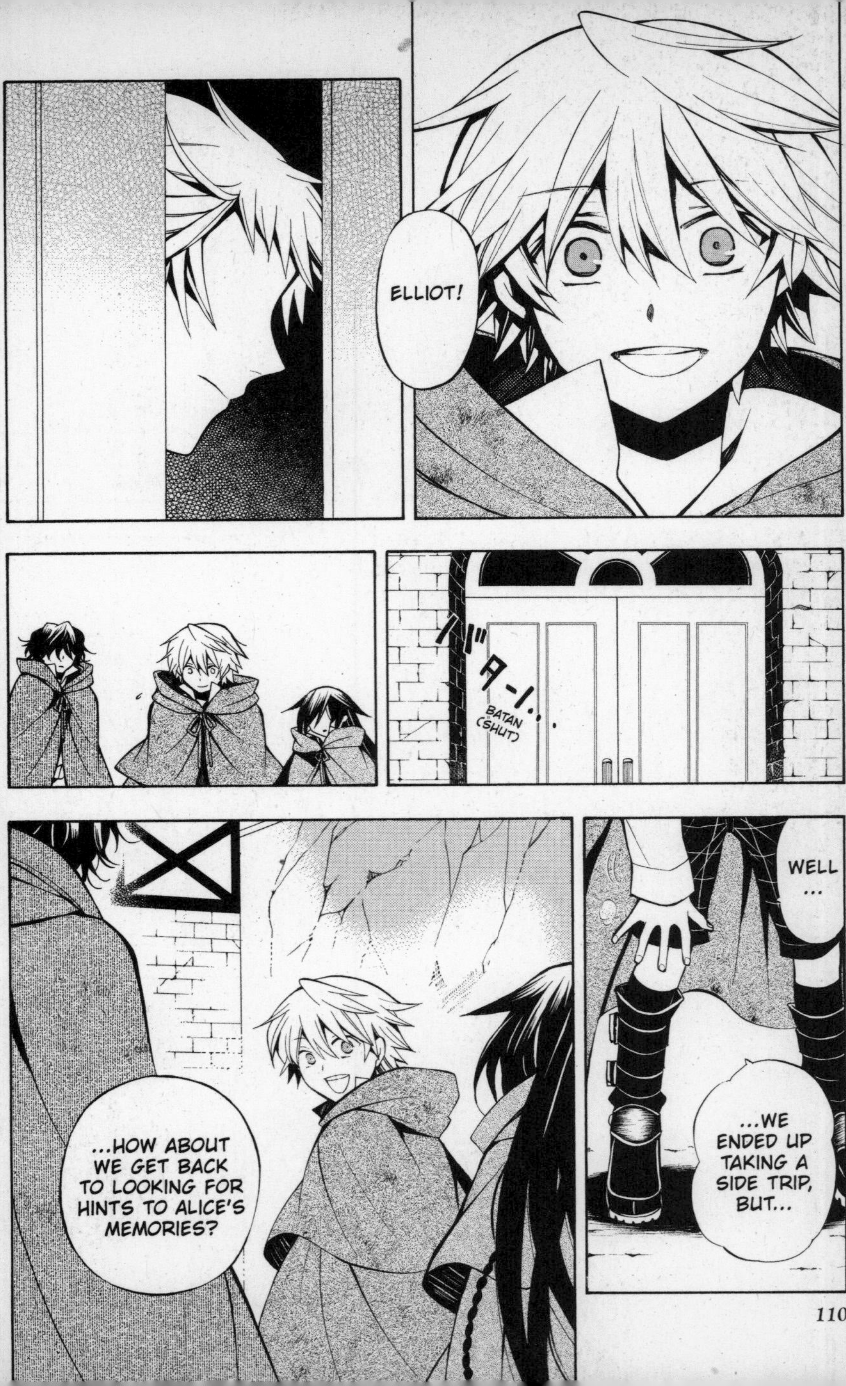
ELLIOT!
バタ—ン…
BATAN (SHUT)
WELL ...
...WE ENDED UP TAKING A SIDE TRIP, BUT...
...HOW ABOUT WE GET BACK TO LOOKING FOR HINTS TO ALICE'S MEMORIES?

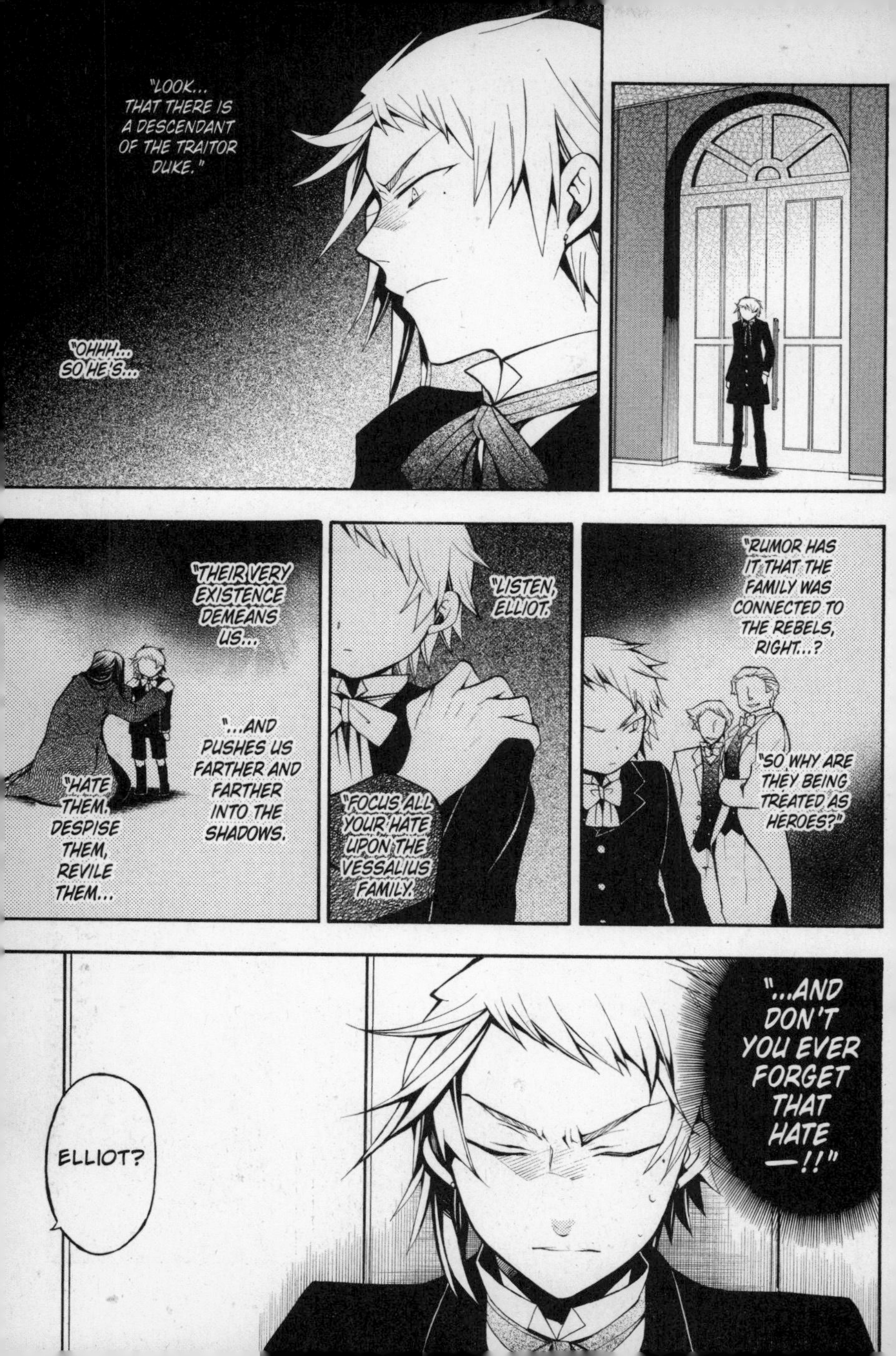
"LOOK... THAT THERE IS A DESCENDANT OF THE TRAITOR DUKE."
"OHHH... SO HE'S...
"RUMOR HAS IT THAT THE FAMILY WAS CONNECTED TO THE REBELS, RIGHT...?
"SO WHY ARE THEY BEING TREATED AS HEROES?"
"LISTEN, ELLIOT.
"FOCUS ALL YOUR HATE UPON THE VESSALIUS FAMILY.
"THEIR VERY EXISTENCE DEMEANS US...
"...AND PUSHES US FARTHER AND FARTHER INTO THE SHADOWS.
"HATE THEM. DESPISE THEM, REVILE THEM...
"...AND DON'T YOU EVER FORGET THAT HATE—!!"
ELLIOT?

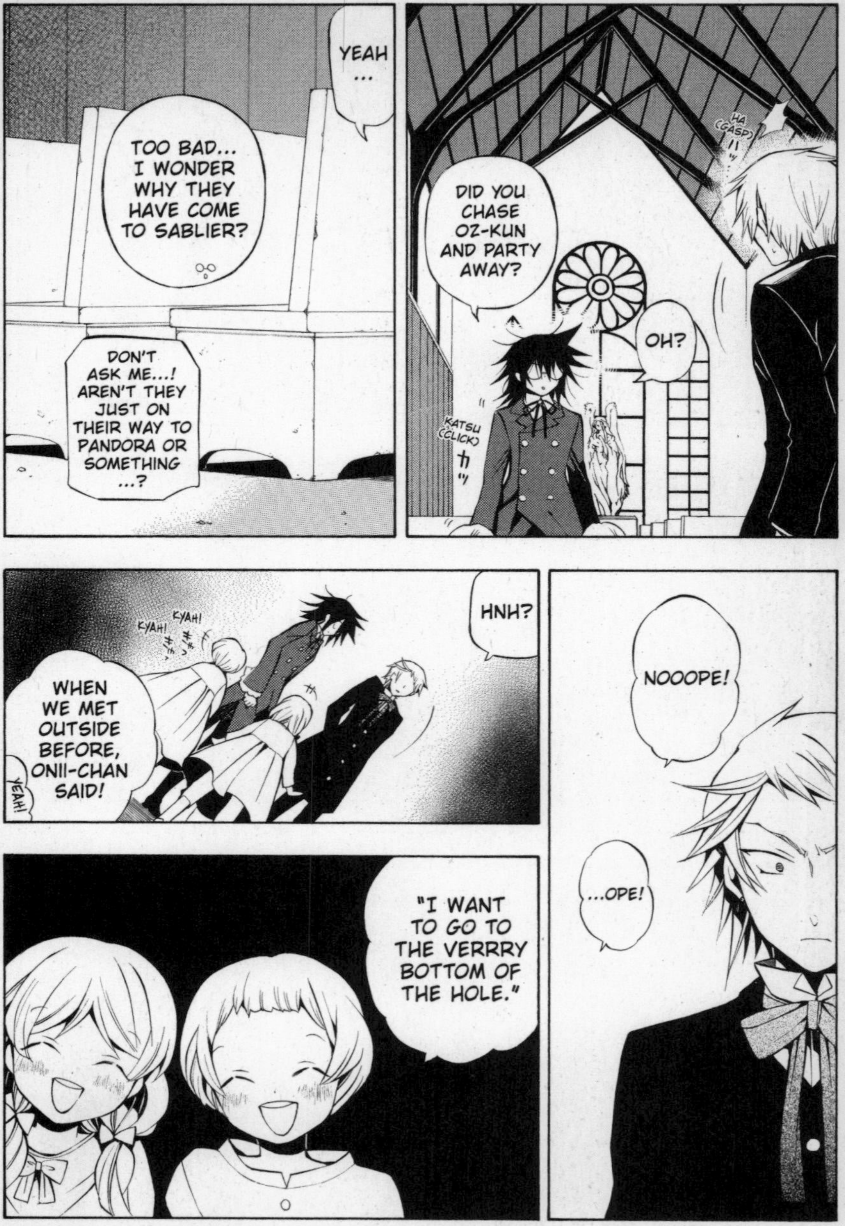
HA (GASP)
DID YOU CHASE OZ-KUN AND PARTY AWAY?
OH?
KATSU (CLICK)
カッ
YEAH ...
TOO BAD... I WONDER WHY THEY HAVE COME TO SABLIER?
DON'T ASK ME...! AREN'T THEY JUST ON THEIR WAY TO PANDORA OR SOMETHING ...?
NOOOPE!
...OPE!
HNH?
KYAH!
KYAH!
WHEN WE MET OUTSIDE BEFORE, ONII-CHAN SAID!
YEAH!
"I WANT TO GO TO THE VERRRY BOTTOM OF THE HOLE."

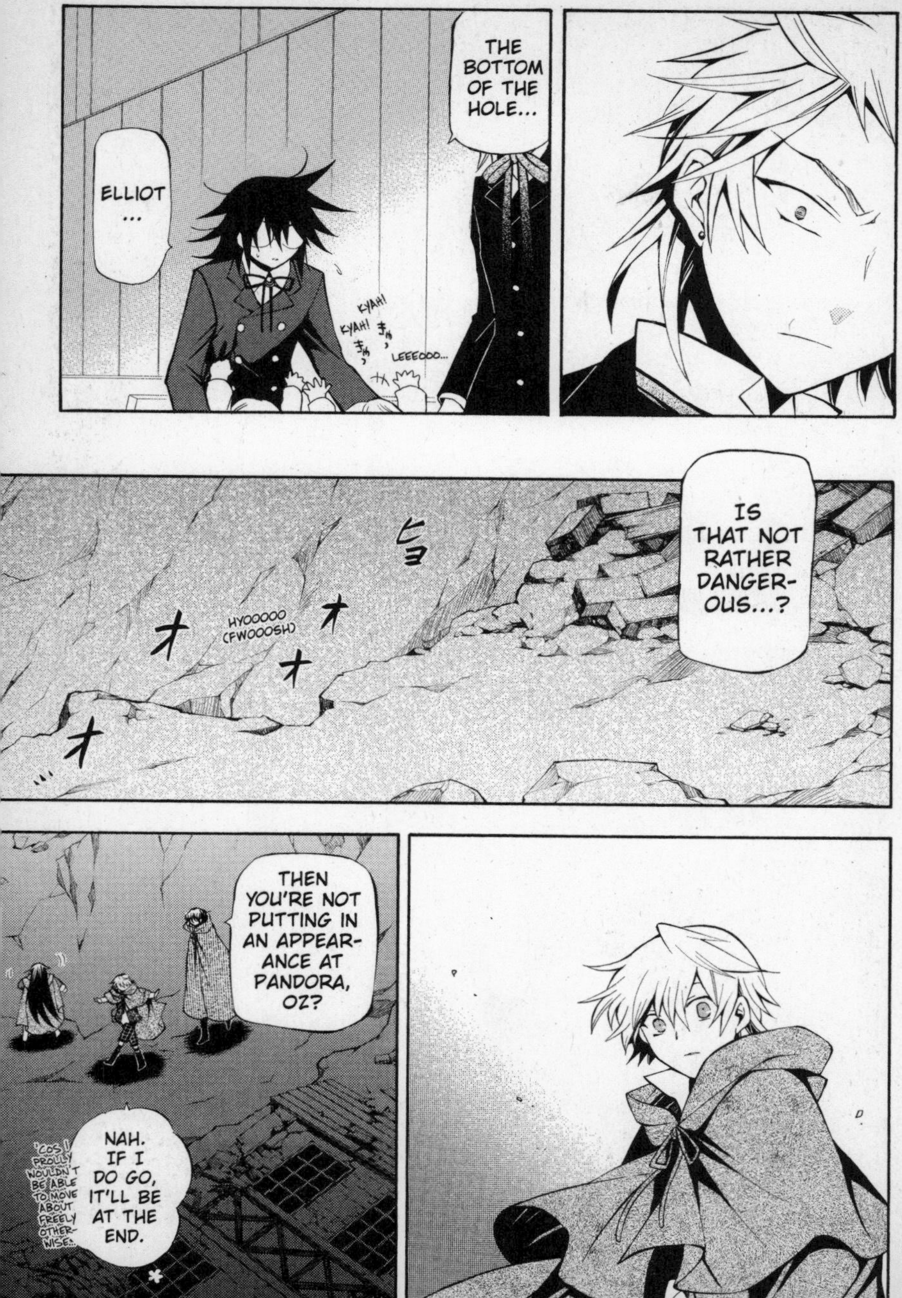
THE BOTTOM OF THE HOLE...
ELLIOT ...
KYAH! KYAH! きゅ きゅ
LEEEOOO...
IS THAT NOT RATHER DANGER-OUS...?
ヒョ
オ オ オ オ
HYOOOOO (FWOOOSH)
THEN YOU'RE NOT PUTTING IN AN APPEAR-ANCE AT PANDORA, OZ?
NAH. IF I DO GO, IT'LL BE AT THE END.
'COS I PROLLY WOULDN'T BE ABLE TO MOVE ABOUT FREELY OTHER-WISE...

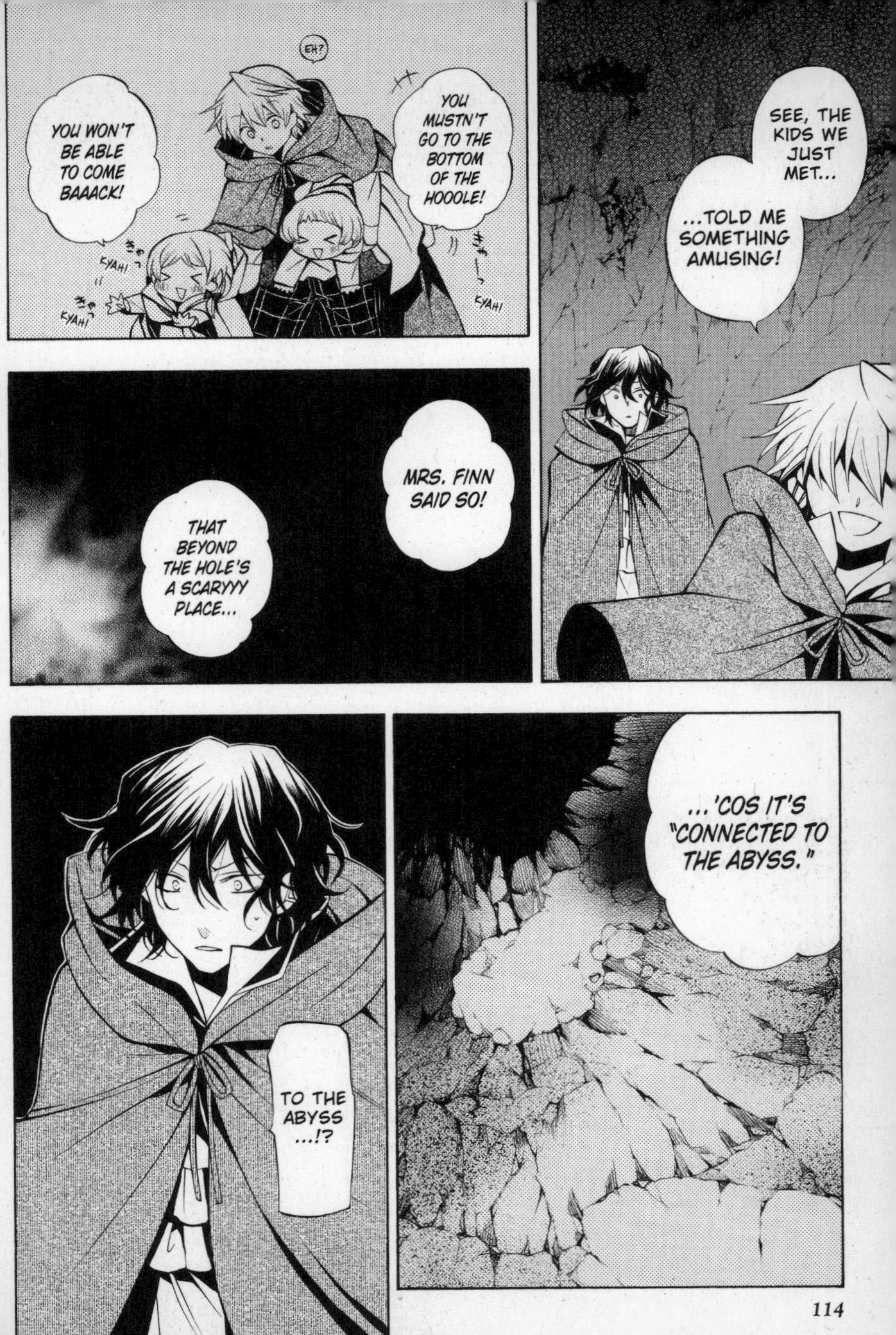
SEE, THE KIDS WE JUST MET...
...TOLD ME SOMETHING AMUSING!
EH?
YOU MUSTN'T GO TO THE BOTTOM OF THE HOOOLE!
YOU WON'T BE ABLE TO COME BAAACK!
KYAH!
KYAH!
KYAH!
MRS. FINN SAID SO!
THAT BEYOND THE HOLE'S A SCARYYY PLACE...
...'COS IT'S "CONNECTED TO THE ABYSS."
TO THE ABYSS ...!?

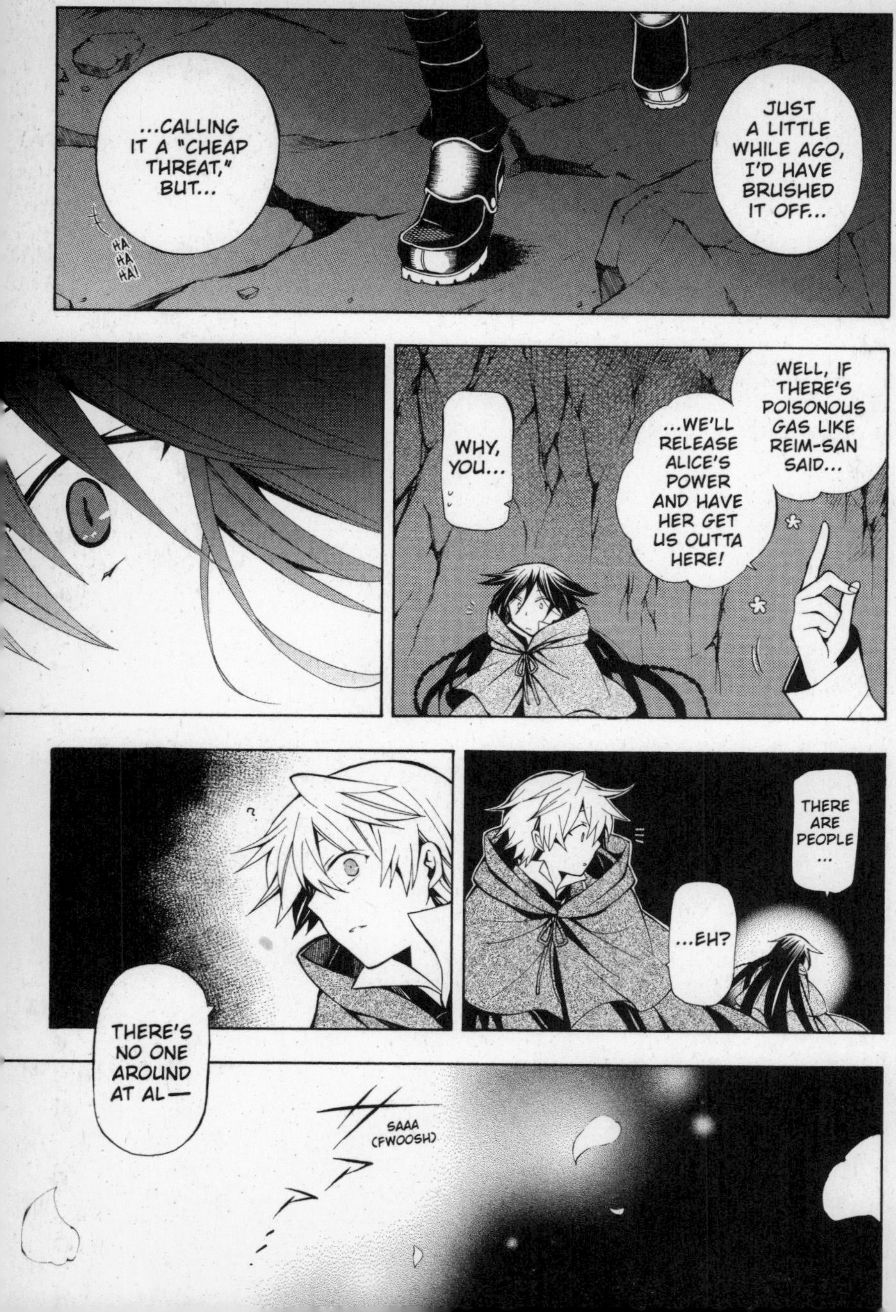
JUST A LITTLE WHILE AGO, I'D HAVE BRUSHED IT OFF...
...CALLING IT A "CHEAP THREAT," BUT...
HA HA HA!
WELL, IF THERE'S POISONOUS GAS LIKE REIM-SAN SAID...
...WE'LL RELEASE ALICE'S POWER AND HAVE HER GET US OUTTA HERE!
WHY, YOU...
THERE ARE PEOPLE ...
...EH?
THERE'S NO ONE AROUND AT AL—
SAAA (FWOOSH)

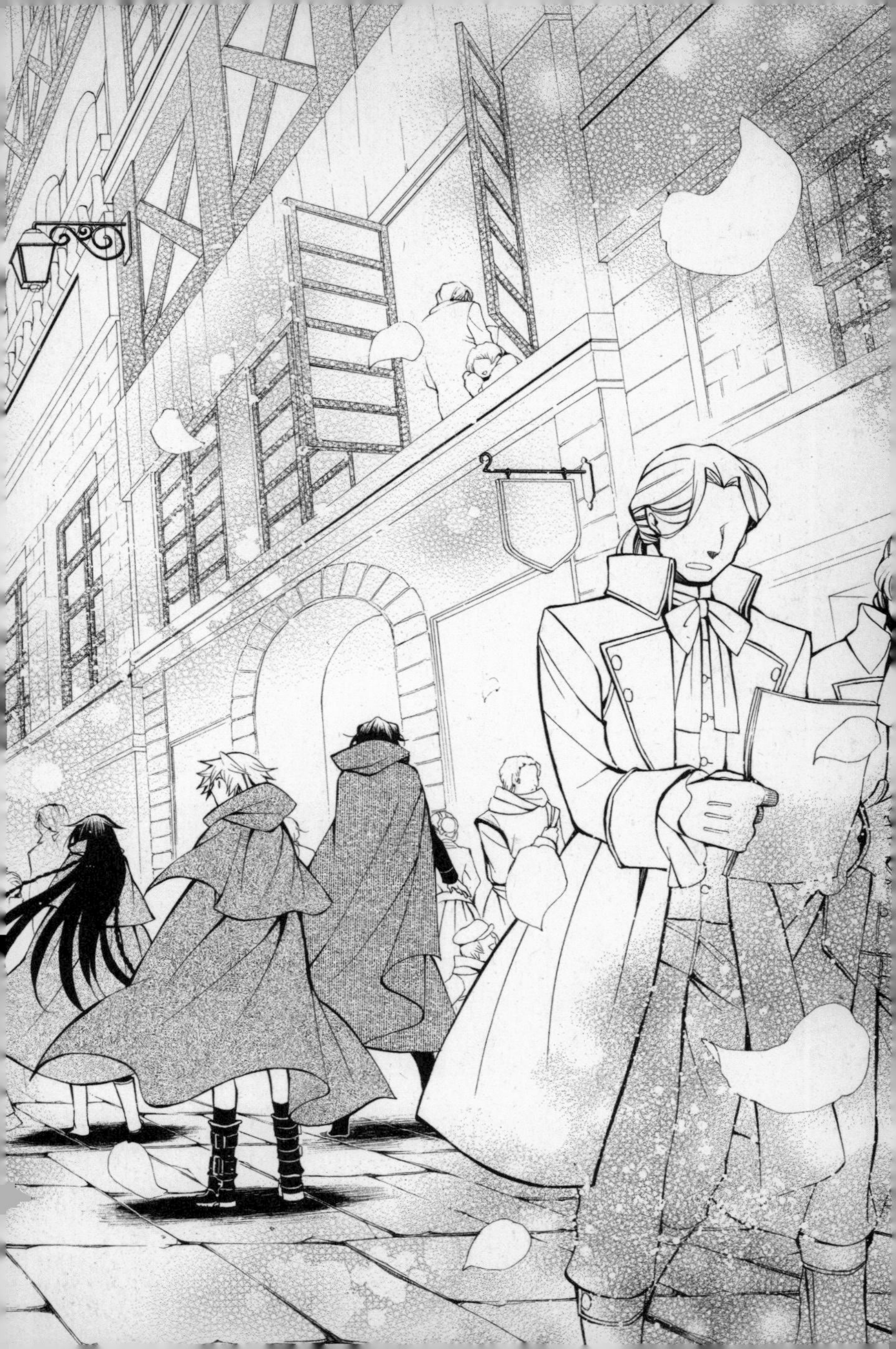

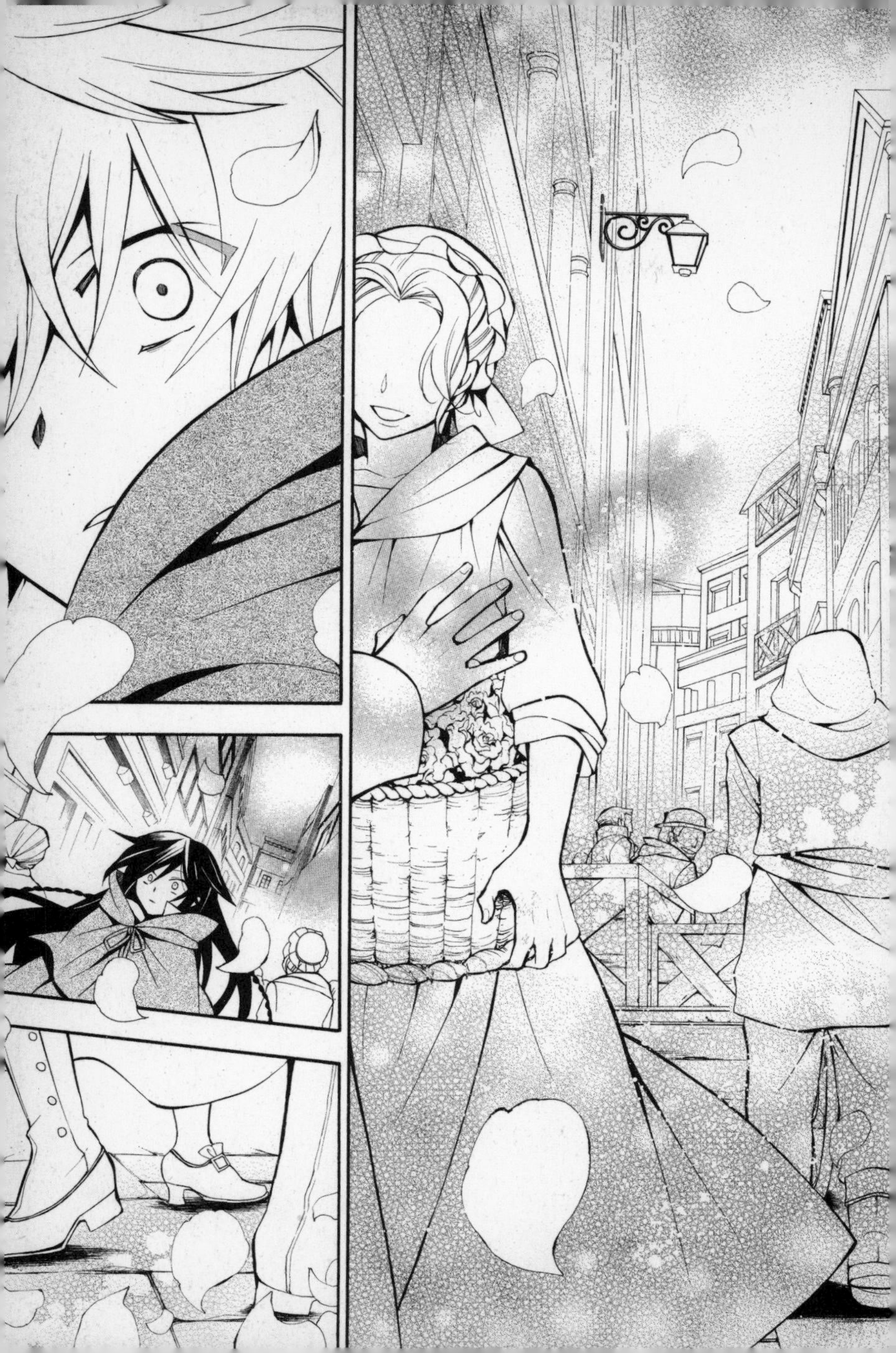

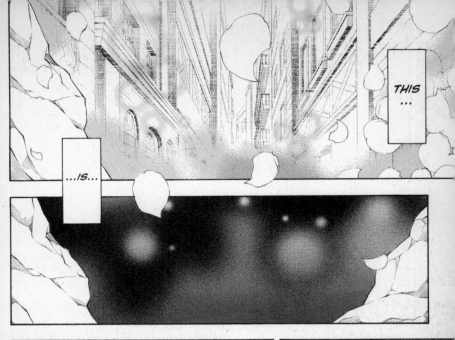

THIS...

...IS....

NO WAY...
SABLIER OF A
HUNDRED
YEARS...!?

...IT'S
AN ILLUSION
SHOWN TO
US BY THE
POWER OF
THE ABYSS.

...?

WHAT?

DUE
TO THE
TRAGEDY
OR WHAT-
EVER...

...IT
SEEMS THE
POWER OF THE
ABYSS GETS
STRONGER
THE FARTHER
WE DESCEND.

KUH-KUH...

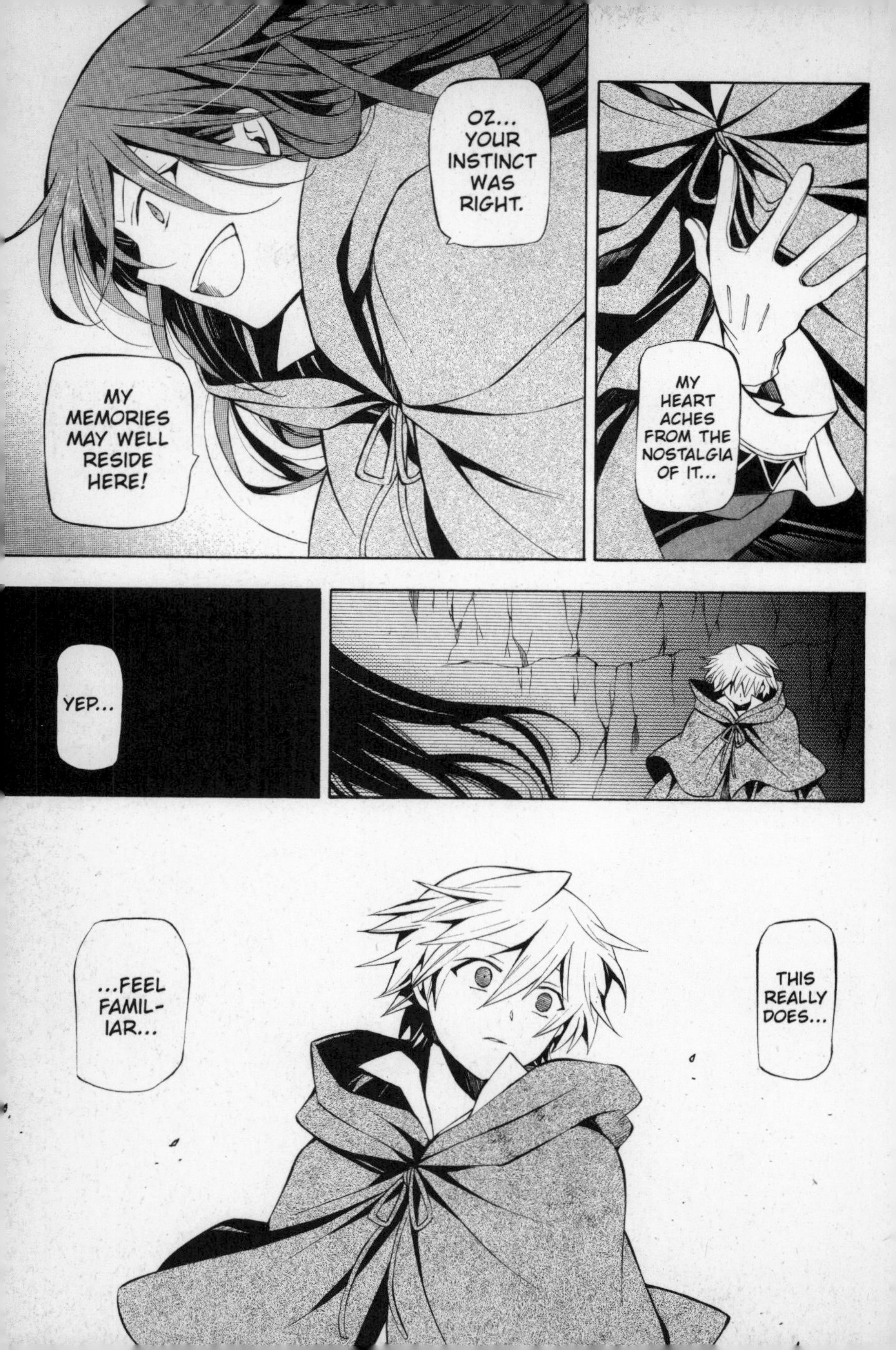
MY HEART ACHES FROM THE NOSTALGIA OF IT...
OZ... YOUR INSTINCT WAS RIGHT.
MY MEMORIES MAY WELL RESIDE HERE!
YEP...
THIS REALLY DOES...
...FEEL FAMILIAR...

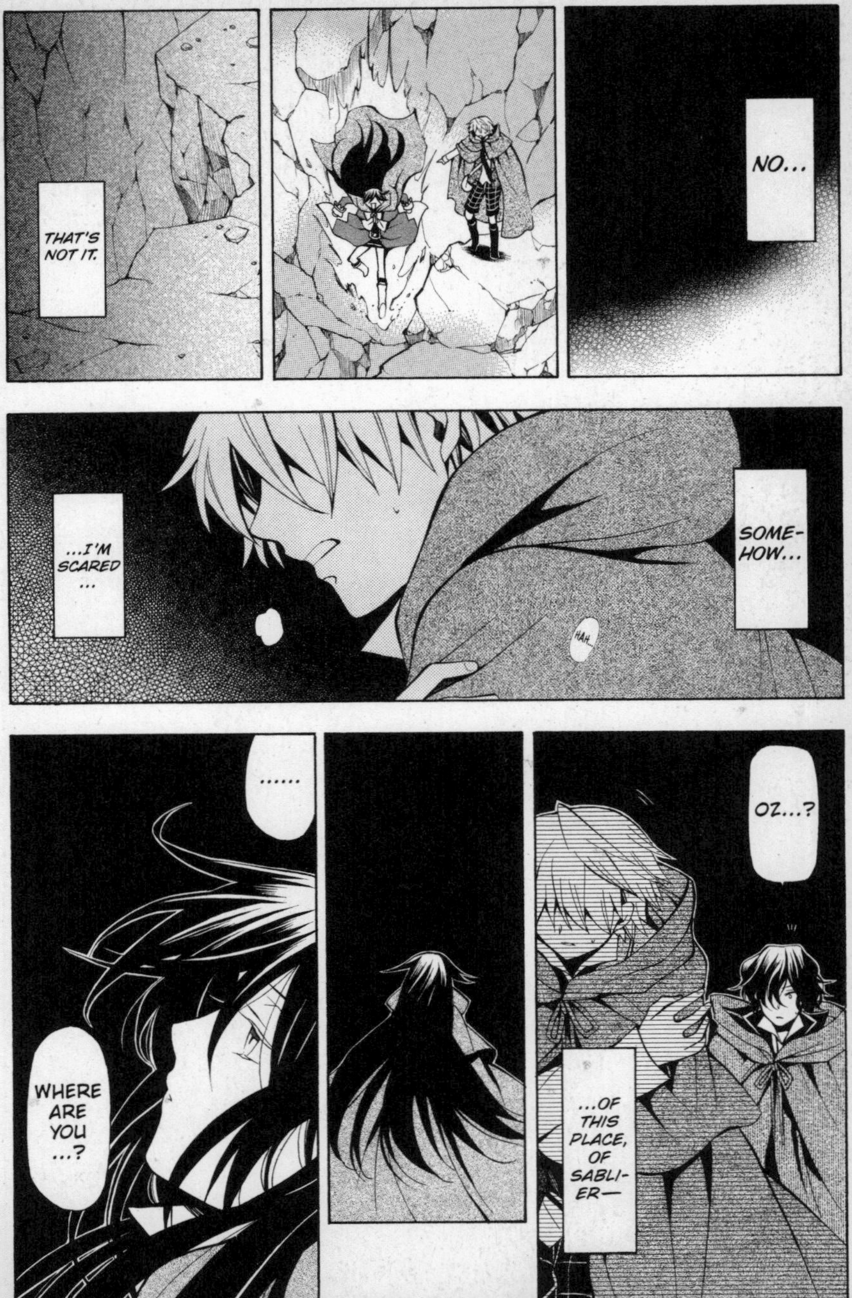
NO...
THAT'S NOT IT.
SOME-HOW...
HAH...
...I'M SCARED ...
OZ...?
...OF THIS PLACE, OF SABLI-ER—
......
WHERE ARE YOU ...?

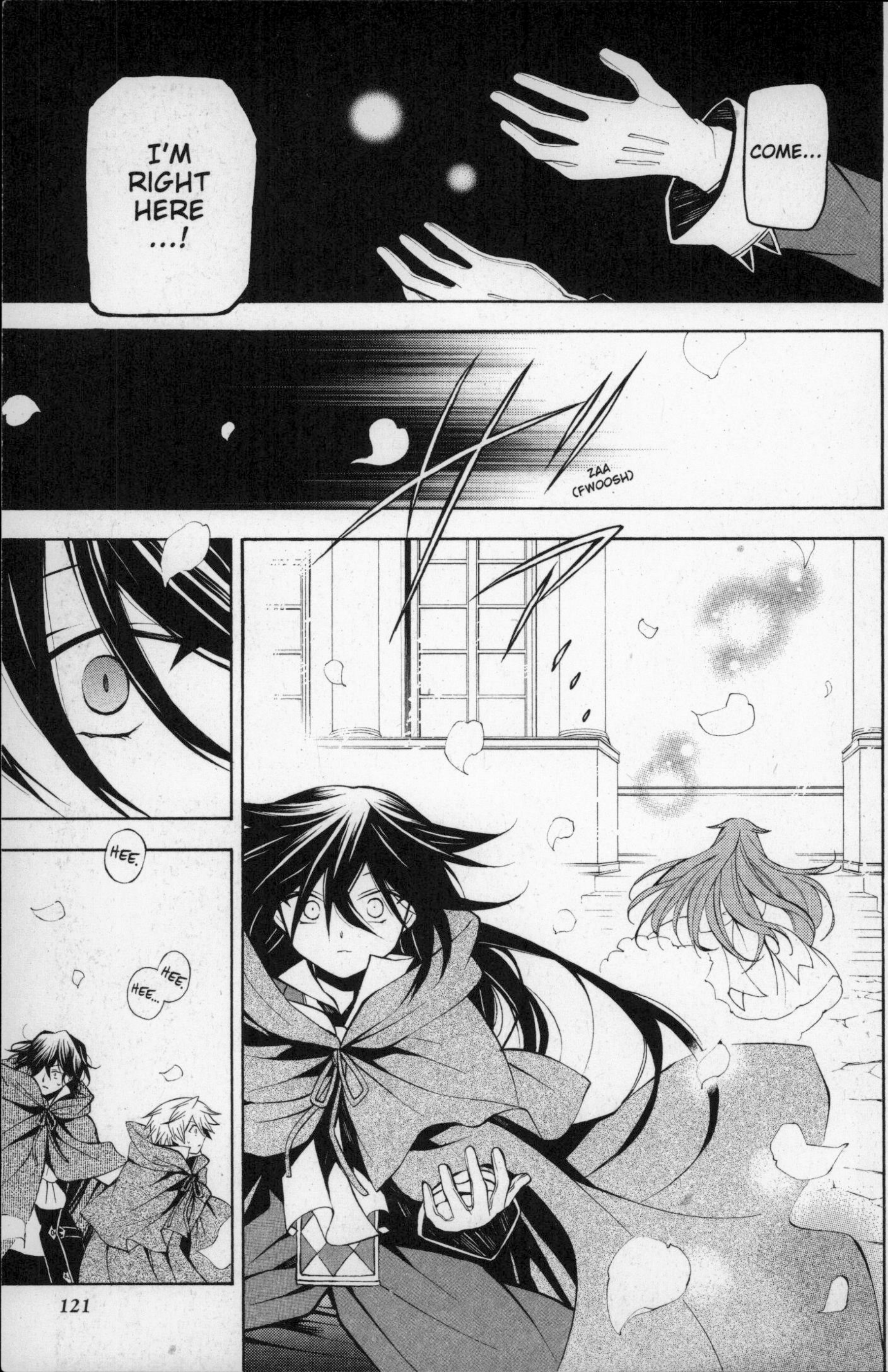
COME...
I'M RIGHT HERE ...!
ZAA (FWOOSH)
HEE.
HEE. HEE...

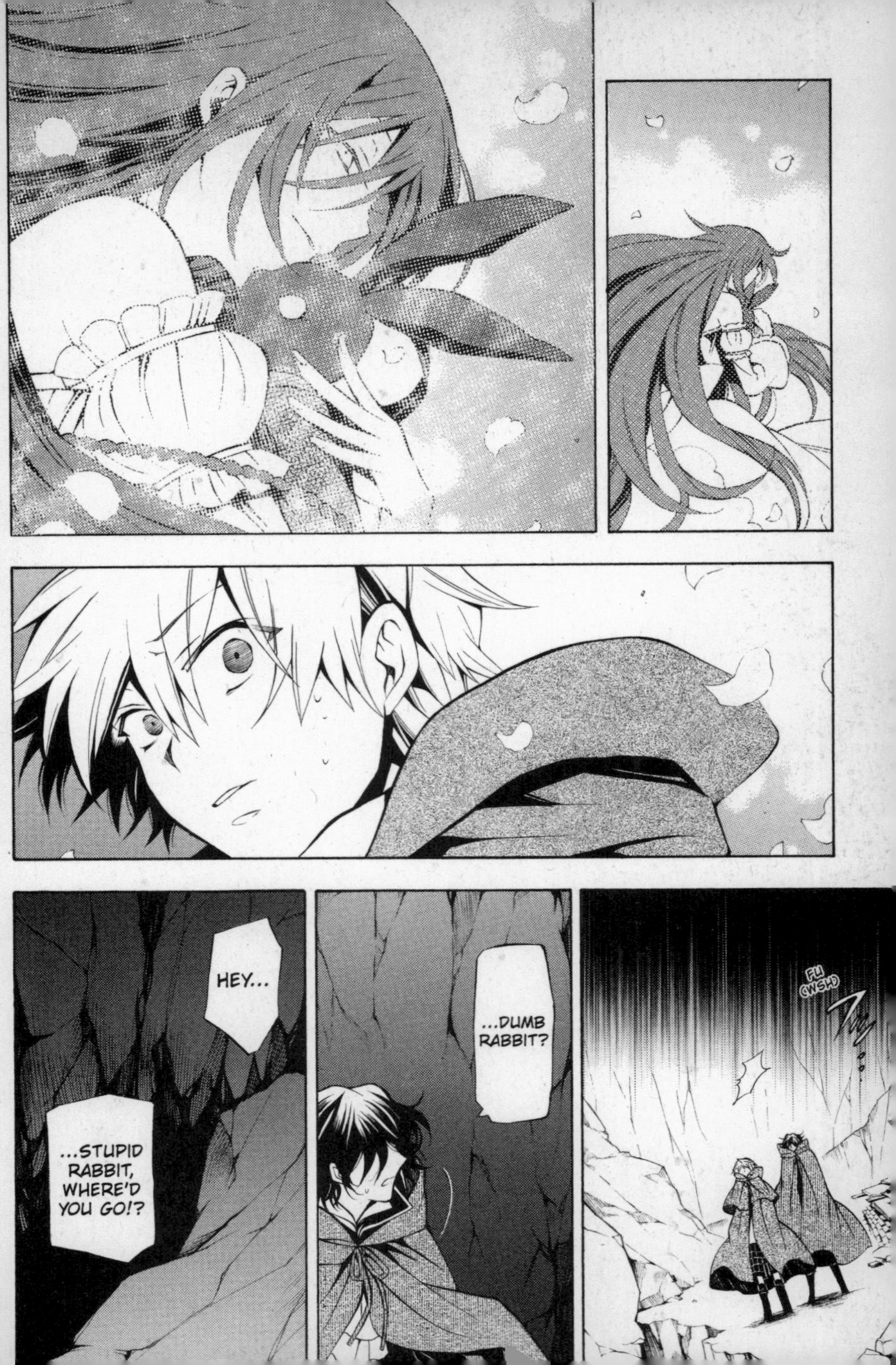
FU (WSH)
...DUMB RABBIT?
HEY...
...STUPID RABBIT, WHERE'D YOU GO!?

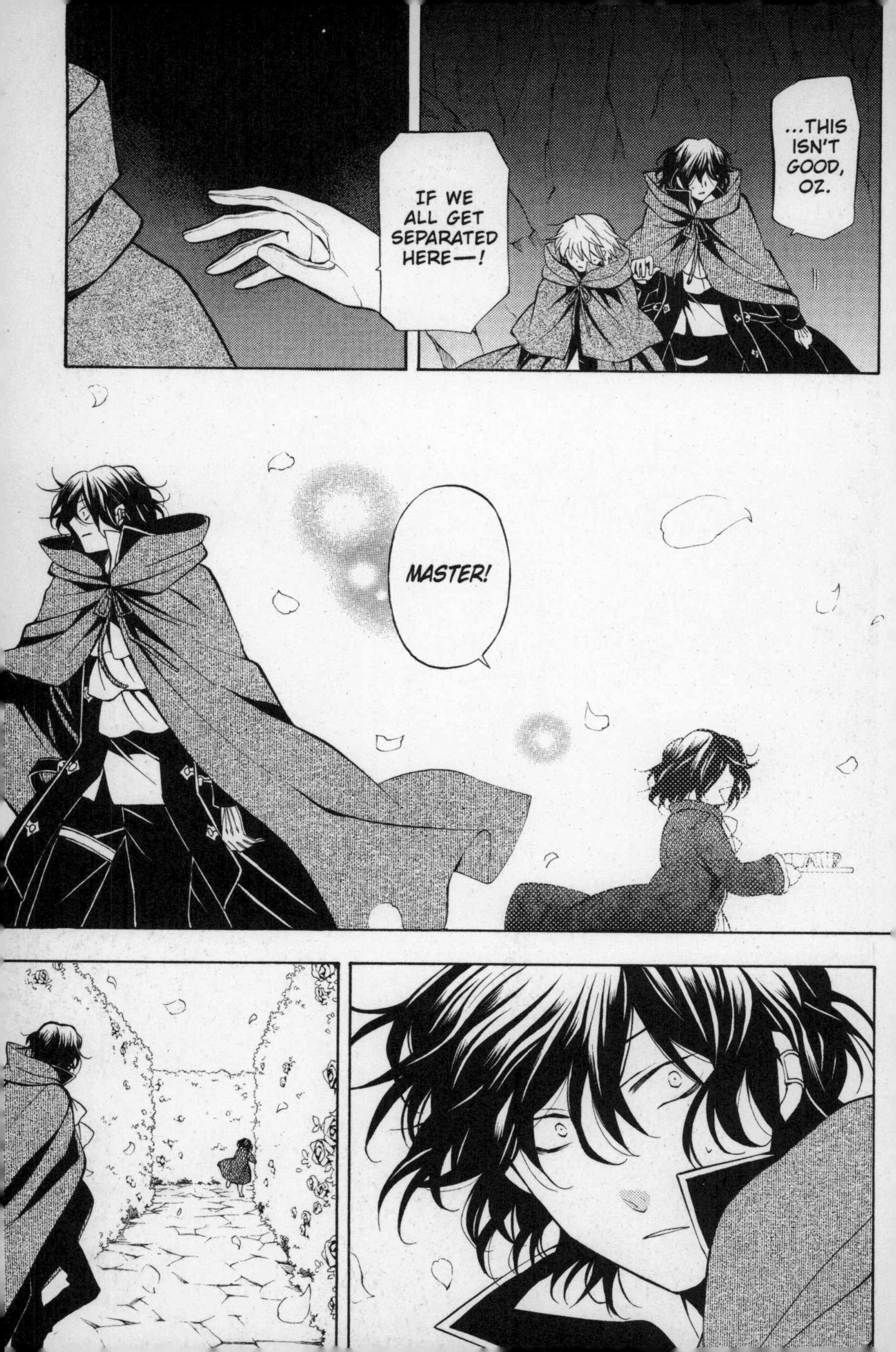
...THIS ISN'T GOOD, OZ.
IF WE ALL GET SEPARATED HERE—!
MASTER!

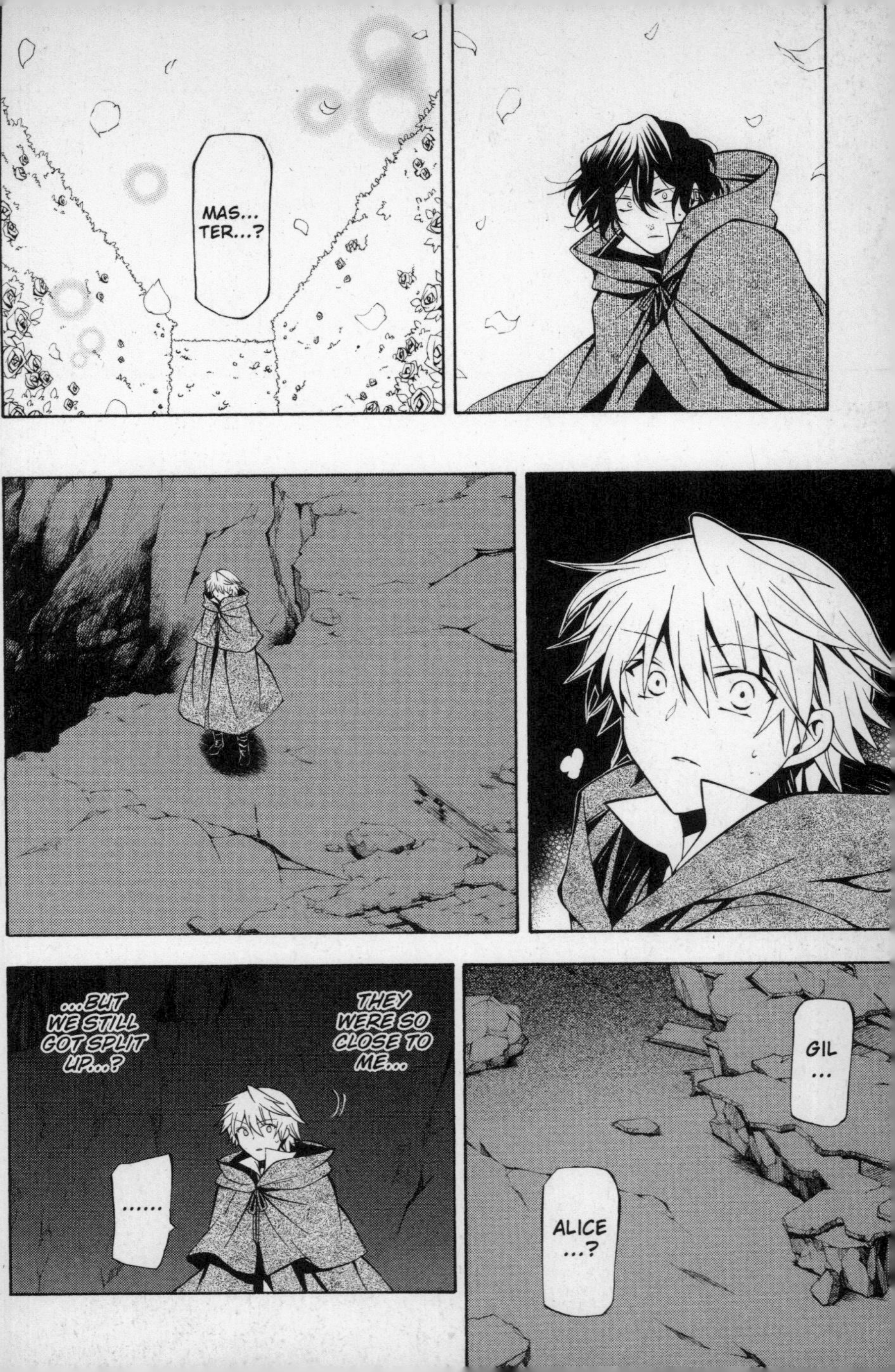
MAS... TER...?
GIL ...
ALICE ...?
THEY WERE SO CLOSE TO ME...
...BUT WE STILL GOT SPLIT UP...?
......

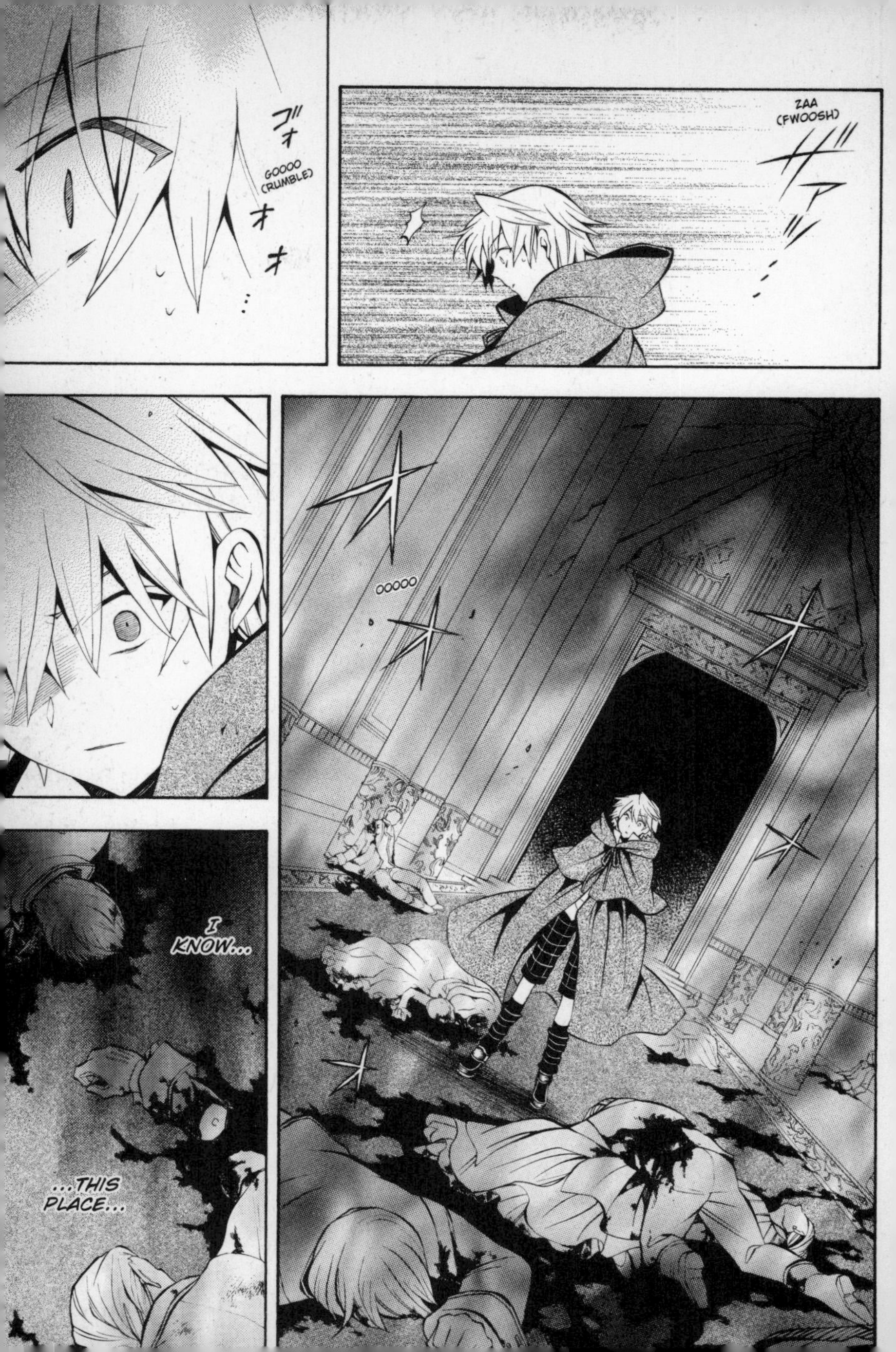
ZAA
(FWOOSH)
GOOOO
(RUMBLE)
OOOOO
I KNOW...
...THIS PLACE...

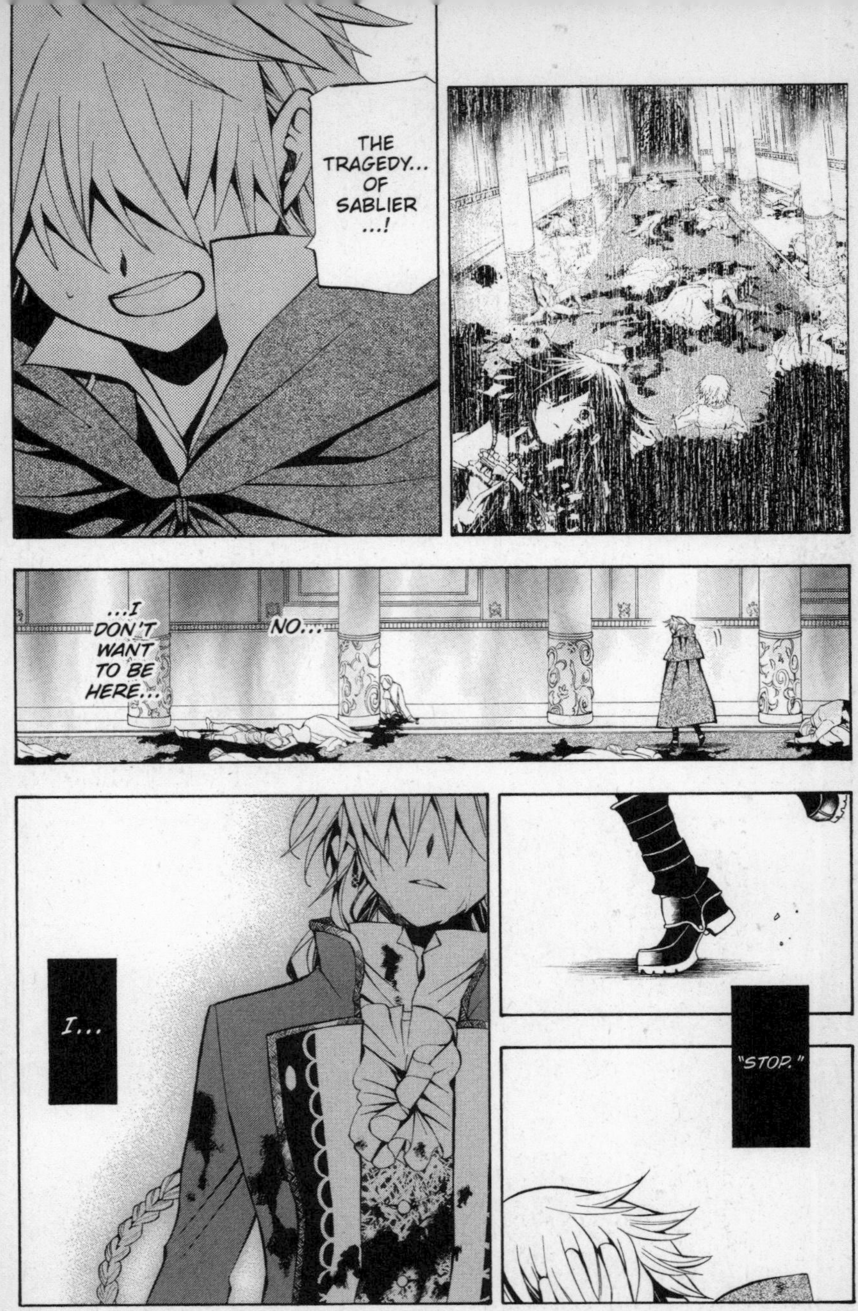
THE TRAGEDY... OF SABLIER ...!
NO...
...I DON'T WANT TO BE HERE...
"STOP."
I...

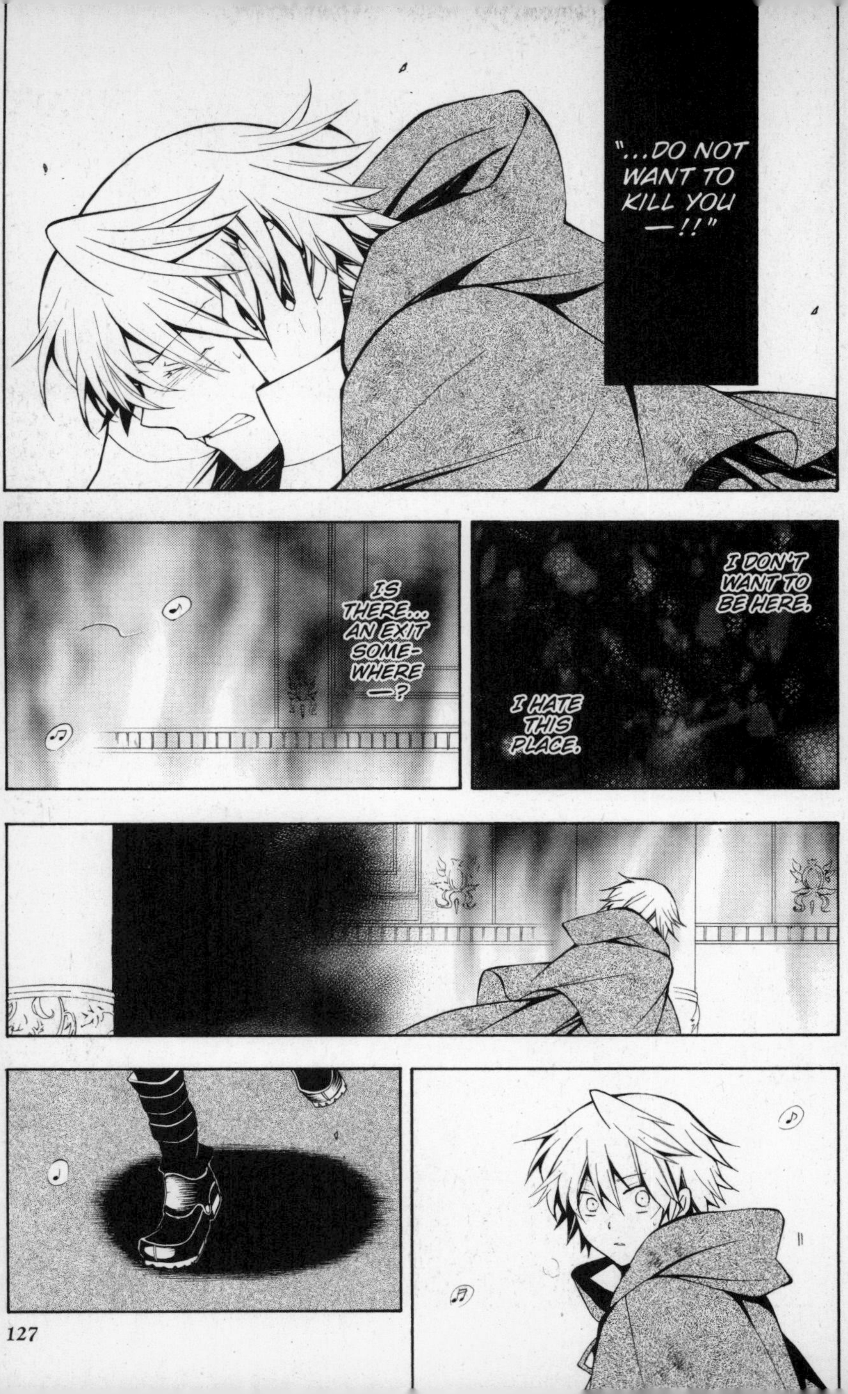
"...DO NOT WANT TO KILL YOU—!!"
I DON'T WANT TO BE HERE.
I HATE THIS PLACE.
IS THERE... AN EXIT SOME-WHERE—?

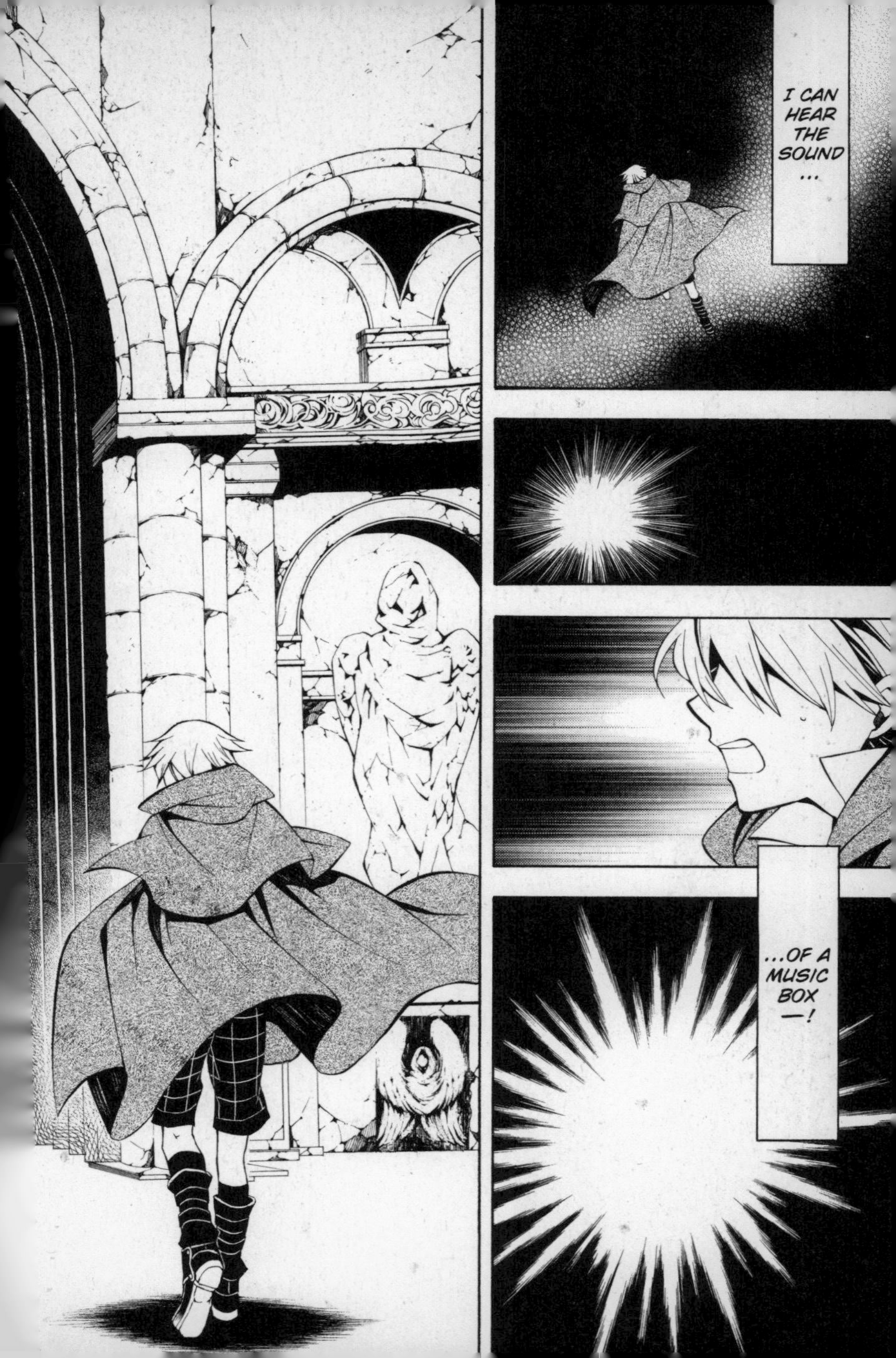
I CAN HEAR THE SOUND ...
...OF A MUSIC BOX —!

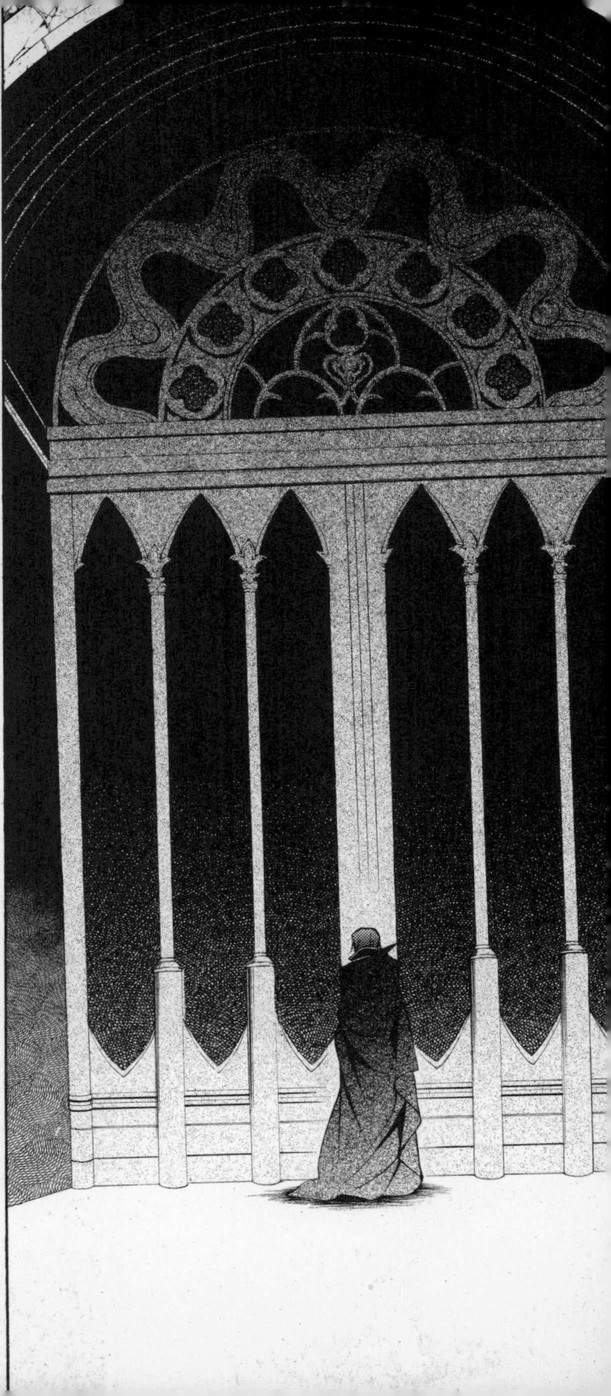
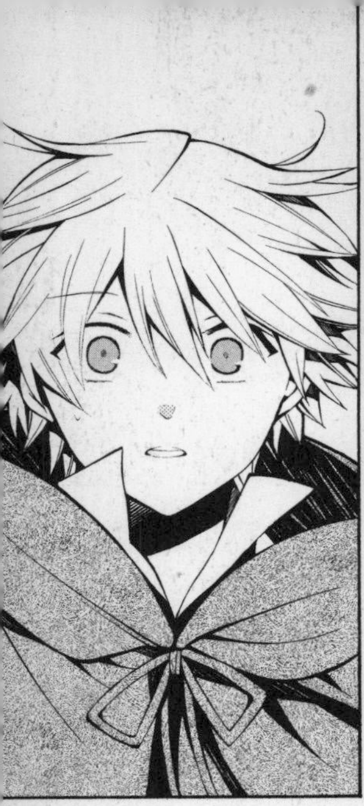
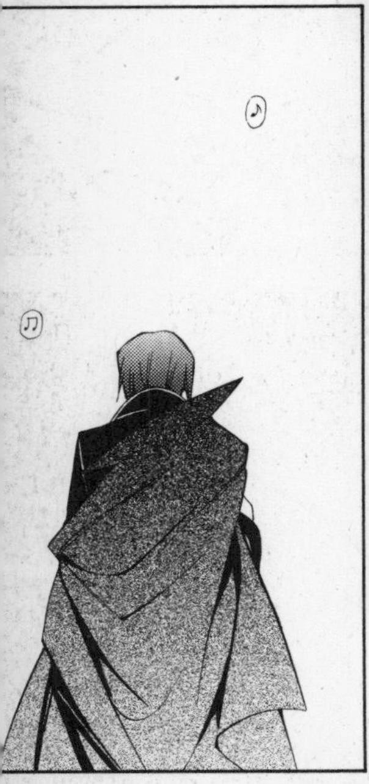
♪
♫

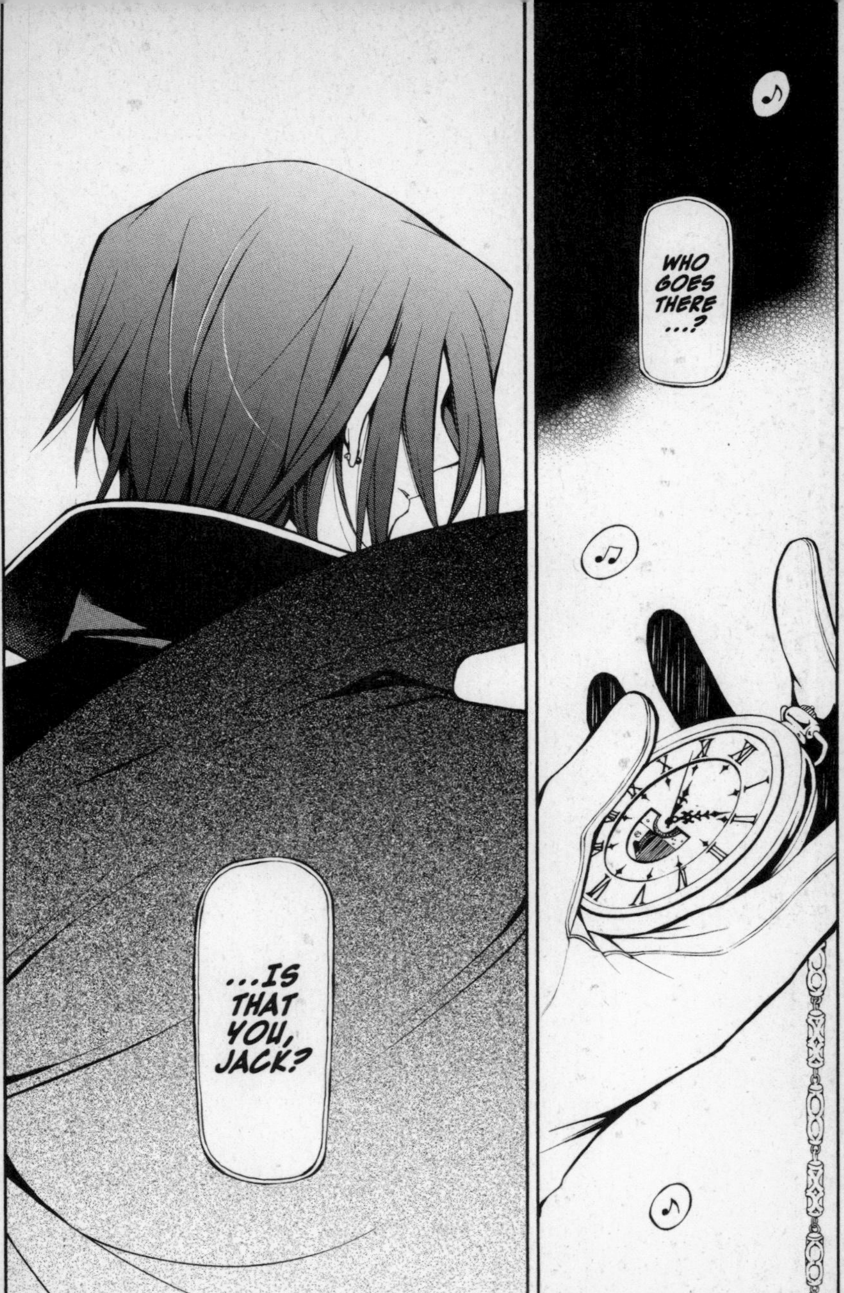
WHO GOES THERE ...?
...IS THAT YOU, JACK?

Retrace:XXXVII Glen Baskerville

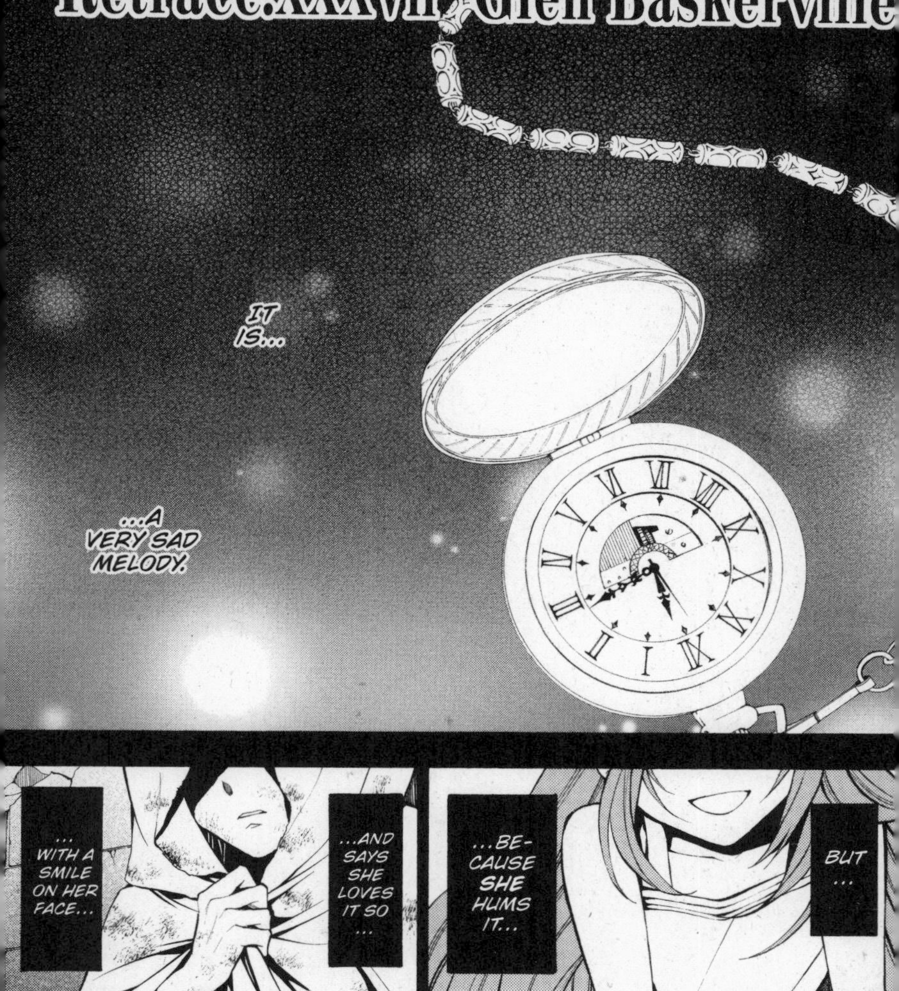
IT IS...
...A VERY SAD MELODY.
BUT...
...BE-CAUSE SHE HUMS IT...
...AND SAYS SHE LOVES IT SO...
...WITH A SMILE ON HER FACE...

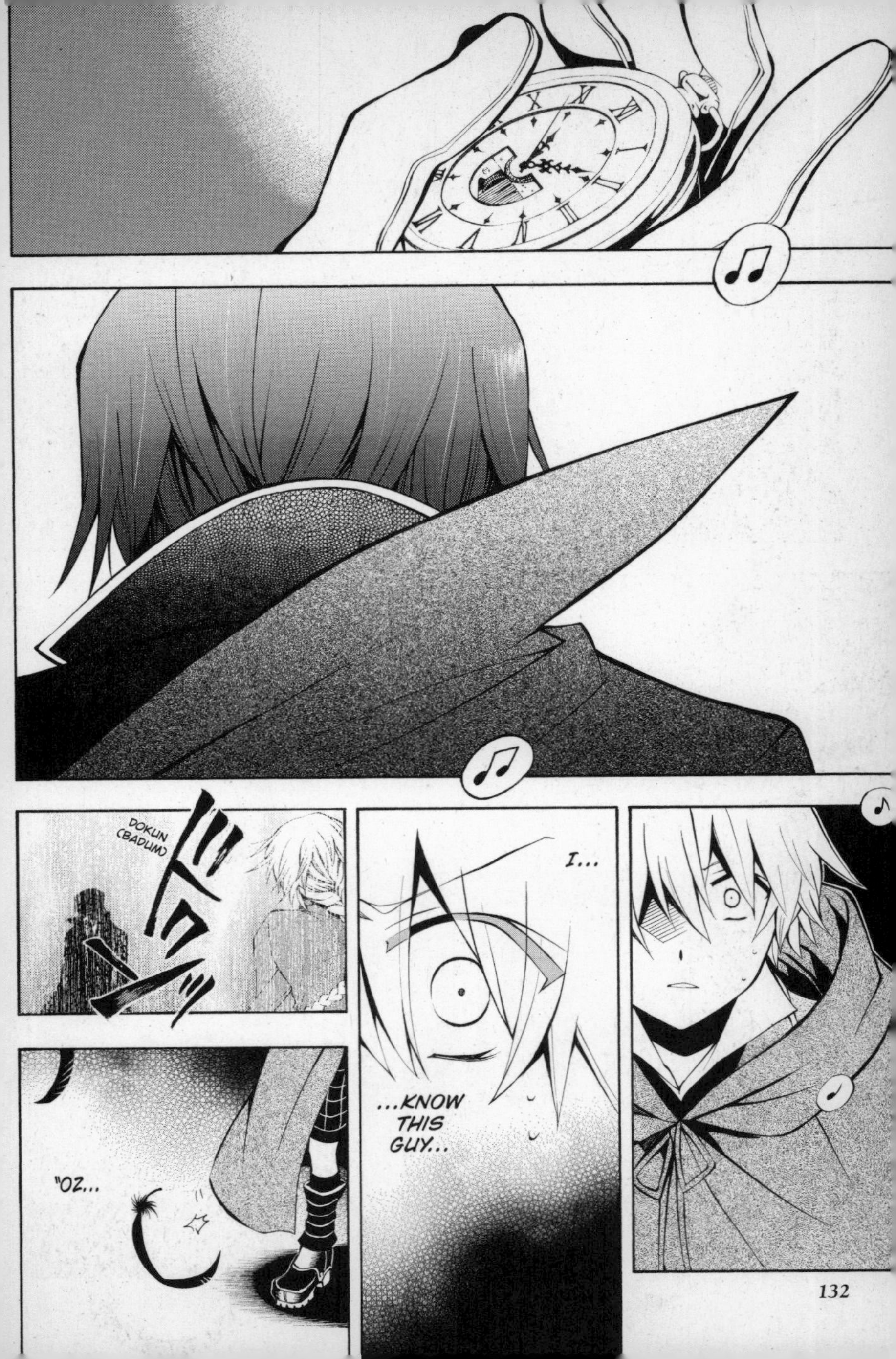
I...
...KNOW THIS GUY...
DOKUN (BADUM)
"OZ...

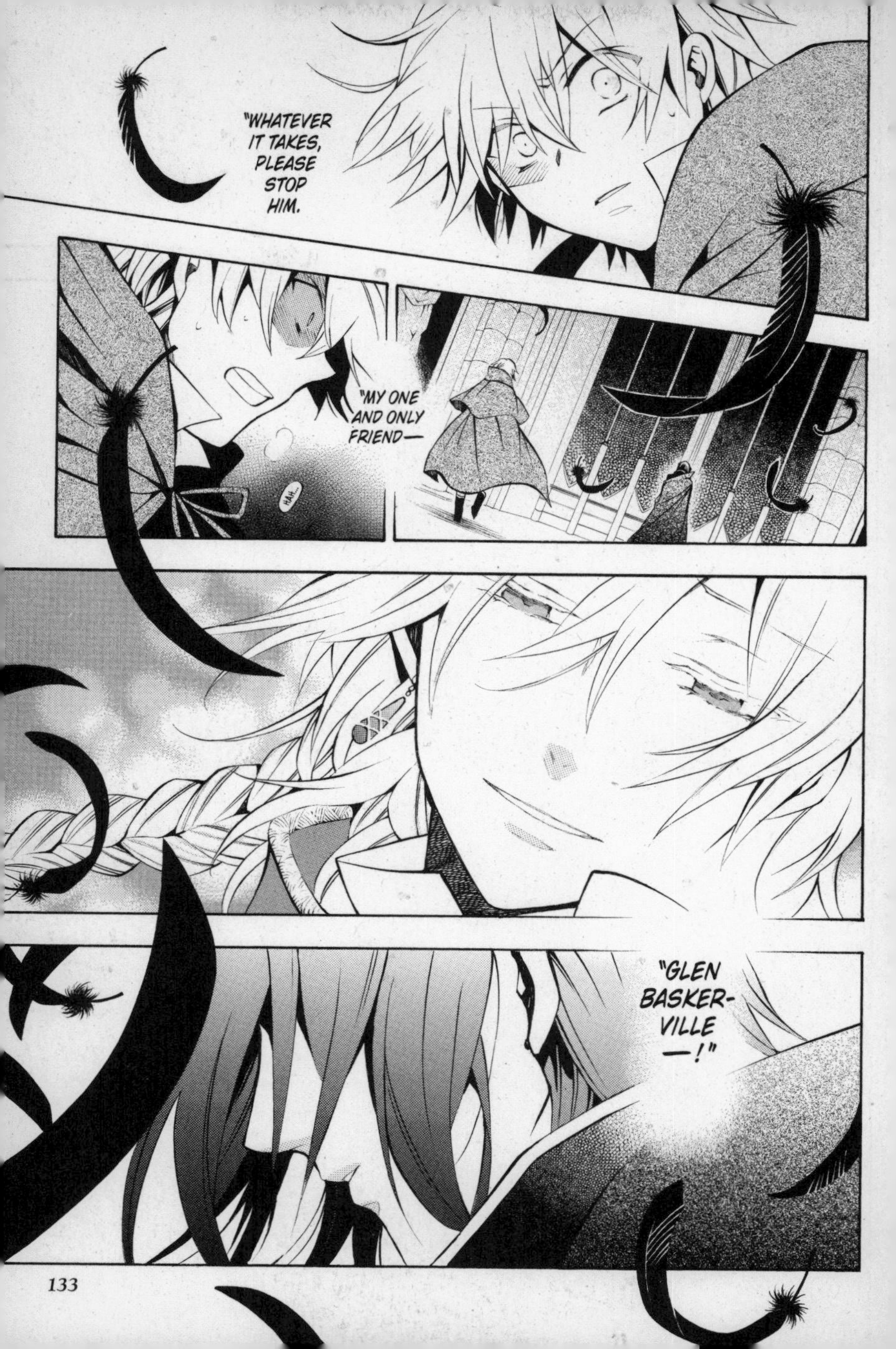
"WHATEVER IT TAKES, PLEASE STOP HIM.
"MY ONE AND ONLY FRIEND—
HAH...
"GLEN BASKER-VILLE—!"

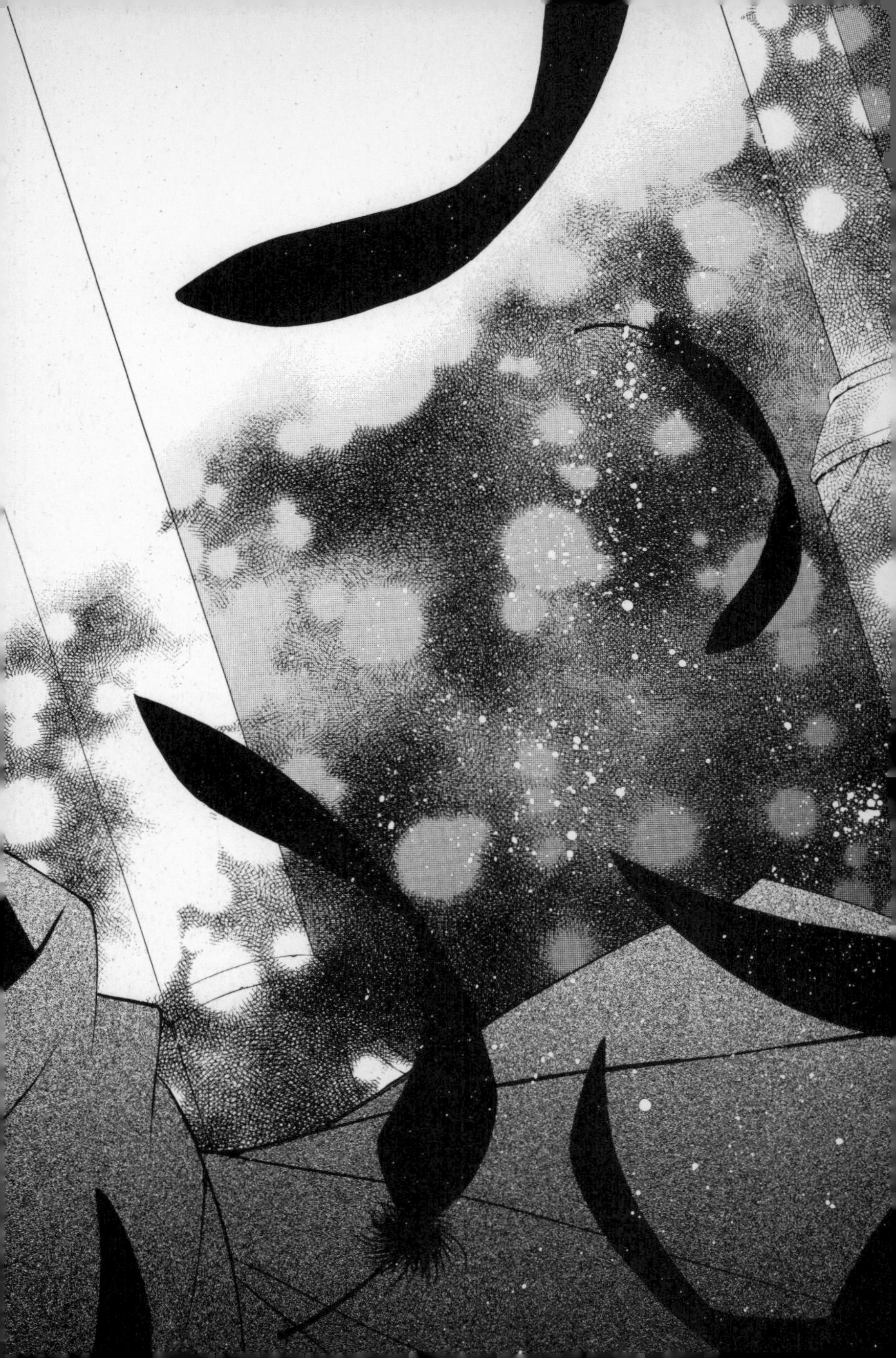

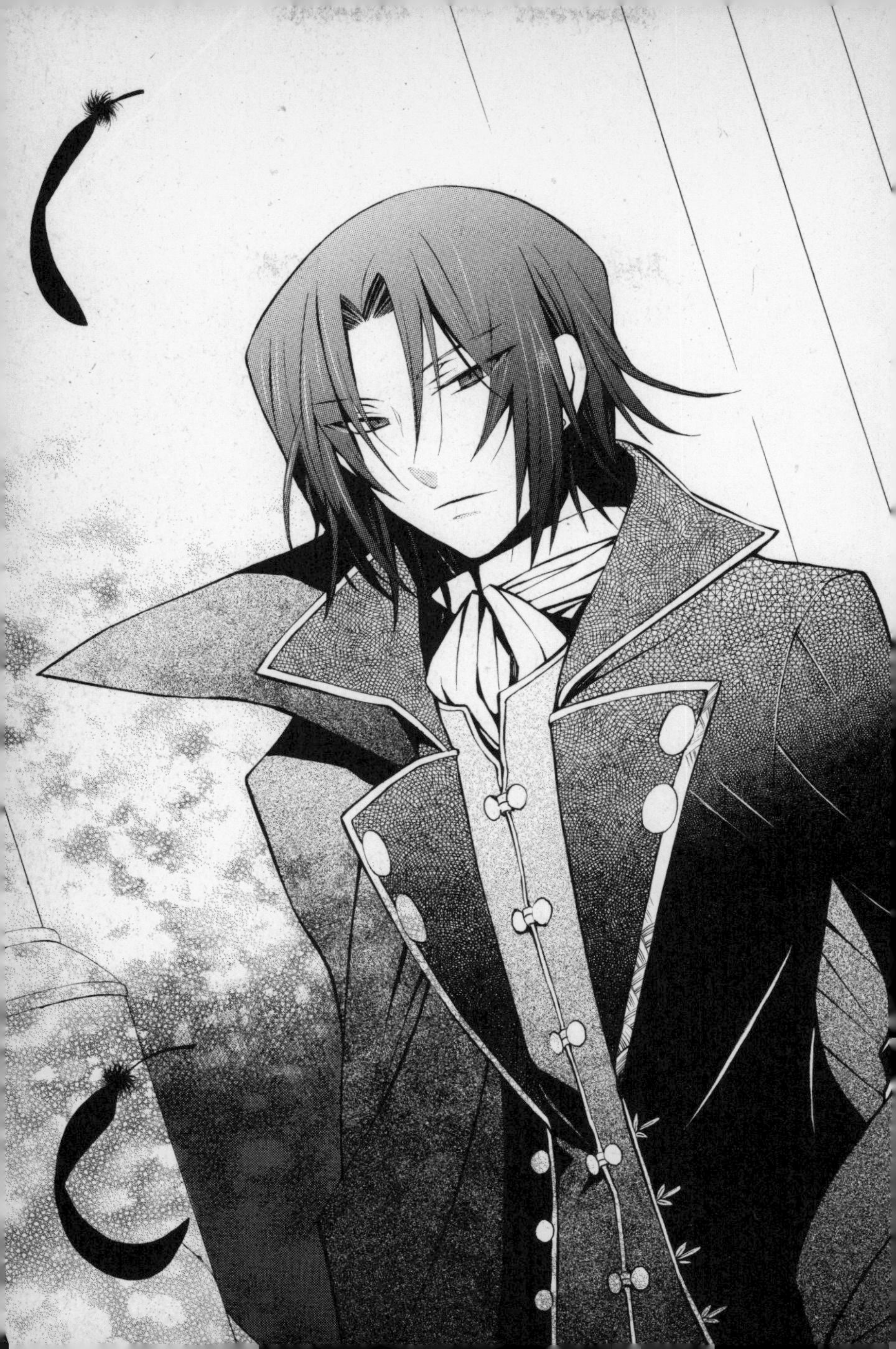

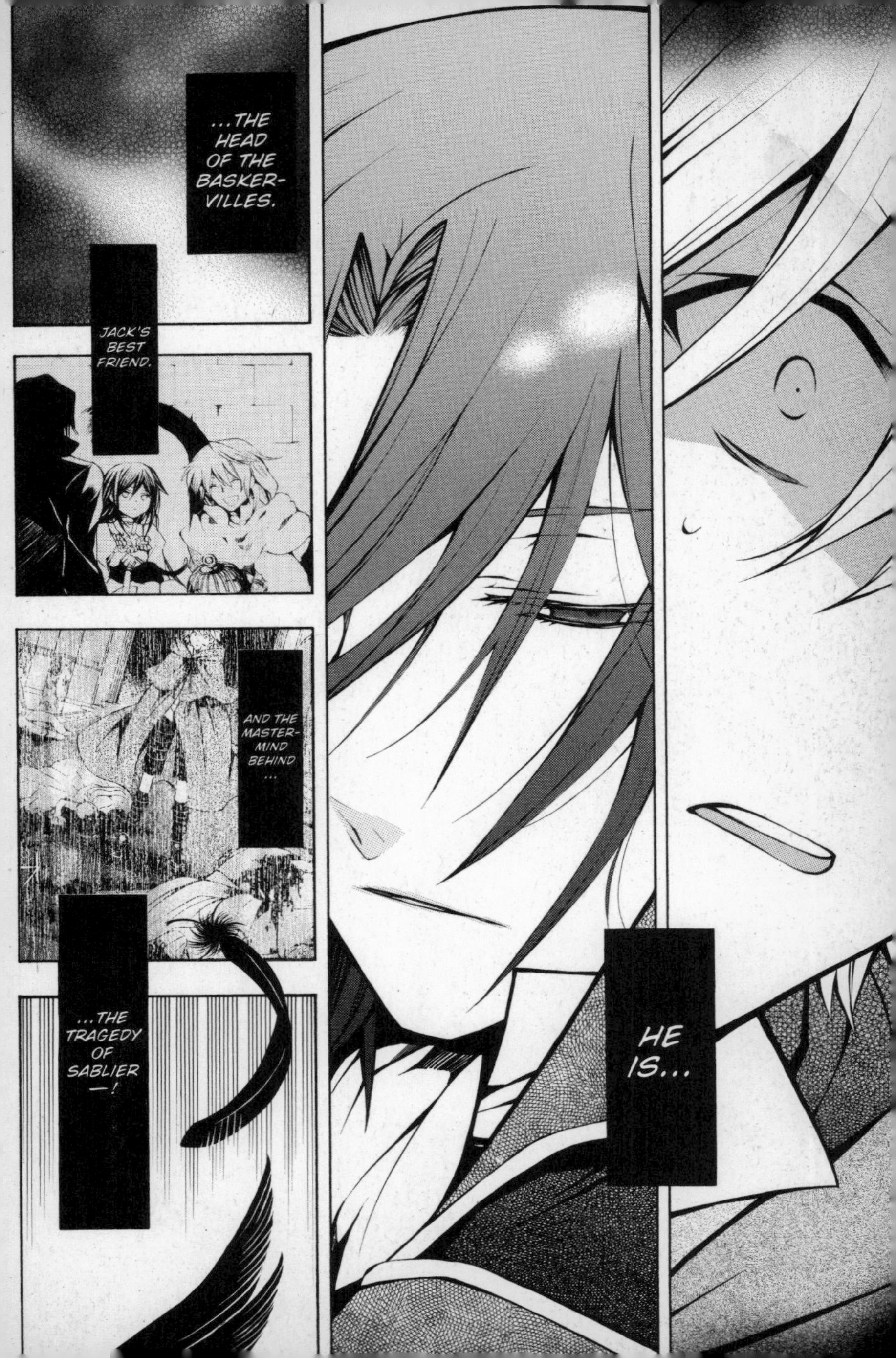
HE IS...
...THE HEAD OF THE BASKER-VILLES.
JACK'S BEST FRIEND.
AND THE MASTER-MIND BEHIND...
...THE TRAGEDY OF SABLIER—!

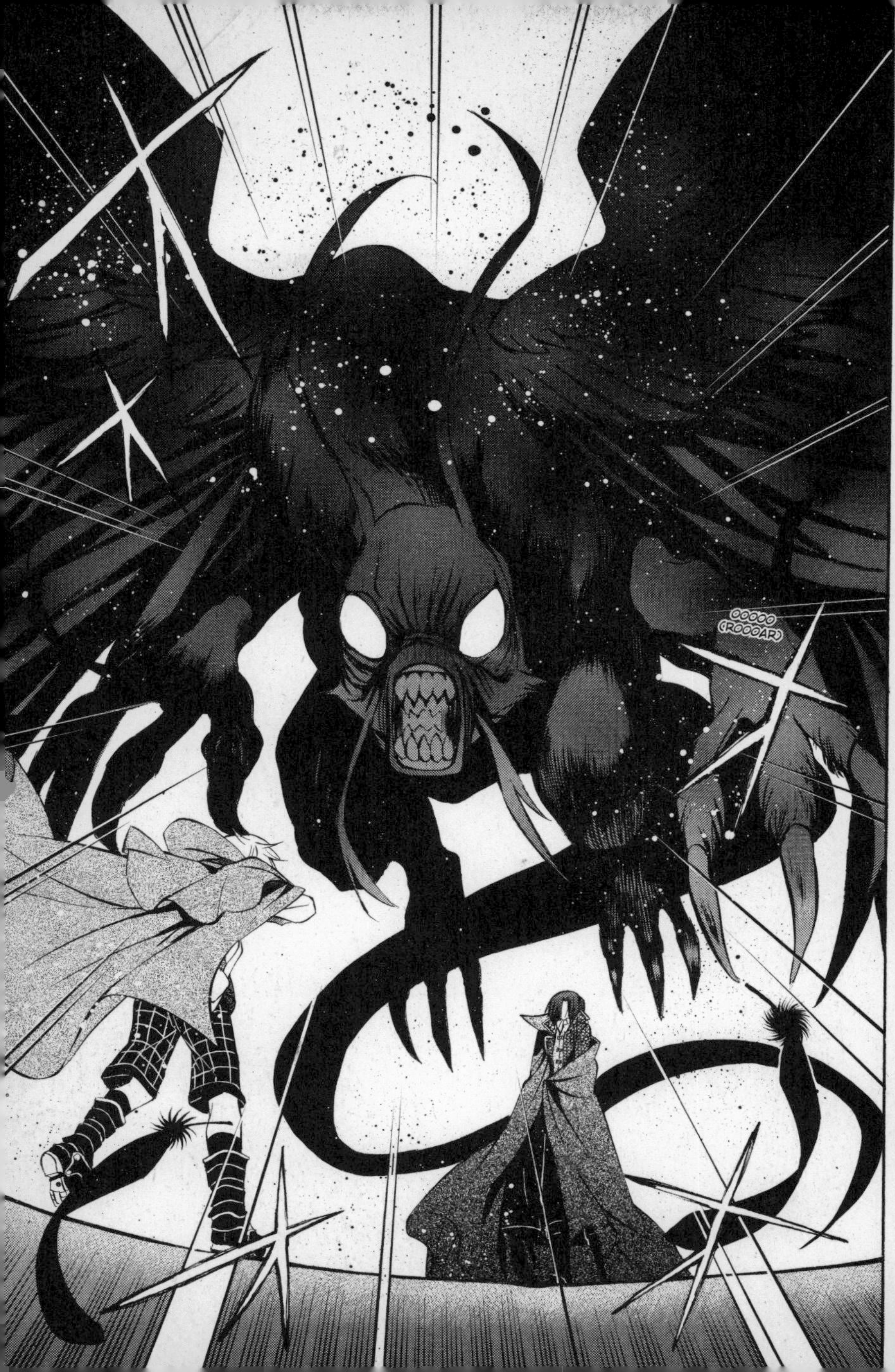
OOOOO
(ROOOAR)

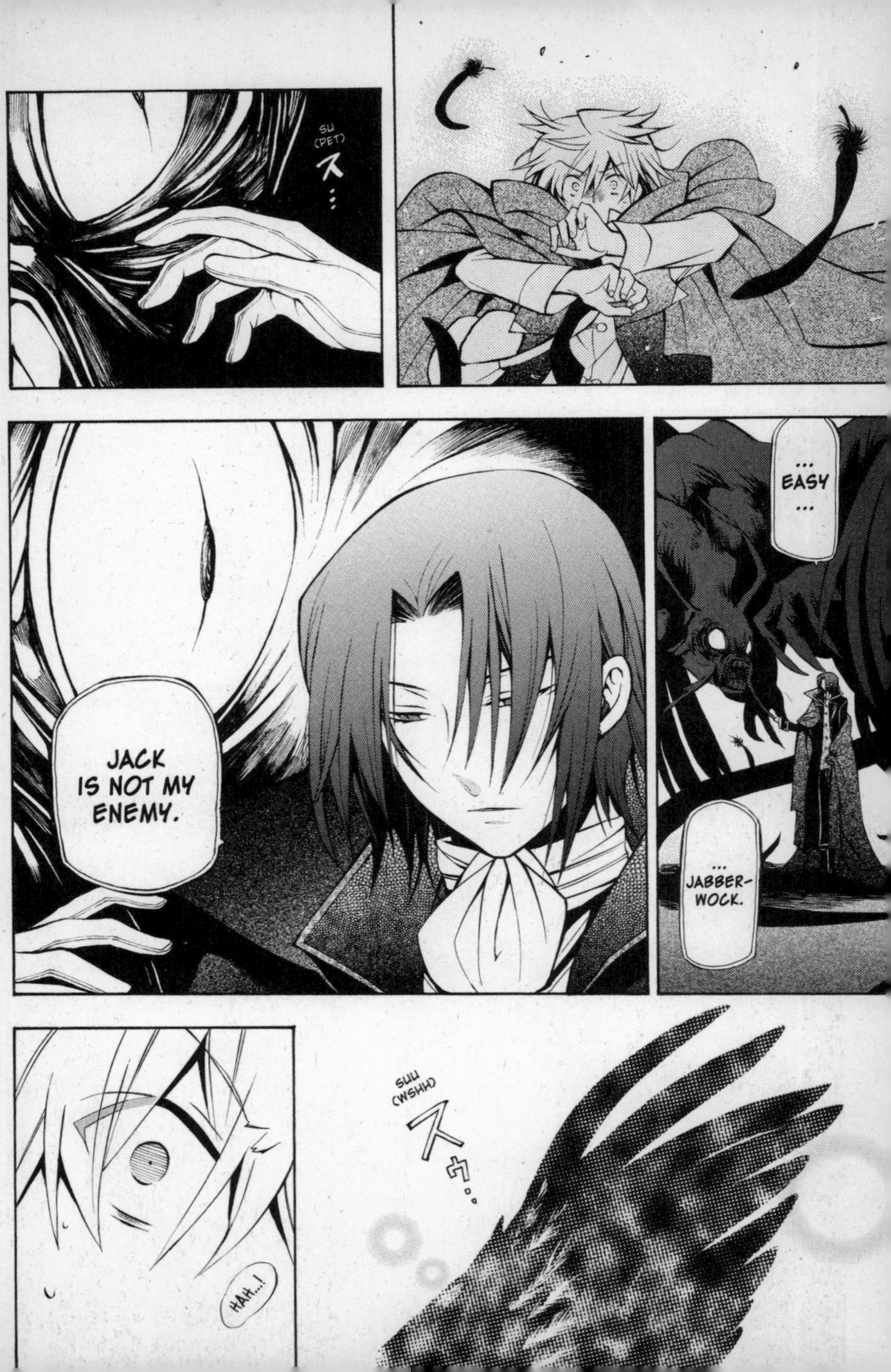
SU (PET)
ス…
...EASY...
...JABBER-WOCK.
JACK IS NOT MY ENEMY.
SUU (WSHH)
スゥ
HAH...!

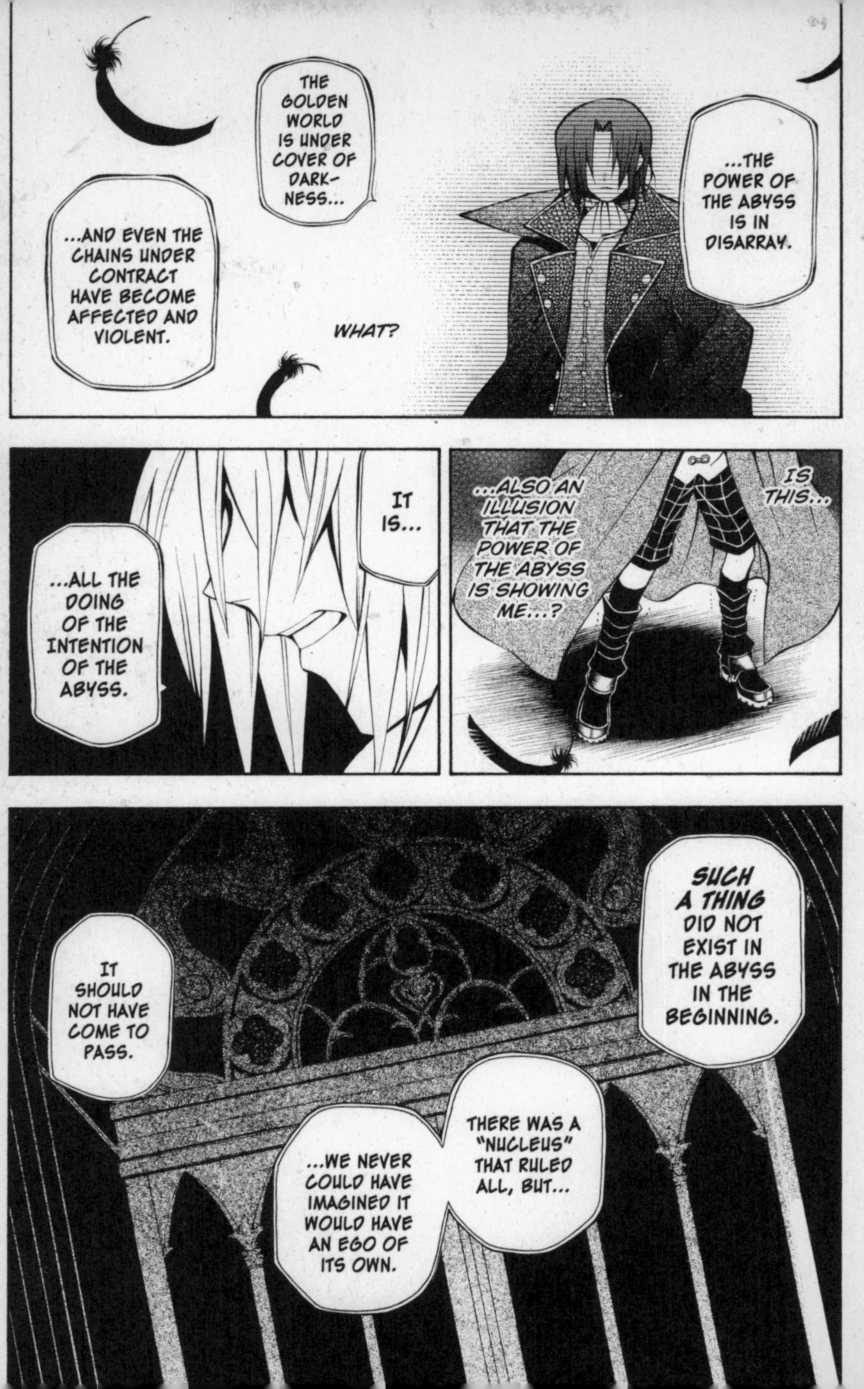
...THE POWER OF THE ABYSS IS IN DISARRAY.
THE GOLDEN WORLD IS UNDER COVER OF DARKNESS...
...AND EVEN THE CHAINS UNDER CONTRACT HAVE BECOME AFFECTED AND VIOLENT.
WHAT?
IS THIS...
...ALSO AN ILLUSION THAT THE POWER OF THE ABYSS IS SHOWING ME...?
IT IS...
...ALL THE DOING OF THE INTENTION OF THE ABYSS.
SUCH A THING DID NOT EXIST IN THE ABYSS IN THE BEGINNING.
IT SHOULD NOT HAVE COME TO PASS.
THERE WAS A "NUCLEUS" THAT RULED ALL, BUT...
...WE NEVER COULD HAVE IMAGINED IT WOULD HAVE AN EGO OF ITS OWN.

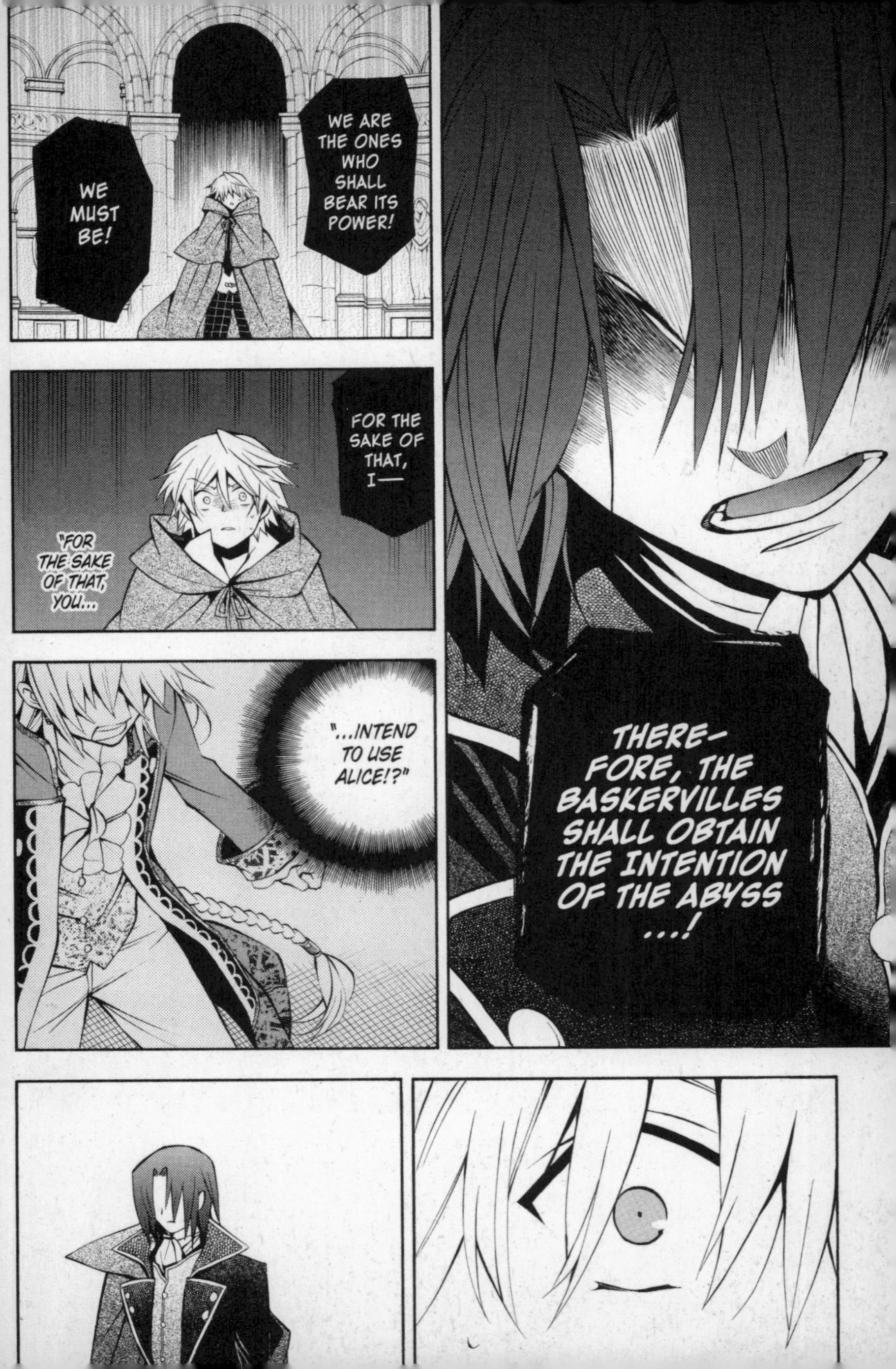
THERE-FORE, THE BASKERVILLES SHALL OBTAIN THE INTENTION OF THE ABYSS ...!
WE ARE THE ONES WHO SHALL BEAR ITS POWER!
WE MUST BE!
FOR THE SAKE OF THAT, I—
"FOR THE SAKE OF THAT, YOU...
"...INTEND TO USE ALICE!?"

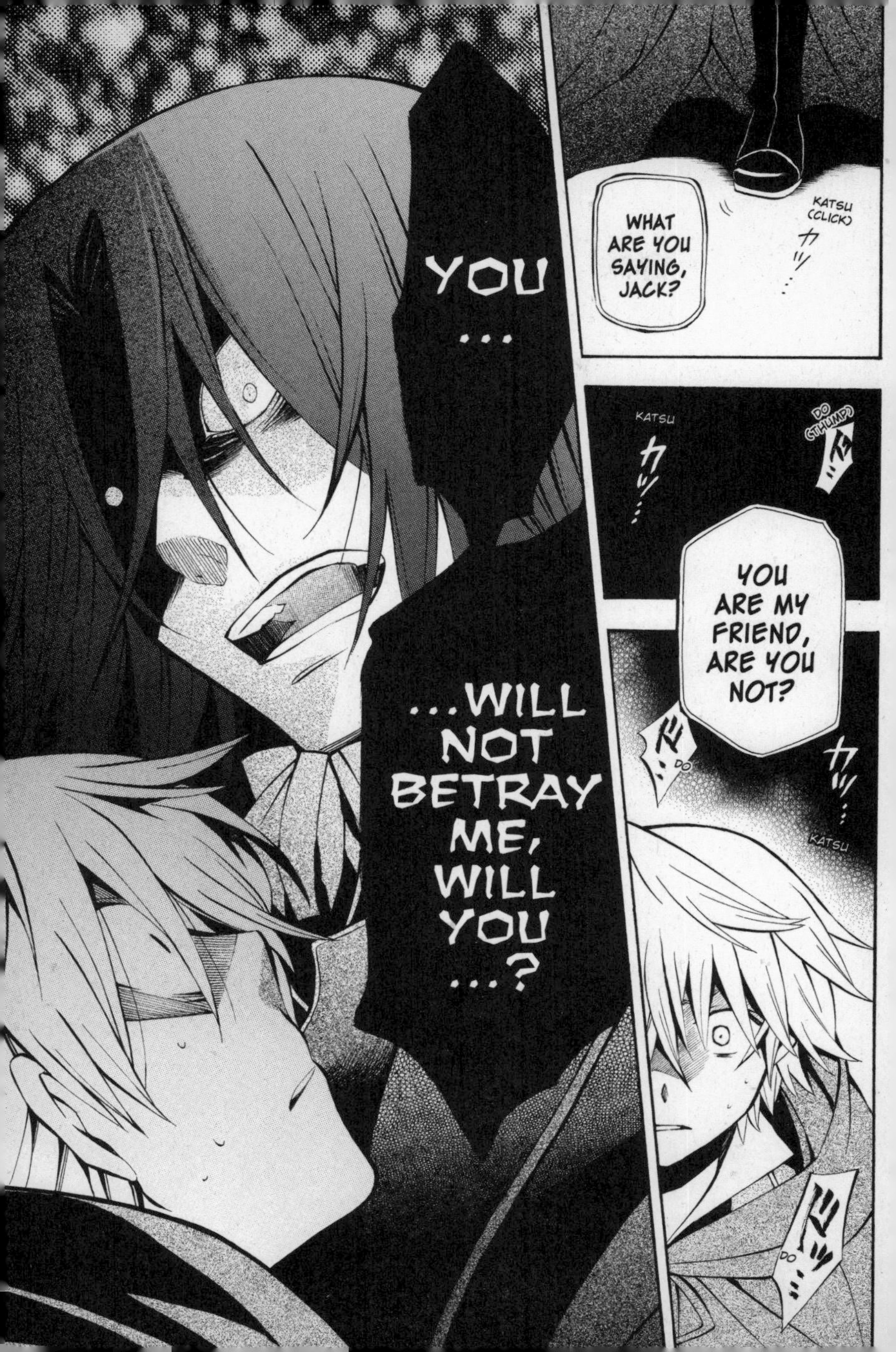

KATSU (CLICK)
カッ…
WHAT ARE YOU SAYING, JACK?
DO (THUMP)
ド
KATSU
カッ…
YOU ARE MY FRIEND, ARE YOU NOT?
カッ…
KATSU
ド
DO
ドッ
DO
YOU ...
...WILL NOT BETRAY ME, WILL YOU ...?

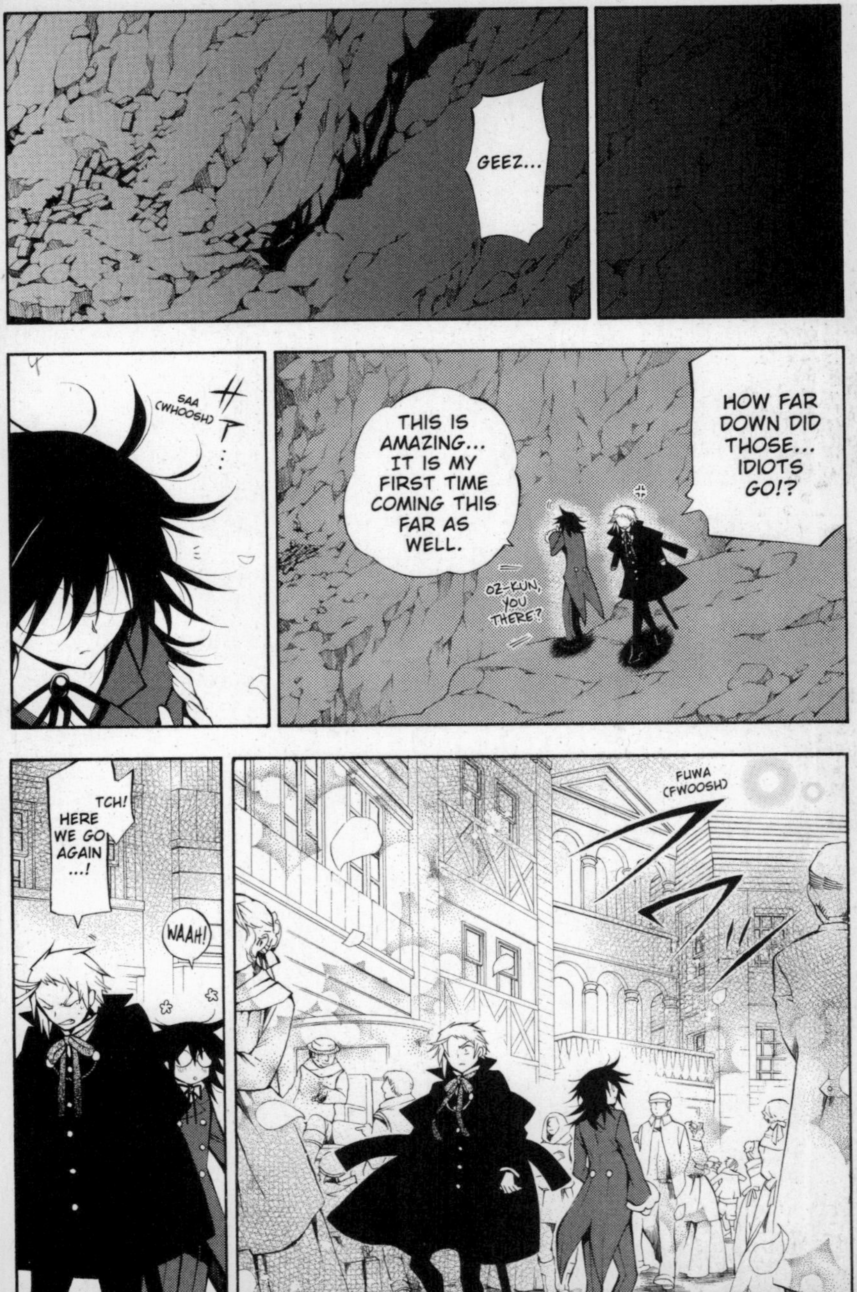
GEEZ...
HOW FAR DOWN DID THOSE... IDIOTS GO!?
THIS IS AMAZING... IT IS MY FIRST TIME COMING THIS FAR AS WELL.
OZ-KUN, YOU THERE?
SAA (WHOOSH)
FUWA (FWOOSH)
TCH! HERE WE GO AGAIN ...!
WAAH!

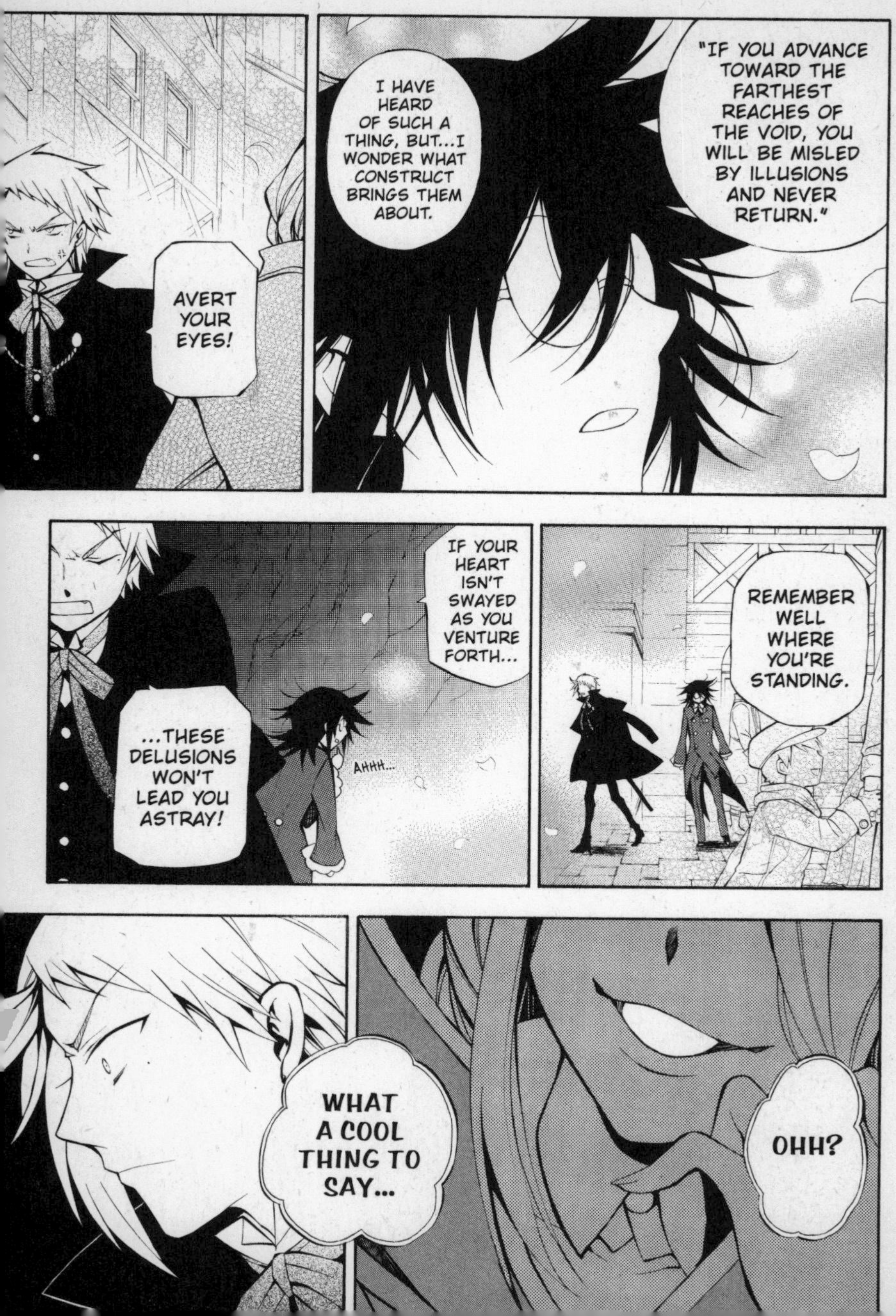
"IF YOU ADVANCE TOWARD THE FARTHEST REACHES OF THE VOID, YOU WILL BE MISLED BY ILLUSIONS AND NEVER RETURN."
I HAVE HEARD OF SUCH A THING, BUT...I WONDER WHAT CONSTRUCT BRINGS THEM ABOUT.
AVERT YOUR EYES!
REMEMBER WELL WHERE YOU'RE STANDING.
IF YOUR HEART ISN'T SWAYED AS YOU VENTURE FORTH...
...THESE DELUSIONS WON'T LEAD YOU ASTRAY!
AHHH...
OHH?
WHAT A COOL THING TO SAY...

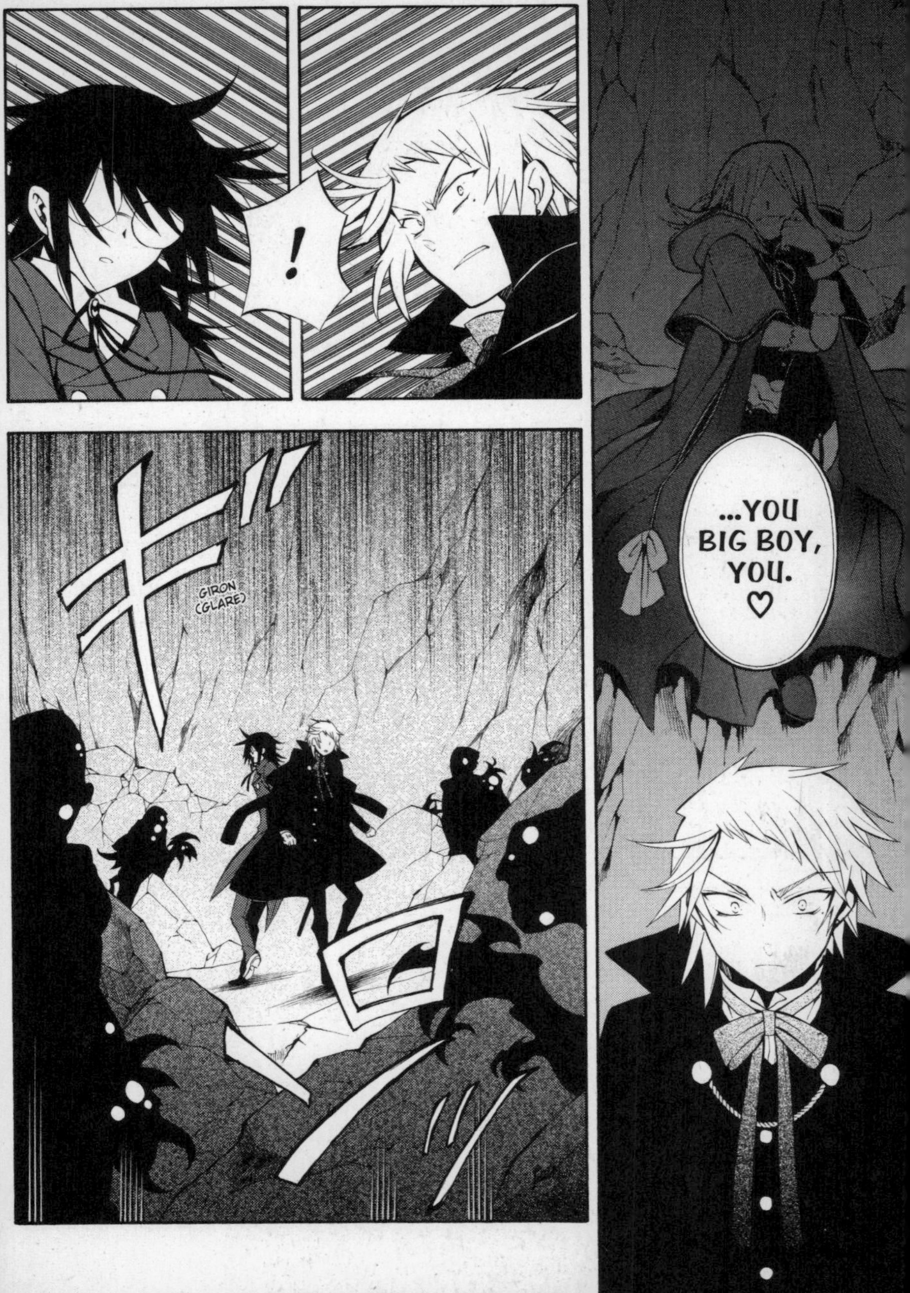
...YOU BIG BOY, YOU. ♡
!
GIRON (GLARE)

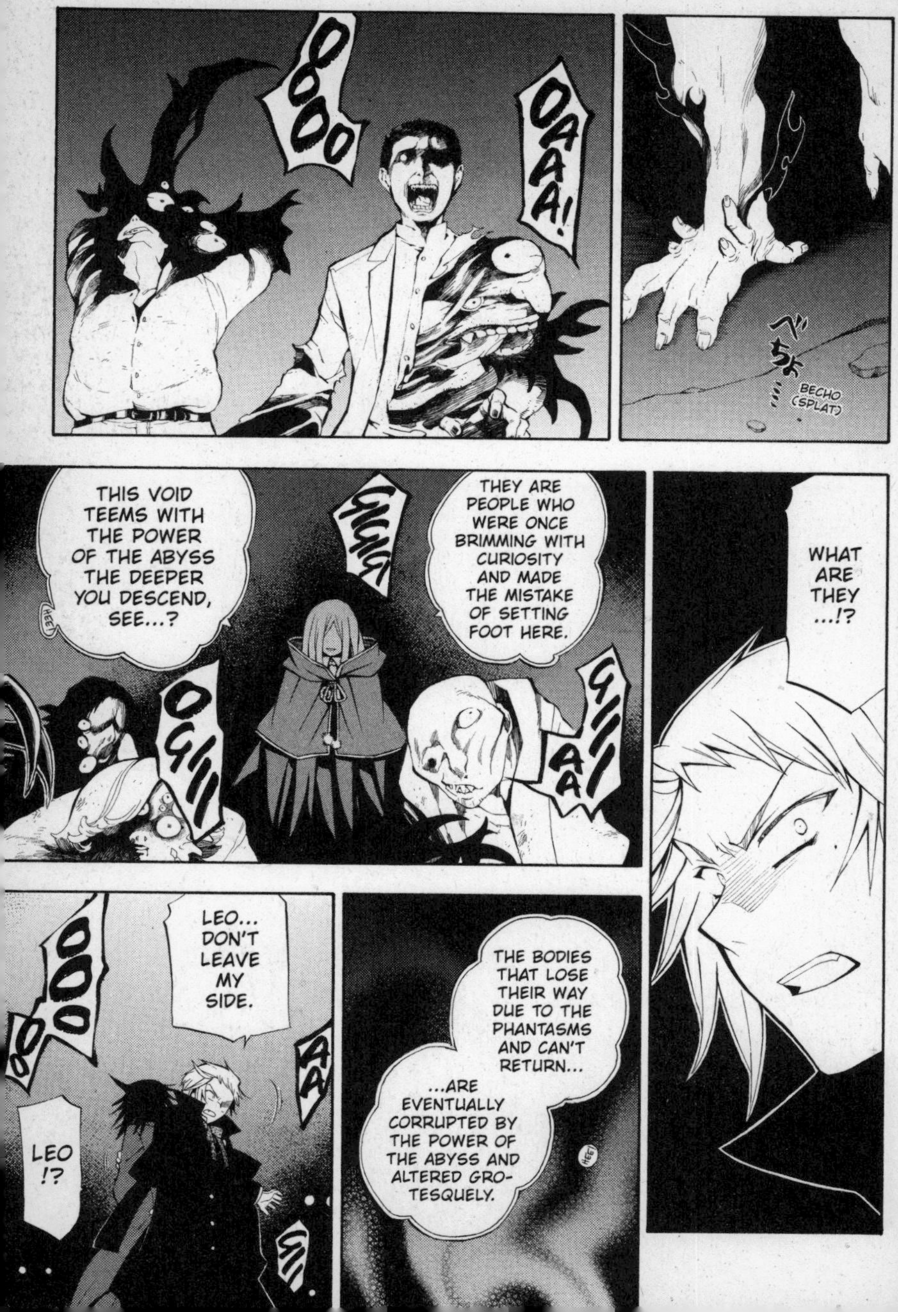

べちょ…
BECHO (SPLAT)
OAAAA!
OOOO
WHAT ARE THEY ...!?
THEY ARE PEOPLE WHO WERE ONCE BRIMMING WITH CURIOSITY AND MADE THE MISTAKE OF SETTING FOOT HERE.
GIGIGI
THIS VOID TEEMS WITH THE POWER OF THE ABYSS THE DEEPER YOU DESCEND, SEE...?
HEE
GIII AAA
OGIII
THE BODIES THAT LOSE THEIR WAY DUE TO THE PHANTASMS AND CAN'T RETURN...
...ARE EVENTUALLY CORRUPTED BY THE POWER OF THE ABYSS AND ALTERED GRO-TESQUELY.
HEE
LEO... DON'T LEAVE MY SIDE.
OOOOO
AA
LEO !?
GII

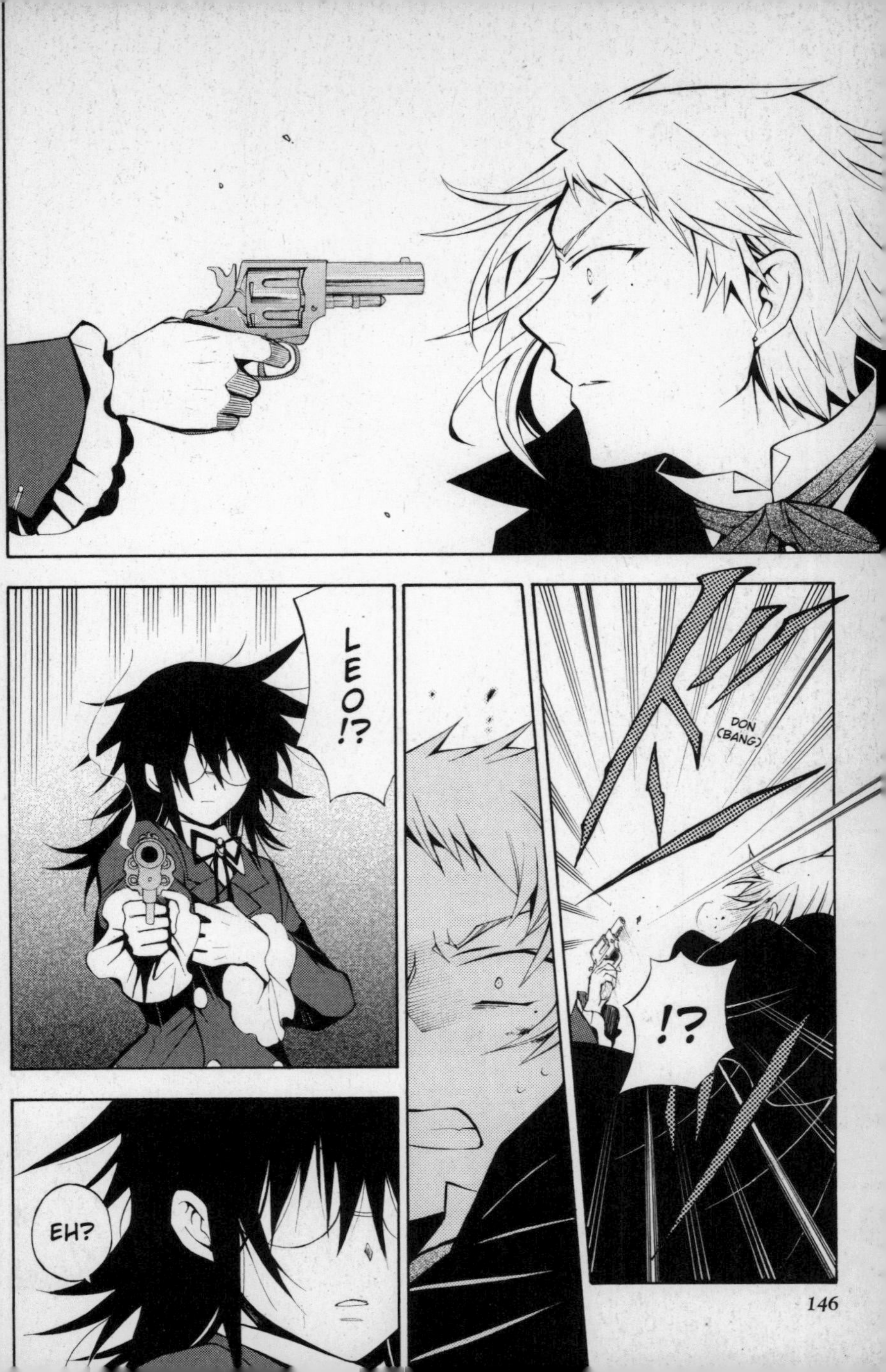
DON (BANG)
!?
LEO!?
EH?

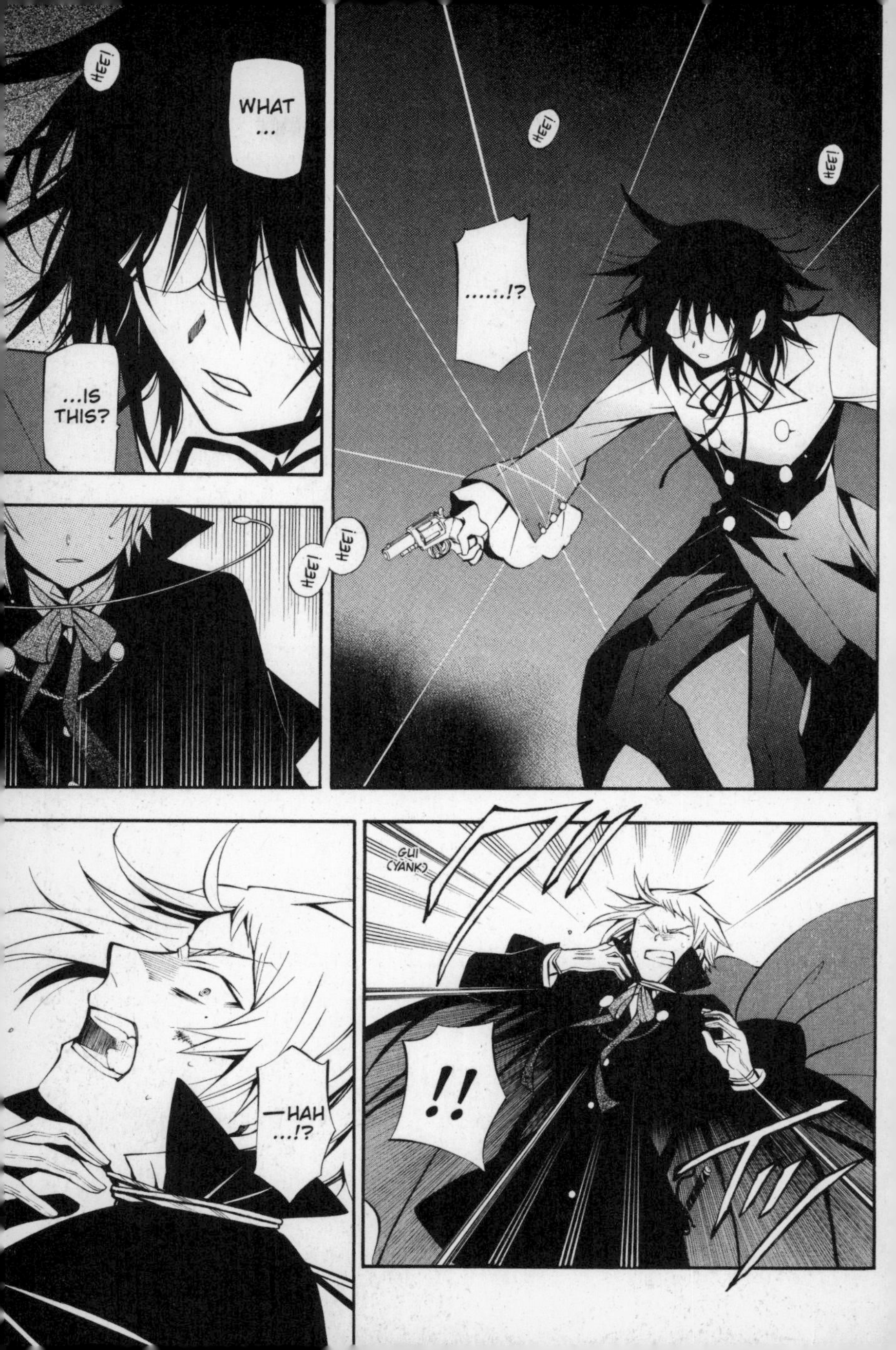
HEE!
HEE!
......!?
WHAT ...
HEE!
...IS THIS?
HEE!
HEE!
GUI (YANK)
!!
—HAH ...!?

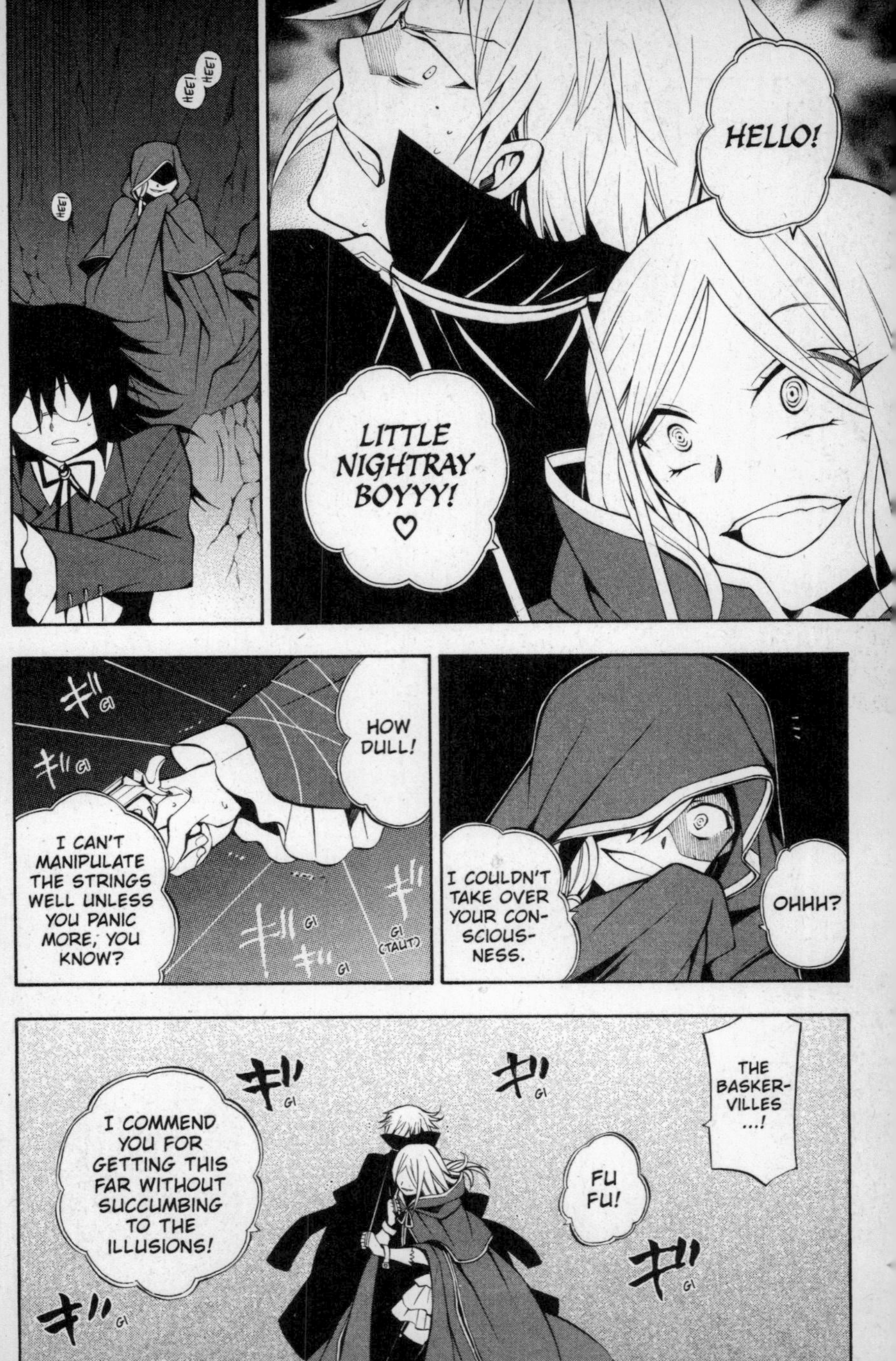
HELLO!
LITTLE NIGHTRAY BOYYY! ♥
HEE! HEE!
HEE!
OHHH?
I COULDN'T TAKE OVER YOUR CON-SCIOUS-NESS.
HOW DULL!
I CAN'T MANIPULATE THE STRINGS WELL UNLESS YOU PANIC MORE, YOU KNOW?
ギリ GI
ギリ GI
ギリ GI (TAUT)
ギリ GI
ギリ GI
THE BASKER-VILLES ...!
FU FU!
I COMMEND YOU FOR GETTING THIS FAR WITHOUT SUCCUMBING TO THE ILLUSIONS!
ギリ GI
ギリ GI
ギリ GI
ギリ GI

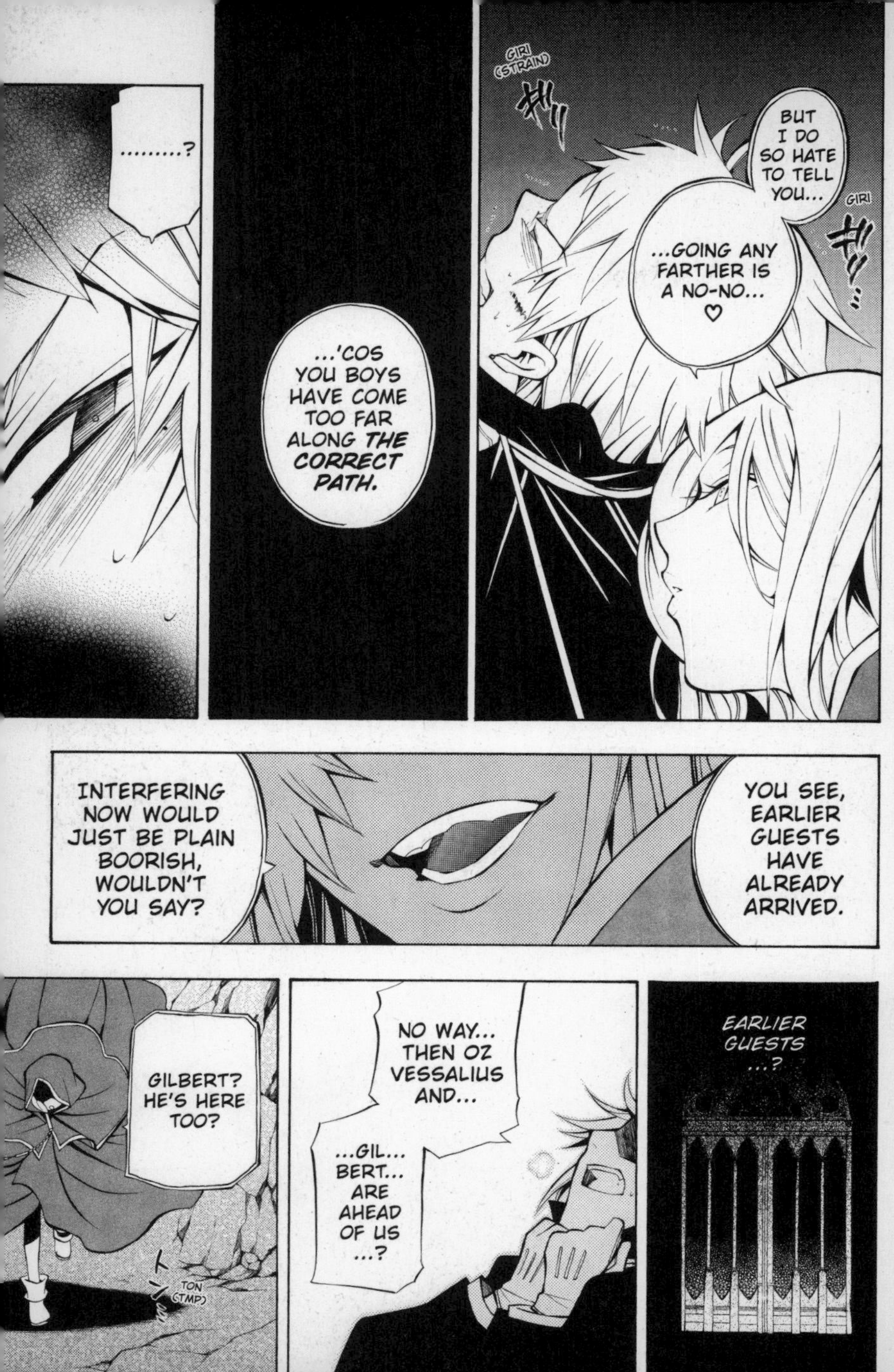
GIRI (STRAIN)
BUT I DO SO HATE TO TELL YOU...
GIRI
...GOING ANY FARTHER IS A NO-NO... ♡
...'COS YOU BOYS HAVE COME TOO FAR ALONG *THE CORRECT PATH.*
.........?
YOU SEE, EARLIER GUESTS HAVE ALREADY ARRIVED.
INTERFERING NOW WOULD JUST BE PLAIN BOORISH, WOULDN'T YOU SAY?
EARLIER GUESTS ...?
NO WAY... THEN OZ VESSALIUS AND...
...GIL... BERT... ARE AHEAD OF US ...?
GILBERT? HE'S HERE TOO?
TON (TMP)

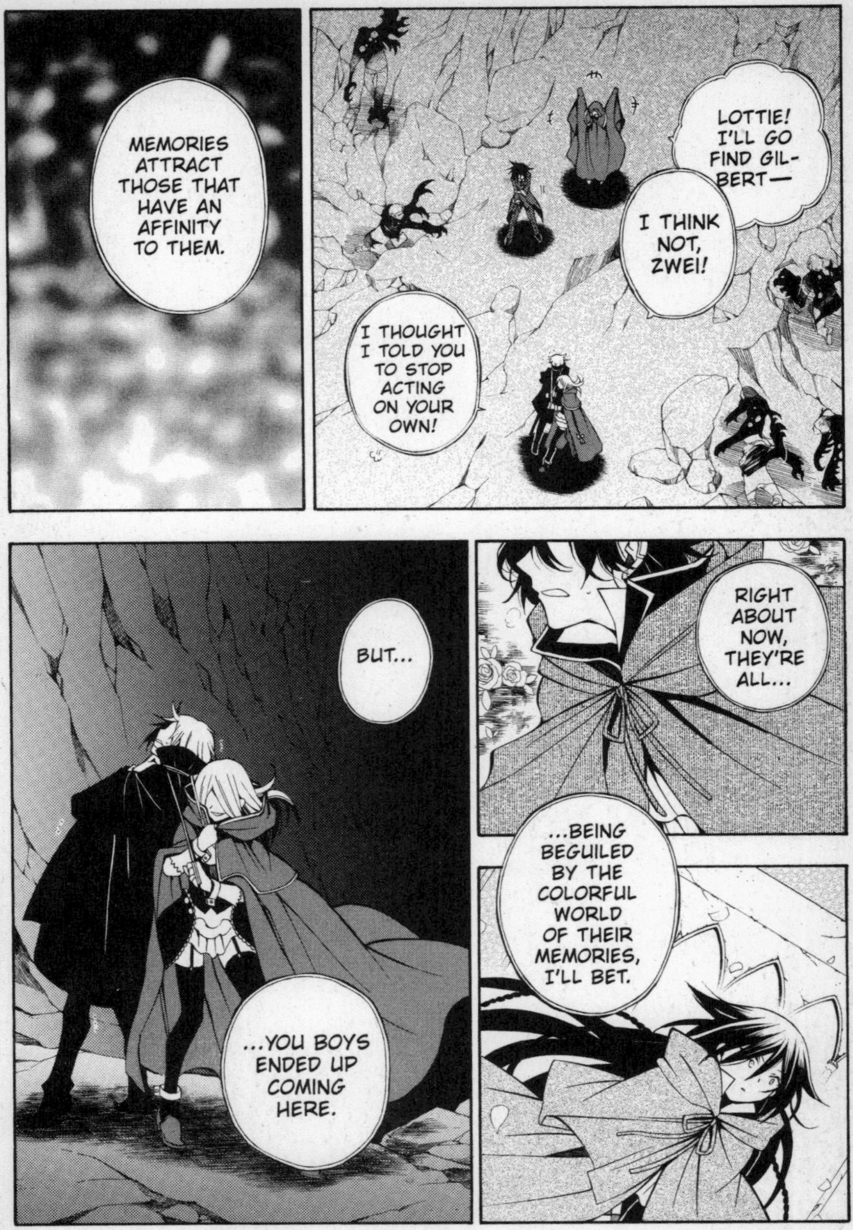
LOTTIE! I'LL GO FIND GIL-BERT—
I THINK NOT, ZWEI!
I THOUGHT I TOLD YOU TO STOP ACTING ON YOUR OWN!
MEMORIES ATTRACT THOSE THAT HAVE AN AFFINITY TO THEM.
RIGHT ABOUT NOW, THEY'RE ALL...
...BEING BEGUILED BY THE COLORFUL WORLD OF THEIR MEMORIES, I'LL BET.
BUT...
...YOU BOYS ENDED UP COMING HERE.

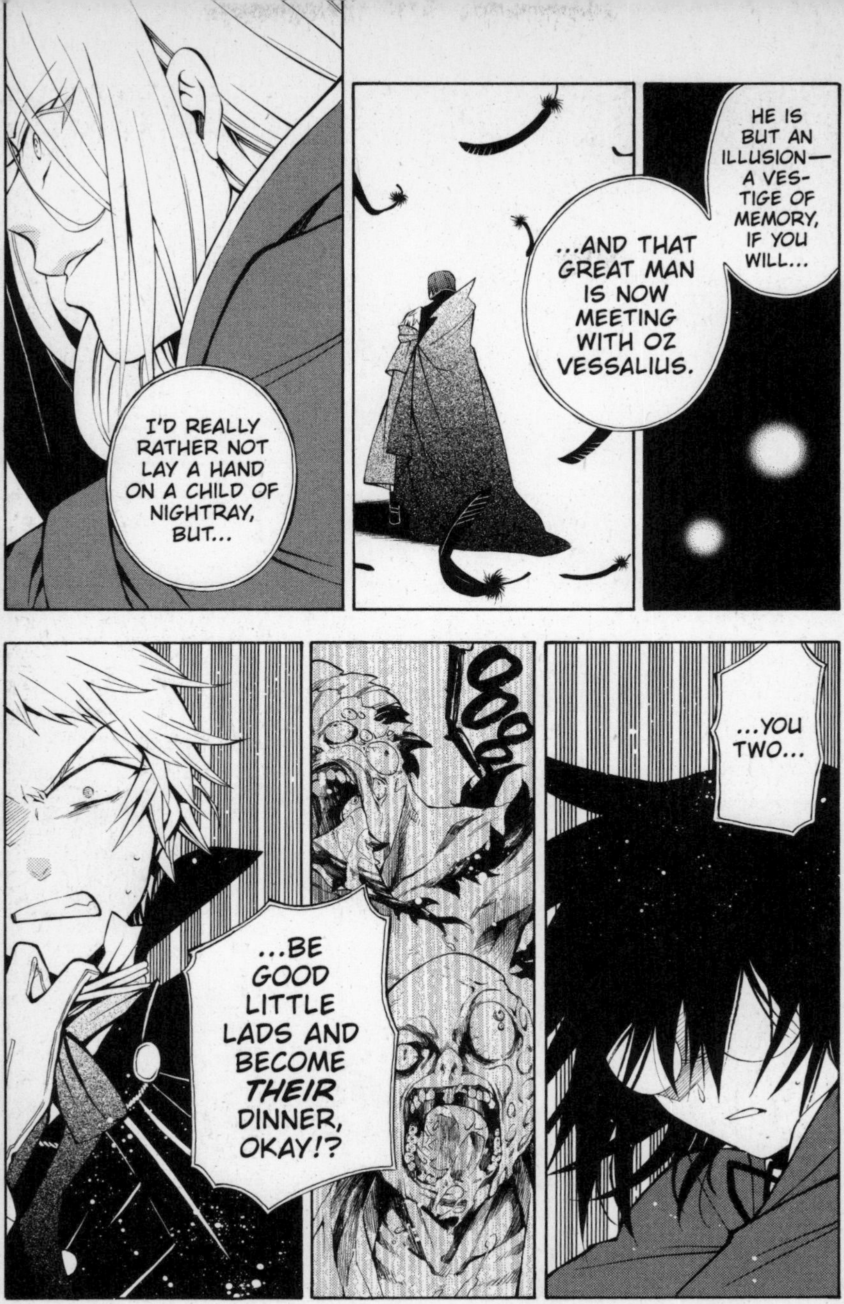

HE IS BUT AN ILLUSION— A VESTIGE OF MEMORY, IF YOU WILL...
...AND THAT GREAT MAN IS NOW MEETING WITH OZ VESSALIUS.
I'D REALLY RATHER NOT LAY A HAND ON A CHILD OF NIGHTRAY, BUT...
...YOU TWO...
...BE GOOD LITTLE LADS AND BECOME *THEIR* DINNER, OKAY!?

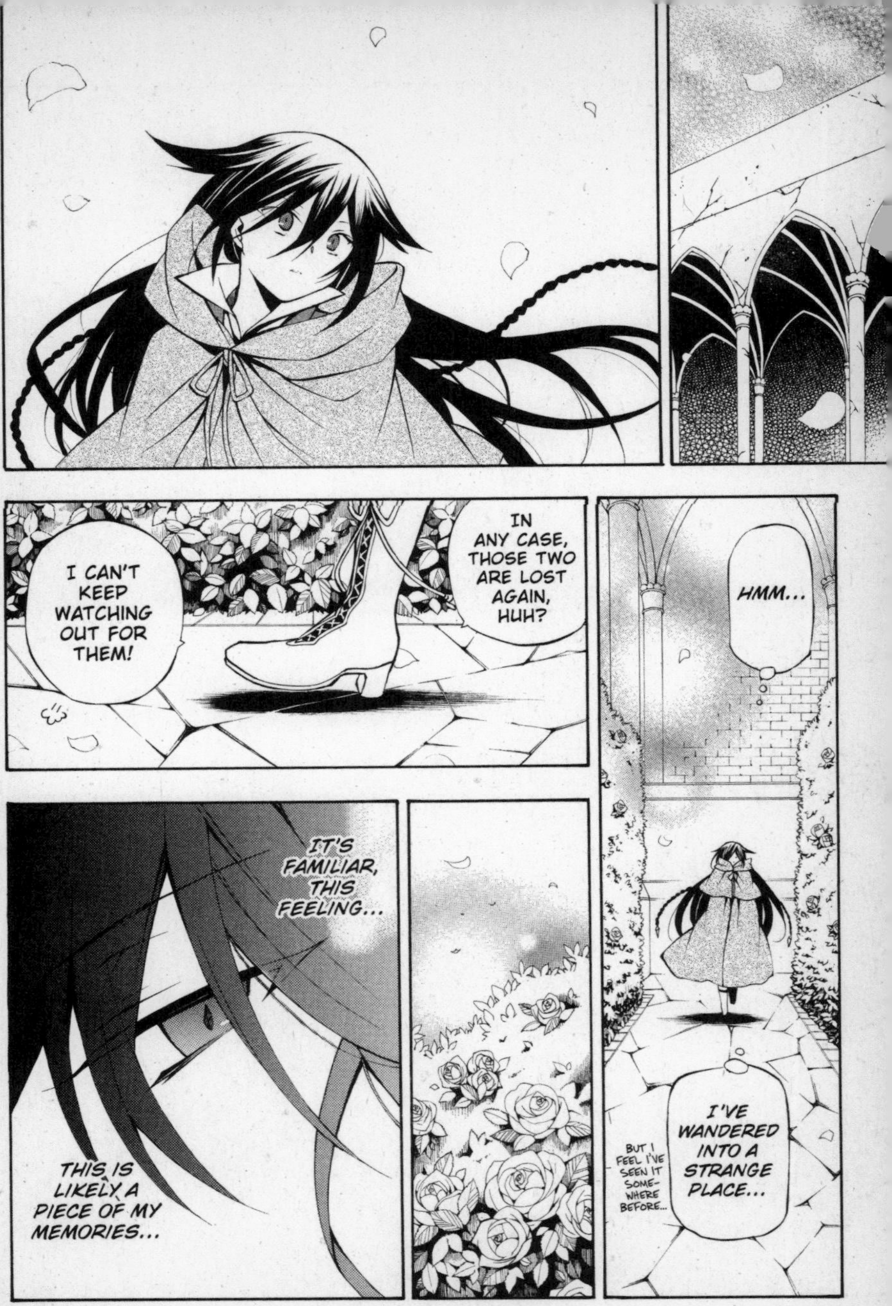
HMM...
I'VE WANDERED INTO A STRANGE PLACE...
BUT I FEEL I'VE SEEN IT SOME-WHERE BEFORE...
IN ANY CASE, THOSE TWO ARE LOST AGAIN, HUH?
I CAN'T KEEP WATCHING OUT FOR THEM!
IT'S FAMILIAR, THIS FEELING...
THIS IS LIKELY A PIECE OF MY MEMORIES...

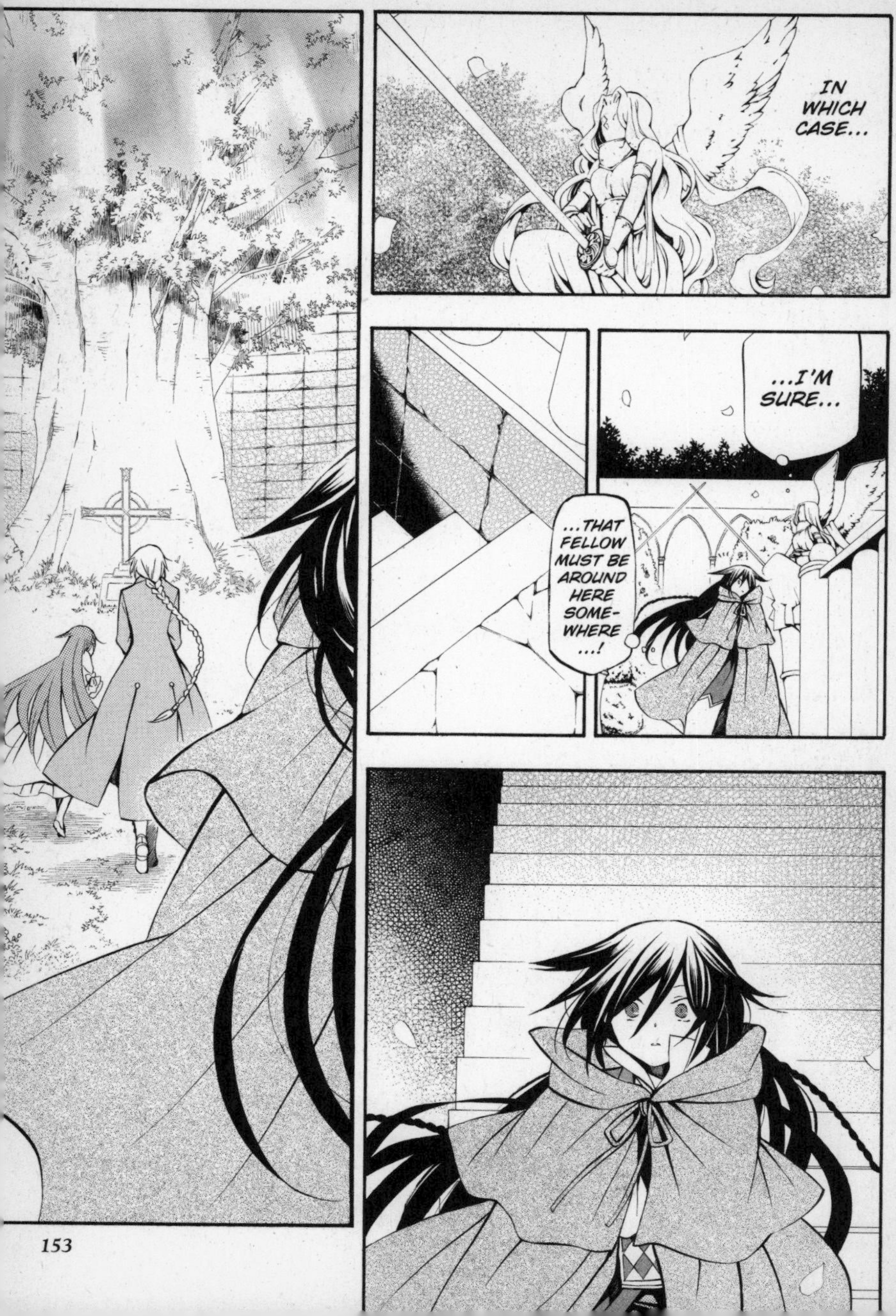
IN WHICH CASE...
...I'M SURE...
...THAT FELLOW MUST BE AROUND HERE SOME-WHERE ...!

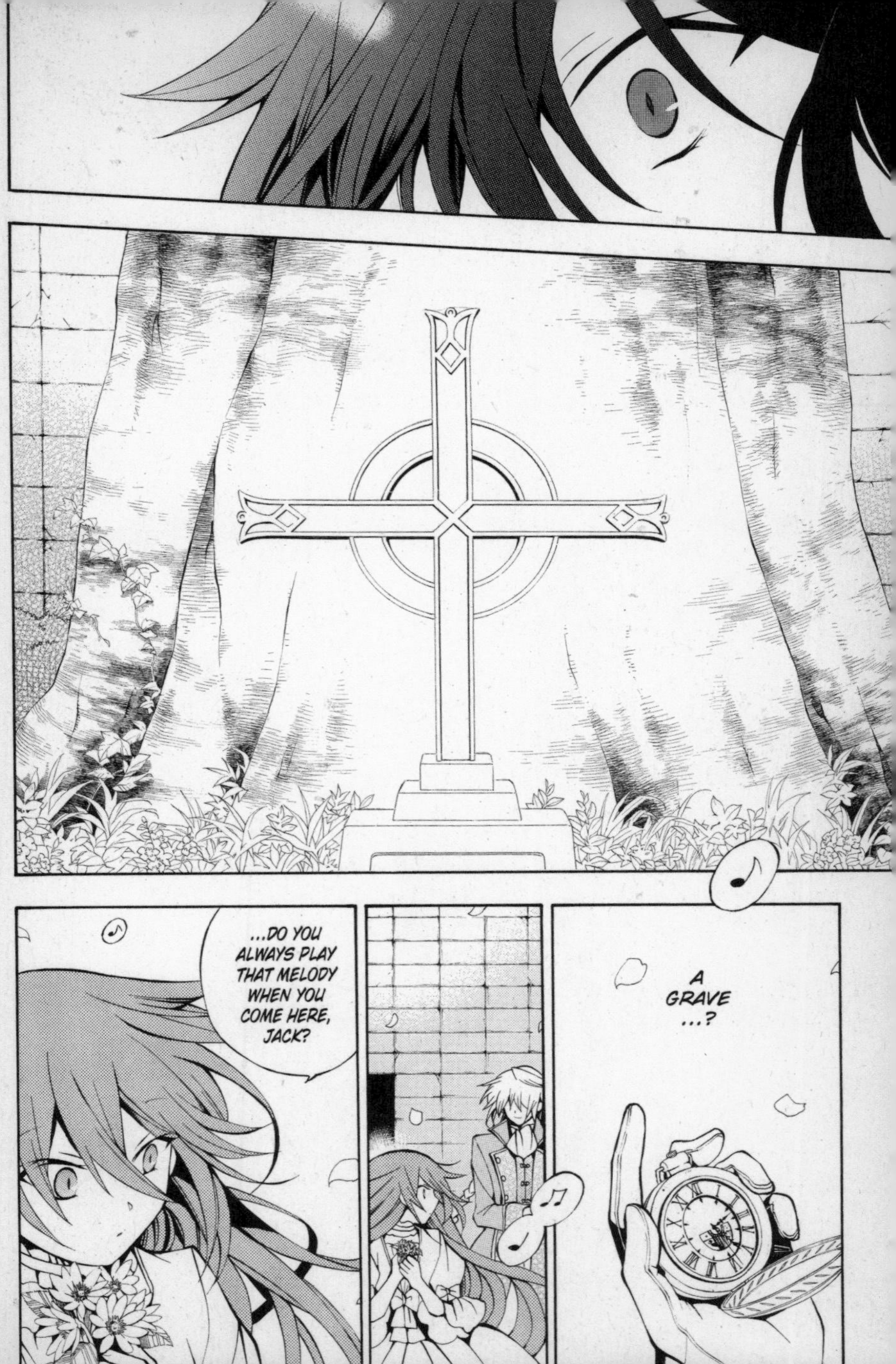
A GRAVE ...?
...DO YOU ALWAYS PLAY THAT MELODY WHEN YOU COME HERE, JACK?

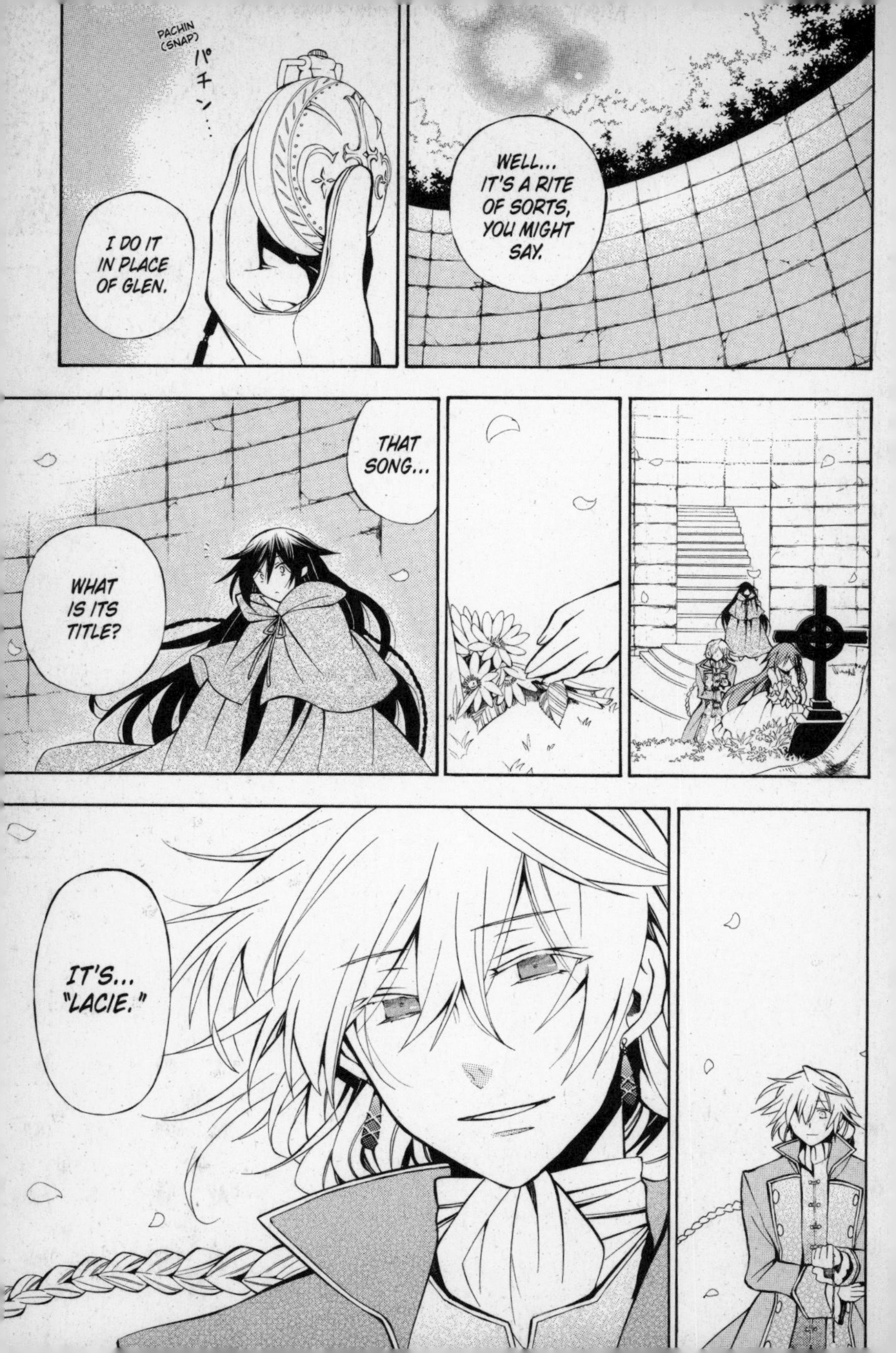
WELL... IT'S A RITE OF SORTS, YOU MIGHT SAY.
PACHIN (SNAP)
パチン…
I DO IT IN PLACE OF GLEN.
THAT SONG...
WHAT IS ITS TITLE?
IT'S... "LACIE."

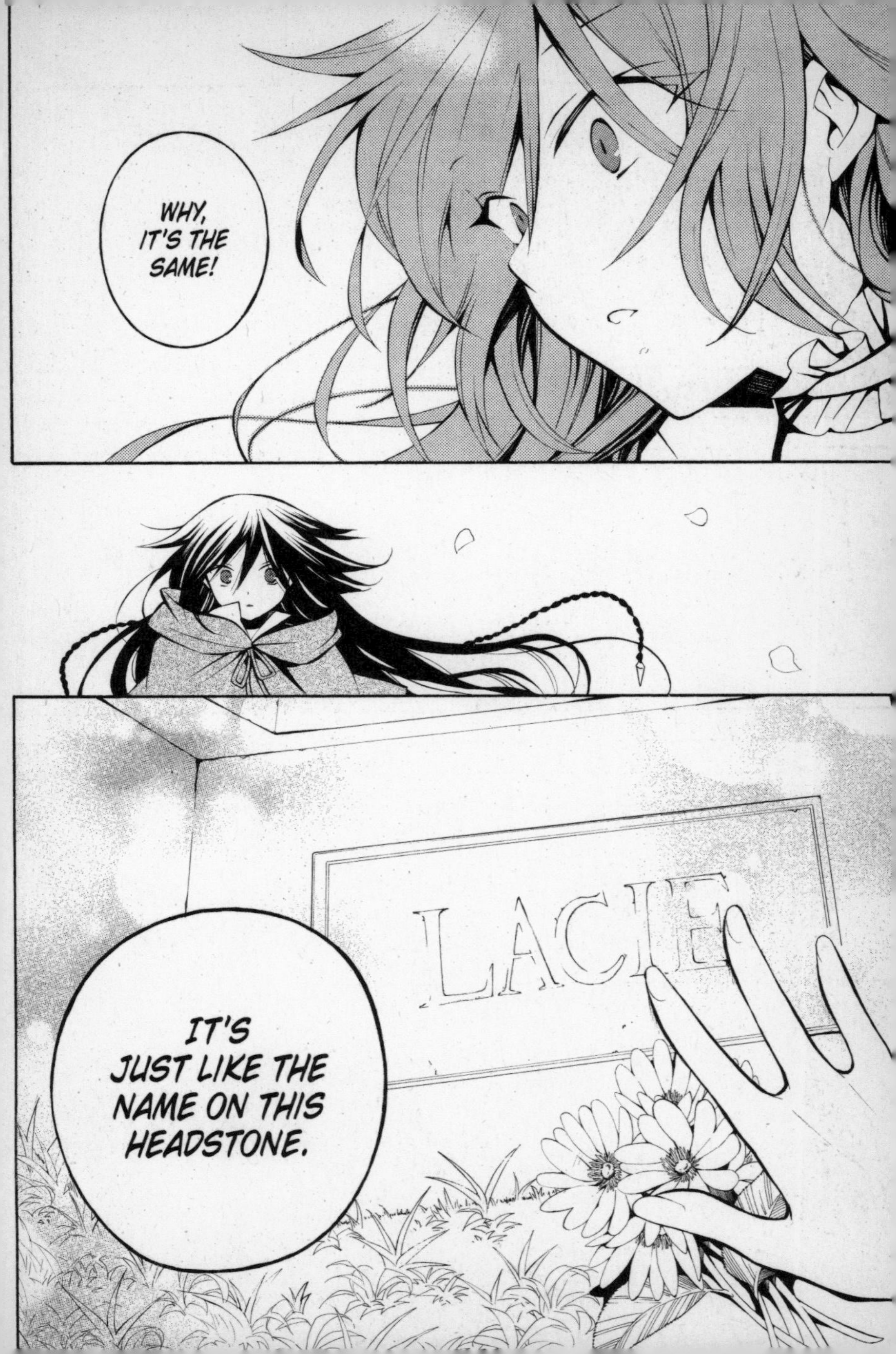
WHY, IT'S THE SAME!
LACIE
IT'S JUST LIKE THE NAME ON THIS HEADSTONE.

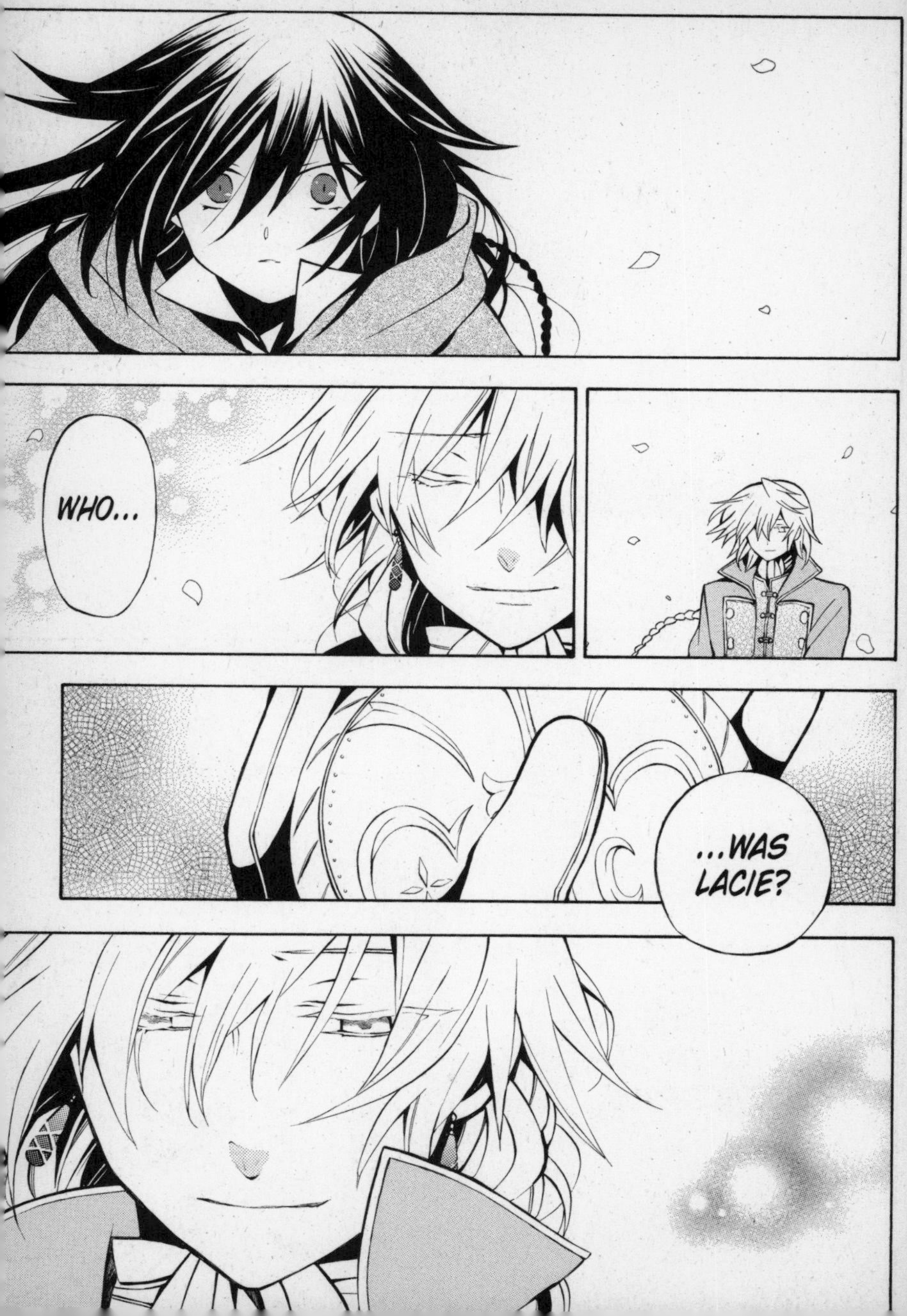
WHO...
...WAS LACIE?

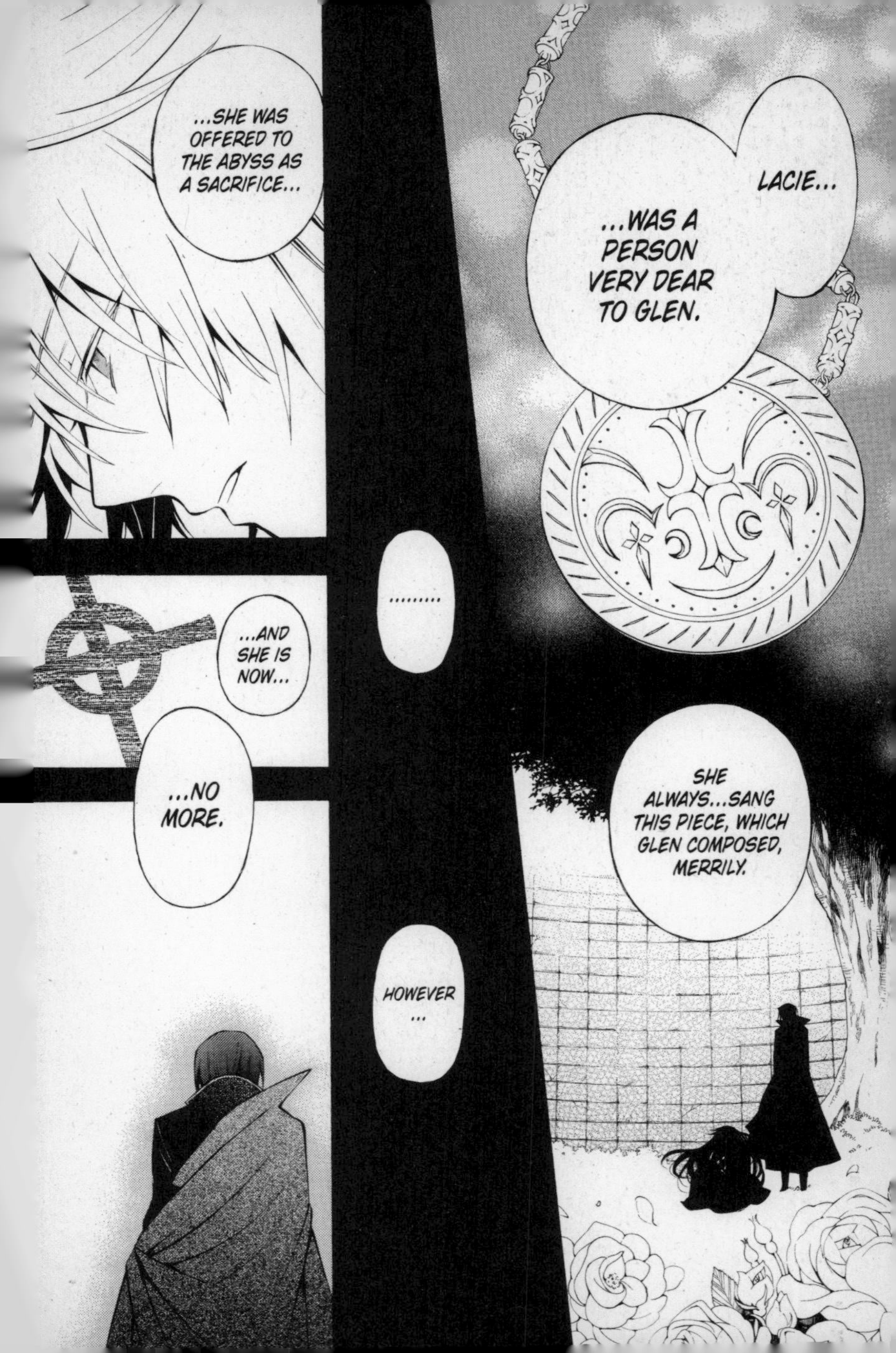
LACIE...
...WAS A PERSON VERY DEAR TO GLEN.
SHE ALWAYS...SANG THIS PIECE, WHICH GLEN COMPOSED, MERRILY.
....
HOWEVER ...
...SHE WAS OFFERED TO THE ABYSS AS A SACRIFICE...
...AND SHE IS NOW...
...NO MORE.

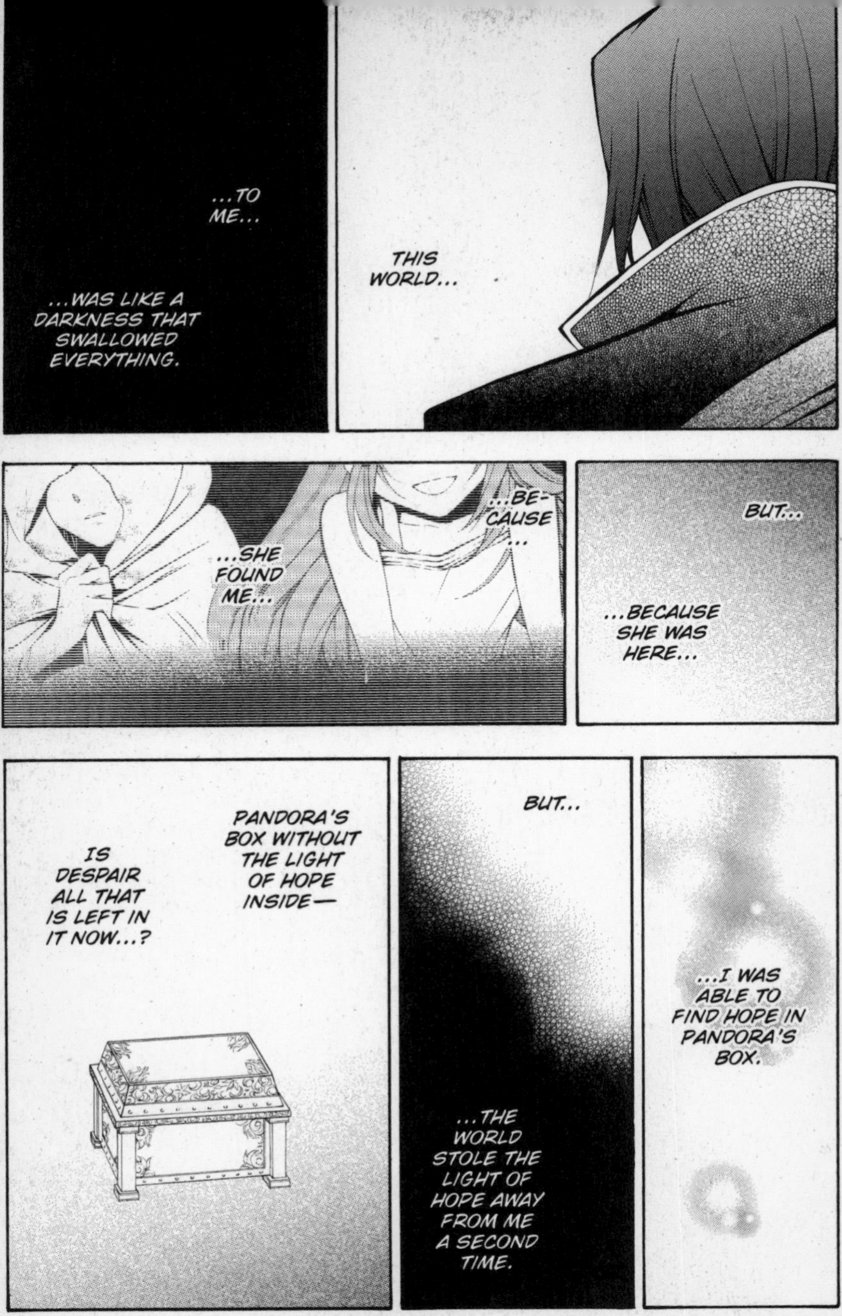
THIS WORLD...
...TO ME...
...WAS LIKE A DARKNESS THAT SWALLOWED EVERYTHING.
BUT...
...BECAUSE SHE WAS HERE...
...BE-CAUSE...
...SHE FOUND ME...
...I WAS ABLE TO FIND HOPE IN PANDORA'S BOX.
BUT...
...THE WORLD STOLE THE LIGHT OF HOPE AWAY FROM ME A SECOND TIME.
PANDORA'S BOX WITHOUT THE LIGHT OF HOPE INSIDE—
IS DESPAIR ALL THAT IS LEFT IN IT NOW...?

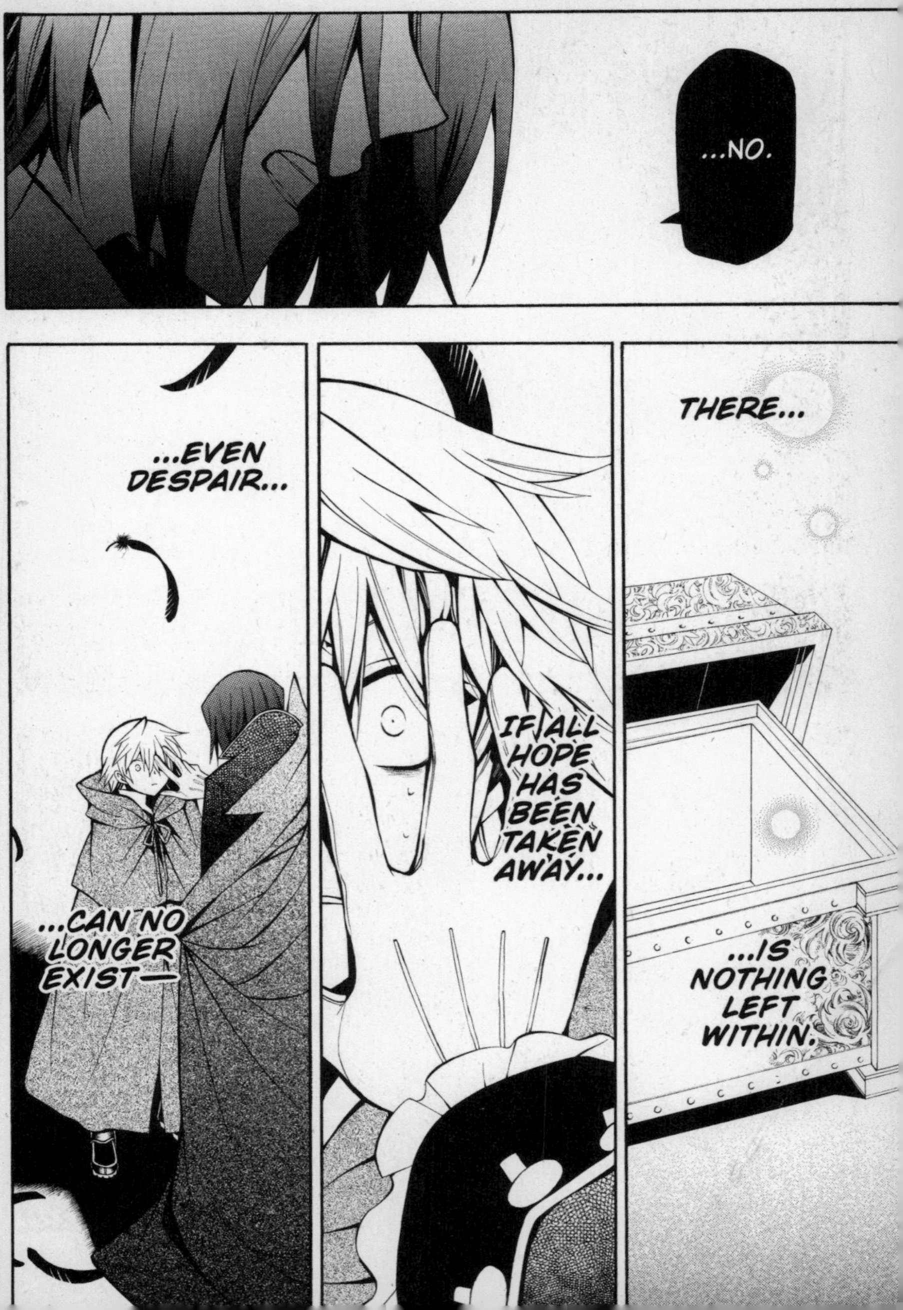
...NO.
THERE...
...IS NOTHING LEFT WITHIN.
IF ALL HOPE HAS BEEN TAKEN AWAY...
...EVEN DESPAIR...
...CAN NO LONGER EXIST—

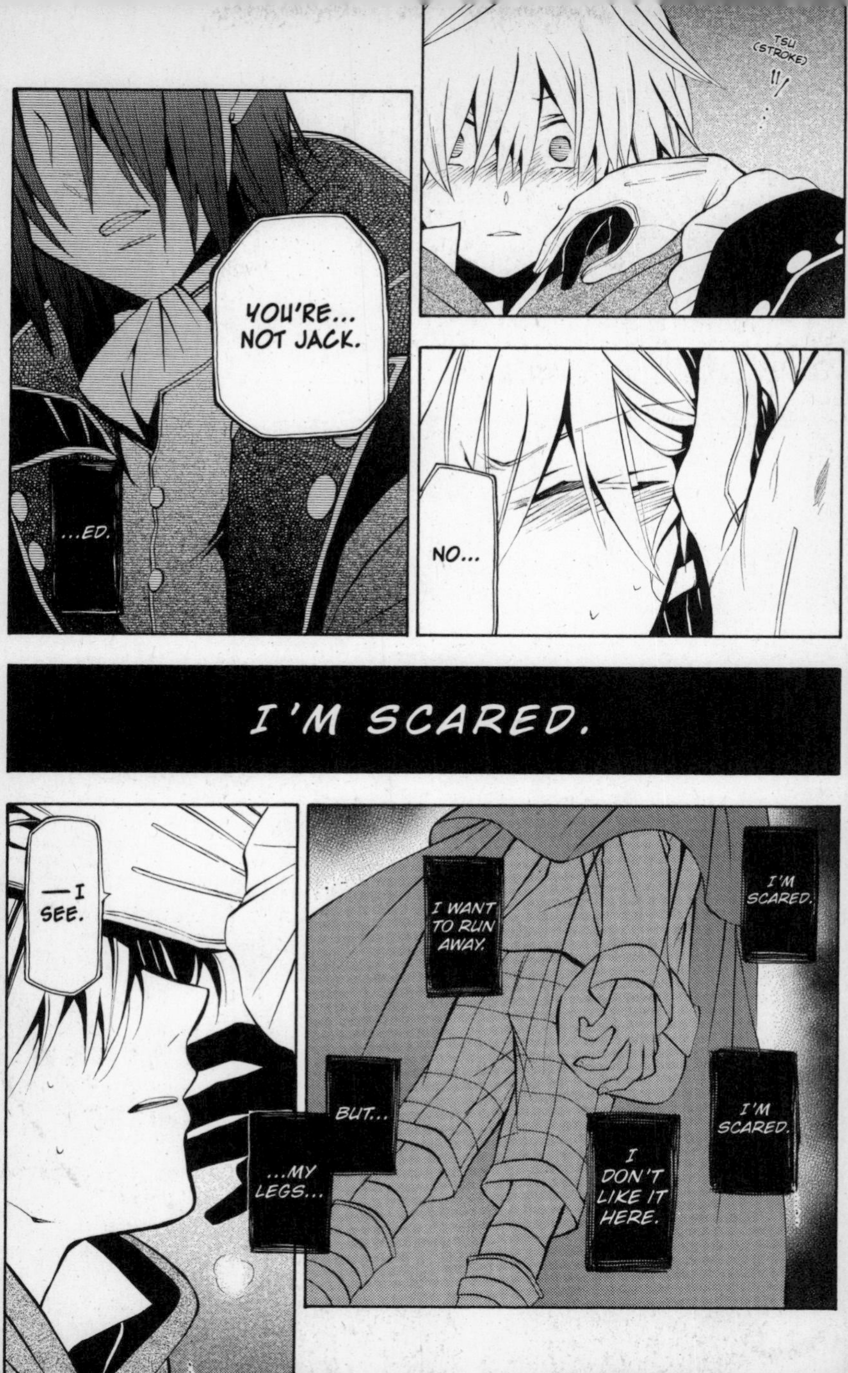
TSU (STROKE)
NO...
YOU'RE... NOT JACK.
...ED.
I'M SCARED.
I'M SCARED.
I WANT TO RUN AWAY.
I'M SCARED.
I DON'T LIKE IT HERE.
BUT...
...MY LEGS...
—I SEE.

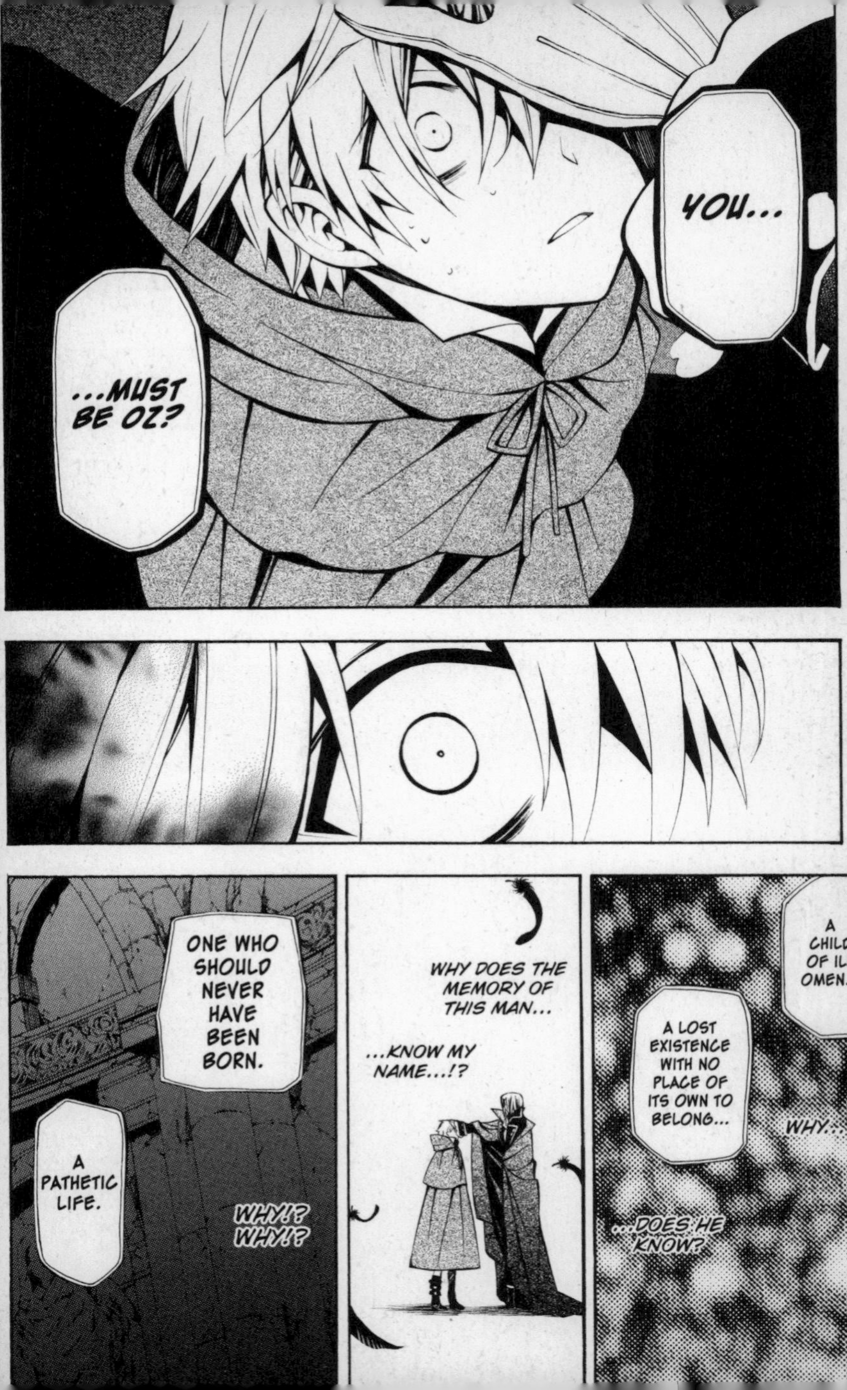
YOU...
...MUST BE OZ?
A CHILD OF ILL OMEN...
A LOST EXISTENCE WITH NO PLACE OF ITS OWN TO BELONG...
WHY...
...DOES HE KNOW?
WHY DOES THE MEMORY OF THIS MAN...
...KNOW MY NAME...!?
ONE WHO SHOULD NEVER HAVE BEEN BORN.
WHY!? WHY!?
A PATHETIC LIFE.

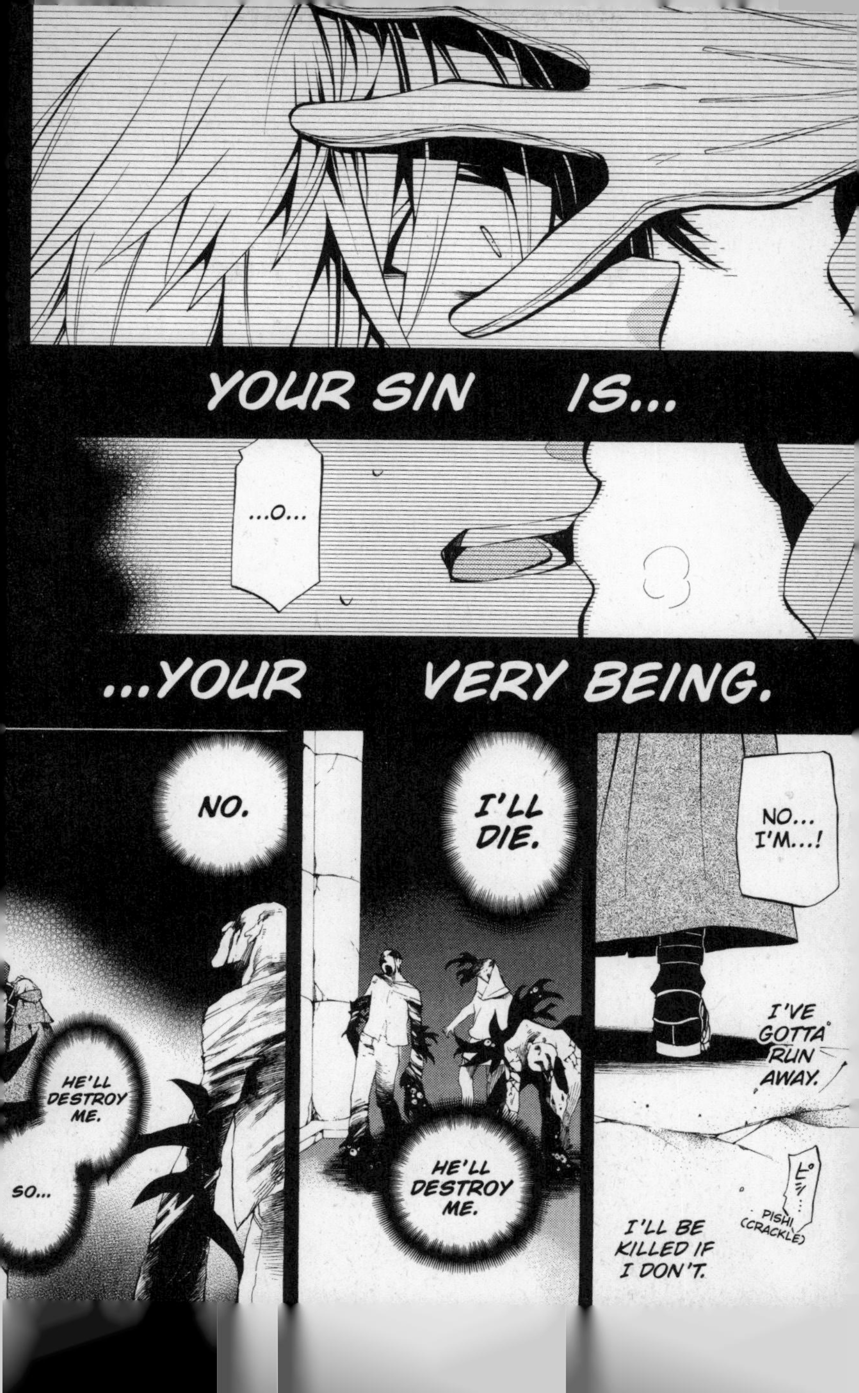
YOUR SIN IS...
...O...
...YOUR VERY BEING.
NO... I'M...!
I'VE GOTTA RUN AWAY.
ピシッ…
PISHI (CRACKLE)
I'LL BE KILLED IF I DON'T.
I'LL DIE.
HE'LL DESTROY ME.
NO.
HE'LL DESTROY ME.
SO...

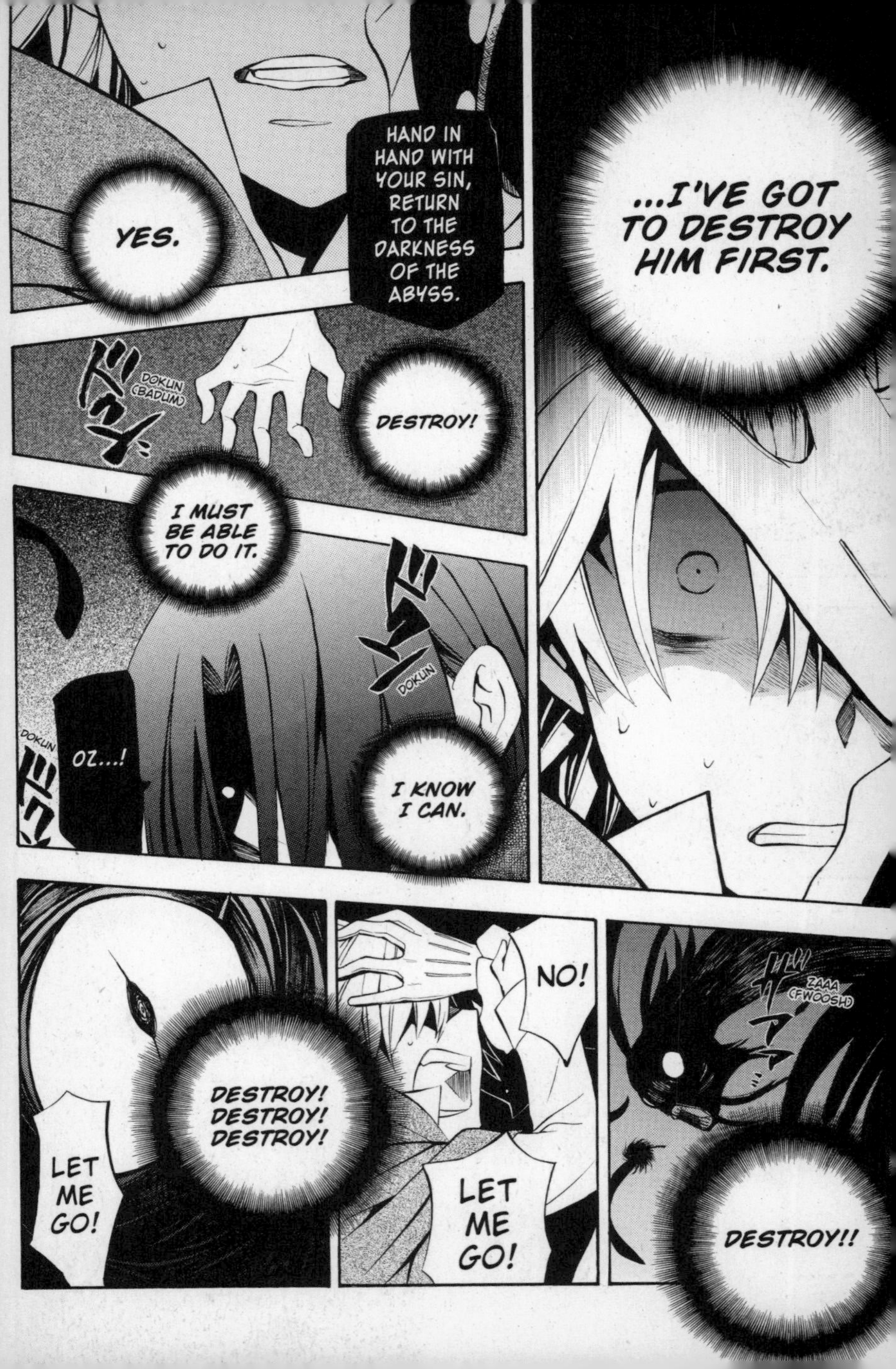
...I'VE GOT TO DESTROY HIM FIRST.
HAND IN HAND WITH YOUR SIN, RETURN TO THE DARKNESS OF THE ABYSS.
YES.
DESTROY!
DOKUN (BADUM)
I MUST BE ABLE TO DO IT.
DOKUN
I KNOW I CAN.
OZ...!
DOKUN
ZAAA (FWOOSH)
DESTROY!!
NO!
LET ME GO!
DESTROY! DESTROY! DESTROY!
LET ME GO!

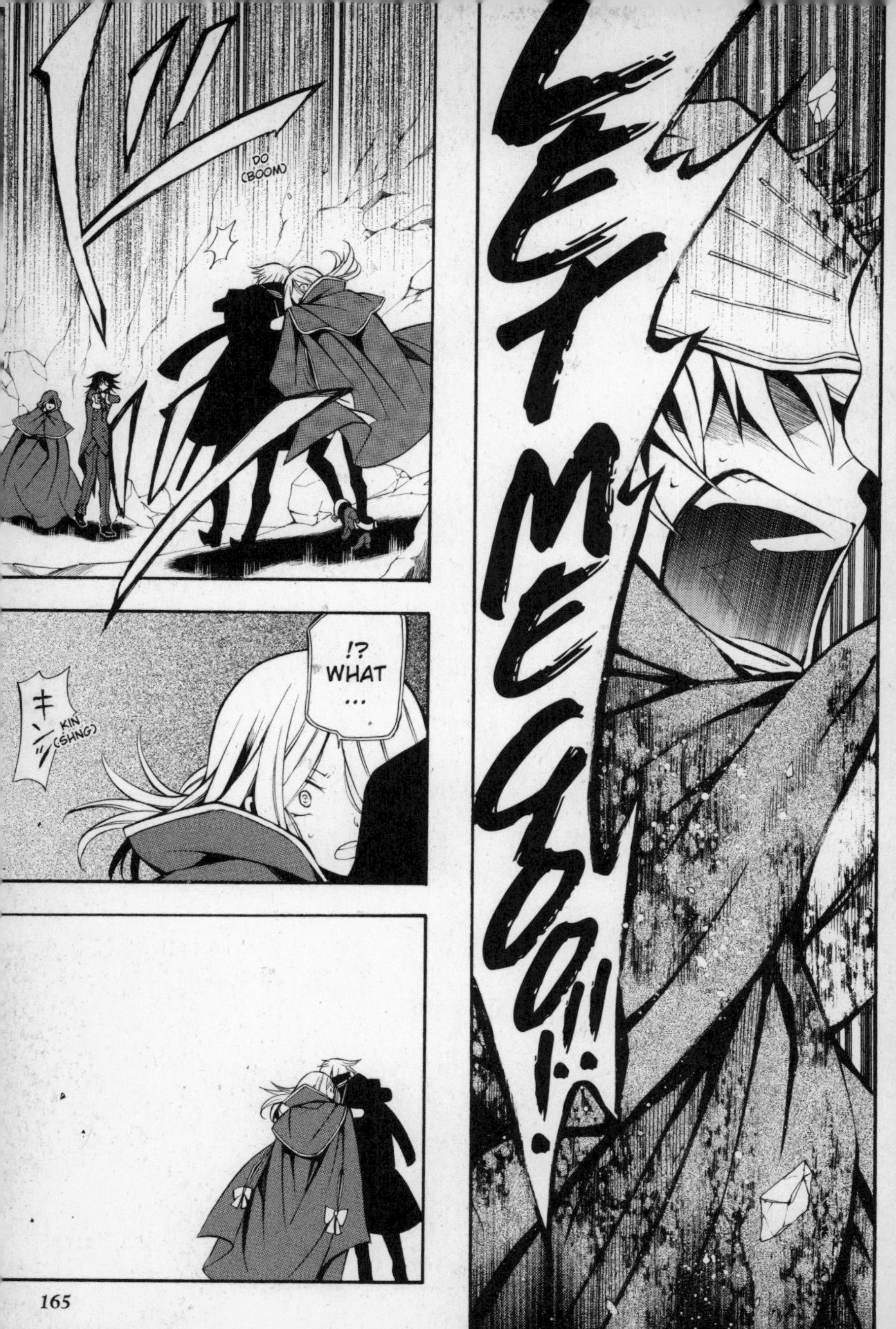
LET ME GO!!!
DO (BOOM)
!? WHAT ...
KIN (SHNG)

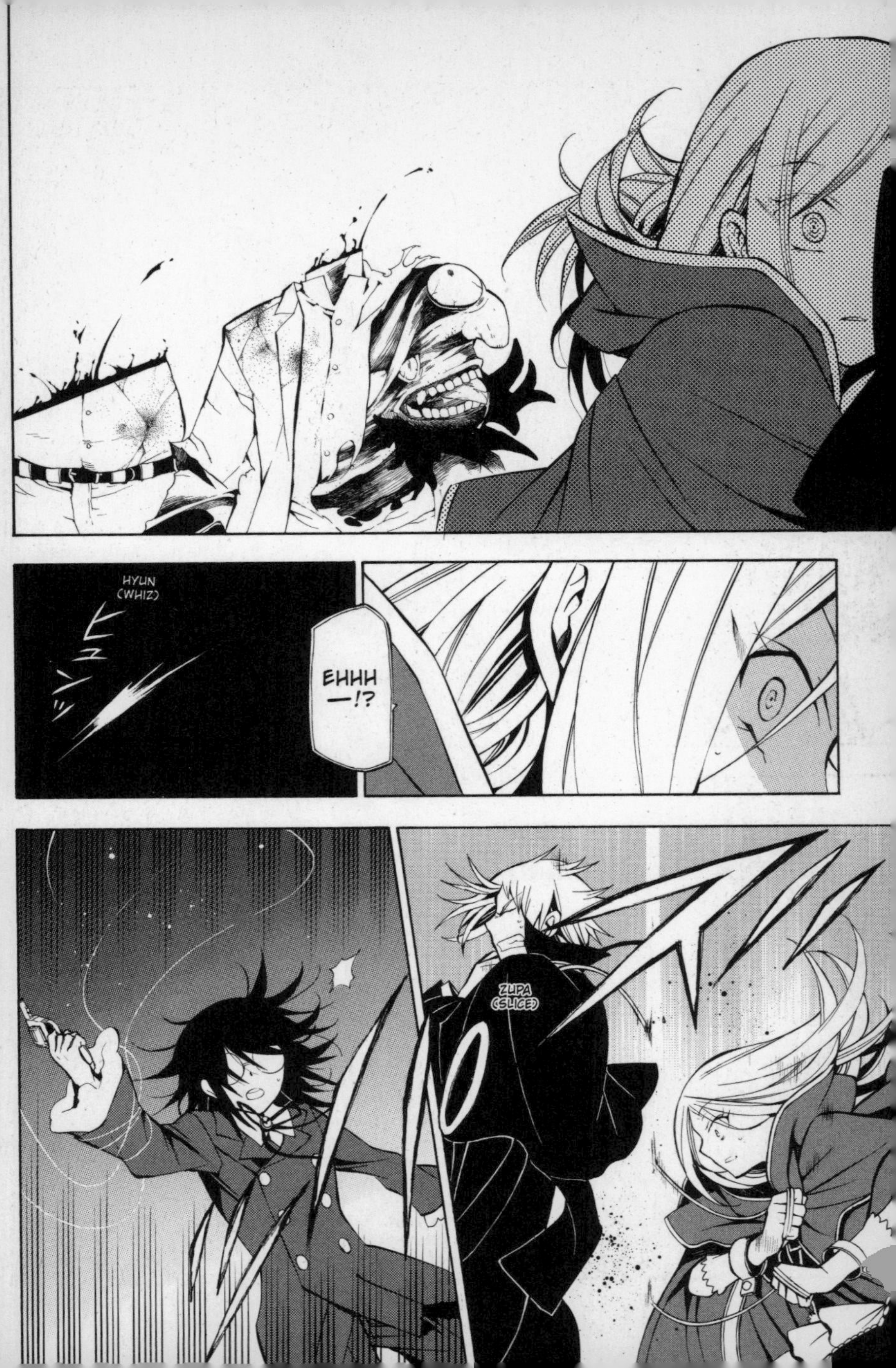
EHHH—!?
HYUN (WHIZ)
ZUPA (SLICE)

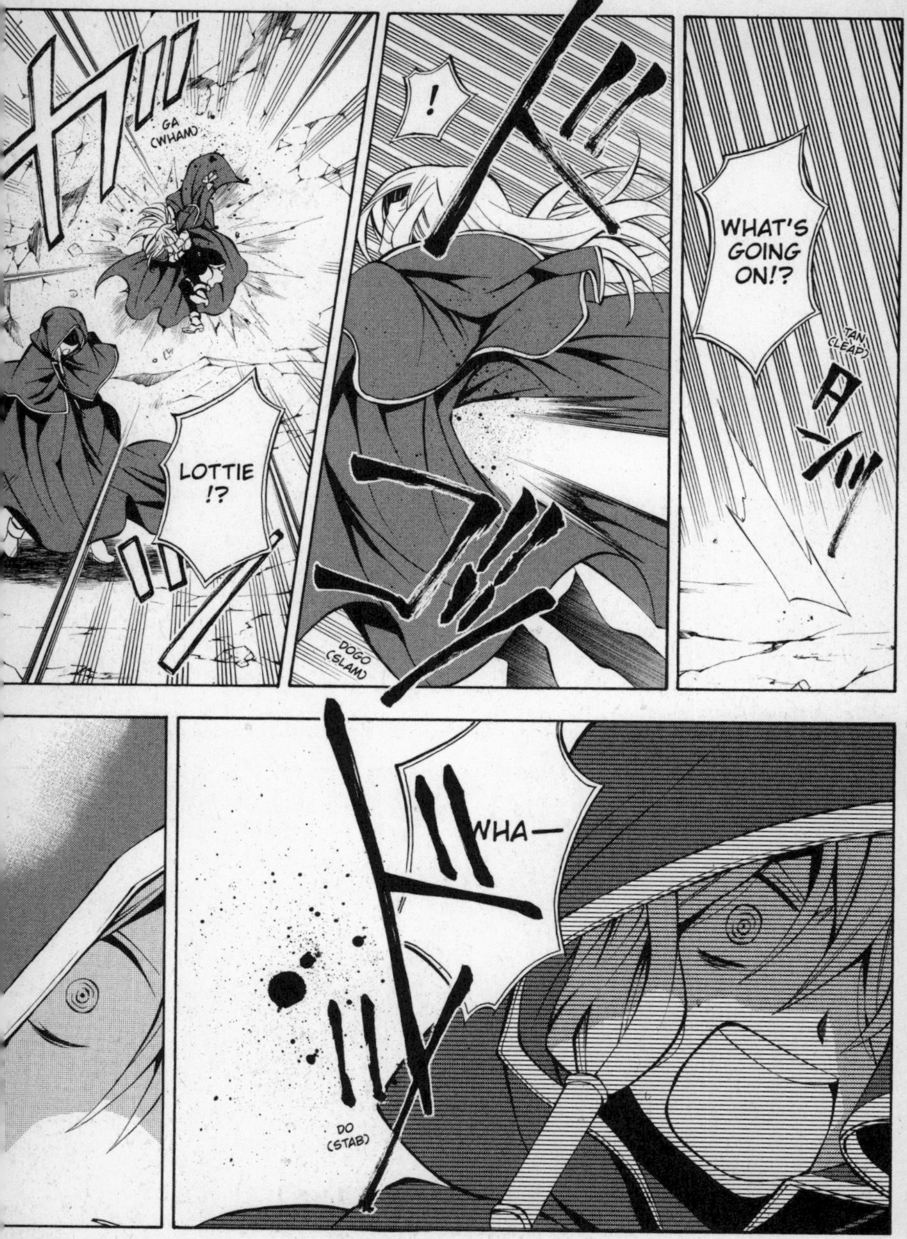
WHAT'S GOING ON!?
TAN (LEAP)
!
DOGO (SLAM)
GA (WHAM)
LOTTIE !?
WHA—
DO (STAB)

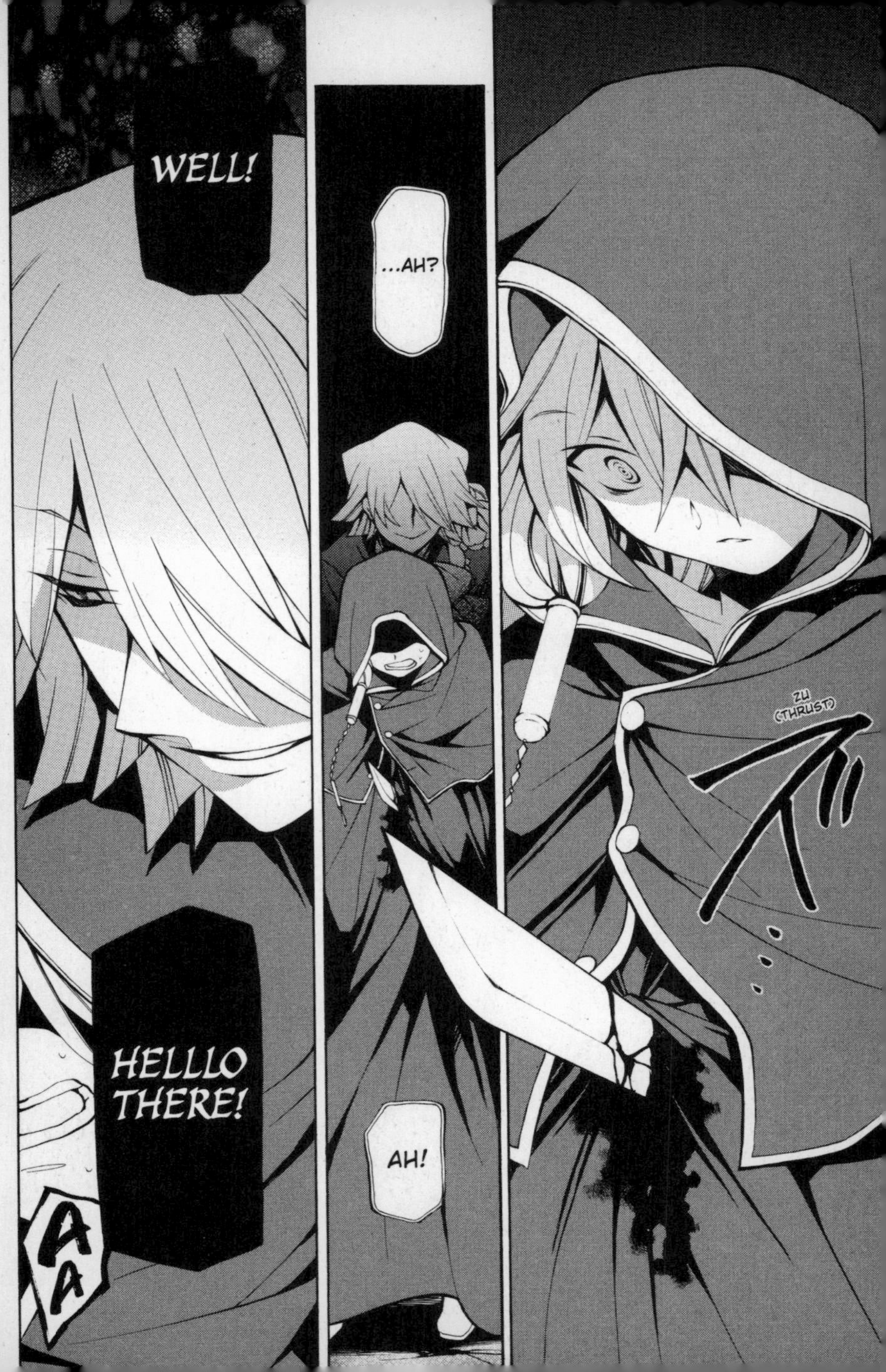
ZU (THRUST)
...AH?
AH!
WELL!
HELLLO THERE!
AA

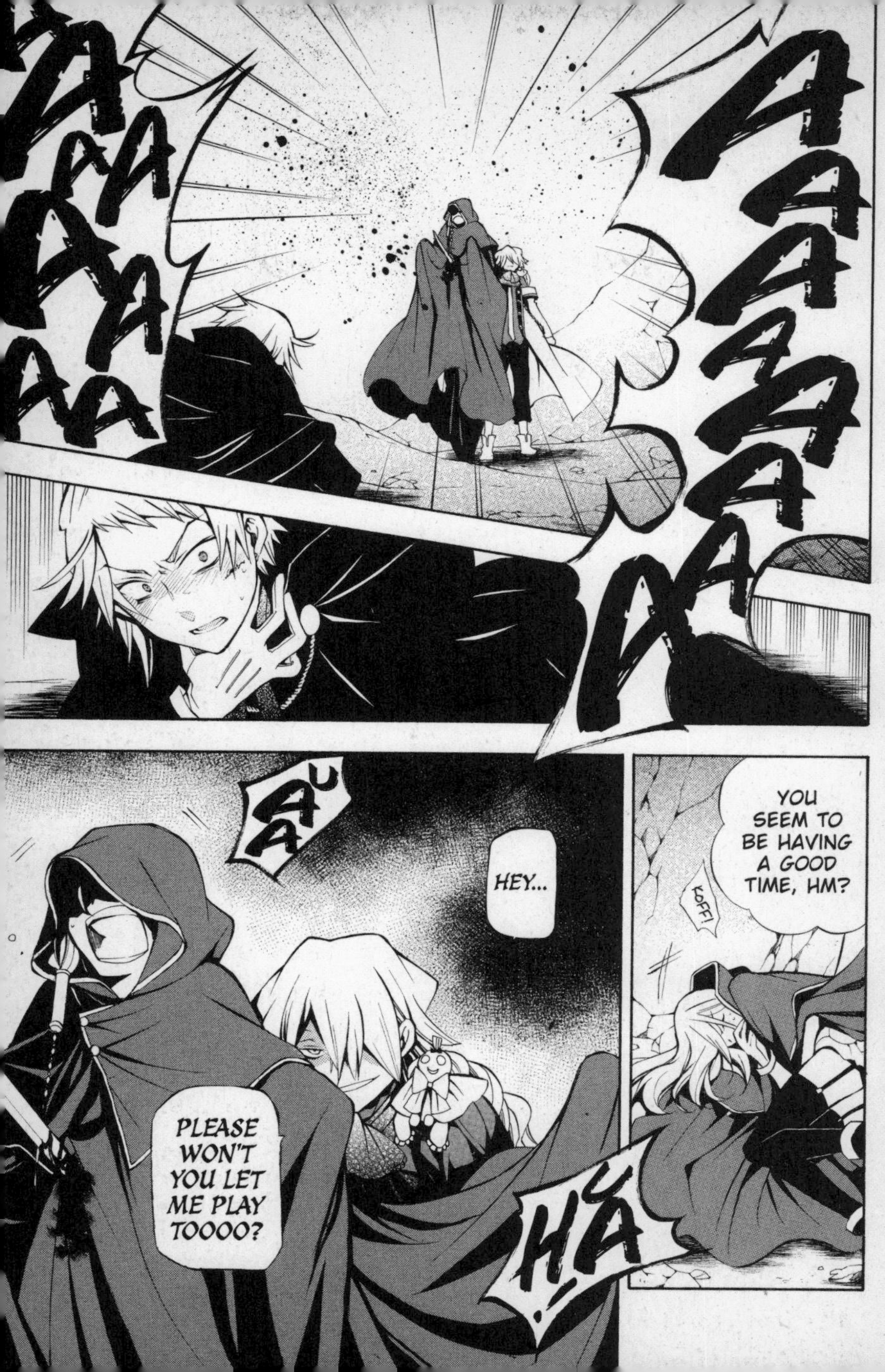
AAAAAAAAA
AAAAAA
YOU SEEM TO BE HAVING A GOOD TIME, HM?
KOFF!
AAU
HEY...
PLEASE WON'T YOU LET ME PLAY TOOOO?
HAU

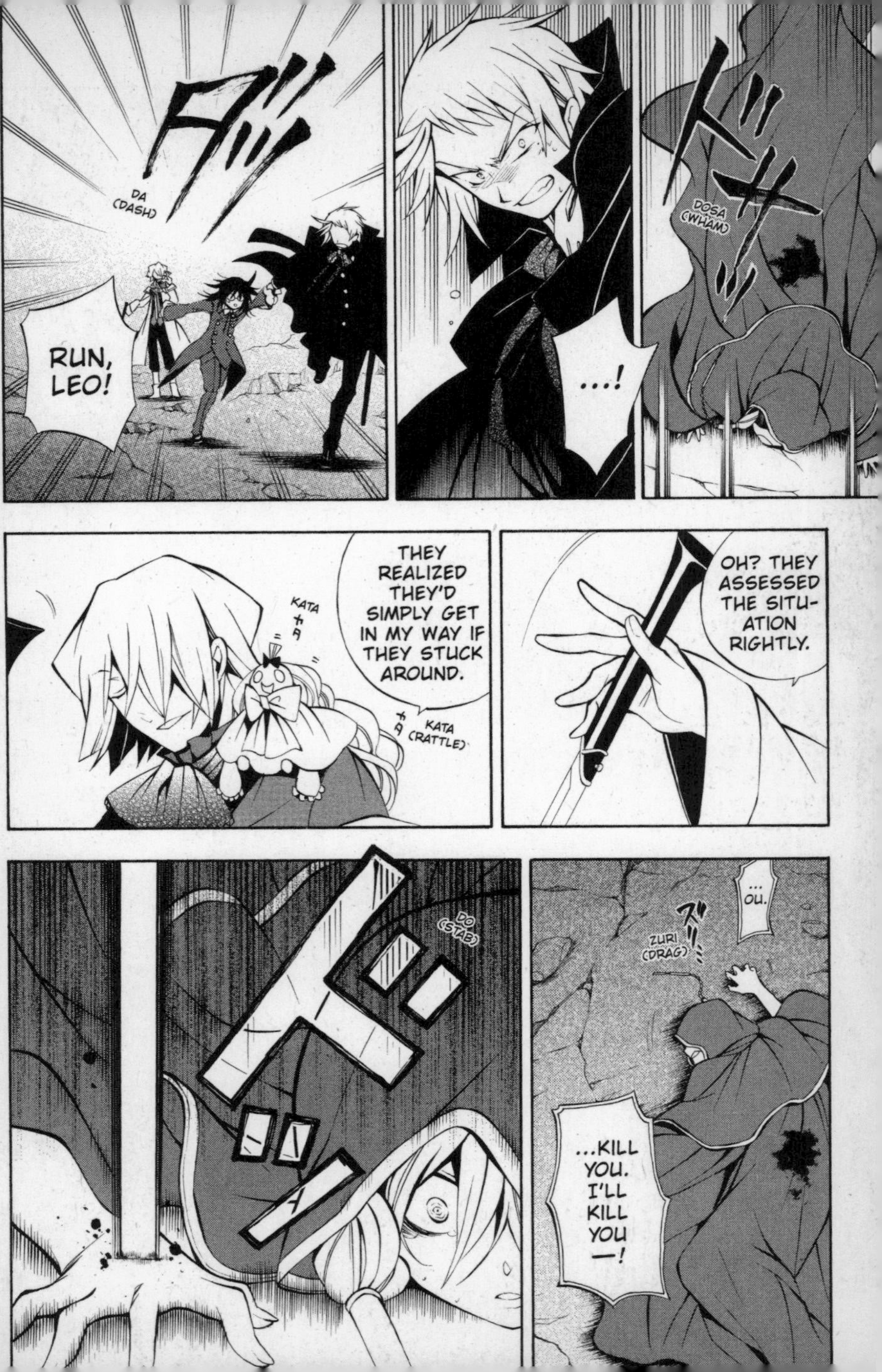
DOSA
(WHAM)
...!
DA
(DASH)
RUN, LEO!
OH? THEY ASSESSED THE SITU-ATION RIGHTLY.
THEY REALIZED THEY'D SIMPLY GET IN MY WAY IF THEY STUCK AROUND.
KATA
KATA
(RATTLE)
... OU.
ZURI
(DRAG)
...KILL YOU. I'LL KILL YOU—!
DO
(STAB)

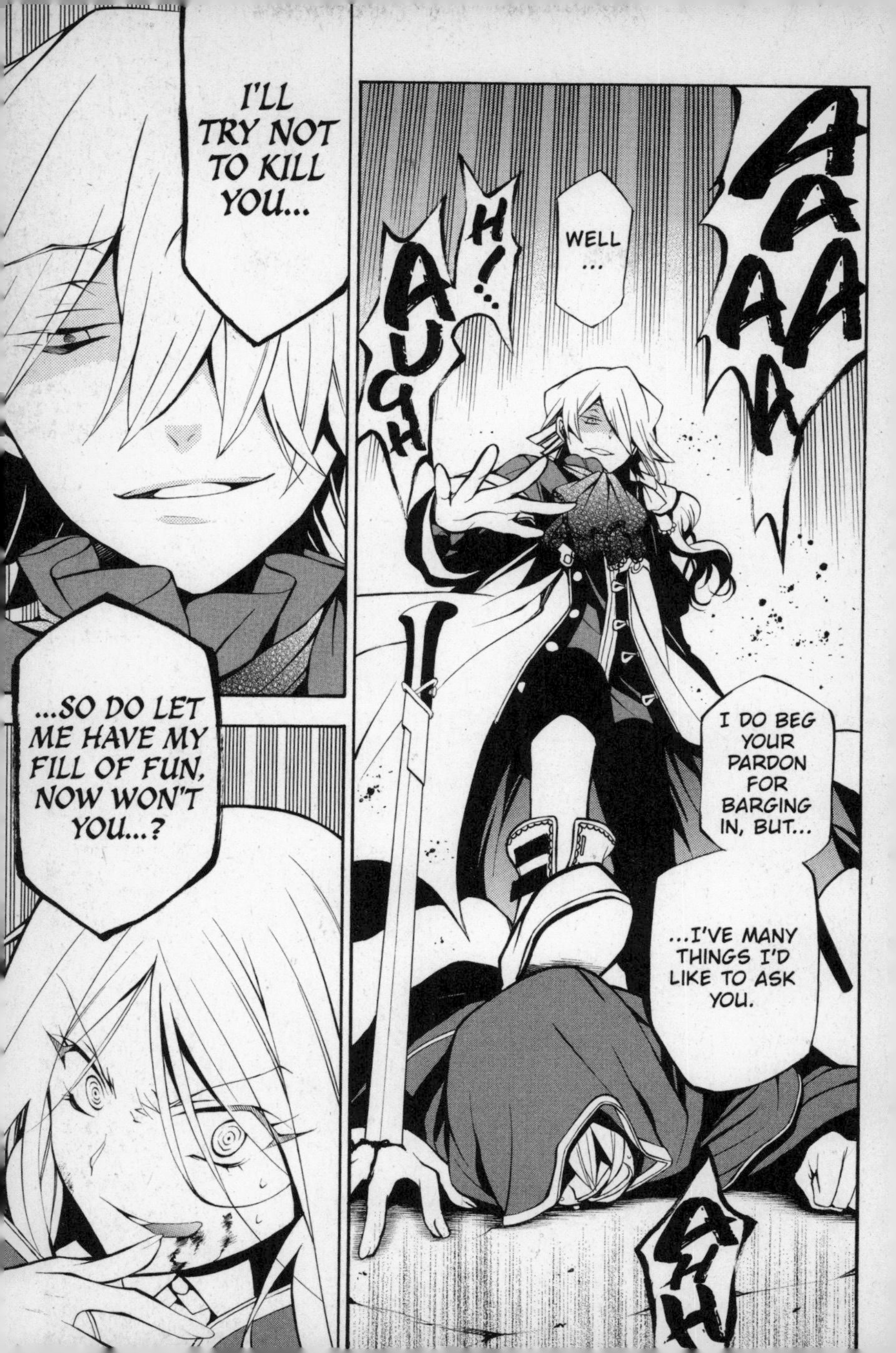
AAAAAA
WELL ...
H!...
AUGH
I DO BEG YOUR PARDON FOR BARGING IN, BUT...
...I'VE MANY THINGS I'D LIKE TO ASK YOU.
AHH
I'LL TRY NOT TO KILL YOU...
...SO DO LET ME HAVE MY FILL OF FUN, NOW WON'T YOU...?

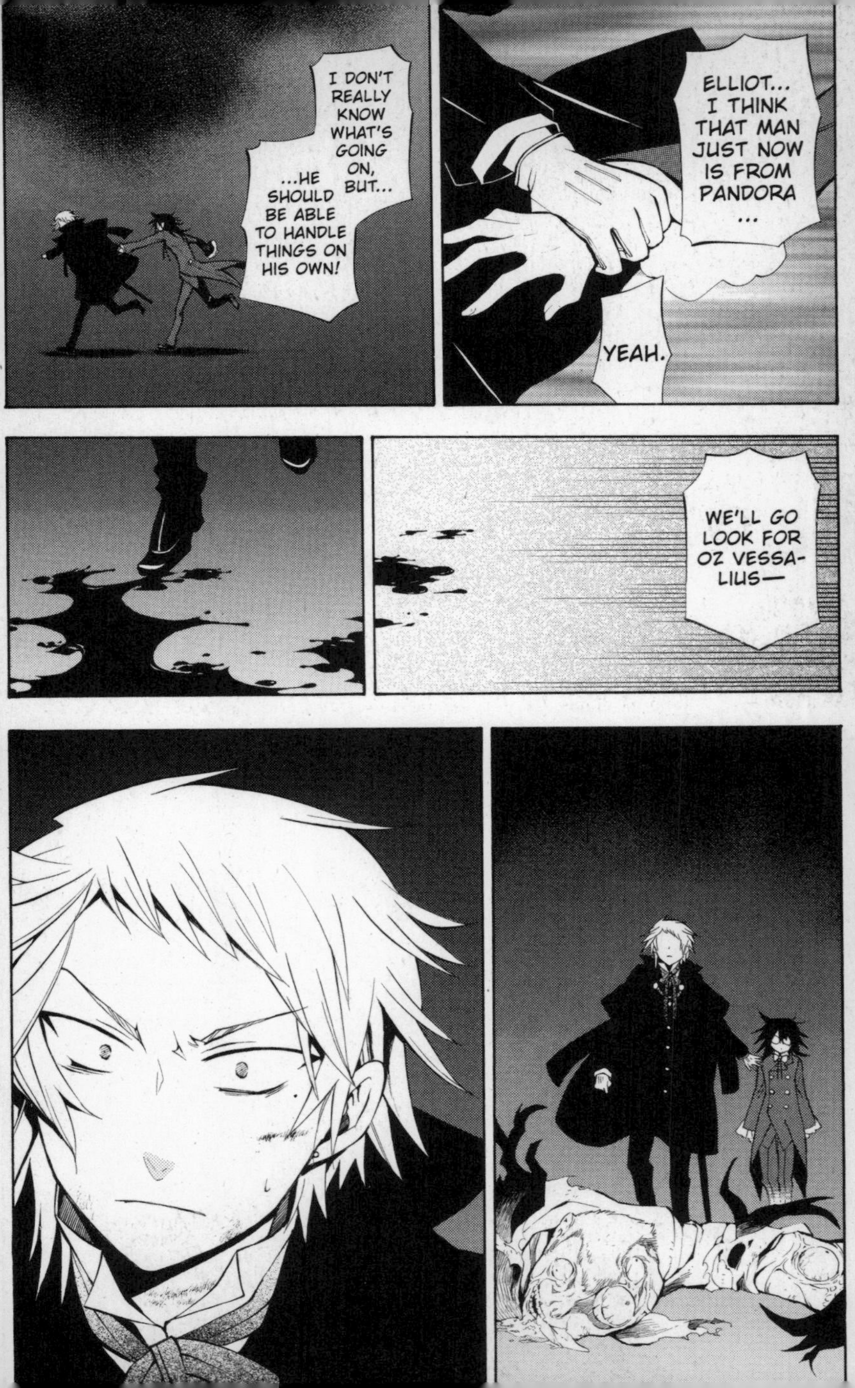
ELLIOT... I THINK THAT MAN JUST NOW IS FROM PANDORA ...
YEAH.
I DON'T REALLY KNOW WHAT'S GOING ON, BUT...
...HE SHOULD BE ABLE TO HANDLE THINGS ON HIS OWN!
WE'LL GO LOOK FOR OZ VESSA-LIUS—

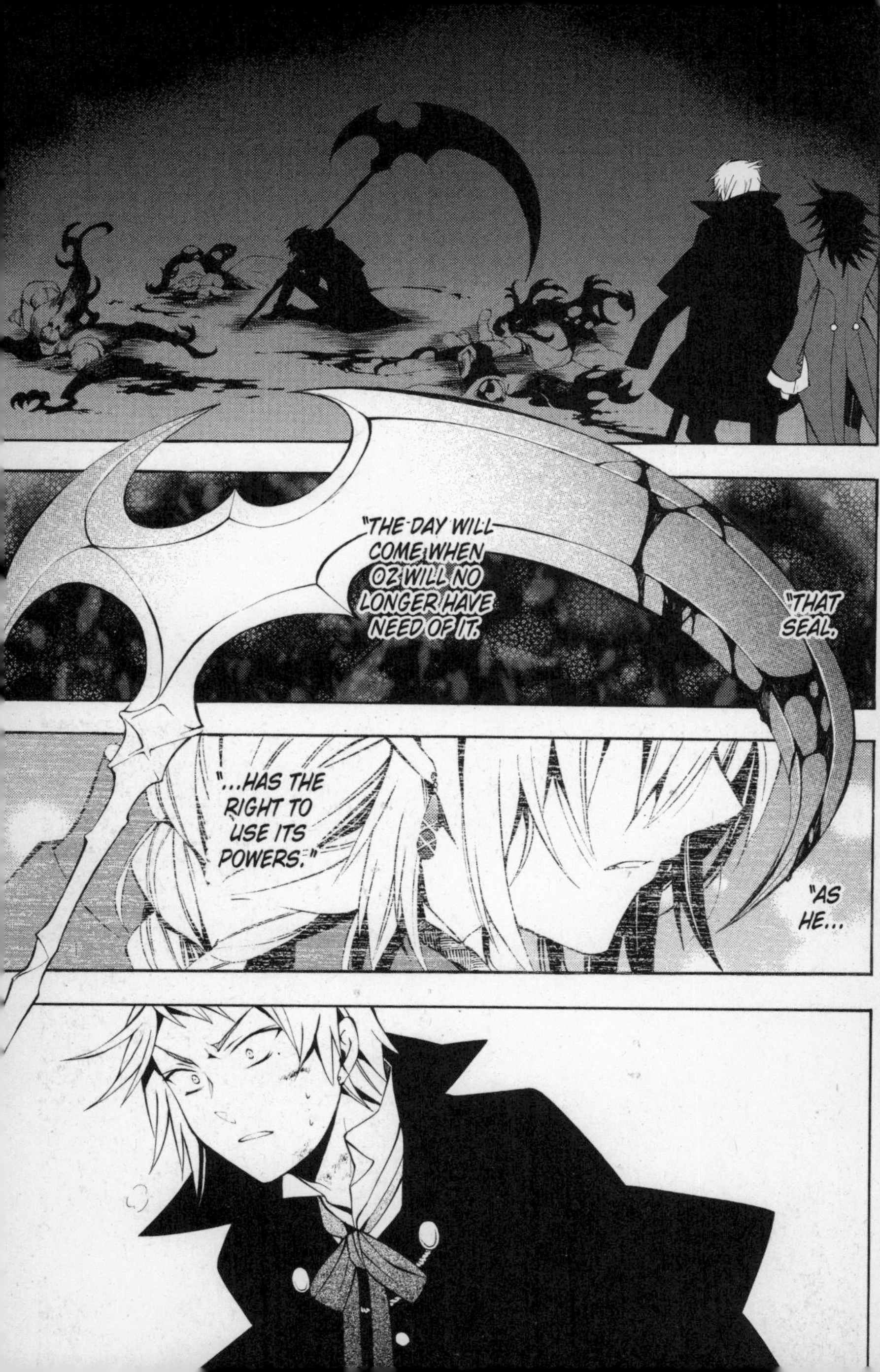
"THAT SEAL.
"THE DAY WILL COME WHEN OZ WILL NO LONGER HAVE NEED OF IT.
"AS HE...
"...HAS THE RIGHT TO USE ITS POWERS."

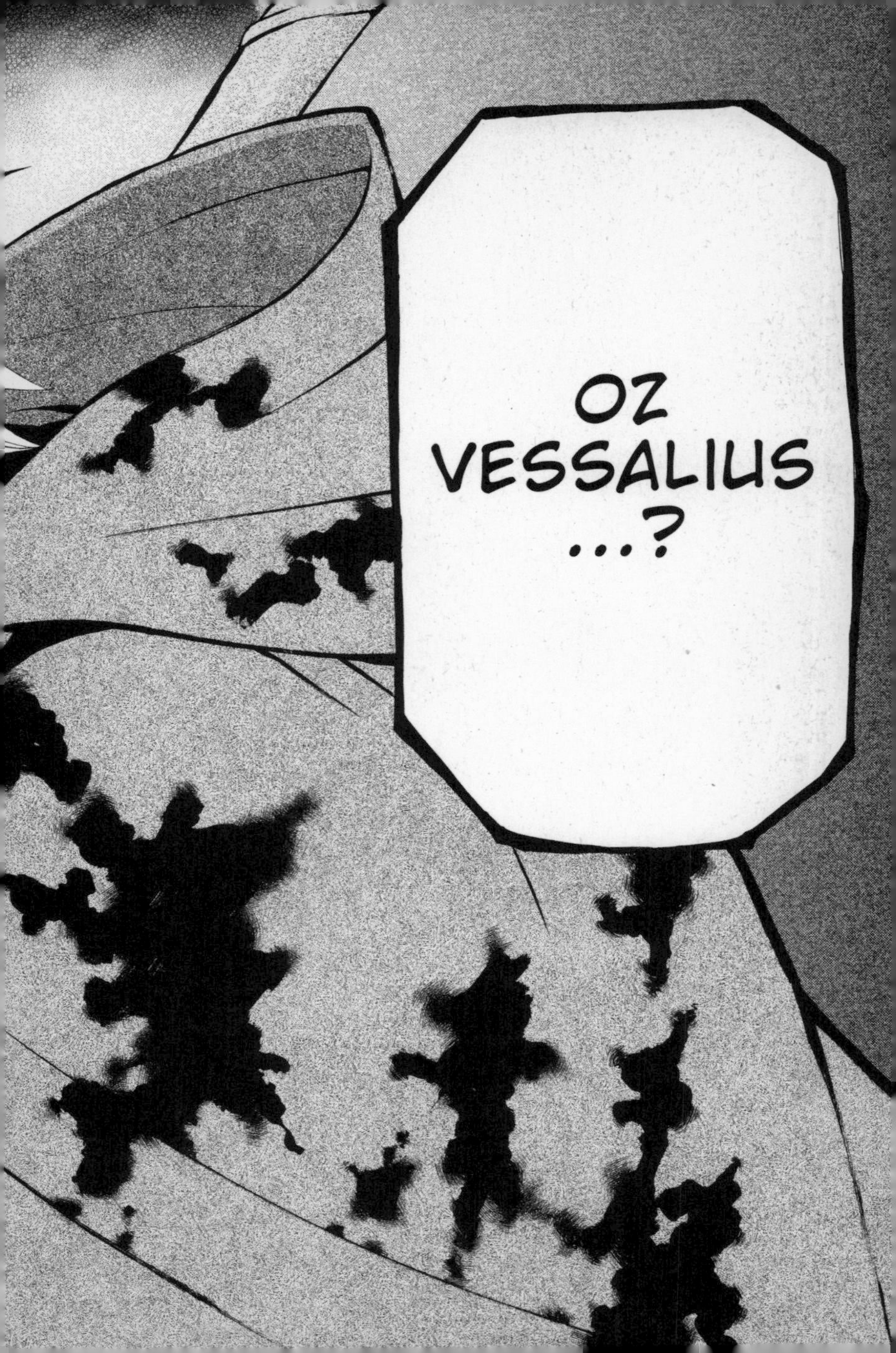
OZ VESSALIUS ...?

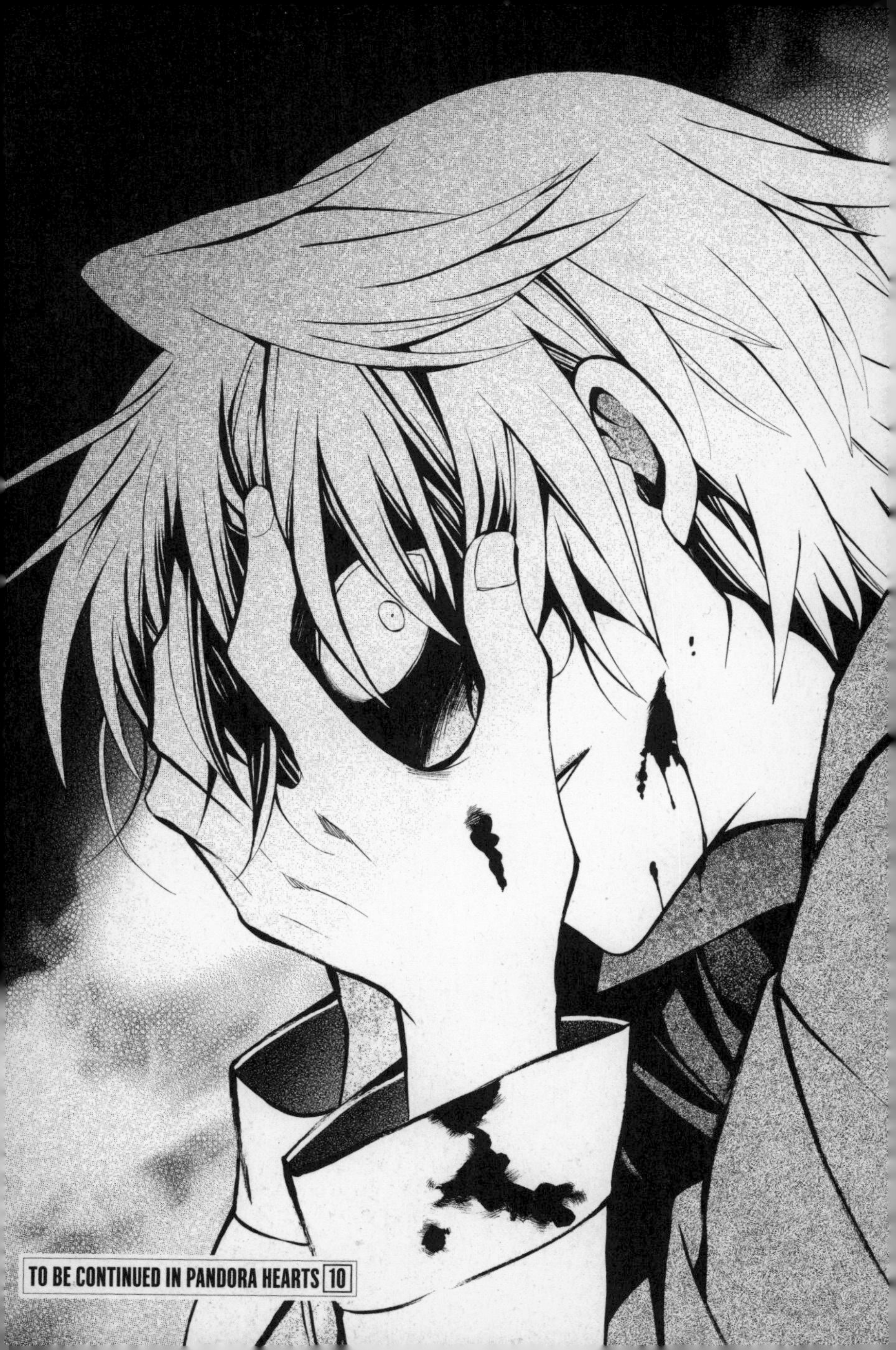
TO BE CONTINUED IN PANDORA HEARTS 10

BONUS: "OOH...MY DEAR HARISEN WOMAN"

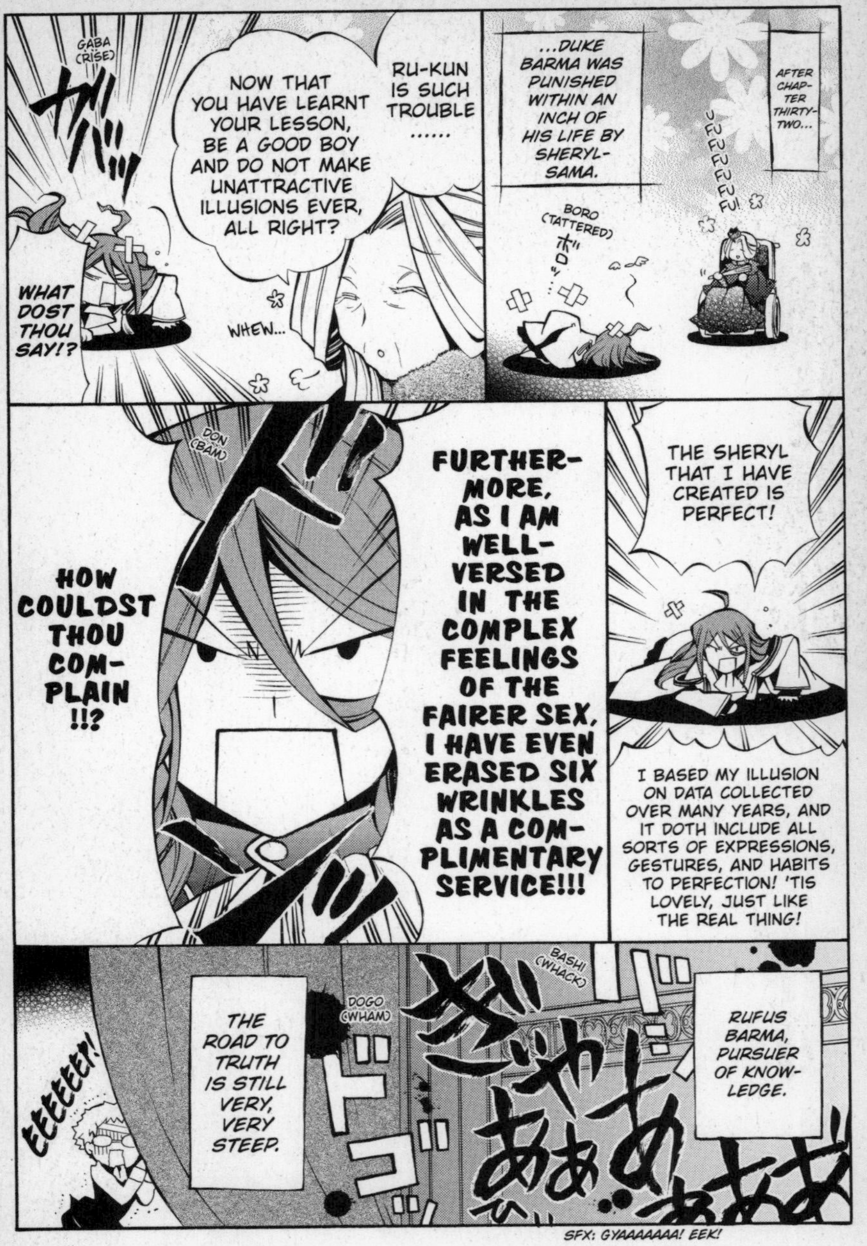
AFTER CHAPTER THIRTY-TWO...
...DUKE BARMA WAS PUNISHED WITHIN AN INCH OF HIS LIFE BY SHERYL-SAMA.
U FU FU FU FU FU FU!
BORO (TATTERED)
RU-KUN IS SUCH TROUBLE......
NOW THAT YOU HAVE LEARNT YOUR LESSON, BE A GOOD BOY AND DO NOT MAKE UNATTRACTIVE ILLUSIONS EVER, ALL RIGHT?
WHEW...
GABA (RISE)
WHAT DOST THOU SAY!?
THE SHERYL THAT I HAVE CREATED IS PERFECT!
I BASED MY ILLUSION ON DATA COLLECTED OVER MANY YEARS, AND IT DOTH INCLUDE ALL SORTS OF EXPRESSIONS, GESTURES, AND HABITS TO PERFECTION! 'TIS LOVELY, JUST LIKE THE REAL THING!
FURTHERMORE, AS I AM WELL-VERSED IN THE COMPLEX FEELINGS OF THE FAIRER SEX, I HAVE EVEN ERASED SIX WRINKLES AS A COMPLIMENTARY SERVICE!!!
DON (BAM)
HOW COULDST THOU COMPLAIN!!?
RUFUS BARMA, PURSUER OF KNOWLEDGE.
BASHI (WHACK)
DOGO (WHAM)
THE ROAD TO TRUTH IS STILL VERY, VERY STEEP.
EEEEEEP!

SFX: GYAAAAAAA! EEK!

Special Thanks

FUMITO YAMAZAKI SEIRA MINAMI-SAN

SOUICHIRO-SAN SAEKO TAKIGAWA-SAN

SHUKU ASAOKA-SAN HAI-SAN

YAJI RYOU BIG BROTHER

EKU-SAN AKKII-SAN

SOU MINAZUKI-SAN

YUKINO-SAN

MY EDITOR
TAKEGASA-SAMA!

and You!

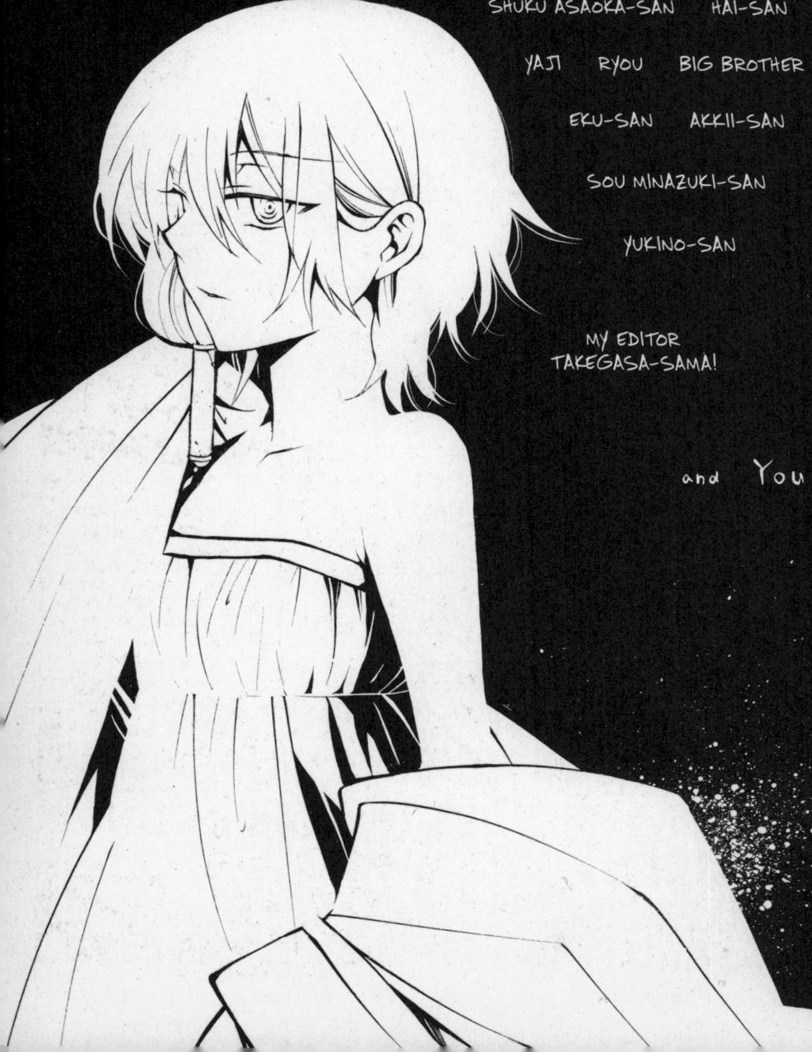

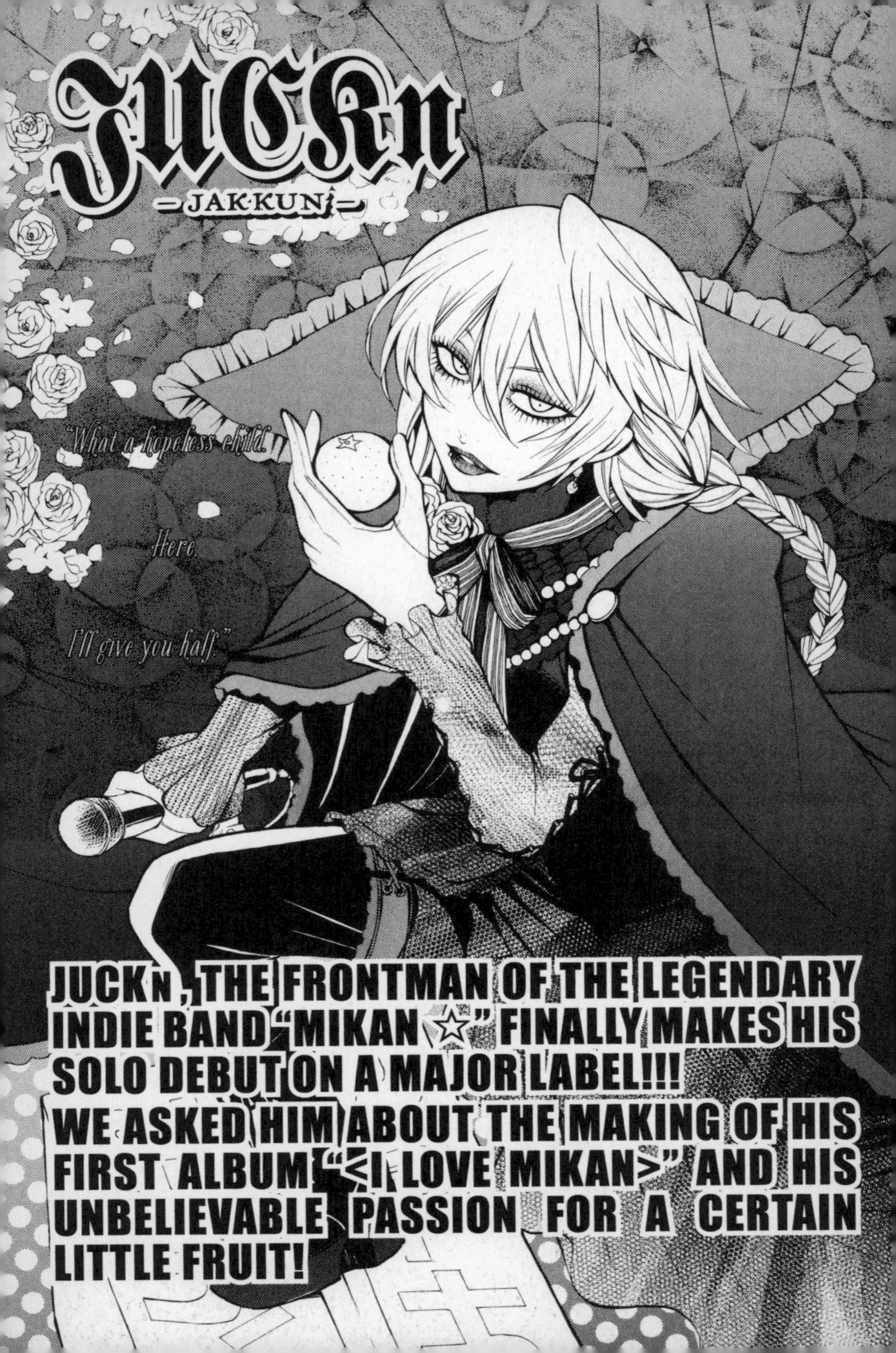
JUCKn
—JAKKUN—
"What a hopeless child.
Here.
I'll give you half."
JUCKn, THE FRONTMAN OF THE LEGENDARY INDIE BAND "MIKAN ☆" FINALLY MAKES HIS SOLO DEBUT ON A MAJOR LABEL!!!
WE ASKED HIM ABOUT THE MAKING OF HIS FIRST ALBUM "<I LOVE MIKAN>" AND HIS UNBELIEVABLE PASSION FOR A CERTAIN LITTLE FRUIT!

"HA-HA-HA. I eat *mikan* every morning, noon, and night. But if I eat too many, my skin might turn the color of *mikan*, so I cry and control myself (*smile*)."

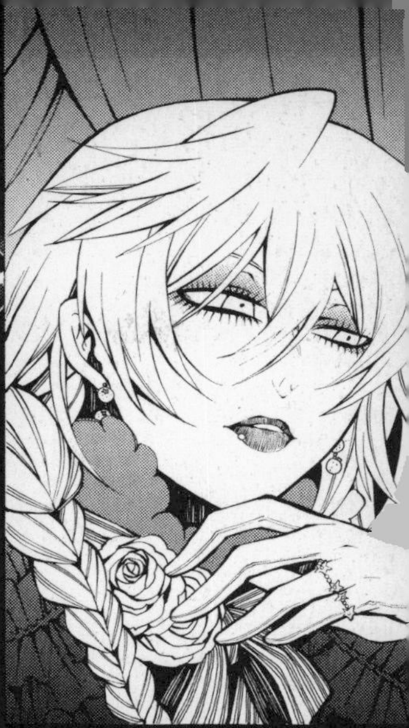

—The name of your previous band and now the title of your new album both contain the word "*mikan*." How did you first encounter *mikan*?

"HA-HA-HA. I first encountered it in a play called "*Pandora Haachu*." My role was to simply sit in a *kotatsu* and say "The mikan's tasty!", but the moment I took that small, round beauty in my hand, my heart was stolen by its texture, form, color, perfume......everything about the existence known as the *mikan* captured my heart."

—So you fell in love with it (*smile*).

"Yes. I felt uneasy about having people around me call me a "hero," but I don't mind being called a "*mikan* hero." Actually, I'd prefer it if folks called me that more often!"

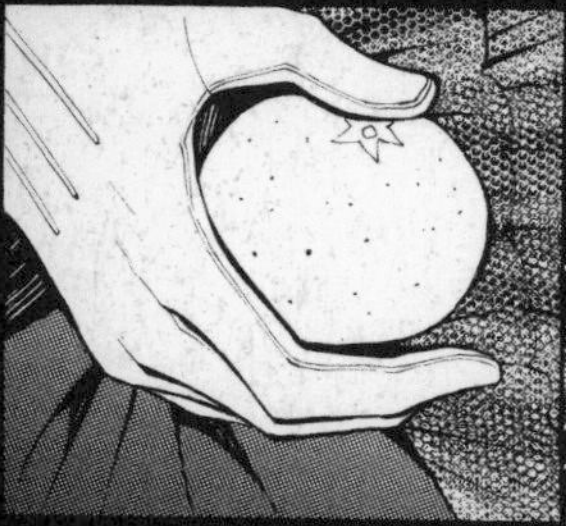

—Your new album, which drops soon, is also chock-ful of your well-rounded *mikan* love.

"HA-HA-HA, exactly! How to grow *mikan*, how t choose the right *mikan* at the store, how to hold a *mikan* how to peel a *mikan*, details of the sublime moment you put a *mikan* in your mouth—all I know about *mikan* i right there in my album! As many already know, a *mikan* is very nutritious and contains Vitamins C and A, citri acid, synephrine...even the white bits contain hesperidin which is supposed to help prevent arterial sclerosi—"

—Thank you very much.

THE LONG-ANTICIPATED DEBUT "〈I LOVE MIKAN〉" DROPS SOON!?

—Tracklisting—

1. I'm Just An Insignificant Music Box Maker
2. Shall I Peel You A *Mikan*, My Lady?
3. Don't Say Orange, Say *Mikan*!
4. Aah, When Will I Get My Turn to Appear?
5. Answer Me, Glen!
6. E●me Is My Holy Land
7. Hello From Inside The *Mikan* Box
8. Please Do Not Call Me A Hero ~Album ver~
9. Do You Eat The White Bits of *Mikan*?
10. *M•I•K•A•N* Forever

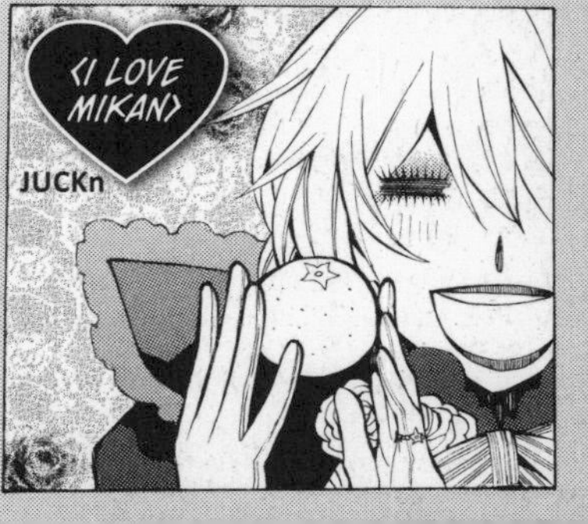
〈I LOVE MIKAN〉
JUCKn

COMMON HONORIFICS

no honorific: Indicates familiarity or closeness; if used without permission or reason, addressing someone in this manner would constitute an insult.

-san: The Japanese equivalent of Mr./Mrs./Miss. If a situation calls for politeness, this is the fail-safe honorific.

-sama: Conveys great respect; may also indicate that the social status of the speaker is lower than that of the addressee.

-kun: Used most often when referring to boys (though it can be applied to girls as well), this indicates affection or familiarity. Occasionally used by older men among their peers, but it may also be used by anyone referring to a person of lower standing.

-chan: An affectionate honorific indicating familiarity used mostly in reference to girls; also used in reference to cute persons or animals of either gender.

boku
page 28

In the original edition, Noise refers to herself with personal pronouns that are more suited to a young boy or man. It's possible that this personality identifes as male.

Jabberwock
page 138

A monstrous foe with horrific claws and teeth from Lewis Carroll's nonsensical poem, "Jabberwocky," which appears in *Through the Looking Glass*, the sequel to *Alice's Adventures in Wonderland*. The appearance of Glen's chain bears some resemblance to the famous illustration of the creature done in 1871 by John Tenniel, the man who illustrated Carroll's Alice books.

JUCKn (Jakkun)
page 178

This volume's cover *omake* is a parody of a Japanese rock aesthetic known as visual-*kei* (or "style"), which is characterized by its bold makeup, elaborate hairstyles, and ornate costumes. The types of rock played by these bands varies. Though the movement originated in the 1980s, visual-*kei* is still used by bands to describe their style today.

mikan
page 178

A kind of citrus fruit that resembles its clementine, satsuma, and tangerine relatives closely and is seedless and sweet.

PandoraHearts

I check each and every volume multiple times with my assistants, but we can never get rid of typesetting errors. They're formidable enemies that we tend to ignore the more serious they are. How terrifying!!

MOCHIZUKI'S MUSINGS

VOLUME 9

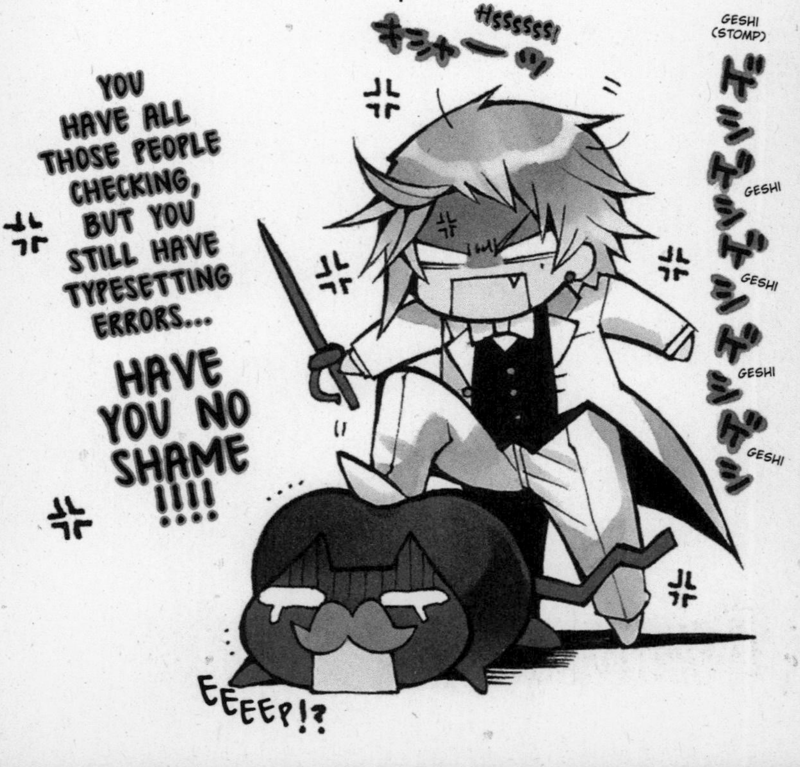
GESHI (STOMP)
Hssssss!
GESHI
GESHI
GESHI
GESHI
YOU HAVE ALL THOSE PEOPLE CHECKING, BUT YOU STILL HAVE TYPESETTING ERRORS...
HAVE YOU NO SHAME!!!!
EEEEP!?

PandoraHearts

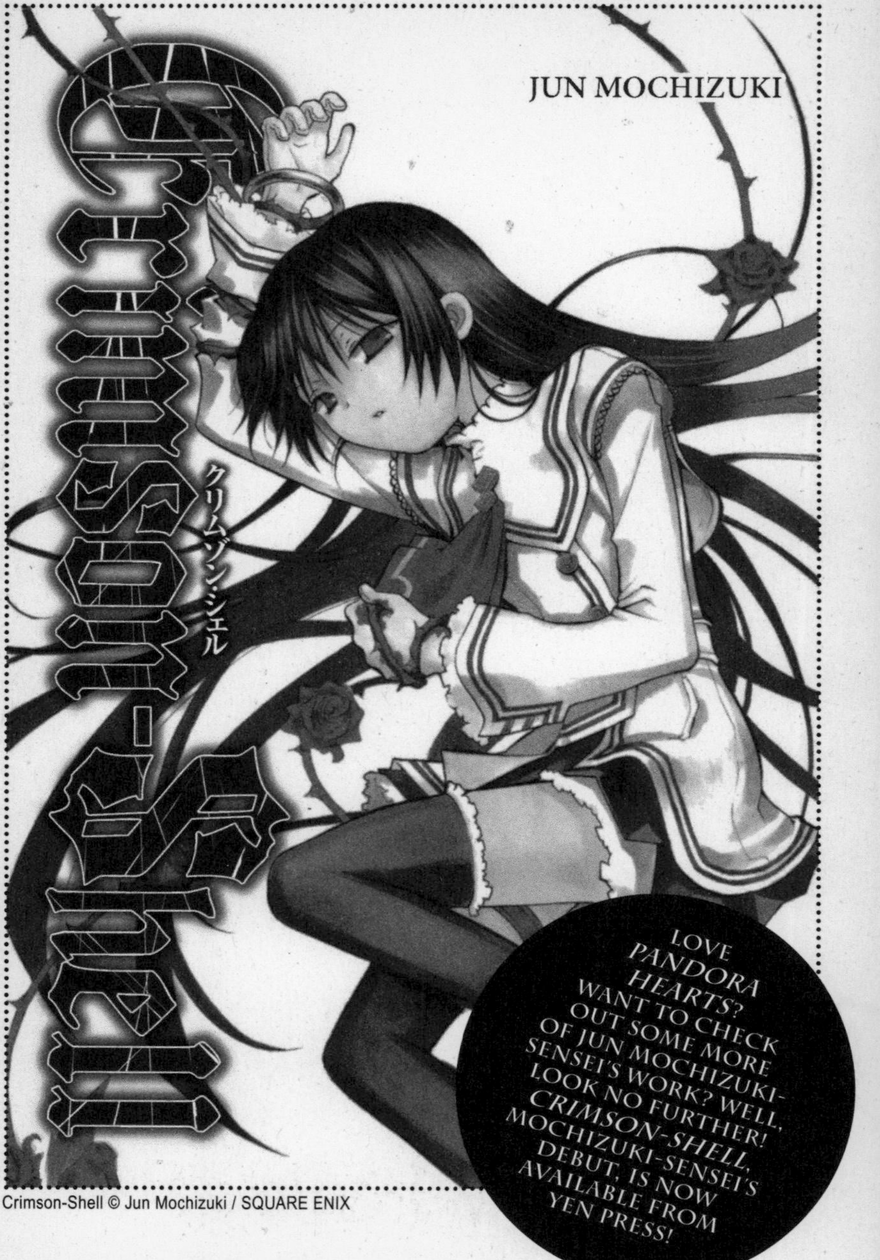
JUN MOCHIZUKI
Crimson-Shell
クリムゾン・シェル
LOVE *PANDORA HEARTS*? WANT TO CHECK OUT SOME MORE OF JUN MOCHIZUKI-SENSEI'S WORK? WELL, LOOK NO FURTHER! *CRIMSON-SHELL*, MOCHIZUKI-SENSEI'S DEBUT, IS NOW AVAILABLE FROM YEN PRESS!

PandoraHearts

Can't wait for the next volume? You don't have to!

Keep up with the latest chapters of some of your favorite manga every month online in the pages of YEN PLUS!

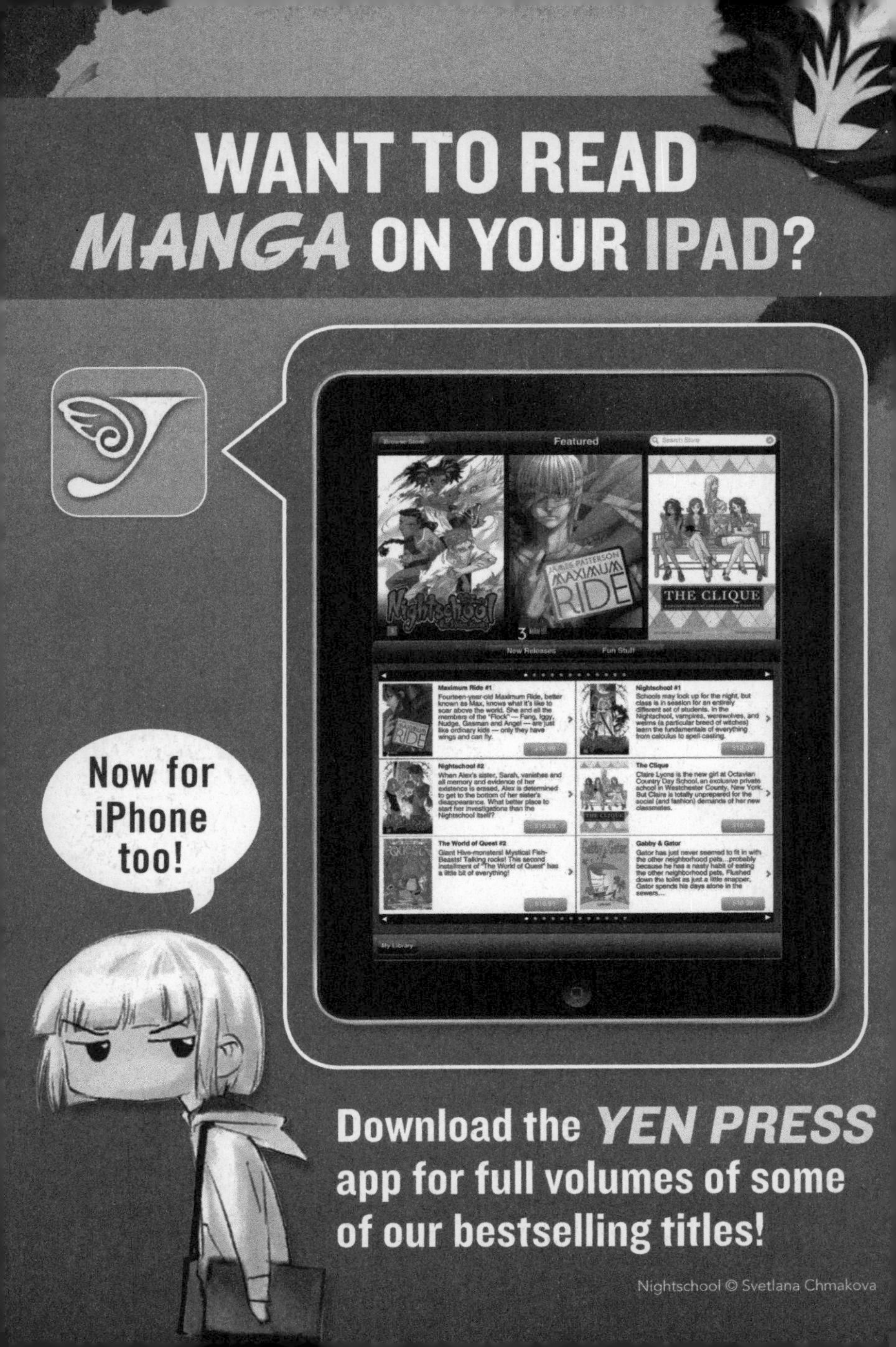
WANT TO READ MANGA ON YOUR IPAD?
Now for iPhone too!
Download the YEN PRESS app for full volumes of some of our bestselling titles!
Nightschool © Svetlana Chmakova

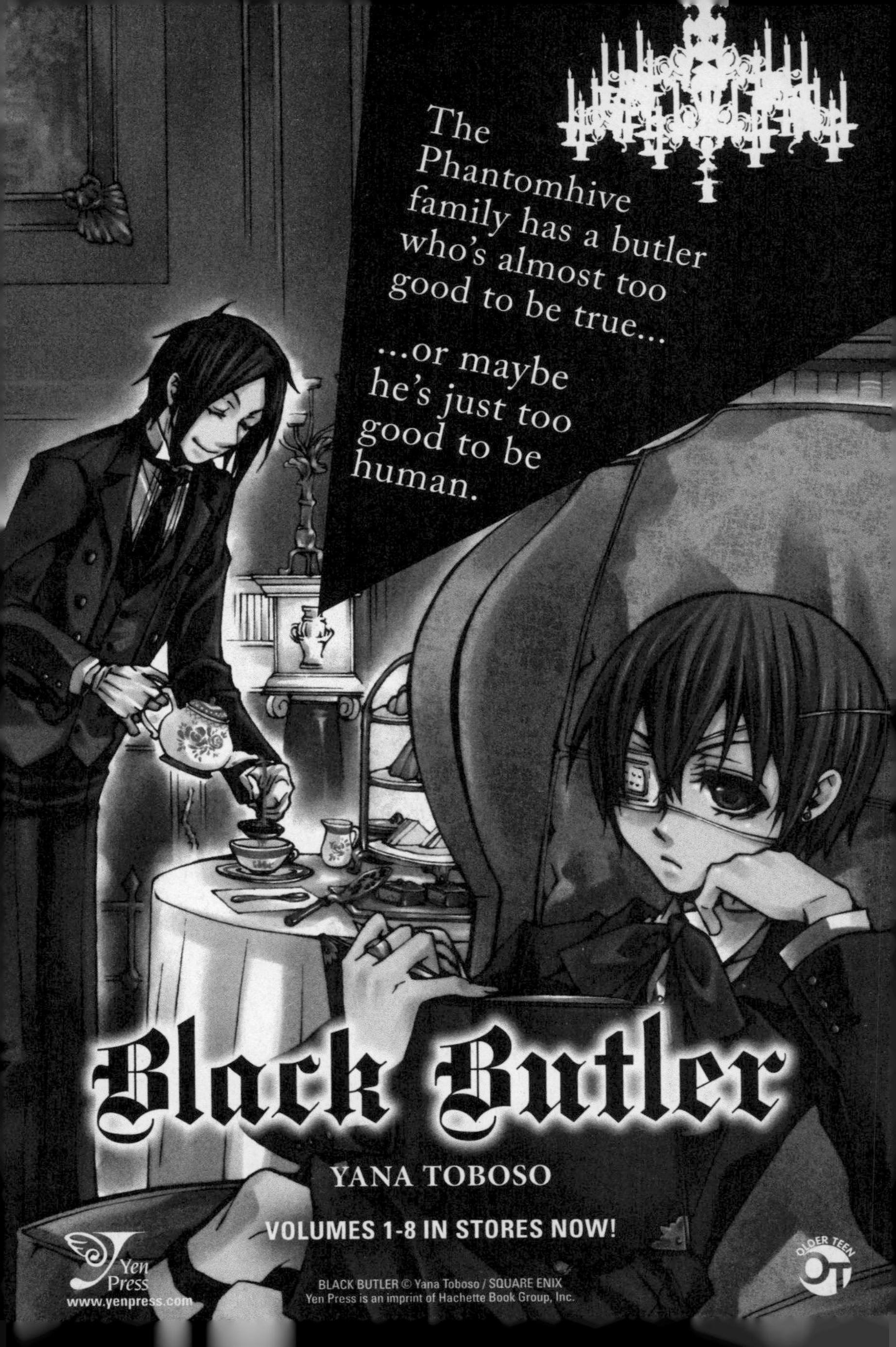
The Phantomhive family has a butler who's almost too good to be true...
...or maybe he's just too good to be human.
Black Butler
YANA TOBOSO
VOLUMES 1-8 IN STORES NOW!
Yen Press
www.yenpress.com
BLACK BUTLER © Yana Toboso / SQUARE ENIX
Yen Press is an imprint of Hachette Book Group, Inc.
OLDER TEEN
OT

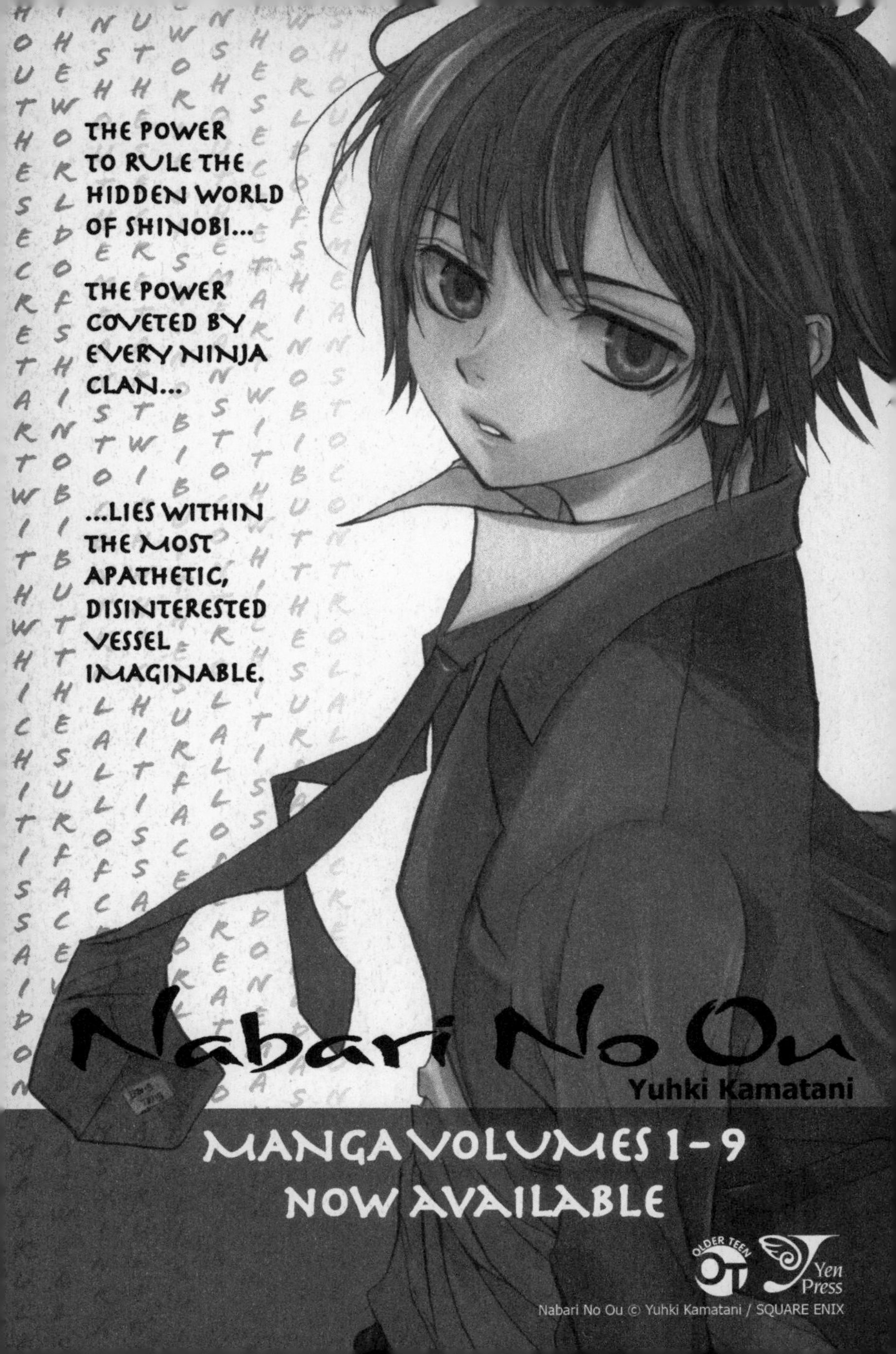
THE POWER TO RULE THE HIDDEN WORLD OF SHINOBI...
THE POWER COVETED BY EVERY NINJA CLAN...
...LIES WITHIN THE MOST APATHETIC, DISINTERESTED VESSEL IMAGINABLE.
Nabari No Ou
Yuhki Kamatani
MANGA VOLUMES 1–9
NOW AVAILABLE
OLDER TEEN
OT
Yen Press
Nabari No Ou © Yuhki Kamatani / SQUARE ENIX

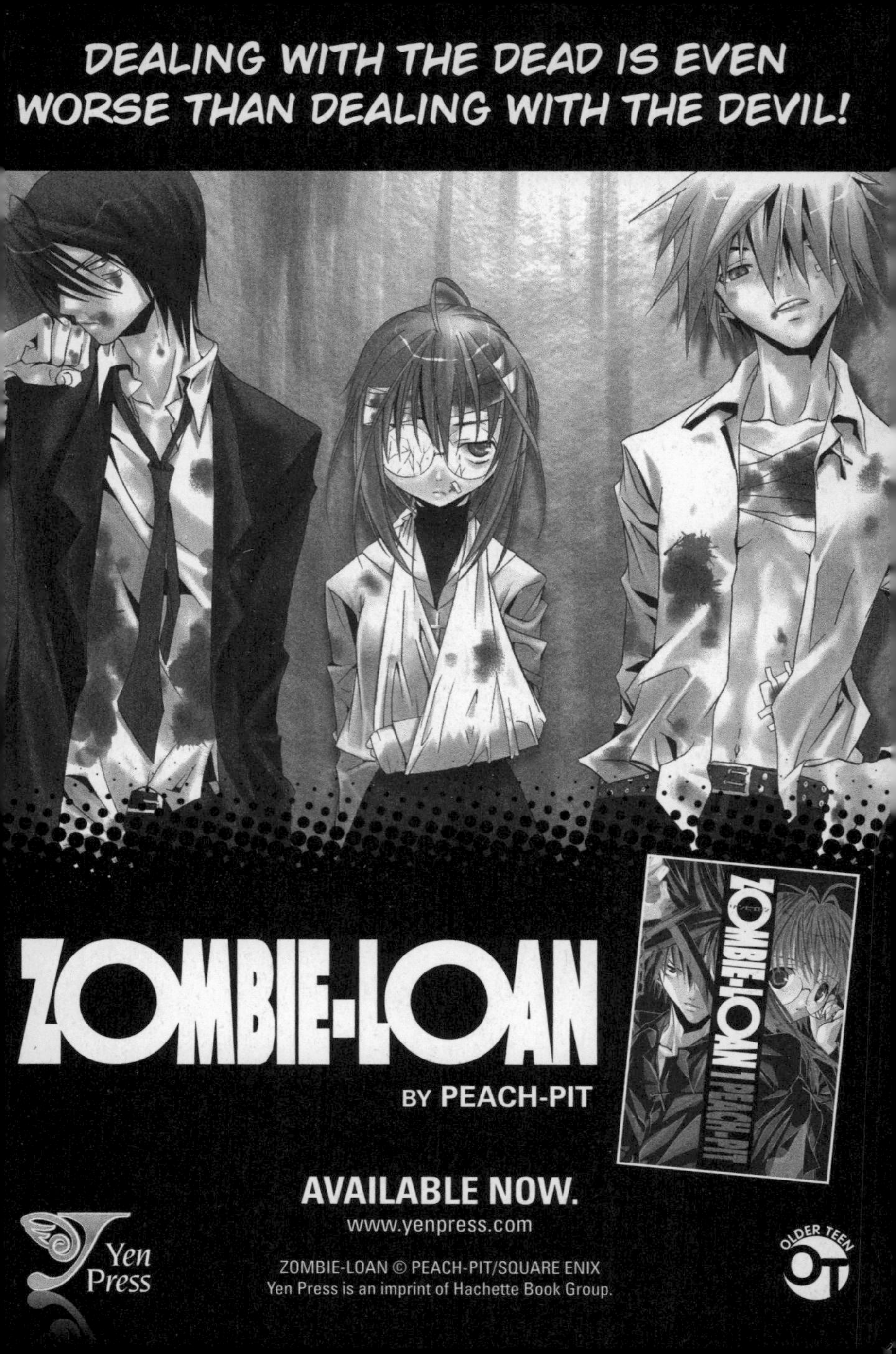
DEALING WITH THE DEAD IS EVEN WORSE THAN DEALING WITH THE DEVIL!
ZOMBIE-LOAN
BY PEACH-PIT
AVAILABLE NOW.
www.yenpress.com
Yen Press
ZOMBIE-LOAN © PEACH-PIT/SQUARE ENIX
Yen Press is an imprint of Hachette Book Group.
OLDER TEEN
OT

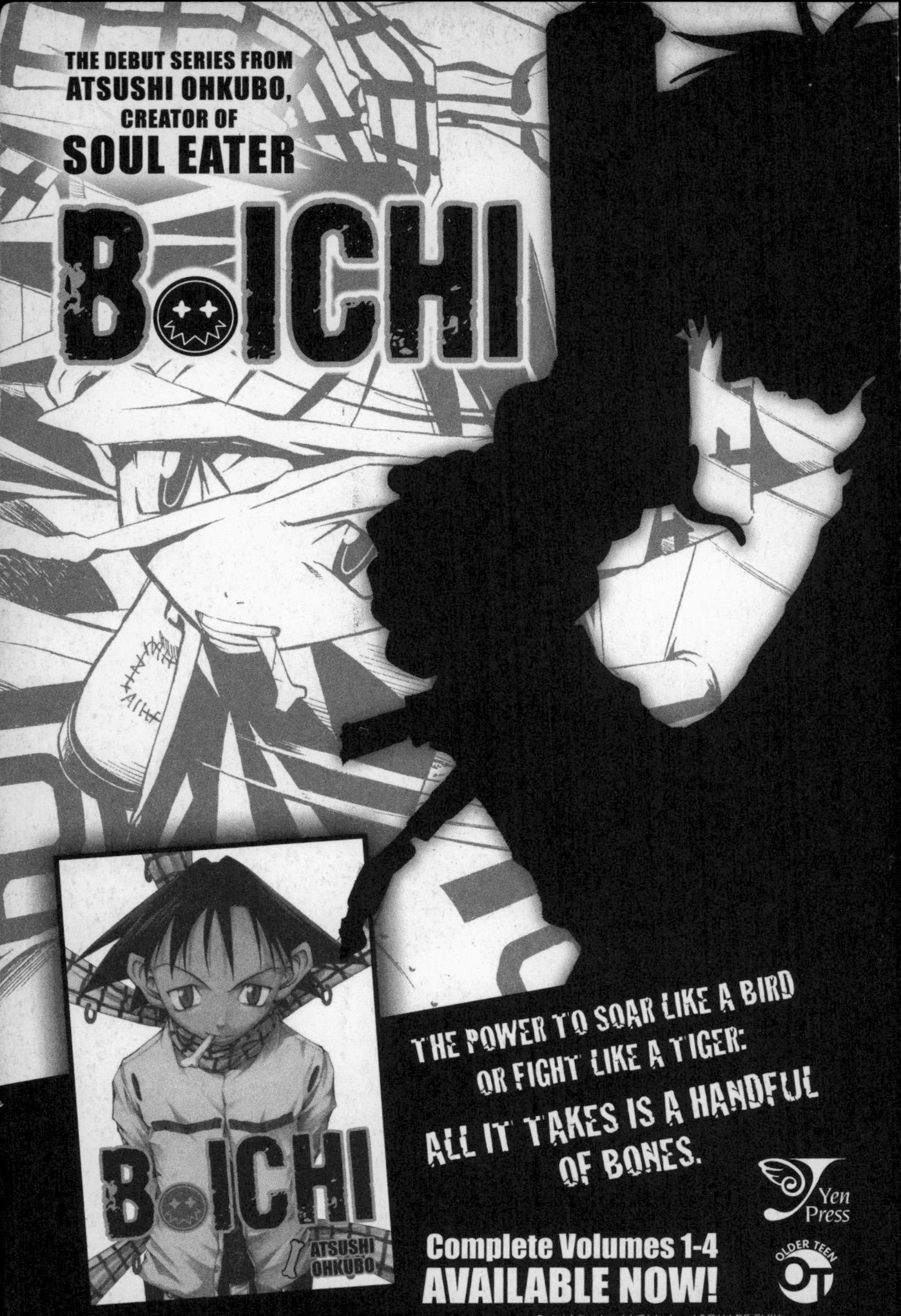
THE DEBUT SERIES FROM ATSUSHI OHKUBO, CREATOR OF SOUL EATER
B ICHI
THE POWER TO SOAR LIKE A BIRD OR FIGHT LIKE A TIGER:
ALL IT TAKES IS A HANDFUL OF BONES.
B ICHI
ATSUSHI OHKUBO
Yen Press
Complete Volumes 1-4
AVAILABLE NOW!
OLDER TEEN
OT